Rogue Archives

Rogue Archives

Digital Cultural Memory and Media Fandom

Abigail De Kosnik

The MIT Press
Cambridge, Massachusetts
London, England

This book was set in Stone Serif and Stone Sans by Toppan Best-set Premedia Limited.

Library of Congress Cataloging-in-Publication Data

Names: De Kosnik, Abigail, author.
Title: Rogue archives : digital cultural memory and media fandom /
    Abigail De Kosnik.
Description: Cambridge, MA : The MIT Press, [2016] | Includes bibliographical
    references and index.
Identifiers: LCCN 2015044395 | ISBN 9780262034661 (hardcover : alk. paper)
    ISBN 9780262544740 (pb)
Subjects: LCSH: Fan fiction--Archival resources. | Digital media--Social aspects. |
    Collective memory. | Digital preservation.
Classification: LCC PN3377.5.F33 D425 2016 | DDC 026/.8083--dc23 LC record
    available at https://lccn.loc.gov/2015044395

For Benjamin, my husband
and
Rosita, my late mother
Both computer programmers
Both creative fans
Both loving and beloved
Mahal na mahal kita

Contents

Acknowledgments

Thanks to Benjamin for your endless reserves of love and warmth. Thanks to all of the members of my large family and my wonderful friends, for your care and affection, and for always encouraging me to watch as much television as I wanted. Thanks to my fantastic professors at Northwestern University, especially Samuel Weber, Lynn Spigel, Alexander Weheliye, and Jeffrey Sconce, for your invaluable mentorship, training, and advising as I launched this project. Thanks to all of the phenomenal faculty, staff, and students at the University of California, Berkeley, with whom I have worked, especially those at the Berkeley Center for New Media and in the Department of Theater, Dance, and Performance Studies, for giving me a tremendous amount of help and motivation as I labored on this manuscript. Special thanks to Shannon Jackson, Catherine Cole, Mark Griffith, Ken Goldberg, Greg Niemeyer, Laurent El Ghaoui, San San Kwan, Angela Marino, David Bates, Shannon Steen, Lisa Wymore, Brandi Wilkins Catanese, and Peter Glazer for your support and feedback, and for believing in my potential. Infinite thanks to all of my students who played crucial roles in bringing this book into being, especially Andrea Horbinski, Andrew Godbehere, Adam Hutz, Lisa Cronin, Renée Pastel, Julia Havard, Kate Mattingly, Megan Hoetger, Kelsey Wong, and all of the undergraduate transcribers. My heartfelt thanks also to all of the fan archivists, fan authors, fan artists, and fan readers who contributed their works and words, and who have long been my inspiration. Eternal gratitude to Henry Jenkins, Diana Taylor, Lisa Nakamura, and Wendy Chun for your brilliant input, insights, and advice. My deepest appreciation to my editor, Doug Sery, and the team at the MIT Press, particularly Susan Buckley and Judith Feldmann, for allowing me to share this work with the world.

The research projects through which I collected the primary data for this book were made possible by grants from the Hellman Fellows Fund, the

Humanities Research Fellowship, the UC Berkeley Committee on Research, and the Townsend Center for the Humanities. Many thanks to each of those organizations.

An earlier version of Break 0 was published in *Transformative Works and Cultures*, vol. 18 (2015).

Every reasonable attempt has been made to identify owners of copyright. Errors or omissions will be corrected in subsequent editions.

Introduction

Memory Escapes the State

Memory has gone rogue. What I mean by this, first of all, is that memory has *fallen into the hands of rogues*.

From the late nineteenth through the late twentieth century, memory—not private, individual memory, but public, collective memory—was the domain of the state. Writes Tony Bennett in *The Birth of the Museum*, "Museums, galleries, and, more intermittently, exhibitions played a pivotal role in the formation of the modern state and are fundamental to its conception as, among other things, a set of educative and civilizing agencies." Bennett points out that "all developed nation-states" have consistently prioritized funding for their memory institutions, and have benefited from these institutions serving as "mechanisms for the permanent display of power," and as "influential cultural technologies" that testify to the states' "ability to command, order, and control objects and bodies, living or dead" (Bennett 1995, 66). Achille Mbembe argues that "the term 'archives'" is first of all understood as referring to "a public institution, which is one of the organs of a constituted state. ... There is no state without archives" (Mbembe 2002, 19, 23).[1]

But when digital networked media began displacing earlier forms of transmission (television, radio, cinema, print) as what Philip Auslander calls "the cultural dominant" (Auslander 2008, 23) in regions with widespread Internet access, the ties binding public memory to the state began to loosen, and memory started to forge links with many other masters: people who never underwent training in library and information sciences (LIS) but designated themselves "archivists" anyway, built freely accessible online archives, and began uploading (or assisting users with uploading) whatever content they deemed suitable for digital preservation. Digital archiving, while of increasing interest to traditional memory institutions, has been most enthusiastically embraced by nonprofessionals—by amateurs, fans, hackers, pirates, and volunteers—in other words, by "rogue" memory workers. Digital archives of cultural content, not associated with any physical museum, library, or archive, populate the Internet, to the point that many people refer to the Internet as a giant archive. (For example, Lev Manovich states in *The Language of New Media*, "The Internet … can be thought of as one huge distributed media database" [Manovich 2001, 55].)

Rogue archivists explore the potential of digital technologies to democratize cultural memory. With digital tools and networks, they construct repositories that are accessible by all Internet users, and can choose to preserve either vast quantities of information (they do not have to choose to save some types of content and discard other types because of physical space restrictions) or highly specific materials (such as the documents of subcultures or minority groups) that have been consistently excluded or ignored by traditional memory institutions. In *Rogues*, Jacques Derrida relates the *"roué"* or "rogue," the figure of licentiousness and debauchery in French culture since the eighteenth century, to democracy: "Democracy, the passage to democracy, *democratization*, will have always been associated with license, with taking too many liberties, with the dissoluteness of the libertine, with liberalism, indeed perversion and delinquency, with malfeasance, with failing to live according to the law, with the notion that 'everything is allowed,' that 'anything goes'" (Derrida 2005, 21). In other words, the process of ending monarchy and inaugurating democracy in France depended on rogues willing to "take liberties" with the very notion of liberty and make themselves over from king's subjects into republican citizens. Similarly, since the late-1980s advent of what we might call the public Internet (that is, the time when the Internet ceased to be a network usable only by government, university, and research lab employees, and became a network with which millions of people engaged on a daily basis),[2] rogue archivists have acted on the assumption that "anything goes" on the network, taking the initiative to design, found, and run their own cultural memory institutions without waiting for traditional institutions to set any precedents for online archiving, and achieving a degree of democratic inclusion and access for which brick-and-mortar archives never even aimed. What I call *rogue archives* are defined by: constant (24/7) availability; zero barriers to entry for all who can connect to the Internet; content that can be streamed or downloaded in full, with no required payment, and no regard for copyright restrictions (some rogue archivists digitize only what is already in the public domain); and content that has never been, and would likely never be, contained in a traditional memory institution.

One digital archivist interviewed by my research team, who uses the pseudonym "jinjurly" and runs what is called the Audiofic Archive, sums up the rogue's attitude toward traditional ideas about the institutional qualifications required for archival work:

[I used to say] "I've got an archive, but I'm not an archivist." I don't have an archivist degree. But what does that mean? Okay, when I was cooking in restaurants, I was writing menus and composing recipes and running a line and hiring and firing and running a kitchen, but I wasn't a chef, because I don't have a chef education or whatever. But again, what does that mean? I really, honestly think that—well, okay, everything takes practice—but anyone can do these things. (jinjurly 2012)

jinjurly's words may have been scandalous in an earlier era, but as digital culture develops, her idea that "anyone can do these things"—meaning that anyone can build a digital archive if she cultivates the necessary technical skills, dedicates sufficient time and resources, and commits to serving a public over a long time period of time through an enduring online resource—is becoming more and more common. Indeed, the "scandal" caused by rogue archivists consists precisely of their transforming "archives" and "archiving" from terms that signify exclusivity into terms that signify commonness, so that instead of locked rooms, the word "archives" connotes websites that operate as information commons, and instead of the concealed workings of a rarified circle of experts, "archiving" refers to acts of database design and maintenance that "anyone can do," that are commonplace. And scandals such as these, caused by *roués*, Derrida claims, can beget serious social and cultural transformations.

Derrida emphasizes rogues' abilities to bring about change, even on the scale of sweeping, radical revolutions. The rogues of digital archiving have effectuated cultural memory's escape from the state; memory will never again be wholly, or even mostly, under the control of the state or state-approved capitalists. Having fallen under the sway of rogues, cultural memory has become more democratic. But this is not the only way that memory is different in the digital era than it was before.

Memory and Making

Memory has gone rogue in another sense: where it used to mean the *record* of cultural production, memory is now the *basis* of a great deal of cultural production. Digital technologies facilitate what Lawrence Lessig (2008) and many others call "remix culture," that is, the appropriation and transformation of mass media texts (including films, television episodes, recorded music, video games, comic books, novels, and so on) into alternate versions, with traces of the "source" texts lingering in the new "takes," the remixes. The people formerly known as the "audience" or as "consumers," whom many media scholars conceived of as passive recipients of popular culture, have shown themselves to be quite active users of culture instead. Media users have seized hold of all of mass culture *as an archive*, an enormous repository of narratives, characters, worlds, images, graphics, and sounds from which they can extract the raw matter they need for their own creations, their alternatives to or customizations of the sources.

Cultural memory has thus gone rogue with respect to its own temporality, its own place in the order and timing of things. Engagement with cultural memory is therefore not only what comes after the making and distribution of cultural texts, it also now often precedes that making, or occurs at every step throughout the process of making. So many digital works begin as acts of memory, with a user remembering a loved (or hated) mass culture text and isolating, then manipulating, revising, and reworking, specific elements of that text. In the past, the chain of media production appeared to conclude with the culture industries' distribution of a finished product. At present, each media commodity becomes, at the instant of its release, an archive to be plundered, an original to be memorized, copied, and manipulated—a starting point or springboard for receivers' creativity, rather than an end unto itself. (And it is not only audiences who generate these extensions of the source text; the culture industries are now deeply committed to building franchises and transmediations around their successful properties, constantly seeking to multiply one hit concept into a series of interlinked films, video games, television series, comics, "webisodes," and toys [see Jonathan Gray's (2010) rich analysis of mass media's "paratexts"].)

Memory has gone rogue in the sense that it has come loose from its fixed place in the production cycle. It now may be found anywhere, or everywhere, in the chain of making. And of course, it still may also be found in its typical place, at the tail of the chain, as media users seek to archive their remixes. Many "rogue" digital archives have, as their primary mission, the collection and storage of users' versions, digitizations, and transmediations of media texts. Much of digital culture emerges through iterative, serial, and distributed modes of production. Traditional memory institutions were not designed to safeguard cultural texts that proliferate indefinitely. Numerous untraditional digital archives, however, have been designed specifically for this purpose.

Memory as the "Cultural Dominant"

Memory has always been intrinsic to making, of course, but the relation between the two has increasingly come to the forefront of popular consciousness since the late 1970s, with the beginnings of postmodern appropriation in visual art, architecture, cinema, hip hop, and other creative genres. Today, in the third decade of the public Internet, digital culture cannot be thought separately from memory-based making, so prominently do postmodern makers' techniques (influenced by earlier movements, including Dada, surrealism, and situationism), such as collage, bricolage, intertextuality, *détournement*, culture jamming, and nostalgic reference, feature in digital creativity. In fact, both postmodernism and new media have been declared the post-print, post-television "cultural dominant" over the past thirty years, and I argue that the contemporary preeminence, if we can call it that, of both phenomena must be understood as not only simultaneously occurring but also inextricably intertwined.

In 1984, Frederic Jameson declared postmodernism to be the "cultural dominant" of the late twentieth century (Jameson 1984, 55–58), based on a style of production that he perceived to be transpiring in multiple spheres of activity. But scholars who have taken up the term "cultural dominant" from Jameson have used it to refer to a specific technological medium rather than to a style or mode of making. For example, in *Liveness*, performance scholar Philip Auslander writes, "I consider television, not film, to be the dominant cultural medium of the second half of the twentieth century" (Auslander 2008, 11), and states that the "televisual" is "the cultural dominant" (23). And in "What Is the Post-cinematic?" film scholar Steven Shaviro (2011) periodizes the starting point of the "post-cinematic" to the early twenty-first century, when film "has been 'surpassed' by digital and computer-based media." (Shaviro notes that he places "surpassed" in quotation marks "to guard against giving this term a teleological meaning"— and yet, there is a progression of media formats as "cultural dominants" from film to television to digital, if we follow the development of the term from Auslander to Shaviro.)

Digital media is currently the cultural dominant in the sense that Auslander and Shaviro mean, marking one media form as ascendant over all others. But let us also retain the meanings that Jameson assigned to the term when he coined it, which have to do with how we make culture, and what we do with culture. Jameson was prescient in naming postmodernism "the cultural dominant," as digital culture is rife with the postmodern moves of referentiality, citation, and appropriation that Jameson discusses.

Contemporary media users do with cultural texts whatever they like, disregarding print and analog's boundaries of textual cohesion (where a text begins and ends), authorial ownership (who made the text), or historical time (when a text was created), and this postmodern style of making has proliferated wildly as digital media has facilitated the operations of cutting, copying, mixing, and distributing far better than previous media have done. By this reasoning, the cultural dominant of the early twenty-first century is postmodern digital media production.

Another way to say this is: memory-based making—facilitated by digital tools, published on digital networks, and saved mostly in "rogue" digital archives—is the cultural dominant of the early twenty-first century.

The Rise of Repertoire

"Archive" in this book has multiple valences. I am writing about actual digital archives, websites you can visit, such as the Internet Archive, ibiblio, Project Gutenberg, and Open Library. I am also writing about metaphorical archives, archives that are opened up by each media text put into circulation, archives that audience members enter into, plunder for usable material, and then augment and expand when they deposit their transformations and variations back into the archive of the source.[3] The actual archives and the metaphorical archives are not identical, but they bear close relation to one another; the actual digital networked archives serve as the distribution and preservation mechanisms of the archival, or what I call "archontic," productions of media users. The dual notion of "archive," then, as constructed site/conceptual entity, is this book's central object of investigation.

But something strange happens when one investigates both the built and metaphorical instances of "archive" in the digital age. The closer one comes to "archive," the more scrutiny one devotes to it, the larger another, seemingly opposite, idea looms: the idea of "repertoire." The reader who begins this book thinking that she will learn all about "archive" in the digital era will finish the book realizing that she has, in fact, been reading intensively about "repertoire." For every actual and virtual archive in the digital age depends heavily on repertoire, and can even be said to rely more on repertoire—by which I mean physical, bodily acts of repetition, of human performance—than seems readily apparent.

Here is how repertoire works in actual archives: The scores of nonprofessional archivists who found and maintain online archives must labor endlessly to keep their archives operational, and I mean "endlessly" literally, for whenever they stop investing their labor, their sites stagnate and/or shut down. Their archival labor consists of a repertoire, a series of actions that they must perform over and over, which consists of moves such as paying for server space, processing submissions (even if an archive has an auto- mated intake process, in which contributors can upload their own content without an archivist's assistance, the archivist must still constantly over- see, debug, and improve the automated system), responding to users' ques- tions, migrating the data when necessary, and representing the archive to interested members of the public or press. The very fragility of digital data and Internet sites, the fact that digital content is so prone to disappearance and loss, means that no Internet archive should be regarded as a structure that will last into perpetuity. Most, if not all, digital archives that currently exist will not survive into the next century. But I predict that the methods and means that rogue archivists have developed for assembling, coding, and operating idiosyncratic archives will survive. In other words, the reper- toire of digital archive building that has been pioneered over the past few decades will likely outlast any actual archives that have been built.

Here is how repertoire works in metaphorical archives: The action of treating media texts as archives has always been implicit or ignored in print culture but explicit and universally acknowledged in performance cultures. Humans are playback machines (Gaines 1991) that record what they see, hear, and otherwise experience sensorially, and then play back those experi- ences, transforming them in the process. A music fan sings a popular song in the shower, putting his personal "take" on it; a professional DJ creates an extended mix of a hit recording by mashing it up with samples lifted from twelve other tracks. A child pretends to be a superhero or a monster after seeing a slew of genre films; a theater company mounts the thou- sandth production of a classic musical. All of these reperformers have put the source text into their repertoires. They play back, with a difference, what they have stored in their memories. Digital makers who appropriate literary works, still and moving images, video games, and other cultural productions in recorded or "archival" formats, do the same: they add the texts they experience to their repertoires, and, using their bodies (at the least, their fingers and wrists interfacing with computer keyboards, their eyes and ears gauging their inputs and outputs), they reperform what they have stored.

Therefore, I understand the increasing popularity of postmodern digital remix, of memory-based making, of what I call *archontic production*, as an elevation of the logics and methods of performance, and as a sharp spike in the cultural significance of repertoire. Yet another way in which memory in the digital age has gone rogue is in its dramatically shifting the balance of power between archive and repertoire. Where print culture consistently privileged the memory mode of archive over repertoire, digital culture does not sustain this privilege. At present, repertoire may not currently carry greater importance than archive as a modality of memory, but repertoire is certainly on the rise as digital culture evolves.

Above, I stated that memory-based digital making is the cultural dominant. I will now elaborate on that statement: memory-based digital making manifests in both actual and virtual archives, through the modalities of both archive and repertoire. For repertoire factors heavily into built and metaphorical archives. Repertoire is a key driver of both categories of digital archive.

Archive and Repertoire

In my discussion of archive and repertoire, I am referencing Diana Taylor's theoretical explorations of the two concepts in her landmark work of performance studies, *The Archive and the Repertoire* (2003), and subsequently in her essay "Save As ...: Knowledge and Transmission in the Age of Digital Technologies" (2010). In *The Archive and the Repertoire*, Taylor argues that print culture's hierarchy of memory logics ranks archive over repertoire. Print-analog culture valorizes "'archival' memory," which, Taylor states, "exists as documents, maps, literary texts, letters, archeological remains, bones, videos, films, CDs, all those items supposedly resistant to change" (Taylor 2003, 19), and denigrates repertoire, which Taylor defines as "embodied memory: performances, gestures, orality, movement, dance, singing—in short, all those acts usually thought of as ephemeral, nonreproducible knowledge" (20). Although Taylor points out that while archive and repertoire often "work in tandem" (21) (she gives the example of ceremonies such as flag-planting complementing the writing of histories of colonial conquest), the Global North's "tendency has been to banish the repertoire to the past" (21) and to characterize repertoire, as historian Jacques Le Goff does, as "ethnic memory" (21), and as "traditional, authentic, now lost," as opposed to archival memory, which is "present," "modern," and "global" (22).

Often, Taylor argues, a binary is drawn between archive as "mediated" and repertoire as "unmediated" (22). But she resists these definitions, and flags the ascent of digital media as a moment that will push against print-analog culture's opposition of archive to repertoire: "Other systems of transmission—like the digital—complicate any simple binary formulation" (22).

Taylor's essay "Save As ..." delves deeper into the question of what the digital might do to alter the long-entrenched "embodied/documented divide": "If the repertoire consists of embodied acts of transfer and the archive preserves and safeguards print and material culture—objects—what to make of the digital that displaces both bodies and objects as it transmits more information far faster and more broadly than ever before?" (Taylor 2010, 3).

Taylor questions whether print culture's hierarchy of memory modes will persist through the transition of media regimes. I argue that not only are we witnessing the rise of repertoire in actual archive building and in the archontic productions of media users, we are seeing repertoire assert its significance, even its primacy, in multiple other arenas of memory-based making in digital culture. For example, as I will argue in chapter 6, users perform bodily in digital networks, not only when they record their physical bodies acting or singing and circulate their recordings online but when they determine (in text, icons, screen grabs, GIFs, game play, animations, or art) the actions of avatars (which represent themselves) and what I call "marionettes" (which represent fictional characters)—these are instances of repertoire.

But the history of digital culture also still shows moments of strong division between repertoire and archive. For example, in chapter 5, I will describe the anxiety of a female subculture as it faced mass migration from physical meeting spaces to online virtual spaces. I perceive the subculture's early mistrust of the Internet as a fear that their cultural memory, which had been encoded largely as repertoire (embodied transmissions from experienced members to newcomers), or as repertoire combined with printed "zines," would not survive a mass migration into the text-only sphere of the Internet.

This book, then, investigates a range of ways that digital media are drastically altering long-standing definitions of cultural memory. I am studying how cultural memory has become a question mark, how it has become an unfixed and dynamic concept, how it has gone rogue. The expansion of the meanings of "archive," the growing prominence of "repertoire," and the constantly shifting relation between the two memory modes are key topics in every chapter.

The Promise of Democratization

I study rogue memory in large part because of the promise of democratization that inheres in it. Earlier, I cited Derrida's proposition that large-scale change depends on rogues, and that democracy itself emerged in modern

Europe as a result of the liberties taken by rogues. In the upending of old assumptions about what cultural memory is and how it works by rogue archivists and rogue media users, I see a number of exciting political possibilities, including:

• The possibility for vast quantities of cultural content to be preserved and made accessible to a broad public—marking an end, in certain spaces, to what Raymond Williams ([1961] 2001, 66–69) calls "the selective tradition," which always grants priority to the culture that supports the narratives and identities of the dominant group.
• The possibility for subcultural and marginalized groups to have archives of their own, on digital networks, constructed and operated by members of their communities, instead of (or in addition to) lobbying traditional memory institutions for recognition and admission of their cultural materials.
• The possibility for "mass audiences" to invert the sociocultural hierarchy that places them at the bottom of the power structure of media, and to exhibit, en masse, their ability to treat the culture industries' products as the incomplete, often impoverished, basic matter from which they construct meaningful texts for themselves and their affinity-based communities.
• The possibility for a style of memory-based making in the mode of repertoire—that is, an everyday making, an individualized and personalized style of reperformance, a holding-in-common of all culture as shared resource and property—to challenge the barriers of copyright and antiduplication technologies erected around archival genres such as printed text and image, sound, and video recordings.

Rogue cultural memory is not essentially the product or tool of marginalized and minority groups; it may certainly be used to serve the interests of dominant classes and groups. But, over the past few decades, it has been effectively developed and deployed to strengthen the positions and fuel the activities of subordinated individuals and collectives, and to further the projects of democratization outlined above. This book will document some of the ways in which digital technologies and networks, and the memory-based making they enable, have subverted and counteracted traditional power structures. I have stated that memory has fallen into the hands of rogues, and what this explicitly means is: memory has fallen into female hands, into queer hands, into immigrant and diasporic and transnational hands, into nonwhite hands, into the hands of the masses.

Factors of identity, wealth, and geographic location continue to facilitate the "digital divide,"[4] and I do not claim that the spread of digital archiving is closing gaps in computing access or skill between large numbers of people. The focus of this book is on how people who are usually marginalized in narratives of technological development are innovating new media practices in ways that will likely alter how cultural memory takes form, becomes institutionalized, and operates going forward. Sarah Florini states, "Digital media studies often erase users of color. ... When users of color do receive scholarly attention, most often they are cast as victims with limited technological access and resources. The consistent scholarly focus on the 'digital divide' all too often frames people of color as technological outsiders and has served to obscure the many people of color who *are* online" (Florini 2014, 224). Like Florini, I aim to fill in some of the blanks that persist in new media studies around the activity of nonwhite, nonmale, nonheteronormative individuals and collectives on digital networks. As a woman of color from the Global South, and as an ally of queer people and politics, I have a vested interest in increasing the representation of these groups in new media scholarship. I have therefore selected, as my primary case study, a set of online communities that are predominantly female and largely queer.

The Case of Fan Fiction Archives

Though this book will make reference to, and offer descriptions of, many digital archives as examples of rogue memory, my chief example throughout will be Internet fan fiction archives. Cultural memory in the digital era—or digital cultural memory—can be imagined as a double helix structure, like DNA: one strand consists of memory-based making in the form of appropriations, remixes, and transformative works, and the other strand consists of actual archives that exist online which publish and preserve a great deal of digital content, much of which is appropriative in nature. Media fans provide an ideal case for investigating digital cultural memory because they were early developers and practitioners of both online archive building and archontic production. In Internet fan fiction communities, we find a full expression of the double helix of digital cultural memory.

Media fan cultures populate the Internet and their creations run rampant through it; hoards of appropriations and remixes, transmediations and transformations, macros and parody vids and "Fuck Yeah" Tumblrs[5] and other responses to mass media traverse digital networks. I argue that Internet fan cultures are archival cultures in multiple ways: their core operations concern the apprehension of media *as* archive, the unconstrained plundering of that archive, and the construction of both virtual archives (the overarching archives opened by media texts—for example, the "Cinderella archive" or the "Batman archive," which fans continually expand with their new variations and versions) and actual digital archives (websites on which fan archivists store their communities' creative works). I view fan cultures as exemplary of Internet culture at large, and the actions of fan cultures as therefore illustrative of the shifting memory logics of the digital era: in online fan fiction communities and archives, the binaries and oppositions that print-analog culture established between archive and repertoire fade and blend.

By studying online fan archives and archivists—a group of users that began dedicating themselves to digital cultural memory work in the early 1990s, just as the Internet and the World Wide Web were becoming integral to daily life for a broad user base in the United States—we can gain insights into how rogue memory has operated so far: what digital preservation has required in the way of technical and organizational labor, how it has evolved as network technologies and network cultures have rapidly changed, and how appropriation and remix practices rely as much on performance-oriented, embodied means of transmission as on archival media. In other words, through analyzing Internet fan fiction archives, we can understand the circumstances, motivations, and decisions that have shaped rogue digital memory.

Gender, Sexuality, and Digital Archiving

Internet fan fiction archives are also valuable as objects of study because they are archives of women's digital culture and queer digital culture. Fan fiction is created primarily by people and for people who self-identify as female or as not-male, many of whom identify as nonheterosexual or not exclusively heterosexual (I present qualitative and quantitative data on the femaleness and queerness of fan fiction archive contributors and users in chapter 3). Women and queer individuals and collectives occupy minoritarian positions on and in digital networks, although they participate in these networks heavily.

Despite the cyberutopian hopes of Norbert Wiener and other early pioneers of computing culture, who saw in information systems "model[s] of an egalitarian, democratic social order" and "metaphors for the democratic creation of order from below" (Turner 2006, 24), inequality persists in Internet use, and gender is no less a constant marker of disparity in the digital sphere than other identity traits. "One of the most enduring technological inequalities is the gender divide," write Laura J. Dixon et al. (2014, 992): "Research has detailed a variety of ways in which women lag behind men in the ownership of technology and the development of technological skills. For example, men own and use computers and the Internet more than women, spend more time online, take more technology classes, and show more motivation to learn digital skills" (992; see also Cooper 2006; Correa 2010; Livingstone and Helper 2007; Seiter 1999). While "women have a long history in computing," according to Janet Abbate, whose *Recoding Gender* seeks to restore the work of generations of female programmers to the historical record, "women today [in the United States and UK] hold a relatively low percentage of computer science degrees and technical computing jobs, and popular stereotypes of male computer geeks abound" (Abbate 2012, 2). Lisa Parks states, "Despite feminist efforts to claim the computer as a platform for social transformation, the dominant social, economic, and cultural discourses continue to position computer technologies as domains of masculine activity, authority, and control" (Parks 2004, 141). That millions of girls and women use the Internet daily does not obviate the fact that, in the early decades of the twenty-first century, technoculture remains strongly gendered male, not only in the Global South (Intel Corporation 2012), but in the Global North as well. This gendering is evident in the preponderance of men in technology sector jobs, particularly in top positions (Forrest 2014; Linshi 2015; Williams 2014), in the scarcity of women inventors and coders in histories of hardware and software (as Abbate points out), and in the commonality of harassment (including rape threats and death threats) directed at women who, through their blogging or social media activity, gain large followings or otherwise attain public prominence (see Dockterman 2014; Hess 2014; Sierra 2014).

Tech corporations may value women's social media use and e-commerce activity (Lee 2011), and women may be more active participants on many social networks than men (Duggan 2013; Duggan and Brenner 2013), but women do not exercise the majority of financial, managerial, and cultural control over tech corporations, and they have not derived most of the profits, or power, generated by them over their recent period of explosive growth. As I have argued elsewhere,[6] women's online activities, including fannish participation on social networks, often constitute a type of free labor that increases the value of the networks themselves, as well as of various products—labor on which companies have come to rely for the generation and maintenance of audience interest in, and the spread of "buzz" or "hype" around, their commodities and platforms. In other words, while women may gain personal pleasure and satisfaction from their contributions to social networks, what they do online constitutes a form of production from which capitalist enterprises extract significant amounts of economic value, and for which those enterprises do not have to pay wages. (Women are hardly alone in this respect—the vast majority of Internet users donate free labor to tech companies when they use social media sites—but I wish to emphasize that, even if women currently participate in social networks in greater numbers than men, the economic and managerial structures of new media corporations are not gender balanced.)

The fact that women do not shape or direct the infrastructure or operations of the majority of the Internet has had serious consequences for their digital cultural productions: female fan communities have experienced large-scale content "takedowns," in which site owners/moderators delete fans' work from websites without fans' advance knowledge or permission (Fanlore, "Strikethrough and Boldthrough"; Supernatural Wiki 2011; Jardin 2007), and attempts by Hollywood stakeholders to create rule-bound, monitored spaces—gated digital neighborhoods—for fan fiction online, and to monetize the production of fan works (without making any provisions for financially compensating fan creators) (Cupitt 2008; Jenkins 2007a; Fanlore, "FanLib"). Corporate-owned Internet platforms, either because they fundamentally misunderstood the purpose and significance of female-driven online fan communities, or because they have aimed to co-opt and exploit women fans' labor, thus have sought to actively curtail and suppress women's digital cultures, and have challenged their right to exist.

Other threats to women's online expression have arisen in recent years, and may rise again soon: millions of Internet users successfully protested in 2012 against the Stop Online Piracy Act (SOPA) and the PROTECT IP Act (PIPA), which the Electronic Frontier Foundation and many other organizations criticized for posing dangers to freedom of online expression and access to information (Samuels and McSherry 2012), but the US Congress only tabled these acts; it did not withdraw them from consideration altogether. Proposed laws such as these, if passed, could render Internet communities primarily populated by user-generated content, including women's fan communities, vulnerable to sudden and massive takedowns or closures. Internet cultural creation—especially that which lies outside, or deliberately confounds, the realm of normative, conventional, socially acceptable discourse—could swiftly be "chilled" if users felt that sharing their creativity would subject their works, or themselves, to hostile surveillance or policing. Laws aside, if large-scale social networks such as YouTube, Facebook, or Tumblr were to simply place greater restrictions on the types of cultural expression they allow, the same chilling effect would occur. Female fan expression, which is considered by many, as Henry Jenkins writes, to be a "scandalous category" of cultural production, well outside the bounds of "'good taste,' appropriate conduct, or aesthetic merit" (Jenkins 1992, 16), would be among the most likely categories of online expression to suffer under increased Internet regulation—and unless users remain vigilant and actively protect their rights, as they did in 2012 with respect to SOPA and PIPA, such regulation may very well come to pass.

As far as LGBTQ participation on the Internet, online targeting and shaming of self-identifying queer people, especially among young users, is commonplace. A 2013 report by the Gay, Lesbian & Straight Education Network (GLSEN) states that LGBT youth "experience nearly three times as much bullying and harassment online as non-LGBT youth" (GLSEN 2013), and several suicides of teens and college students have been linked to the victims' being cyberbullied because of their queer sexualities (New York Times 2012; Huffington Post 2012; Pitts 2010). The censorship and harassment of adult LGBTQ users online is also well documented (Cossman 2013; boyd 2006a). At the same time that the Internet offers LGBTQ youth opportunities to "find greater peer support, access to health information and opportunities to be civically engaged" than they typically can access in "real life" (GLSEN 2013), networked technologies often work to suppress queer expression and communication, both through identifiable, visible modes such as harassment, and through far less detectable means, such as deletion of content, or the prevention of content posting. As Brenda Cossman writes, the Internet "is a site of censorship [of LGBTQ expression] that is not well understood; much of it [the logic governing this censorship] remains locked in confidential algorithms, allowing what we do see and do not see to remain in a kind of digital closet" (Cossman 2013, 46). And queer studies scholars have expressed concerns over tech firms' exploitative attitudes toward queer users that mirror my concerns over these corporations' reliance on the free labor of women users. Kate O'Riordan and David J. Phillips state,

Through the 1990s, ownership and control of the infrastructure of the internet ... became increasingly the domain of fewer, larger, and more integrated media corporations. [Joshua] Gamson has noted that this has entailed a "transformation of gay and lesbian [Internet] media from organizations answering at least partly to geographical and political communities into businesses answering primarily to advertisers and investors." ... [John Edward] Campbell, too, has pursued the political and cultural representations of this transformation, as "Janus-faced ... online portals ... present themselves as inclusive communities to gay and lesbian consumers while simultaneously presenting themselves as surveilling entities to corporate clients." (O'Riordan and Phillips 2007, 5)

Countering the depriving, threatening, suppressing, or exploitative attitudes and moves to which women and LGBTQ are frequently exposed on digital networks, Internet fan fiction archives serve as "safe spaces" for the production, publication, distribution, access, and safeguarding of female and queer digital culture. bell hooks states that the second-wave US women's movement articulated the need for "'safe' spaces where groups of presumably like-minded women [can] come together, sharing ideas and experiences without fear of silencing" (hooks 1994, 76);[7] LGBTQ and other equality movements have since applied the concept of "safe spaces" to both real-world and online collectives (New Tactics 2013; Ferguson 2014; Craig 2014). Drawing on the discourse of safe space, fan studies scholars Alexis Lothian, Kristina Busse, and Robin Anne Reid characterize Internet fan fiction communities as "queer female space" (Lothian, Busse, and Reid 2007).[8] Many fan fiction archivists have taken great care to construct and operate their archives on servers and URLs that they own, to avoid any censorial pressure or "TOS'ing"[9] from corporate site owners; also, no fan archivists charge fees for access to their sites, and most also refuse to permit advertising on their archives (although some archives fundraise to cover the costs of server space). Fan archives explicitly position themselves as friendly and open to female and queer makers and users, especially for the making and use of cultural texts that pertain to female and queer affect and sexuality. These archives may be regarded as spaces of safety in that they stand apart from corporate-owned sites, they commit to preserving women's and queer people's content and to protecting that content from censorship (and the content producers from harassment) as much as possible, and they do not seek to transmute women and queer users' voluntary digital labor into profits for majority male and straight owners.

Internet fan fiction archives also provide another function for women and queer digital culture. Achille Mbembe states that archives confer *status* on their contents, and on the culture and society that produced those contents: "The archive ... is fundamentally a matter of discrimination and of selection, which, in the end, results in the granting of a privileged status to certain written documents, and the refusal of that same status to others, thereby judged 'unarchivable.' The archive is, therefore, not a piece of data, but a status" (2002, 20). The status that the archive awards is, first of all, according to Mbembe, the foundational status of existence, of a person or a culture having existed: "The archive becomes ... something that does away with doubt, exerting a debilitating power over such doubt. It then acquires the status of proof. It is proof that a life truly existed, that something actually happened. ... The final destination of the archive is therefore always situated … in the story that it makes possible" (20–21). Fans, fan fiction, and fan communities have historically been granted incredibly low status in cultural hierarchies (Jenkins 1992, 9–23; Coppa 2006b, 230–233), and online archives of fan works will not likely alter that ranking. But Mbembe illuminates the power of digital communities' self-made archives to award those communities with the minimal status of *having truly existed*, of their individual and collective cultures *having actually happened*, and therefore of making possible their insertion into history. In the absence of archives of their work, female and queer uses/users of the Internet would risk disappearance and erasure; their cultures would remain unknown and unknowable to subsequent generations, as the existence of so many women's and queer people's cultural expressions in earlier eras have been excluded from the historical record.

Fans who found and operate their communities' digital archives do not guarantee that they or their works will be remembered, but they create the conditions of possibility for persistence and recollection. Perhaps the last quarter-century of digital fan archiving will matter to no one a quarter-century from now; but perhaps digital fan productions made between 1990 and 2015, and many genres of user-generated Internet content from the same time period, will be widely regarded as critically important forms of early digital networked culture, just as silent films hold a venerable place in cinema history and amateur ham radio operators are understood to be the direct ancestors of the broadcasting industries. Maybe successive generations of girls and women and LGBTQ people will benefit from the first twenty-five years of fan archiving; maybe future historians will value the ability to access evidence of what it was to be female and queer online in the first wave of mass Internet use. Fan archivists cultivate this chance, this *may-be*.

Fans' archive building and archive maintenance constitute attempts to prove to the future that particular queer and female ways of being and making existed. If fan archivists did not carefully assemble such proof, women and queer fans' digital collective actions would almost certainly be forgotten, go unlearned, or simply be, as Mbembe puts it, the subjects of doubt, of disbelief that they ever *were*. In part this forgetting or doubt would result from the ephemerality of digital production, against which all digital archivists must tirelessly work, but it would also arise from the tendency of hegemonic discourse to elide and ignore what it cannot incorporate.

What I have said here of women and queer fans can be said of every non- and counterhegemonic group that forges a community online and seeks to archive its communications and cultural expressions. Rogue archival efforts are political efforts, for, as Derrida argues, "There is no political power without control of the archive, if not of memory. Effective democratization can always be measured by this essential criterion: the participation in and the access to the archive, its constitution, and its interpretation" (Derrida 1995, 11). Those on the edges of power, in real life and in virtual life, continually invent new cultural forms and genres online, prolifically generate and actively spread their digital productions, and establish digital archives, first of all, in order to demonstrate that their cultures and their creations exist and deserve the status and recognition of *being*, and second, to refuse those at the center of power complete "control of the archive." Rogue archivists insistently pry open "the archive"—digital cultural memory writ large— to include their idiosyncratic repositories, and thus foist some measure of democratization onto the field of contemporary archival practice.

Objects and Methods

I define rogue digital archives as Internet sites that can be accessed by all online users, with no paywalls or institutional barriers; that allow all content to be streamed or downloaded in full; that do not delete, hide, or edit content based on copyright holders' allegations of legal infringement or for any other reason; that are committed to the persistent publication and long-term preservation of all content that they store; that have search-and-retrieval features so that users can locate specific texts; and that have either weak ties or no affiliations with traditional memory institutions such as government archives, university libraries, and brick-and-mortar museums. There are many sites and platforms that are commonly referred to as "archives" that do not meet these criteria, such as YouTube, Tumblr, and Wikipedia. (YouTube frequently deletes user-uploaded content because of copyright-related complaints; Tumblr is not searchable and has shown little interest in the long-term preservation of content published there; and Wikipedia allows readers to view summaries of many texts, but not the texts in full.) I do not discuss in detail any of these sites.

My examples of rogue archives include the Internet Archive, Project Gutenberg, ibiblio, the Rhizome ArtBase, and many smaller, lesser-known archives founded by specific subcultures, minority groups, and artists' collectives. I discovered a great deal of information about these archives from news articles and various texts written by their archivists that have been published online.

However, one category of archives—fan fiction archives—serve as my core case study because, as stated above, fan fiction communities have a long history of archive building, and their primary modes of cultural production are remixing and appropriation, making fans exemplary digital memory workers at the level of content production as well as content preservation. I gathered much more primary data about Internet fan fiction archives than about any other type of rogue archive. From June 2012 through March 2013, I directed an oral history project titled "Fan Fiction and Internet Memory" or FFIM, funded by the UC Berkeley Committee on Research and the Townsend Center for the Humanities. Undergraduate Lisa Cronin, PhD candidate Andrea Horbinski, and I conducted 56 interviews with 50 participants who had a history of activity in fan fiction archives, as archive-builders and/or maintainers, as authors, as dedicated readers and reviewers, or as all of these. Participation was by invitation only, and we extended invitations to individuals whom we knew personally, or knew *of*, from our own histories of online fan activity; we also welcomed suggestions from our interviewees of additional individuals that we should invite. We were able to recruit participants who had been involved with Internet fan archives from the early 1990s, when the first archives opened, through the time of our interviews in 2012 and 2013. In other words, we succeeded in gathering descriptions and recollections of every phase of Internet fan fiction archives from the fans that we interviewed, with many interviewees having actively participated in online fandom from its inception. All interviews were conducted in English, and participants discussed primarily, though not exclusively, Anglophone media and English-language fandoms. We cite all interviewees by their chosen names; some participants chose their legal names, and others chose pseudonyms (in Internet fandoms, the use of pseudonyms is a common practice). The appendix contains detailed information about the FFIM oral history project, including the demographics of our participants in table form and as visualizations.

The temporal range covered in the personal histories shared by our FFIM participants allows me to make some generalizations about how fans think and feel about fan fiction archives. It would be a mistake for me, or any researcher, to presume that fans are more similar than they are different; the FFIM project reinforced what I already knew from my participation in fan communities, which is that fans' experiences of online fandom are, for the most part, distinctive and unique, and a number of contentious issues arise in online fandom on which every fan has her own personal opinion. There are as many pathways through Internet fandom, as many attitudes toward fandom, and as many intellectual frames for understanding the "fan experience," as there are individual fans. However, I was able to identify several clusters of opinions, attitudes, and experiences from our interviews, and I have done my best to accurately represent our participants' views in the chapters that follow.

In addition to the oral history research team I assembled, I put together a different but related team of digital humanities researchers, for a project called "Fan Data," funded by the Hellman Fellows Fund and the UC Berkeley Committee on Research, and supported in part by URAP (the Undergraduate Research Apprentice Program at UC Berkeley). The Fan Data team collaborated to build a series of "data scrapers"—Python scripts that could be used to extract and analyze large sets of information from websites—to perform various quantitative analyses of a diverse range of Internet fan fiction archives. The conclusion includes numerous visualizations and graphics that show the size and scale of these archives, as well as their rates of production, growth over time, and (for some archives) the number of authors, reviewers, and readers who have participated in them. Over the years that I have worked on this project, I have repeatedly been asked for numerical statistics about the phenomenon of Internet fan fiction. I specifically designed the Fan Data project to quantify the "world" of fan fiction archives, and am pleased to present our results here.

As for my theoretical methods: I have already begun to discuss Internet archives using the language of performance, and I will continue to employ performance-related vocabulary throughout this book. At UC Berkeley, I am a scholar "housed" in two campus units: the Berkeley Center for New Media (BCNM) and the Department of Theater, Dance & Performance Studies (TDPS). Given that my two academic "homes" are new media studies and performance studies, it should not be surprising that performance studies is crucial to my thinking about new media, and vice versa. My analyses will be suffused with terms and concepts borrowed from performance, even though—or, I would say, *because*—I am examining new media objects. In break 0, which follows this introduction, I offer the reader a genealogy of the decades-long interrelation of performance studies and new media studies; I intend this work to be a contribution to that important, if largely unknown, tradition of scholarship.

Chapters and Breaks

This book contains two types of sections: "chapters" and "breaks." The breaks and the chapters alternate, so following this Introduction, the reader will encounter the somewhat clumsily numbered break 0, then chapter 1, then break 1, then chapter 2, then break 2, and so on. I have written the chapters in what I consider to be a straightforward academic style, and have written the breaks somewhat differently. I would say that some of the breaks are more informal, some are more experimental, and the rest are simply less rounded-out and more fragmentary than the chapters. I have taken the term "breaks" from hip-hop culture; here is a definition from S. Craig Watkins (2005): "[Grandmaster] Flash and his DJ friends believed that in every great record there is an even greater part, what they called 'the get down part.' That part of the song is more formally referred to as the break" (27). I would not claim that this book's breaks are "greater" than its chapters, but I do think of the breaks as "the get down parts." I generated them more in the spirit of jamming or freestyling, while I crafted the chapters in order to advance specific arguments.

I have explained that I conceive of digital cultural memory as being composed of both actual and metaphorical archives. Some of the chapters and breaks therefore concentrate on digital archives located on the Internet, while other chapters and breaks investigate archives at a more conceptual level. The idea of repertoire will be a consistent thread through all of my varied approaches to different archival entities and genres; I will make the case that many forms of repertoire penetrate, suffuse, and define many archival practices.

Break 0, "A Glossary of Key Terms," will serve to define several concepts that I have only alluded to in this introduction: digital cultural memory, archontic production, the connection of new media studies and performance studies, fan fiction, and fan fiction archives. This break aims to help the reader gain an understanding of what I mean by each of these terms, and why I think them important, which will help the reader as she progresses through the subsequent sections and repeatedly encounters these key concepts.

Chapter 1, "Memory Machine Myth: The Memex, Media Archaeology, and Repertoires of Archiving" strives to dispel the widespread perception that the Internet is a vast archive, and surfaces the fears of the "digital dark age" expressed by professional and amateur archivists alike. I argue that only dedicated archival labor, which I frame as "techno-volunteerism," can "save" digital information, and I characterize the activities of techno-volunteer archivists as a repertoire of what is referred to in design studies as "infrastructuring."

In break 1, "Canon and Repertoire," I argue that there can be no "canon" of rogue digital archives, and that in fact, such archives are intrinsically opposed to the very notion of canonicity. Instead, I propose that we place more importance on defining the repertoires of digital use and Internet preservation.

Chapter 2, "Archival Styles: Universal, Community, and Alternative Digital Preservation Projects," describes a diverse set of digital archives that I think exemplify the ascent of rogue cultural memory. I posit three major archival styles or categories: universal archives, community archives, and alternative archives, and I list several specific archives in each category. I then list various fan fiction archives, and explain how fan fiction archives function as universal, community, and alternative archives simultaneously.

Break 2, "Archive Elves," discusses digital archival work in relation to theories of free labor and creative labor, especially theatrical labor.

In chapter 3, "Queer and Feminist Archival Cultures: The Politics of Preserving Fan Works," I describe how fan archives serve women and queer users, and how their value as cultural resources derives largely from their operation as archives for these communities.

Break 3, "Fan Time versus Media Time," argues that fan fiction archives support a temporality that queers and feminizes the time of mass media synchronization.

In chapter 4, "Repertoire Fills the Archive: Race, Sexuality, and Social Justice in Fandom," I explore how a number of digital archivists seek to diversify their databases through what I call the "repertoire of archive contribution," attempting to attract content in categories that they deem lacking. I examine several fanworks "challenges" that explicitly set the goal of diversifying fan fiction archives by incentivizing fans to produce stories about characters that are non-white, non-Western, and/or practice non-normative sexualities. I argue that these challenges invite fans to enact a kind of "carnival repertoire," in which they work (play) together, for delimited periods of time, to invert and subvert the systemic privileging of whiteness in mass media representations, and to add more stories of difference to both fan archives and the total archive of media.

Break 4, "'Works' or 'Performances'?," investigates the traditional distinctions between the kinds of cultural productions that constitute archivable "works" and unarchivable, ephemeral "performances," and asks how these differentiations blur when we examine the output of online communities.

Chapter 5, "Print Fans versus Net Fans: Women's Cultural Memory at the Threshold of New Media," describes the period in the history of media fandom when the Internet was new, and fans understood that they were facing the imminent migration of their culture from the real world to the virtual network. I explain that many female fans did not think that their culture, which had always been transmitted through face-to-face and embodied practices—that is, through repertoire—would survive a "translation" to the digital, and I read their doubt against the background of a larger cultural imaginary, found in cyberpunk narratives and other forms of popular discourse, that framed women as the last defenders of humanity against the encroaching reign of machines.

Break 5, "A Femslash Parable of the Print-to-Digital Transition," is a close reading of one piece of fan fiction, a *Star Trek: Voyager* story in which Captain Janeway and one of her crew members, the female cyborg Seven of Nine, embark on a sexual relationship. I interpret the popularity of Janeway/Seven fan fiction as a desire among female fans for "print fans" (an older generation of fans, who had entered fandom as a face-to-face enterprise that traded printed zines) to reconcile and merge with "net fans" (younger fans, who had only known fandom as a digitally networked enterprise.)

Chapter 6, "The Default Body and the Composed Body: Performance through New Media," argues that the Internet is a *body medium*, that is, a place where users perform through virtual bodies. I argue that when users appropriate the faces and bodies of actors for their online interactions and representations, they are performing through "composed bodies," while their own physical bodies are "default bodies." I claim that fan fiction illustrates very well how embodiment is crucial to Internet-based performances—in other words, we do not at all leave embodiment behind when we "go" online.

Break 6, "Body and Voice in Fan Production," details several kinds of performances common in media fandom that are different from fan fiction: real-world performances (such as "cosplay" or costume play, and childhood play), audiofic performances (in which fans record themselves reading fan fictions aloud), and fan casting (in which fans imagine a media property cast with actors of their choosing; fans often "genderswap" or "racebend" known characters).

Chapter 7, "Archontic Production: Free Culture and Free Software as Versioning," considers archontic production as a cultural analog to the free software movement (launched by programmer Richard Stallman) and GNU/Linux development, and also puts archontic production in relation to postcolonial, ethnic minority, and feminist theories of culture-as-archive, and of appropriative-writing-as-performance, that predated the digital age.

Whereas chapter 7 proposes similarities between free culture and free software, break 7, "Licensing and Licentiousness," examines an important difference between GNU/Linux hacking and the segment of free culture constituted by fan production: free software is deeply concerned with licensing (e.g., Stallman's GNU General Public License, which developers use to "modulate" copyright and permit others to lawfully modify their code), while most fans do not concern themselves with questions of the legality of their practices, and simply "take license" with the media they consume. Building on Derrida's linking of licentiousness to democracy, I suggest that fan archivists, and all rogue archivists, seek not to resist current legal or cultural structures but to bring a new kind of democracy into being, one that fulfills democracy's promises regarding diversity and transformability.

The concluding chapter, "Fan Data: A Digital Humanities Approach to Internet Archives," presents the results of a data-scraping project that I led from 2012 through 2014. An array of data visualizations illustrates the scale and rate of growth of various fan fiction archives and indicates the massive size of rogue archiving projects.

Break 0   A Glossary of Key Terms

It may seem strange to begin the body of this book with a break—a "break 0," a break from a work that has not even properly begun yet—but I intend this break to be a launching pad, a delivery of fundamental ideas and concepts that will, I hope, prove helpful to the reader's intake of all of the sections that follow.

In the introduction, I briefly mentioned a number of terms—such as "digital cultural memory," "the intersection of new media studies and performance studies," "archontic production," "fan fiction," and "fan fiction archives"—that warrant elaboration. At the very least, the reader should be aware of how I think about each of these constructs, and what I find to be significant about them. Therefore, the text below can be read as a glossary of terms. It is divided into five subsections, each dedicated to a different question:

- What Is Digital Cultural Memory?
- What Is "Global Theater"? (or, What Does New Media Studies Have to Do with Performance Studies?)
- What Is Archontic Production?
- What Is Fan Fiction?
- What Are Fan Fiction Archives?

While the subsections may not at first appear to have much to do with one another, I think that by the end of this break—or at any rate, by the end of this book—it will be clear that these topics are closely interlinked.

What Is Digital Cultural Memory?

As I wrote in the introduction, I think of *digital cultural memory* as a double helix, composed of two intertwining strands. The first strand is made up of what I call *archontic productions* (see below). The second strand is made up of actual Internet archives. Here I will offer a short background for my think-ing on this second strand, the phenomena of archives that exist online (but I will occasionally make reference to the first strand, the genre of digi-tal appropriations and remixes that many digital archives are devoted to preserving).

My idea of digital cultural memory starts with the fact that "memory institutions," such as libraries, museums, and archives, understand their mission to be the keeping and transmission of "cultural memory," usu-ally meant in a vernacular rather than an academic way. For these institu-tions, preserving cultural memory means ensuring that significant artifacts representing the histories of the wider cultures in which they, the institu-tions, operate, are accessible by successive generations. Guy Pessach defines memory institutions as "social entities that select, document, contextual-ize, preserve, index, and thus canonize elements of humanity's culture, his-torical narratives, individual and collective memories" (Pessach 2008, 73).[1] Memory institutions have been aware since at least the 1994 Commission on Preservation and Access that the future of cultural artifacts, both those born digital and those born analog, will be largely digital, and that, as Julie Holcomb (2000) writes, "the long-term preservation of digital resources" is equivalent to "preserving our cultural memory." The archival and heritage professions are well aware that the cultural and the digital are increasingly bound together, that more and more predigital and nondigital cultural materials must be transcribed or remediated into digital formats (Pascha-lidis 2008, 5; Bolter and Grusin 2000), and that more and more cultural productions, as well as cultural preservation efforts, are being launched digitally, as a result of which, states Gregory Paschalidis, "a whole new economy of social memory has emerged" (Paschalidis 2008, 4). This econ-omy is composed not just of professional preservationists and intellectuals authorized to curate and administer cultural materials for laypeople; it also encompasses amateur cultural producers and amateur digital archivists.

Paschalidis writes that the "development and diffusion of modern communication media" which has made possible the "democratization and pluralization of social memory" (2008, 4) offends and repulses large numbers of cultural workers. In the context of discussions and debates taking place among memory, heritage, and information resource profes-sionals, digital cultural memory means cultural memory that lives in and as digital media, and the fact that vast swaths of nonprofessionals are under-taking micro- and macro-sized missions pertaining to digital cultural mem-ory gives the entire field an "unregulated, decentralized and multi-voiced character [that] plays havoc with our inherited routines and established protocols. ... It is no accident, then, that many teachers and intellectuals, the presumed guardians and characters of cultural memory, revolt against this new social organization of social memory, whose confusing lack of order, center or discipline seems to them as disorienting as amnesia," Paschalidis states (2008, 4). A condemnation of amateur digital activity, including amateur archiving, can be found in many cultural critics' writings from the 2000s;[2] this attitude is well represented by a 2007 article in the *Guardian* that opines, in relation to the Museum of Online Museums, "Nowhere has [the Internet] been more successful than in the field of meaningless rubbish. Here, vast swathes of tat are housed in one handy place for easy navigation" (cited in Terras 2010, 426).

But some information scholars, such as Melissa Terras, have taken a different position on the growing ranks of amateur digital archivists, arguing that "the uncharted territory of digital resources created outside traditional memory institution boundaries can provide a rich source of materials for both the general public and academic researchers. Additionally, those creating such online materials are generally more successful in interacting with their relevant online communities than memory institutions are. ... The best digital resources created by enthusiasts, in their own time and at their own expense, can inform the library, archive, and cultural heritage community about best practice in constructing online resources, and reaching relevant audiences in the process" (Terras 2010, 425–426). Mizuko Ito (2006), Charles Leadbeater and Paul Miller (2004), Ruth Finnegan (2005), Clay Shirky (2008), Matthew Kirschenbaum et al. (2009), and Robert Stebbins (1992, 2001) are among those who laud the cultural memory work performed by amateur archivists, both now in the digital era and at every point in the history of memory institutions, as amateurs have always played a large part in founding and growing organizations for the preservation of social and cultural histories, some of which have fed into, or become, museums and academic research disciplines.[3] Leadbeater and Miller (2004) propose the term "Pro-am" as suitable for referring to a person who "pursues an activity as an amateur, mainly for the love of it, but sets a professional standard" (20), and Stebbins (1992, 2001) employs the phrase "serious leisure" to describe the commitment and effort that some hobbyists dedicate to their chosen pursuits; Terras (2010) uses these framings of amateurs' labor in her discussion of amateur digital archivists, suggesting that amateur archivists execute digital cultural memory projects that are different from professional preservationist work but comparable to it, and that deserve consideration as serious, rather than ridiculous or random or trivial, enterprises.

Digital cultural memory thus refers to a moment in time, a turning point in the history of memory institutions: the mid-1990s through the present have been a period of transition from analog to digital formats for libraries, museums, and other predigital archives, and a period of emergence for amateur digital archivists. The role that amateur archivists are playing in the field of digital cultural memory is growing, and has compelled acknowledgment by the archival professions, acknowledgment that has manifested as condemnation by some circles, and as approbation by others.

The phrase *digital cultural memory* also flags an uneasy overlap of new media studies with the research field defined as "memory studies," which analyzes the historical, political, and philosophical significance of personal and collective recollection. Memory studies goes back at least as far as Plato's (2005 [360 BCE]) *Phaedrus*,[4] but the field in its contemporary form[5] was initiated by Maurice Halbwachs's *Social Frameworks of Memory* (1925, in *On Collective Memory* [1992]), in which Halbwachs articulated his theory of collective memory. Halbwachs argues that, as individuals form their memories in society, "It is also in society that they recall, recognize, and localize their memories. ... [Memories] are recalled to me externally, and the groups of which I am a part at any time give me the means to reconstruct them" (Halbwachs 1992, 38). Jeffrey Olick, Vered Vinitzky-Seroussi, and Daniel Levy summarize Halbwachs' theory of collective memory when they write, "All individual remembering ... takes place with social materials, within social contexts, and in response to social cues" (2011, 19). One implication of Halbwachs's work is that a society's technologies for storing and retrieving its memories influence and inform how and what individuals recollect; as Halbwachs states, the "means to reconstruct them [memories]" are given by the society to the individual. Thus, how digital technologies affect collective "remembering" is a point of interest for memory studies.

Jan and Aleida Assmann, drawing on Halbwachs's theories and on Aby Warburg's 1930s writings on social memory, advanced their idea of cultural memory beginning in the 1980s.[6] Jan Assmann (1995) points out that Halbwachs's and Warburg's thinking resisted the nineteenth-century notion that collective memory depended on biological inheritance ("racial memory" [125] and "survival of the type" [125–126]), and proposed the alternative that cultural memory is the technology by which a society survives. Each generation transmits culture to the next, not through genetic inheritance, but through the conservation and repeated reexamination or reuse of cultural objects and rituals—"cultural formation[s] (texts, rites, monuments) and institutional communication (recitation, practice, observance)" (129)—that constitute a society's "objectivized culture" (128). Assmann uses Warburg's capacious idea of objectivized culture, which included "not only works of high art," but also "posters, postage stamps, costumes, customs, etc." (129), which, Warburg argued, possess a type of "mnemonic energy" (129).

Taking up the Assmanns' and Warburg's arguments that objects and practices—including those that originate in so-called low and everyday culture—are bearers of cultural memory, media scholars over the past twenty years have investigated how collective memory and social identity are consolidated and transmitted through communities' uses of media texts, such as photographs, pop and rock songs, films, television broadcasts, and digital communications.[7] In line with this branch of media studies, fan fiction and other genres of transformative fan works, as well as the source texts that inspire them, can be seen as cultural memory objects, possessing the kind of "mnemonic energy" that Warburg attributed to posters and postage stamps. Fan communities define their group identities in part through what Warburg calls "costumes" and "customs" (dressing up as favorite characters and gathering together at fan- or industry-organized conventions, a type of public performance called "cosplay," is a long-standing fannish tradition that combines costumes and customs), and in part through collecting, circulating, consuming, and discussing fannish objects, both industry issued and fan made. Fan fiction and fan fiction archives help to reinforce fans' sense of participating in a common culture. Within a given fandom, the practices of writing and/or reading fanfic are themselves acts of remembrance (of the source text and of the affective charge fans experience when interacting with the source text), and archives of that fandom's fiction writing are aggregators of fans' remembrances, which are plural and diverse, but recognizable as all belonging to a specific fandom. Fic archives thus embody and convey the cultural memory of specific fandoms, as well as the cultural memory of the larger enterprise of media fandom. For all fan archives, and the practices and rituals involved in making and using fan archives, perpetuate the cultural memory of what it is to be a media fan.

However, even as communities regard digital artifacts as instantiations and transmitters of cultural memory, and eagerly build Internet archives in order to preserve their access to these objects and practices, there is great uncertainty about digital media's capacity to serve as a vehicle for cultural memory over long periods of time. Digital technologies are not perfect archival technologies; rather, they tend toward loss and disappearance. Paschalidis, citing Robert Darnton, states that the "singular, distressing law that governs digital evolution" is that "hardware and software become obsolete so rapidly as to condemn all digital texts 'to belong to an endangered species'" (Paschalidis 2008, 6; Darnton 2008, 79). The rapidity with which digital material is vanishing raises alarms in Geert Lovink that echo the fears of cultural amnesia expressed by memory studies scholars. Lovink writes, "Because of the speed of events, there is a real danger that an online phenomenon will already have disappeared before a critical discourse reflecting on it has had the time to mature and establish itself as institutionally recognized knowledge" (Lovink 2011, 8). In other words, if digital objects and practices do not remain accessible long enough to be thoroughly understood by the society that produces them, there may be no digital cultural memory at all. Jan Assmann writes that "cultural memory comprises that body of reusable texts, images, and rituals specific to each society in each epoch, whose 'cultivation' serves to stabilize and convey that society's self-image" (Assmann 1995, 132), and if digital texts are not reusable, if Internet rituals that arise around those texts are not reenactable, then societies in this epoch, at the dawn of the digital age, cannot be stabilized. Even as people increasingly use digital networks and platforms to create and archive cultural productions, the relationship between digital technologies and cultural memory is tenuous at best.

In chapter 1, I will explore some of the questions that arise from thinking "digital cultural memory" together with "memory studies": How can communities employ digital tools in making and preserving culture, while at the same time, digital texts become inaccessible or unusable so rapidly that digital technologies are sometimes characterized as *anti*archival? How *can* cultural memory, as defined by memory studies, be served by digital platforms that are never permanent? Are online communities, and other communities reliant on digital tools to bear their group identities into the future, condemned to short life spans commensurate with the abbreviated utility of these tools?

I will argue that online archives can only be made stable, reliable, and accessible over the long term by human labor. One of my central claims is that digital technologies are not innately archival, but must be *made* to serve archival purposes by the constant efforts of archivists. Thus, the second referent of digital cultural memory is a labor requirement: communities must work to conserve their digital artifacts and rituals, or risk losing them to the digital's proclivity for ephemerality and loss.

What Is "Global Theater"? (or, What Does New Media Studies Have to Do with Performance Studies?)

What does performance studies have to do with new media studies? Or: Why use performance studies in an analysis of Internet cultures and digital phenomena? My answer is: New media studies has had quite a long history of borrowing metaphors and frameworks from the fields of drama, theater, and performance, and while this genealogy may not be well known to either performance scholars or new media scholars, it is an important one; I situate my work within this robust, if unheralded, school of thought. I will briefly review the major intersections between new media studies and performance studies, and then, in the next section, I will explain why I believe that it is useful to think "new media" and "performance" together when studying online fan cultures and fan archiving.

Marshall McLuhan, one of the key founders of what we today call new media studies, first compared new media to performance in 1970, when he sought to replace his 1962 term "global village" with a new term: "global theater." In *From Cliché to Archetype*, McLuhan (1970) writes, "Since Sputnik [launched in 1957] put the globe in a 'proscenium arch,' and the global village has been transformed into a global theater, the result, quite literally, is the use of public space for 'doing one's thing'" (12). The "global village" has become the "global theater" (apparently in 1957, even before McLuhan first mentioned the "global village," but let us not scrutinize McLuhan's chronology too closely) as a result of the telecommunications networks that cross the world, making every place on the planet a potential performance space.[8]

McLuhan's replacement of "village" with "theater" as his preferred metaphor is read by John Tinnell as a commentary on live video transmission. Tinnell (2011) writes, "Widespread televisual applications of satellite technology cultivated a tele-performative space, which ... added an awareness that whatever took place in the presence of various electronic recording devices could be broadcast to and seen by large audiences all across the world, in real time and for all time. This awareness becomes a force of enculturation; one does not need to possess a video camera to be ontologically affected by the cultural (f)act of televisual recording and worldwide broadcasting." While I agree with Tinnell that McLuhan had global live television in mind when he declared that the world is now a theater, the implications of McLuhan's "global theater" extend well beyond the medium of television.

The Internet, more than television (indeed, the two are increasingly converging), is a public space for "doing one's thing," each participant generating his or her own content, putting on his or her own show, as it were. The Internet "turns the globe into a repertory theater to be programed" (McLuhan 1970, 9–10) by its participants. The Internet realizes McLuhan's vision of a space that serves as a stage that is theoretically open to an infinite number of players, each doing their thing for others to witness, and thus contributing "programming" to the nonstop theater. McLuhan is even clearer in his prediction of a networked participatory culture in his 1972 book, *Take Today: The Executive as Dropout* (coauthored with Barrington Nevitt), when he writes of "the institution of a new kind of global theater, in which all men become actors and there are few spectators. The population of the world is both the cast and content of this new theater. The repertory of the theater consists of a perpetual *happening*, which can include the retrieval or *replay* of any previous happenings that men choose to experience" (McLuhan and Nevitt 1972, 145).

Thus McLuhan introduces the link between new media and theater, predicting future telecommunications platforms that will be open to participation by all (all who can gain access to the platforms and have the knowledge to use them, that is). From McLuhan's phrase "perpetual *happening*," and his statement that "all men become actors and there are few spectators" we can see the influence of 1950s and 1960s performance culture—specifically, the famous "Happenings" by Allan Kaprow and others—on early 1970s new media theory. The connection that McLuhan perceives between performance and new media is *interactivity*, and McLuhan would not be the only new media theorist to see this resonance: in *The New Media Reader*, Noah Wardrip-Fruin and Nick Montfort (2003) write that "the *idea of interaction* associated with Happenings [in the fifties and sixties] was profoundly inspiring and has remained so for decades" as that idea "reflected and provoked a desire to break down distinctions between creator and audience—a desire and activity now central for many new media practitioners. ... The 'Happenings' are a touchstone for nearly every discussion of new media as it relates to interactivity in art" (83).

Numerous new media theorists after McLuhan (though none cite him) have argued that all human–computer interaction (HCI), and not only computer-based art-making, is most fruitfully conceptualized as a form of interactive performance. Brenda Laurel's *Computers as Theater* (1991), Sherry Turkle's *Life on the Screen* (1995), Allucquére Rosanne Stone's essay "Will the Real Body Please Stand Up?" (1991), and Stone's book *The War of Desire and Technology at the Close of the Mechanical Age* (1996) all argue that new media actions and engagements are types of performance because they invite, and often require, computer users' interactions with hardware and software and/or other users via digital networks. Laurel, an interface designer, relates that designers often regard theatergoing as a model for HCI: "As researchers grapple with the notion of interaction in the world of computing, they sometimes compare computer users to theatrical audiences"

(1991, 16). Laurel's own view is that users resemble actors more than they do audience members: "People who are participating in the representation [of actions on their computer screens] aren't audience members anymore. ... They *become* actors—and the notion of 'passive' observers disappears. In a theatrical view of human–computer activity, the stage is a virtual world" (17). Turkle writes that the interactivity of computer use has the potential to boost each user's sense of being an autonomous individual, of "being an actor in one's life" (1995, 274). Stone states that "Computers are arenas for social experience and dramatic interaction, a type of media more like a public theater" than like prior forms of electronic media, such as cinema (1996, 16).

Erving Goffman's 1956 book *The Presentation of Self in Everyday Life* also began to be explicitly cited by new media theorists in the 1980s and 1990s, as performance studies (of which Goffman's *Presentation* is a foundational text) became established as a discipline (or what Shannon Jackson calls an "anti-discipline") in the US academy (Jackson 2004, 30). Goffman proposes that every person is an actor playing a variety of roles in her daily life—that anytime "the individual is in the immediate presence of others," the individual expresses herself and tries to manage others' impressions of her, and in doing so, performs (Goffman 1956, 1–4). Goffman's concept of everyday social performance resonates with McLuhan's notion of a "global theater" in which all are actors; Joshua Meyrowitz's *No Sense of Place: The Impact of Electronic Media on Social Behavior* (1985) was the first to combine Goffman's and McLuhan's concepts. Although Meyrowitz's (1985) analysis centers on television and has limited application to contemporary network technologies, he puts forward the notion that "electronic media [effect] a very discernible rearrangement of the social stages on which we play our roles" (4). Goffman has been, by far, the most influential performance theorist on new media scholars.[9] Goffman's perspective on performance comes through clearly in statements such as this one by Annette Markham in her essay "The Dramaturgy of Digital Experience": "Regardless of which device or interface I'm using, what I'm wearing, or where I'm located I am performing multiple roles on multiple simultaneous stages with a globally distributed range of actual and potential audiences" (Markham 2013, 280).

McLuhan, Laurel, Turkle, Stone, and the diverse and growing group of Goffman-influenced new media theorists all stress that network technologies facilitate what Mark Poster (2012) calls "many-to-many communication." In a global telecom network, everyone can perform; the networks are like open stages that users fill with their performances. Importantly, liveness or presence is not a defining characteristic of performance for any of these thinkers. What is regarded as an essential feature of "performance" to many performance theorists—physical bodies that are copresent with one another at the time and place of action—is not at all necessary for "performance" as conceived by new media studies. Stone addresses this issue directly, stating, "We have to rethink some assumptions about presence," as major "shifts in cultural beliefs and practices" are giving on to "repeated transgressions of the traditional concept of the body's physical envelope and of the locus of human agency" (Stone 1996, 16). In other words, human agency, and therefore human presence, is no longer located exclusively *in* the human body. Stone claims that the computer is "a technological object that acts as a channel or representative for [physically] absent human agencies" (16–17) (Stone acknowledges her indebtedness to Laurel on this point). But Stone is rare among new media theorists who explicitly deal with the challenge that metaphors of online-interaction-as-performance pose to definitions of performance-as-presence. The vast majority of new media scholars simply assume that bodily presence is not necessary for performance, and that, following McLuhan, Goffman, and the aforementioned theorists, every person performs on the virtual stage of the Internet each time he or she posts a comment, shares a link, publishes a fan work, or builds an Internet archive.[10]

Therefore, when I draw on metaphors and vocabularies of theater, drama, and performance to describe the activities of Internet fan archivists, I feel myself to be working within a well-developed branch of new media theory that was founded more than four decades ago.

What Is Archontic Production?

My theory of *archontic production* is that many readers, filmgoers, gamers, and television viewers engage deeply with the "archive" of media culture, which is the array of perceptible cultural artifacts distributed widely for mass consumption. From this archive of source texts, media users select the texts they want to work with, and from those texts, they extract what they like and what they need, using those extractions as the raw materials for their own cultural productions, such as fan fiction.

A virtual archive—let us call it a "meta-archive"[11]—is opened by each source text, and encompasses not only that source text but all variations and transformations of it produced by readers, viewers, listeners, scholars, critics, and fans. These meta-archives, comprising every version of a source text that have ever been imagined, told, played, sung, written, or recorded in an audiovisual medium, are conceptual rather than perceptible.

I have appropriated the word "archontic" from Jacques Derrida's essay "Archive Fever," in which Derrida states that no archive can ever be said to be finished or fully completed. "The archive is never closed. It opens out of the future" (Derrida 1995, 45), he writes. Derrida recalls the original ties of the concept and term "archive" to the *archons*, the lawmakers or "superior magistrates" (9) in Greek society who housed the official documents of the *polis* in their homes. "The archons are first of all the documents' guardians. They do not only ensure the physical security of what is deposited and of the substrate. They are also accorded the hermeneutic right and competence. They have the power to interpret the archives" (10). I use "archontic" to signal a new identification of the "archons" of culture. Who has the power to interpret the archives of mass media? I argue that it is the audiences, the consumers, the *users* of media.

And I would also argue that it is these new archons who have taken it upon themselves to "ensure the [digital] security of what is deposited and of the substrate" in the meta-archives of mass media. A great deal of digital cultural memory is composed of archontic producers on the one hand, and archivists of archontic productions on the other.

What Is Fan Fiction?

Fan fiction (also called "fanfiction," "fanfic," or simply "fic") refers to stories written by fans of mass-produced texts (of any genre and all media, from comics to video games to novels to television programs to popular music) that appropriate the characters of the textual universe, and occasionally other elements as well, such as story arcs, settings, narrative themes, and so on, but are original stories. The practice of revising and augmenting received stories is ancient—the creation of folklore, mythology, and tall tales depends on this practice[12]—but the beginning of fan fiction as it is currently understood, as a form of creative appropriation by predominantly female communities organized as "fandoms" around mass media productions, can perhaps be dated to the first issue of the first *Star Trek* fanzine, *Spockanalia*, printed and released in 1967 (Fanlore, "Spockanalia").[13] Beginning in the early 1990s, fans began to post fan fiction on the Internet (in chapter 5, I discuss the period of transition from zine-based, or "print" fandom, to Internet-based, or "Net" fandom), and today, the vast majority of fan fiction is published and distributed online rather than in printed formats.

Fan fiction stories usually expand on potentialities that inhere in the "source" texts: adventures that the characters could have had but never did; relationships or sexual encounters they might have had but didn't—or which were never portrayed onscreen; events in the characters' lives that may have taken place before, after, or in between the events described in the source material. Many "fics" do not adhere very closely to their source texts, and only borrow characters in order to put them in "alternate universe" or "crossover" settings: for example, two characters in a movie about a postapocalyptic wasteland might be "ficced" as a couple who meet in a contemporary coffee shop, or in a Regency-era ballroom, or at Hogwarts School of Witchcraft and Wizardry; two straight-identifying characters might be "ficced" as having a same-sex relationship; a character who is male in the source text might be written as a female in a fanfic. The attitude of fan fiction to its source material is thus usually a strange combination of fidelity and infidelity: a work of fanfic may be much the same as the source in certain respects but very different in others. It is this hybridity of repetition and difference in fan fiction that has led fan scholars to make a strong case that performance studies and theater studies offer the best frameworks for understanding fan fiction.

Kurt Lancaster (2001) uses Richard Schechner's theory of "restored behavior" (1985, 35–36) to describe fan fiction writing and reading: "Memories of ... actors' performances of their characters reside within the fan texts, and writers as well as readers restore these performances through this work. ... A fan fiction author places strips of behavior garnered from watching episodes of [a television show] into new contexts. The reader of the fanfic imagines the immaterial behaviors occurring in the story as being concrete, or *performed*" (Lancaster 2001, 132–133). Schechner argues that all performance, "from shamanism and exorcism to trance, from ritual to aesthetic dance and theater, from initiation rites to social dramas," consists of restored behavior, by which Schechner means "living behavior treated as a film director treats a strip of film. These strips of behavior can be rearranged or reconstructed" (Schechner 1985, 35). In Lancaster's conception of fan fiction, fan writers do not physically rearrange or reconstruct the strips of behavior that they witness actors performing into new live performances ("living behavior"), but they effectuate such reconstructions through their fanfic stories, and so produce performances in their readers' imaginations. Fan fiction stories therefore resemble performances, and operate according to performance principles, more than other kinds of fiction stories do, because fan stories, at least those that are based on audiovisual media texts, intentionally and explicitly strive to evoke actors' physicality (their facial expressions, styles of movement, and vocal intonations) in written form, and readers of fanfic understand that they should create mental images of specific actors performing the original scenes that the fan author describes—they know that they should envision those actors "playing" the scenes that the fan author has written for them.

Lancaster's reasoning suggests a comparison between fan fiction and screenplays, and Francesca Coppa's essay "Writing Bodies in Space" (2006) makes this comparison explicit. Coppa relates that "some fan fiction has been written in script or teleplay form, often by fans who aspired to write for [a] produced show. ... To write in script form would be a sign of a writer's aspiring professionalism" in the 1970s and 1980s (Coppa 2006b, 234–235). "But the script form has always been unpopular among readers," Coppa states, "so a fan whose primary audience was other fans rather than the television industry was more likely to tell her dramatic story in prose" (235). Coppa's point is that even though most fan fiction stories are written as prose rather than in teleplay format, all fan stories are essentially scripts: "The existence of the teleplay [as a format that fan authors occasionally use] helps to demonstrate fan fiction's roots as an essentially dramatic literature, but the larger part of my argument is that fan fiction directs bodies in space even when it's not overtly written in theatrical form" (235). Coppa echoes Lancaster when she writes that fan writers and readers "bring our memories of [actors'] physicality to the [fan] text, so the [fan] reader is precharged" (236), that is, ready to imagine the actors playing out the scenarios written by the fan writer. "We've met these characters already, and now we're seeing them again. In theatre, we call that a *production*," writes Coppa (236).

To think of fan fiction as a performance genre is a similar move to the one that the "global theater" thinkers make in identifying networked communications, including textual communications, as performances, as theater. For Lancaster and Coppa, as for the global theater theorists, writing can be performance. But the concept of global theater is that each person puts on a performance online, that each of us is an actor on the virtual stage constituted by digital networks, while Lancaster and Coppa propose that fan writers script and direct the action of what Coppa calls "bodies in space," the actors whose screen performances fans admire, and the fan-directed enactments of these bodies take place on a virtual stage that is not online, but in fan writers' and readers' imaginations. We know, from the existence of fanzines and other earlier print-based forms of archontic fiction, that fan fiction-as-performance predates the Internet; the virtual stage on which archontic productions take place—the "mind's eye" of audiences—certainly has a longer history than the virtual stage of telecommunications networks on which global theater plays out.

What Are Fan Fiction Archives?

Fan fiction archives are repositories of fan fiction stories, where authors can deposit their fics and readers of fics can retrieve them. Morgan Dawn (2012) spoke to my research team about donating her large store of fanzines to the University of Iowa Libraries' Zine and Amateur Press Collections (http://www.lib.uiowa.edu/sc/resources/zineresources/), following the lead of her friend and fellow fan organizer Sandy Herrold, and other zine collectors have done the same. The University of Iowa Collections constitute what is currently the most visible and widely accessible archive of fan fiction (and other forms of fan works, including fan art and fan commentary) published from the 1960s through the 1980s. But Internet fan-fiction production has, from the 1990s to the present, been archived primarily in fan-built digital archives (I describe a number of major online fic archives in chapter 2). Typically, online fan fiction archives are databases that contain all of the stories submitted to the archivists by authors; archivists organize the stories according to various categories of metadata (source title, story title, author name, characters [prominently featured in the fanfic], rating [from general to mature], genre, etc.), to make the databases easily searchable by readers.

If, following Lancaster and Coppa, we consider fan fiction to be performances, as stagings, as variants of source texts that are not "derivative" but are simply diverse productions of popular texts, and if we also take into account that these sorts of fan performances are far older than electronic network technologies, we must define fan fiction archives as something other than simply periodically updated databases.

Every fan fiction archive is, in some sense, a concrete, visible incarnation of a wide variety of performances based on that source material. The *Lord of the Rings* archive, the *Avengers* archive, the *Romeo and Juliet* archive are all virtual meta-archives, as I explained above. A meta-archive cannot be seen; it is a construct, a metaphor that allows me to describe the relation of adaptations, transmediations, remixes, commentaries and fan texts to one another and to their sources. Lancaster's and Coppa's theories allow me to assert that fan fiction archives embody and make perceptible these formerly only-virtual meta-archives. A meta-archive grows without limit; it keeps growing as long as audiences keep encountering the source material and transforming it. Before Internet fan archives, it would have been impossible to visualize any one always-increasing meta-archive, except possibly by placing every fan fiction zine in a given fandom on the same shelf—and even then, only the fans who had physical access to that shelf would have been able to read through all of the contents of that collection. But Internet fan fiction archives make visible and accessible multitudes of stories that have been written in a given fandom.

Fan fiction archives put all of the (public and published) performances based on a given source text on display, for fan readers' engagement. It is as if Shakespeare enthusiasts were able to see all (or, at least, many) of the performances of *Hamlet* being produced simultaneously, in one giant performing arts building containing innumerable stages, each stage occupied by a different company offering their unique take, revision, or reworking of *Hamlet*. A Shakespeare fan could walk from stage to stage to stage inside that enormous building, watching *Hamlet* after *Hamlet* after *Hamlet*, and when he reached what he thought was the last stage and the last version of *Hamlet*, he might find that the structure had the capacity to expand infinitely, and that new stages, with new performances of *Hamlet* being played out on them, were being added on to the building all the time.

What does it matter whether we can "see" a meta-archive or not? What does it signify that fan archives make visible these constantly growing meta-archives that were, before the Internet, only conceptual? One significance is that fan archives finally put to rest a question that has been asked about consumers of popular culture and popular media for centuries, which is: Are audiences of mass texts passive or active? Do they merely receive ideas and ideological messages that are "injected" into them by the media they consume (the "hypodermic needle" theory of media reception),[14] or is there some kind of active response engendered in them by their acts of consumption (the "active audience" theory of media reception)?[15] For decades, cultural studies scholars have argued that audiences are active, that they make their own meanings of texts, that they are never wholly passive in their intake of media.[16] Fan scholars, without exception, have made the same claims. But online fan archives, and all collections of remix—in fact, the rising popularity of remix as a new literacy, made possible by the affordances of digital and Internet technologies—serve as evidence that audiences actively and imaginatively engage with media texts. Audiences create in response to the media texts they receive. Acts of media reception spur acts of media *production*. Internet archives of fan appropriations and remixes are deeply important because the massive quantities of creative output that they contain constitute a kind of proof that audiences are not "cultural dopes" (Hall 1998, 446), that is, the dupes of mass culture, but are users of mass culture, who take from media texts what they desire to incorporate in their own archontic productions.

1 Memory Machine Myth: The Memex, Media Archaeology, and Repertoires of Archiving

The Internet Is Not a Memory Machine

The Internet, the World Wide Web, and desktop and mobile digital tele-communications devices comprise a system of networked computing that is often framed as a giant memory machine, a comprehensive and infinitely expansive archive, which automatically saves users' posts and emails; the sites they have visited; and the text, image, and video content they have uploaded, downloaded, emailed, or blogged/reblogged/tweeted/pinned/tagged. From this supposed total archive, users will presumably be able to retrieve elements and traces of (what will be) their digital histories far into the future.

However, the system of networked computing fails as an archive much of the time. The Internet, far from autosaving all that we do and share there, is what Wendy Chun (2008) calls an "enduring ephemeral." "The internet may be available 24/7, but specific content may not" (167), Chun writes. In other words, the near-constant availability and functionality of the network itself may suggest that everything that traverses the network is permanent and durable, but this association between the persistence of the Internet and the persistence of online content is a delusion, a false equivalence. In this chapter, I will argue that when the Internet *does* work well as an archive, it is because of the initiative and interventions of what I call "techno-volunteers": self-appointed, mostly nonprofessional individuals and collectives who regard some digital cultural productions and events as worth preserving, and who choose to devote their skills, time, effort, and often their own finances to constructing and maintaining online archives. Networked digital culture is "saved" for future generations, not primarily through any automated operations, but through the labors of human actors.

Origins of the Memory Machine Myth

The myth that the Internet, combined with networked computers, constitutes a massive digital memory machine is as old as the concept of the Internet itself. Vannevar Bush, who served in World War II as Director of the Office of Scientific Research and Development (OSRD) (in which role he coordinated the military research activities of scientists at government and private institutions throughout the United States), first proposed the research project that would become first the ARPANET, than the Internet, in an essay called "As We May Think" that appeared in the *Atlantic* in July 1945. In the essay, Bush outlines his idea for a device called the "memex," which would be a desk-sized machine linked to a large network of information. The memex, writes Bush, will be a "mechanized private file and library," "a device in which an individual stores all his books, records, and communications, and which is mechanized so that it may be consulted with exceeding speed and flexibility," and will serve as "an enlarged intimate supplement to his [a human user's] memory" (Bush 1945, sec. 6). Bush describes the memex as a large desk housing scrolls of microfilm, on which are recorded documents, notes, and "associative trails" (sec. 8), that is, links between specific documents, or mental pathways through sets of material, forged by the user (see figure 1.1).

Bush's memex concept influenced many of the scientists and engineers who architected the Internet and other networked computing technologies, such as J. C. R. Licklider, who wrote seminal papers in the early 1960s proposing interactive networked computers that would be operated through graphical user interfaces (GUIs), and whose 1965 *Libraries of the Future* quotes Bush's "As We May Think" on its first page; Douglas Engelbart, whose Augmented Research Center team invented the computer mouse and did pioneering development on hyperlinking, networking, and GUIs; and Ted Nelson, who coined the terms "hypertext" and "hypermedia." Nelson makes Bush's impact on his thinking clear when he begins a 1972 paper on hypertext with the sentence "Bush was right" (Nelson [1972] 1991, 245) (this paper of Nelson's is entitled "As We Will Think," a direct homage to Bush's "As We May Think").[1] Licklider, Engelbart, and Nelson's work in the 1960s and early 1970s, answering the call issued by Bush in his 1945 essay, gave rise to the Internet and to the system of networked, graphical, hyperlinking, personal computing that forms the basis of contemporary digital culture.

Bush can thus be credited as one of the "fathers" of the Internet. As head of the OSRD, which oversaw the Manhattan Project and the manufacture of

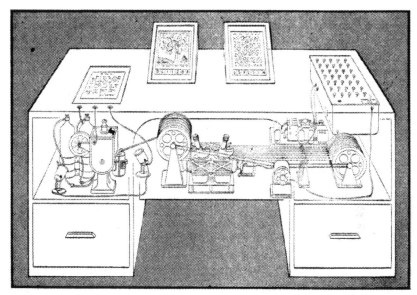

MEMEX in the form of a desk would instantly bring files and material on any subject to the operator's fingertips. Slanting translucent viewing screens magnify supermicrofilm filed by code numbers. At left is a mechanism which automatically photographs longhand notes, pictures and letters, then files them in the desk for future reference.

Figure 1.1
A drawing of Vannevar Bush's proposed "memex" machine. From *LIFE*, September 10, 1945, 123.

the first generation of nuclear weapons, he was also one of the "fathers" of "the bomb."[2] It is not coincidental, I think, that Bush's "As We May Think" appeared in print just one month prior to the US military's August 1945 release of atomic bombs over the Japanese cities Hiroshima and Nagasaki. At the time that he wrote "As We May Think," Bush almost certainly had full advance knowledge of the plan to use atom bombs on Japan, and in the essay, he alludes to the horrors of nuclear warfare and its world-destroying potential—a potential that he knew the entire world would soon learn about—and contrasts it with the world-saving potential of the memex. Bush writes that US scientists, having banded together so effectively during wartime for "the making of strange destructive gadgets," should now turn their talents toward "objectives worthy of their best." In other words, having become creators of killing machines for use in a global armed conflict, one that "appears to be approaching an end," scientists should, in the postwar period, turn their talents to the creation of machines that will have "lasting benefit" to humanity (Bush 1945, sec. 1). His proposal for such a machine is the memex. Bush states: "The applications of science ... have enabled him [the human] to throw masses of people against one another with cruel weapons. They may yet allow him truly to encompass the great record and to grow in the wisdom of race experience. He may perish in conflict before he learns to wield that record for his true good. Yet, in the application of science to the needs and desires of man, it would seem to be a singularly unfortunate stage at which to terminate the process, or to lose hope as to the outcome" (sec. 8).

What *may* take place next in the course of human history, Bush seems to indicate, is the end of human history, that is, the end of the human. The termination of the species may be brought about by the invention of weapons of mass destruction, made possible by scientific research. But Bush proposes that, just as his network of American science and technology researchers has produced weapons that can usher in the final phase of human history— global nuclear war—so can the same network turn itself, in peacetime, to the purpose of augmenting human intelligence—with the memex—to the point that humans will be able to "wield" "the great record" for "his [the human's] true good" (Bush 1945, sec. 8). Bush pits the memex against the atom bomb in a timed race: either human research will bring about the destruction of humanity, or it will increase humans' capacity for learning and thought by such a degree that humans will, at last, be wise enough to serve their own "true good" (a world without war, perhaps?). In Bush's worldview, both the atom bomb and the memex are all-encompassing technologies. Bush seems to perceive postwar humanity as confronting a binary choice: total war, or complete archive. One or the other will be humanity's future, in Bush's immediately pre-postwar prognostication.

The Memory Machine Myth after Bush

The Internet thus began as a fantasy of the perfect archive, a technology that would preserve the vast record of human knowledge in its entirety. That fantasy has accompanied the network from 1945 to the present, becoming pervasive in both scholarly and popular discourses.

Noah Wardrip-Fruin, commenting on Ted Nelson's "dream of hypermedia" as it was laid out in Nelson's groundbreaking *Literary Machines* (first published in 1980 and revised and published nine additional times between 1981 and 1993), points out that Nelson's dream was in large part a vision of "the ultimate archive." Writes Wardrip-Fruin (2000),

Consider the dream of hypermedia, put forth by Ted Nelson and others over the last three decades: That, in a not-so-distant future, we read and write (view and draw, hear and compose) most everything from and to a world-spanning network. That everyone have the ability to produce their own documents, and connect them with any other public documents. That the author may constantly create new versions of his or her own document, and individuals may create their own versions of any public document. ... That historical backtrack and degradation-proof storage allows us to visit any version, any moment in the network's history. To have the ultimate archive, and yet have each element of the archive constantly in process. Dynamism without loss. Impermanence enfolded within permanence.

Nelson's hope continued Bush's: they shared the dream that the system of networked computing would prove to be a more robust, capacious, complete, and durable archive than had ever existed before.

Today, it is not uncommon to come across academic texts that subscribe to the Bush–Nelson line of thinking about the Internet as an archive. For example, the authors of *Digital Humanities* write, "Ubiquitous networks have led and will continue to lead to evolutions in pedagogy precisely because they involve the outsourcing of memory. ... We would be ignoring precedent completely if we assumed that the *allatonceness* of a vast and increasing digital archive accessible anywhere at any time will not affect the way that we learn" (Burdick et al. 2013, 25). The authors do not explain or defend their equation of the Internet with memory, but treat it as self-evident.

In popular discourse, the perception of the Internet as an automated archive circulates widely via truisms such as "The Internet remembers everything." Adults warn youth that they must be circumspect in their speech and actions, since anything they say or do can be recorded and distributed online, reaching larger audiences over longer periods of time than any young person probably intends. "The Internet is written in pen" has become an oft-repeated saying. The notion that the Internet archives children's and teens' foolish antics is reminiscent of a much older type of threat directed at the young, that all their follies and missteps would be documented in their "permanent records." A 2012 *Huffington Post* article by Hemanshu Nigam, former Chief Security Officer of News Corp and MySpace, employs this exact phrasing: "By our own conduct, we build a permanent record of everything we do online. Whether we want them to or not, family, friends, recruiters, employers, enemies and criminals may easily access our lives with a single click of a button. What might seem like a good idea at the time often leads to embarrassment and long-term personal and professional devastation. The Internet remembers, and that is a fact that we must remember too" (Nigam 2012). A host of similar blog posts and op-eds, warning of the impossibility of erasing documentation of one's immature indiscretions from social networks, populate news, parenting, and career advice websites.

Warnings about the Internet's auto-archival nature are sometimes couched within scenarios of tragedy, as in the blockbuster action film *The Dark Knight Rises (TDKR)*, the final installment of director Christopher Nolan's trilogy of Batman films. In *TDKR*, one criminal character, cat burglar Selina Kyle, voices her dismay that she cannot "start fresh," as crime-fighter Batman urges her to do. Selina laments, "There's no fresh start in today's world. Any twelve-year-old with a cell phone could find out what you did. Everything we do is collated and quantified. Everything sticks." In this framing, the Internet-as-memory-machine dramatically undermines the ability of individuals to continually reinvent themselves, an ability that is presented as simultaneously a freedom and an imperative in Western postmodern, postindustrial, neoliberal society. Given that the constant flux of twenty-first-century global capital demands endless flexibility and unfixity from workers at every economic stratum—capital mines the willingness of workers to "start fresh" multiple times over the course of their lives—it is understandable that parents and educators are deeply concerned about what they assume to be the Internet's built-in archival functions, as a young person's adaptability, on which their academic and career success depends, may be thwarted at any moment by the system's recollection of a wrong move from their past.

Warnings of the Digital Dark Age

However widely the myth of the automatically archival Internet has spread over the past seventy years, the fact is that the system of networked computing utterly *fails* as a memory machine. Professionals in the field of library and information sciences (LIS) have issued warnings about digital data's tendency to degrade and disappear since the mid-1990s. They have collectively proclaimed that the Internet and computers do *not* constitute the greatest archive in human history, but rather the reverse. The current historical moment, they argue, may be a "digital dark age," a time of which future generations will have scant records, owing to the short lifespans of our current digital platforms, devices, and applications (as compared to the lifespans of older technologies, such as paper).

As far as I can determine, the first note of caution about digital decay was sounded in 1995, when Michael Lesk, a member of the US Task Force on Archiving of Digital Information,[3] gave a talk called "Preserving Digital Objects: Recurring Needs and Challenges," at Australia's Second National Preservation Office (NPO) conference on Multimedia Preservation. Lesk told a tale of archivists putting their faith into new media that appeared to be betraying them. The abstract of his presentation reads, "Acid process wood pulp paper, used in most books since about 1850, ... threatened cultural memory loss. But digital technology seemed to come to the rescue, allowing indefinite storage without loss. Now we find that digital information too, has its dark side" (Lesk 1995). In other words, Lesk argued, digital storage media at first appeared to be archivists' ideal solution to the degradation of paper, but then turned out itself to be highly degradable. After Lesk's talk came a report by Paul Conway (1996), then head of the Preservation Department of Yale University Library, which pointed out, "Information in digital form—the evidence of the world we live in—is more fragile than the fragments of papyrus found buried with the Pharaohs," because "the permanence, durability, and stamina of newer recording media" have declined steadily over the course of the twentieth century, making the digital age one in which we have "information density" but few options for permanently preserving that information and keeping it accessible. One year later, in 1997, Terry Kuny appears to have coined the phrase "digital dark age(s)" in a paper presented at the Sixty-third IFLA (International Federation of Library Associations and Institutions) Council and General Conference. Kuny (1997) argued that "we are moving into an era where much of what we know today, much of what is coded and written electronically, will be lost forever. We are, to my mind, living in the midst of digital Dark Ages" (1).

Then, in the late 1990s, voices outside of the LIS professions—from the mainstream press, the business world, and humanities research—joined in the chorus cautioning that digital technologies are often antiarchival. In 1998, science and technology journalist James Gleick wrote in a *New York Times Magazine* story, "Many of the world's librarians, archivists, and Internet experts are warning that the record of our blooming digital culture is heading for oblivion, and fast. They note that we have already begun losing crucial scientific data and essential business records. ... In the electronic era, we are stockpiling our heritage on millions of floppy disks and hard drives and CD-ROMs. These flaky objects go obsolete dismayingly fast, with new technologies rolling in on product cycles as short as two to five years" (Gleick [1998] 2002, 197). In 1999, Stewart Brand, an early new media entrepreneur who founded the influential *Whole Earth* magazine, published an essay in *Library Journal* called "Escaping the Digital Dark Age." Brand called for "a long-term strategy for storage," a remedy to the fact that "there is still nothing in the digital world like acid-free paper." Brand quoted an admonition from Peter Lyman, a librarian at the University of California, Berkeley: "We know there is a 500-year life to microfilm properly cared for. But what do we do with digital documents? ... We need a digital equivalent to microfilm, a 500-year solution" (Brand 1999, 46).

One of the most widely cited critics of the myth of the archival Internet is Wendy Chun, who dissects Bush's "As We May Think," criticizing Bush's prognostication that a future technology of networked memory will "make possible the overarching archive of human knowledge in which there is no gap, no absence—a summation of human knowledge" (Chun 2008, 159). Far from fulfilling Bush's goal of a perfect archival technology, writes Chun, "Digital media is not always there. We suffer daily frustration with digital sources that just disappear. Digital media is degenerative, forgetful, erasable" (160).

Chun characterizes networked computer memory as not wholly forgetful, but as unreliable and unpredictable in what it remembers. Reconciling the "Internet remembers everything" narrative with the digital dark age narrative, Chun states, "If things constantly disappear, they also reappear, often to the chagrin of those trying to erase data" (Chun 2008, 167). The system of networked computing sometimes resurrects un-looked-for, unwanted information, and often deletes valuable and longed-for information. Vannevar Bush's perfect memory machine has never existed.

The Wayback Machine: The Real Memex?

And yet, even in digital dark age discourse, one finds echoes of Bush's belief that a combination of the Internet and programmable computers will produce an automated archive. Chun ascribes a kind of ultimate saving power to a different "machine" than Bush's memex: the Internet Archive's Wayback Machine. In 1996, the Internet Archive, an organization I will describe in more detail in chapter 2, began developing software to crawl and download all publicly viewable websites and take "snapshots" of them, in order to record the websites at different intervals over their life spans. This software, and the service that stores, preserves, and makes accessible what it "harvests," is collectively called the Wayback Machine. Chun writes, "Like search engines, the Internet Wayback Machine (IWM)[4] comprises a slew of robots and servers that automatically and diligently, and in human terms obsessively, back up most webpages. ... However, unlike search engines, the IWM does not use this data to render the internet into a library but rather uses the backups to create what it calls a 'library of the Internet'" (Chun 2008, 168). Chun, quoting from the Internet Archive's website, compares the Wayback Machine to libraries, and emphasizes the Wayback Machine's mission of maintaining digital cultural memory:

The need for cultural memory drives the IWM and libraries more generally. Noting the loss of early film archives due to the recycling of early film stock, the archivists state that they are building an "internet library" because "without cultural artifacts, civilization has no memory and no mechanism to learn from its successes and failures." ... The IWM is necessary because the Internet, which is in so many ways *about* memory, has, as [Wolfgang] Ernst argues, no memory—at least not without the intervention of something like the IWM. (Chun 2008, 168–169)

It is curious that, despite her opposition to Bush's idealistic goal of designing a comprehensive memory technology, Chun describes the Wayback Machine as a mechanism that accomplishes Bush's hopes. The line that she excerpts from the Internet Archive's website—"without cultural artifacts, civilization has no memory and no mechanism to learn from its successes and failures"—reiterates Bush's sentiments quite precisely. The storage of civilization's memory in machines that will permit humans to review their entire collective history and their accumulated knowledge, in order to plan and execute the best possible future for humanity, is exactly Bush's dream for the memex.

Chun acknowledges that the Wayback Machine does not capture every detail of every webpage that it archives, "because webpages link to, rather than embed, images, which can be located anywhere, and because link locations always change, the IWM preserves only a skeleton of a page, filled with broken—rendered—links and images" (Chun 2008, 169). But despite the Wayback Machine's imperfect recall, Chun nevertheless attributes to the Machine the same all-encompassing archival power that Bush attributes to the memex. Where others regard the Internet as the descendent of Bush's memex concept, Chun recognizes the Wayback Machine to be the only "real" memex, or memex made real (in other words, in Chun's view, the Internet is *not* the memex, as most people think—but the Wayback Machine *is* a means by which the memex's aims are accomplished). Positioning the Wayback Machine in relation to the digital dark age discourse summarized above, Chun writes, "Blind belief in digital memory threatens to spread [a] lack of memory everywhere and plunge us ... into the so-called digital dark age. The IWM thus fixes the internet by offering us a 'machine' that lets us control our movement between past and future by regenerating the internet on a grand scale" (169).

I greatly admire the Internet Archive's Wayback Machine and appreciate that the Machine's snapshots of websites at different points in time makes it possible for online users to occasionally visit websites that have been taken down, or to see websites in previous incarnations, even if the "saved" versions are, as Chun points out, somewhat "lossy" (with missing images, broken links, etc.). However, I dispute Chun's idea that the Machine successfully preserves digital cultural memory in an automated fashion. Both Bush and Chun fail to recognize that automated archival machines can be easily defeated by their own, or other machines', operational assumptions. For example, the Wayback Machine's policies cause it to delete its records of virtually all websites whose original domain owners have ceased to renew those domain names, which results in losses on a far greater scale than Chun describes. One online fan fiction archivist, whose fan pseudonym is Morgan Dawn (2012) and who was interviewed for my oral history project, explains this particular failing of the Wayback Machine: "Once you lose your domain ownership—so let's say 'Morgan.com,' I allow it to lapse. Somebody, usually bulk resellers, will snap it up, and they'll park a [new web] page [at that URL]. 'This domain available for sale.' They will always put a robot text [robots.txt] file on that parked page. The Internet Archive, Wayback Machine, honors robot text files and next time it scans my—'my'—former website, it will see the robot text and it will retroactively remove my entire history. And this has been a problem that's been known since 2007." Reinforcing Morgan Dawn's assessment, a blog post on the *Economist* website in January 2014 calls robots.txt "the [Internet] archive's kryptonite" (Fleischman 2014). One of the driving questions of Chun's (2008) essay is, What leads to "the resuscibility or the undead of information" (171)? The Wayback Machine, though it sometimes proves very useful for the recovery of "dead" websites, also adheres to policies that cause sites to be erased from its index, sites that it had previously recorded, rendering it an untrustworthy archive that will likely become more unreliable as time goes on, as more domain names expire and more gaps in the Machine's "memory" appear.

Fears of a digital dark age are therefore not necessarily opposed to the myth of an automatically archival Internet. Chun seems to suggest that one answer to the ephemerality of online data is to automate the periodic saving of data through some memex-like technology. In other words, Bush's goal of making a networked technology into a comprehensive archive may have failed, but other automatic archiving machines, however imperfect, may succeed in preserving the cultural memory of these early years of the digital age. A wish for a technological solution to the constant disappearance of human knowledge, culture, and experience lies at the heart of both the myth of the Internet-as-archive and the dread of a digital dark age.

What is missing from both of these discourses is the figure of the human archivist.

Techno-Volunteerism

Automated archival technologies acting alone have not, to date, yielded exceptional results. It is human archivists, working on and with digital tools and networks, that make digital ephemera endure—when it does endure, which is not often. Matthew Kirschenbaum writes,

> As electronic objects begin to accumulate archival identities (by virtue of the libraries, museums, and other cultural repositories increasingly interested in or charged with collecting them), it will become essential to understand ... where the most significant challenges of digital preservation finally lie. ... Those challenges, while massively technical to be sure, are also ultimately—and profoundly—social. That is, ... effective preservation must rest in large measure on the cultivation of new social practices to attend our new media. (Kirschenbaum 2012, 21)

Here Kirschenbaum argues that many of the answers to complex questions about digital preservation lie not in the technical end of archiving, but in the social aspect—in people. People must work together to preserve "electronic objects"; technology alone will not accomplish it. Nonprofessional Internet archivists have dedicated thought, intent, and time to developing the "new social practices" of archiving for which Kirschenbaum calls. At some point in each of their lives, these people decided that what they wanted to do with their spare time was to construct and maintain Internet archives of cultural content. I call these self-designated digital archivists "techno-volunteers."

I will use the terms "techno-volunteers" and "techno-volunteerism" to signal a distinct break from the technological determinist (or "techno-determinist") thinking that has suffused theories of digital archives from 1945 to the present. Technological determinism is a school of thought that emphasizes the agency of technologies in moments of sociocultural change; a simplistic summary of a techno-determinist outlook is, "Shifts in technology cause shifts in society and culture." The methodological school most often opposed to techno-determinism is social constructivism (or social construction of technology [SCOT]), which focuses on how humans' agency and social structures decide what kinds of sociocultural impact specific technologies have; social constructivism's preferred object of analysis is "The social shaping of technology," a framework initially proposed by Donald MacKenzie and Judy Wajcman ([1985] 1999). According to this perspective, "Our technology of production is in many ways the *result* of our social relations," and "technical choices are simultaneously social through and through" (143).

New media studies usually frames the beginnings of the techno-determinist vs. social constructivism opposition as a battle of ideas between Marshall McLuhan (cited as the preeminent technological determinist) and Raymond Williams (as the primary advocate of the social construction perspective) that took place in the 1960s and 1970s. Narratives about this debate then point to the 1980s development and launch of actor-network theory (ANT) by Bruno Latour, Michael Callon, and John Law as a kind of resolution of the dichotomy, as ANT awards the same possibility for agency to all actors, or actants—both humans and nonhumans—that combine to form a sociotechnical system. Nonhuman actants may not have *intentions*, as humans do, but they nevertheless "make others do things" (Latour 2005, 107); for example, speed bumps cause human drivers to slow their vehicles, and so must be taken into account as significant players in social action. In his study of cell phone usage, Gerard Goggin articulates the viewpoint shared by many new media theorists, that ANT offers a middle ground between techno-determinism and social constructivism: Goggin writes that ANT revises "formulaic oppositions between technology and society," as it refuses to subscribe wholly either to the deterministic position or to the "countervailing reaction that society determines technology" (Goggin 2006, 11). Over the past thirty years, ANT has usefully drawn attention to "the necessity of a *composition* of forces to explain [an] action" and has productively asserted that humans and nonhumans are always co-actants, with frequent variance as to which actant, and which type of actant, is the "prime mover" in an action (Latour 1994, 35).

However, in studies and theories of archival technologies, determinism has always been a popular stance. Above, I described how Bush, Bush's adherent Nelson, Bush's critic Chun, and numerous popular writers and texts, have all promoted an idea of the Internet as an automatic archive. Wolfgang Ernst, outlining his proposal for a method of "media archaeology," conceives of recording technologies, beginning with the photographic camera, as "registering the past coldly, in contrast to painterly animation and historical imagination" (Ernst 2013, 47)—painting and history writing being two modes of recording the past that preceded photography. Here is another of Ernst's descriptions of photography as a memory machine: "With the emergence of photography, the idea of the theatrical gaze literally staging the past is displaced by the cold mechanical eye, a technologically neutral code rather than a subjective discourse" (Ernst 2005, 592). While photography is a vastly different technology from the Internet, they are both rendered into devices that record the past in a "mechanical" and "neutral" way in the discourse of Bush and his successors and in the discourse of Ernst and media archeologists.

While human decision and action are presumably necessary to activate the memex's and the photographic camera's documenting and storage functions, Ernst downplays the participation of the human user to the point of claiming that photographs are a non-"subjective discourse," and Chun frames the Internet "snapshot"-taking system of the Wayback Machine as non-reliant on human choice or intent, as do Nigam and others who perceive the Internet as a "permanent record." Even when Ernst writes directly about Internet archives, rather than memory technologies such as photographic cameras, he uses a language of automaticity; for example, discussing "born-digital media art," Ernst asks, "How does dynamic art archive itself?" (2013, 82).

In this book, I will relate the stories of many digital archivists and archive users to reveal how the old category of "archives" is being renewed in and through new media, generating new cultural forms and conflicts. By drawing heavily on my research team's interviews with human actants in digital archival systems, I will be employing a "theatrical gaze," which Ernst is eager to shunt aside in favor of the "cold gaze" of media archeology (see Parikka 2013, 8), in "staging the past" of digital archiving for the reader. While much valuable work on media technologies has resulted from Ernst's cold gaze, with its attention to the physical materiality and engineered operability of machines, a theatrical gaze will capture the participation of human as well as nonhuman actants in the history of Internet archiving. The efforts of what I call techno-volunteers have been so crucial to online archiving that to ignore or marginalize this labor would be to completely misperceive what it means, and what it takes, to "save" the Internet.

Repertoires of Digital Archiving

To say that I advocate techno-volunteerism over techno-determinism as a lens for understanding digital memory means that I wish to emphasize that Internet culture is best preserved by self-designated archivists who perform the labor required to create and sustain online archives, rather than by any built-in functionalities of the network or by any software system.

I argue that techno-volunteers have managed to archive online cultural production through developing archival *repertoires*, that is, through practices and ways of doing that are passed from person to person. "Repertoire" is a mode of memory that, as Diana Taylor (2003) points out, is often held to be the antithesis of the memory mode of "archive" (19–22). "Repertoire" transmits knowledge through processes of embodied mimesis, one person imitating what another person *does*, while "archive" transmits knowledge through recording technologies, such as handwriting, printing, sound records, photographs, film, and so on, one person decoding the knowledge that another person has encoded in fixed form. But Taylor resists the notion that the two modes of transmission form a dichotomy, and points out that archive and repertoire frequently cooperate or operate simultaneously.

I argue that techno-volunteers have developed ways and means of archiving the Internet that form the backbone of digital cultural memory. Without these practices, few, if any, digital archives would be in existence. Thus, if the Internet is ever usable *as* archive, it is made so by repertoire. Internet archiving depends on techno-volunteers' archival repertoires. Thus, it cannot be said that print culture's elevation of archive as a superior memory mode has persisted, unchallenged, into the twenty-first century, as digital culture has become more prevalent. Techniques of repertoire have, so far, mattered at least as much as the technics of archives in the preservation of digital networked culture.

Archiving with digital technologies requires human *enactment* of the archivist's repertoire. (Also, digital archives require a great deal of non-repertoire-based performance: online archiving has been so experimental throughout its first few decades that it often demands creative improvisation, and archivists sometimes wish they had more of a repertoire to rely on.) Print culture opposed archive to repertoire and assigned very different values to them; it placed archival modes in a privileged position over repertoire, linking notions of objectivity, facticity, fixity, whiteness, and modernity to archive, while relegating repertoire to the lesser position, associating repertoire with unreliability, subjectivity, fluidity, non-whiteness, and ancientness or "tradition." In the digital era, repertoire factors so heavily in the making and sustaining of digital archives that its inextricability from the archival mode, and its significance in processes of cultural preservation, cannot be contested.

One might say that print and analog media archives were, and still are, just as dependent on repertoire as digital archives. After all, human archivists have always been necessary for the archiving of cultural materials—a major objective of LIS education programs is to transmit the repertoires of archival labor required by traditional memory institutions to successive generations of workers. But the elaborate repertoires and rituals of librarians and archivists have tended to remain what Erving Goffman ([1956] 1959) would call "backstage" at memory institutions. Digital archives, in contrast, have foregrounded archival repertoires, for three major reasons.

First, because the first generation of Internet archivists have brought these repertoires into existence, their practices and ways-of-doing are more evident to users than the regularized, professionalized practices of LIS workers at traditional archives and libraries. Even if digital archive users do not "see" the vast majority of the work performed by archivists, users do see the differences between various archivists' methods, the upgrades and alterations that archivists make to their sites, and the moments when archives break (for example, when archives lose massive amounts of data) or succeed (for example, when archives experience large influxes of new content or recover data that was presumed lost)—in other words, the irregularities and lack of standardization between digital archives at this time, when the entire genre of online archives is still so young, announce the fact that humans are driving these archives, and those humans are still in the process of inventing and refining the repertoires of digital archival work.

Second, archivists often do a great deal of what Goffman ([1956] 1959) would call "front stage" work, representing their archives to the public and interfacing directly with users, and in general serving as the "face" (or, at least, the name and email address) of their archives. However, oftentimes only one archivist—the lead or founding archivist—is the primary contact for the archive's users; in many cases, a team of workers is required to support an Internet archive, and this support staff's work often is invisible to the public. Also, even if users know who the archivists of a given repository are, and frequently communicate with them, they may know nothing of, or severely underestimate, the type and quantity of labor that the archivists put into keeping their archives up to date and their interfaces easy to use.

The third reason that archival repertoires are more prominent in digital archiving than in print and analog archiving is the tendency of digital archives to fail. As I have been emphasizing, building on Chun's "enduring ephemeral" argument, digital data is so prone to disappearance that constant intervention is required to refresh data storage and keep it retrievable. At the least, data must be migrated to new servers when old servers cease to function optimally. Also, the rental costs of server rack space must be paid, ownership of website URLs must be renewed, sites should be mirrored (redundancy is one of the best methods for staving off accidental data disappearance), and when a lead archivist decides to quit her archival responsibilities, she should recruit her replacement(s) and oversee the smooth transition of the archive into new hands. If librarians had to not only enter books into their records and put them on the shelves of a library, but also had to move the entire library to a new building every few years, and also had to pay the rent and other fees associated with having the library building in the first place, and also had to make sure that for every single book in the library, a copy existed in another library with which they were in direct contact, and if librarians had to personally designate their replacement before resigning their post, or else risk the closure of the entire library, then both librarians and the library-going public would be far more conscious of how much repeated human labor and intervention—which I am calling archival repertoire—goes into the maintenance of a library. (Of course, the type of migration and mirroring labor that I am describing would be far more physically taxing, and would require much more time and many more financial resources, for employees at a brick-and-mortar library than it is for digital archivists, but digital archivists must still devote significant volumes of energy, time, and money to their repositories—just because the digital archive's repertoire is physically easier, and cheaper, to enact than the built-library repertoire does not mean that it isn't *work*.) Users of Internet archives know that archivists are needed to make those archives operational—if only when the archivist goes on a vacation, gets too busy with his or her "real" job or personal life to actively maintain the archive, or leaves the archive altogether because it becomes too much of a drain on his or her personal resources. The day that an online archive dies, or goes dark (that is, becomes inaccessible to the public), is the day when an archivist ceases to enact the repertoire, and this is usually the day when the user base becomes painfully aware of the repertoire's existence, and the necessity of the repertoire's repeated performance.

Repertoires and Scripts in New Media Studies

I am not the first to borrow the term "repertoire" from performance theory and apply it to new media phenomena. The field of digital design studies has thoroughly incorporated "repertoire" into its vocabulary, often using it to refer to the sum of practices and ways-of-doing that designers employ in their work (for example: "A rich repertoire of templates and a developed language for design qualities are two essential components of professional design ability" [Löwgren and Stolterman 1998]; "A repertoire of practice refers to the sum of available tools, techniques, strategies, tactics, ways of working, expertise and know-how from which a practitioner may draw, choose from, and/or combine to suit both known and novel situations or address a particular purpose" [Burrows and Morgan 2010]). This translation of design activity as "repertoire" has been especially useful for design pedagogy, as instructors can encourage students to build their repertoires by demonstrating their own "repertoires of practice" or "repertoires of experience." (For instance, the abstract for a paper by design educators Philippe Saliou and Vincent Ribaud [2004] reads, "Performing good design is a difficult task. To take up this challenge, practitioners rely on their repertoire of experience. Students, however, do not have any such repertoire. We propose an approach aimed at bootstrapping the repertoire.")

However, a richer use of "repertoire" in design studies can be found in Erling Björgvinsson, Pelle Ehn, and Per-Anders Hillgren's 2012 essay "Agonistic Participatory Design." Björgvinsson, Ehn, and Hillgren write about the struggles that often arise among participants in an emerging system, and stress the importance of the designer's leadership in negotiating the various demands placed upon the system: "The design researcher role becomes one of infrastructuring agonistic public spaces mainly by facilitating the careful building of arenas consisting of heterogeneous participants, legitimizing those marginalized, maintaining network constellations, and leaving behind repertoires of how to organize socio-materially when conducting transformative innovations" (Björgvinsson, Ehn, and Hillgren 2012, 143). Substituting "digital archivist" for "design researcher" in this formulation enables me to surface a number of core components of digital archival labor:

• The digital archivist engages in infrastructure building, or *infrastructuring*.[5]
• The archivist infrastructures *public spaces* that are often "agonistic," that is, engaged in conflict (see Mouffe's [2000] argument in *The Democratic Paradox* that "agonistic pluralism" is a better model for democratic interaction and action than consensus building).
• A large part of the archivist's task in building these spaces is moderating the conflicts that arise, such that "marginalized" opinions are registered and taken into account and the "network constellation" made up of "heterogeneous participants" remains operational despite the heterogeneity.
• Therefore, the archivist works from a repertoire, a repertoire of how to organize a system socially and materially (that is, technically), a repertoire of how to bring new digital archives into being, how to grow them, and how to sustain them.

The repertoire of digital archiving, from this perspective, consists at least as much of managing human relations, including arbitrating majority/

minority disagreements, as it does of providing technical services. As an Internet archivist succeeds in enlarging the public space (the archive) she has constructed, and in dealing with the space in a way that honors its "agonistic pluralism" on a continuing basis, the archivist not only adds to her own, individual repertoire of how-to-do-digital-archiving, but potentially to other Internet archivists' repertoires as well: like design students, digital archivists learn from observing one another's repertoires of practice.

Design studies' application of "repertoire" to infrastructuring—the notion that infrastructuring emerges from, and enhances, a designer's (or archivist's) repertoire, and that it involves negotiating between people as well as solving technological problems—reinforces my perspective that the growing phenomenon of digital archiving is better understood when viewed through the lens of techno-volunteerism rather than the lens of techno-determinism. Techno-volunteerism emphasizes the role of human actants in the creation of systems that preserve digital content and Internet content. Archivists are, as I have argued, incredibly important actants in the building of online archives, and their repertoires must include not only technical skills but techniques for receiving and processing users' feedback in the form of demands, complaints, requests, and compliments. In addition, this ongoing dialogue between designers/archivists and archive users illustrates that users of online archives are themselves techno-volunteers whose interactions with online archives help to shape them.

The recognition that users contribute to the design of platforms has been fostered by the subfield of design studies called "Participatory Design" and has also been productively discussed as "collaborative media" by Jonas Löwgren and Bo Reimer in their 2013 book by that title. Löwgren and Reimer (2013) attempt to put to rest the question of technological determinism versus social constructivism by asserting, "People using collaborative media products and services—people who produce media texts with the help of the products and services and people who consume texts—continuously take part ... in the design process" (148). In other words, the "uses" of a technology are never inherent in that technology, and are never completely fixed in place by the designers of that technology, but arise, over time, from interactions between the technology itself, its original designers, and the users who become its codesigners over time. Löwgren and Reimer point to another appropriation of performance language by new media studies—the concept of "scripts"—to make their point that "The designer [is] one actor in a large participatory process, not *the* actor" (144). Löwgren and Reimer cite ANT theorist Madeleine Akrich's argument that, "like a film script, technical objects define a framework of action together with the actors and the space in which they are supposed to act" (208). Akrich does not mean to imply that the "script" that technical objects give to actors wholly determines the performance of the actors with those technologies; like actors in a stage or media production, there is "incessant variation" between "the designer's projected user and the real user," and "the user's reactions ... give body to the designer's project" (209).

Affordances Need Performances

What Akrich describes as a "script" written into a technology's workings and interface, most designers would call a set of "affordances." Löwgren and Reimer credit Donald Norman for importing the term "affordance" into the field of interaction design in 1988, "as a way to understand what it is in a thing that makes it interesting or relevant for a potential user" (Löwgren and Reimer 2013, 25). Yochai Benkler (2006) lauds designers', engineers', and STS (science and technology) scholars' enthusiastic adoption of "affordances," as Benkler argues that the concept allows technology theorists to move away from "a naïve [technological] determinism." Benkler writes, "Different technologies make different kinds of human action and interaction easier or harder to perform. ... Neither deterministic nor wholly malleable, technology sets some parameters of individual and social action. It can make some actions, relationships, organizations, and institutions easier to pursue, and others harder" (17).

But it is possible to move even more definitively away from technodeterminism than Akrich and Benkler do. Rather than being concerned with what is "in" a technology that makes human action/interaction "easier or harder to perform," we can emphasize that *affordances need performances*. Affordances for archiving may inhere in networked computing—Bush insisted that computing have the potential for vast information storage and retrieval in "As We May Think," and his essay influenced subsequent hardware and interface designers to develop this potentiality—but archival *affordances* do not bring archives into being. They may make building archives "easier to pursue," as Benkler would say, but as this book will detail, the building and (especially) the maintaining of digital archives is not at all easily done; little is easy about the task of online cultural preservation. Technologies' affordances, or "scripts," may suggest uses for those technologies, but it is the human actor—let us replace "actant" with the older and more suggestive term "actor" here—who must perform those scripts, and it is the human body that "gives body," as Akrich says, to the

potential inherent in a technological system. The human actor's performance—the mind's decisions and the body's actions—actualizes what is
virtual in machines (their possibilities, their theoretical capacities), and
because volunteerism—human will—is involved, the actuality never maps
directly onto the virtuality. That is, there is never a precise, one-to-one correspondence between a technology's virtual aspects, encoded by its designers, and the technology's actual functioning, as performed by users.

A script is never, and can never be, performed exactly as intended, even
if the intentions of the "authors" are incredibly clear (which is hardly
ever the case). Rather, a script is always brought to life by, in, and through
human performance differently than the script's writers can predict. In fact,
like every script, technologies' scripts are performed differently by every
human actor every time a performance takes place. The laws of performance (different-with-every-actor, different-every-time, even if there is an
underlying resemblance or repetition between iterations as every actor who
engages with a specific technology works with the same "script") trump the
theory of technological determinism, in the case of digital archiving and in
the case of much technological use.

Concepts and terms of performance, as employed in design studies' and
ANT's theories of technological development, thus highlight the fundamental parts that people play in creating infrastructures of digital cultural
memory. "Performance" connotes modes of transmission that are not fixed
(as are text and recorded media), but are processual and evolving, that are
repetitious but are also unique in each instance—and so is an apt descriptor for how digital archiving currently occurs. "Performance" implies that
human actors must embody and execute scripted functions—and so is useful as a metaphor for the necessary collaborations between humans and
nonhumans that produce digital archival infrastructures. The readiness
with which some branches of new media studies are appropriating the language of performance indicates an opportunity for performance studies to
assert its centrality in the digital age. But it also challenges performance
scholars to decouple performance from liveness and physical presence, and
to turn their theoretical attention to the forms of repertoire and enactment
that are arising in and through new media, forms that do not depend on
face-to-face, real-world contact.

Although many have dreamed that computing machines could be built
to house and preserve human knowledge, or have assumed (hopefully
or anxiously) that the Internet and networked computing systems automatically save what users publish online, Vannevar Bush's ultimate memory machine is still a myth. The digital archives that techno-volunteers

construct, drawing on their repertoires of practice and experience, and building on those repertoires as they learn to negotiate the divergent needs and desires of their users and to navigate constant server-side and coding challenges, are currently the only persistent, reliable forms of digital cultural memory. These archives are only as persistent and as reliable as the humans who make them. Even so, they are, so far, more dependable than machines.

Break 1   Canon and Repertoire

The Breakdown and Multiplication of "Canon"

My initial concept for chapter 2 was that it should contain a list and description of some "canonical" digital archives, in order to give the reader a better understanding of the practice of rogue archiving that is this book's subject. But what would it mean to propose a "canon" of such archives? The rise of digital culture has thrown the very concepts of canon, canonization, and canonicity into radical question. I must investigate how networked computing forces a rethinking of "canon" before risking any new deployment of the term.

I will first briefly recapitulate for the reader the fact that the idea of a cultural canon came under fire long before the advent of widespread, everyday digital culture in the 1990s. Starting in the late 1950s and for several decades following, postmodern theorists and artists, including Susan Sontag, Andreas Huyssen, Andy Warhol, and Frederic Jameson,[1] questioned the utility of canonization, of a distinction between "high" culture and "low" culture; they argued that the conferral of elite status on once-shocking and avant-garde works—such as the modernist output of Pablo Picasso, Gertrude Stein, Virginia Woolf, Igor Stravinsky, and others—seemed only to dull the works' oppositionality and transform them into what Jameson (1984) deemed "a set of dead classics" (56). Postmodernists called for a collapsing of high and low categories, or an incorporation of the "pop," "mass," and "commercial" into the cultural canon.

Over the same period of time, from roughly the 1960s through the 1990s, the "canon wars" raged on US university campuses, fought between traditionalists who sought to identify and defend a core curriculum—"the 'basic' things an educated person should know, ... knowledge [that] develops the informed citizenry a democracy needs to thrive"—and reformists, who expressed "increasing discomfort with inherited curricula, ... seen as constrained by issues of race, class, gender, and first-world biases rooted in Eurocentric traditions," write Anne Burdick et al. (2013, 23) in *Digital Humanities*.[2] "The wars over the core," as Burdick et al. call these conflicts in the humanities, multiplied the number and types of cultural canons recognized as legitimate on college campuses, as faculty and students formed new curricula, programs, and research agendas in ethnic studies, gender and women's studies, disability studies, and other previously ignored and marginalized areas.

But Burdick et al. claim that the most dramatic shift in humanistic study effectuated by the canon wars was not the proliferation of different canons (or canons of difference), but the elimination, or extreme diminishment, of "the very idea of sharing common references or approaches." The authors write that "the perspective of … once-excluded materials," incorporated into humanities-oriented scholarship over the course of the canon wars, "carried with them alternative methodologies and different value systems that shattered any illusion of a single belief system within humanistic thought" (Burdick et al. 2013, 23), and so the very notion of canonicity itself, the thought that there should be *any* center of study that would be recognized as such by a group of scholars, faded.

Burdick et al. (2013) make the case that the clearing away of canonicity has opened the possibility for a new "generative humanities" to arise, one that combines traditional forms of scholarly analysis with "computational capacity" (5), and that will depend on, among other methodologies, "enhanced critical curation" (32–34). The authors argue that the digital era calls for heightened emphasis on curation, which they define as the individual scholar's ability "to filter, organize, craft, and, ultimately, care for a story composed out of—even rescued from—the infinite array of potential tales, relics, and voices" being made available via digital collections (34). "In the Digital Humanities, curation refers to a wide range of practices of organizing and re-presenting the cultural record of humankind in order to create value, impact, and quality" (34), they write. The authors argue, in other words, that scholars will never again be able to agree on a "canon," because they now have too much "archive." At best, individuals or teams will decide on selection strategies that they will apply to the panoply of digital archives at their disposal, and form their own curated collections of content, rather than attempting to establish a cultural canon based on broad consensus.

But then, given the potentially overwhelming preponderance of online archives hinted at by Burdick et al., can or should there be a "canon of digital archives" upon which humanities scholars agree, which presumably many scholars would utilize as their sources for primary documents? Surely, such a canon would include large electronic repositories that can be accessed through subscribing memory institutions (school and university libraries, for instance), such as JSTOR, Artstor, and EEBO (Early English Books Online); archives assembled by, or in close cooperation with, memory and heritage organizations, such as Europeana and all of the online portals of museums and libraries that offer access to content; and for-profit archives such as Getty Images. But what about archives that exist separately from the organizational structures that dominated the print era: governments, museums, libraries, universities, and corporations? What about born-digital archives founded, operated, and most often funded, by volunteers/amateurs/hackers/pirates/fans? It is widely accepted that if certain brick-and-mortar institutions have cultural legitimacy, such as the Library of Congress or the Musée du Louvre, then their online archives carry the same legitimacy. Can "rogue" digital archives attain the same legitimacy—can they be "canonized"?

My answer is no. I argue that the new media have ushered a new archival system into being, one that has little to do with print culture's definitions of "archive." Rogue digital archives cannot be canonized, but they do manifest archival styles, or archival repertoires, that can.

Canon/Repertoire and Archive

A cultural canon is usually thought of in relation to a cultural archive. The title of Aleida Assmann's essay, "Canon and Archive," in Astrid Erll and Ansgar Nünning's anthology *Media and Cultural Memory* (2008), prepares the reader for a repetition of the truism that a canon *is* an archive in certain respects, in that whatever literary texts or audiovisual works one could point to as canonical within a given culture constitutes a conceptual archive of what nineteenth-century cultural critic Matthew Arnold (2009) would call "the best which has been thought and said in the world" (5), at least as perceived by members of that culture. What is canonical therefore is, de facto, what is "archived" by the culture and society; canonical works are preserved, both virtually (theoretically everyone knows them and remembers them) and literally (they are conserved in repositories and kept safe from material degradation, as much as possible).

But A. Assmann's essay argues for a new relation between canon and archive. Rather than drawing an equivalence between canon and archive, A. Assmann (2008) aligns canon with *repertoire*, and defines archive as quite different from both of those terms. She explains that *active* or *working* cultural memory differs from *passive* cultural memory. "The institutions of active memory preserve the *past as present* while the institutions of passive memory preserve the *past as past*," she writes (98). She makes clear that working memory transpires through *repeated performances of the canon*—she gives the example of "works of art, which are destined to be repeatedly re-read, appreciated, staged, performed, and commented [on]" (99)—while the archives, the institutions of passive memory, hold cultural materials that are "relicts" (*sic*, 99), that are inert, that await "new contexts" and "new interpretations" by future scholars and artists who may discover them (99). I extrapolate from A. Assmann, though she may not go so far as to put it this way, that a culture's canon is defined by a culture's repertoire. That is, whatever texts a culture continually reperforms, restages, comments upon, rereads, and so on—whatever is reembodied by the individuals of that culture, over time—comprises that culture's canon. When a work drops out of the repertoire, then, and fails to be restaged and reperformed and reread for a generation or longer, one calls it a "forgotten" work. Such a work exits the canon and enters the archive. Also, texts can also move from the unperformed archive into the performed canon. Canon = texts + performance. Archived texts sit unaccessed most of the time, unread most of the time, unperformed most of the time.

For digital culture, the conflation of canon with repertoire holds two interesting ramifications. First, digital archives potentially redefine what A. Assmann calls "active memory" and "passive memory," in the sense that these become highly individualized: all materials contained in an online database are equally available to the user—no materials are any more "hidden" or "stored away" than any other materials, all materials that are indexed can be retrieved from the database—and so users of an Internet archive may "activate" whichever of the materials they wish, constructing their own personal canons based on the materials that they use. In other words, if repertoire *is* canon, then whatever a user finds in an archive and chooses to use *is* a canonical work, for that person. Digital archives erect no physical barriers between categories of information, so conceivably any piece of information, any archived data, can enter into one person's repertoire and canon; thus, there are as many possible canons as there are archive users, and no possibility for a single canon, achieved by a consensus of cultural archive users, that would be distinct from the culture's archive. For each person, of course, "canon" and "archive" would still be separate, though what texts enter a person's repertoire at any given period, and what texts lie unused in the archive, may change frequently. But for the culture at large, the notion of a shared canon becomes tenuous at best when digital databases store much of the cultural memory. This idea that digital archives assist and manifest the predigital trend of infinite-canons, meaning no-canon, dovetails with the ideas of the *Digital Humanities* authors, described above.

A. Assmann (2008) writes, "Although we cannot imagine a culture without an active cultural memory, we can well imagine a culture without a passive storing memory" (105). When A. Assmann writes of "active culture memory" without "passive storing memory" here, she is referencing "oral cultures in which the cultural memory is embodied and transmitted through performances and practices," in which "material relics do not persist and accumulate," and in which "the range of the cultural memory is coextensive with the embodied repertoires that are performed in festive rites and repeated practices" (105). She cites Diana Taylor's works on "indigenous embodied practice as a form of knowing as well as a system for storing and transmitting knowledge" (Taylor 2003, 18). But even though A. Assmann is discussing "indigenous" and "oral" cultures such as those whose culture is now defined by UNESCO as "intangible cultural heritage" (A. Assmann 2008, 105), I think that her definition of "a culture without a passive storing memory" well describes digital culture.

This is not because there is no such thing as "archive" anymore, but because of the flatness of digital databases—the fact that any item can be retrieved from a database with equal ease, without architectural or status barriers separating certain categories of information from others (at least, this is the case for rogue digital archives)—any individual user of an archive may incorporate any content from that archive into their working memory, or canon, rather than leaving it untouched. In other words, when digital archives form the substrate of cultural memory, the literature, music, film, video, and static art that fill up one person's passive cultural memory (in essence, being forgotten, or unused, by that person) may be the very texts that another person actively engages with, constituting that person's working cultural memory. So one can say that digital culture has no "passive storing memory," because that passive memory differs for each individual. The culture as a whole cannot clearly define what lies fallow as "archive," as opposed to what is activated, living, in "repertoire," or "canonical," for every member of that culture.

Digital Doing

At the same time that digital cultural memory collapses broadly applicable demarcations between passive memory and working memory, the possibility for a new kind of canon and repertoire arises with new media: the canon of digital doing, the repertoire of computer use, the routines and rituals of human performances of technological affordances. Over the past quarter-century or so, since the 1991 launch of the World Wide Web and the subsequent explosion in everyday computer use, millions of people have collectively developed vast repertoires for interfacing with digital devices and networks, exploiting the affordances built into technologies by their makers.

What might be considered the core digital repertoire was invented by Doug Engelbart and his team at the Stanford Research Institute (SRI)'s Augmentation Research Center in the 1960s, and presented to the public by Engelbart at the Fall Joint Computer Conference (FJCC) in San Francisco in December 1968. This presentation is popularly known today as "The Mother of All Demos" (Internet Archive 2010), as it introduced a windowing system, the mouse, hypertext, word processing, dynamic file linking, and other elements of computing that are now taken utterly for granted, so fundamental are they to contemporary hardware and software. The repertoire that Engelbart demoed in 1968, which all users have by now adopted, includes: scrolling and pointing with a mouse, clicking to select and open files, creating files and storing them in folders, opening multiple windows on the desktop, inserting hyperlinks that connect two files. On top of that core repertoire, users have built up twenty-five years' worth of bodily actions, performed mainly by fingers, thumbs, wrists, eyes, and heads, such as: dragging-and-dropping, cutting-and-pasting/copying-and-pasting, scrolling up and down, and swiping left and right.

These actions may seem thoroughly determined by the affordances built into networked computing by designers and programmers, with little room left for users' interpretations. But other types of actions routinely performed by computer users are less "scripted." The use of certain acronyms (IMO for "In my opinion," ITA for "I totally agree," YMMV for "Your mileage may vary"); the use of the pound sign (#) to denote a "hashtag" or "tag" by which online posts can be marked as belonging to a specific group, topic, or theme;[3] the use of one pseudonym, or only a handful of pseuds, as one's login or username on multiple sites; the use of email and Web-based platforms (such as blogs, journals, and social media sites) not only to communicate one's own thoughts and emotions, but to share content made by others (jokes, videos, image macros, GIFs), often *as* an expression of oneself—these often-repeated actions were not dictated by the affordances inherent in hardware, software, or networks, but came to be widely agreed upon conventions through human users' actions. The repetition of such actions is not consciously willed by each user; rather, a *collective* memory of digital use, of what kinds of performances are typical and acceptable and effective, has been transmitted from user to user, and not through written handbooks—so that users simply *know* what to do when they begin to use a digital device, they *remember*, in their bodies, how to perform with their machines. They have a working memory of what to do, when, and how, when they wish to engage with other people remotely, via telecommunications networks.

This collective memory of digital use is a digital repertoire because no one reads a manual when they first begin using networked computers to figure out how to be a user. Even when a user tries to build her competency with a new piece of software, or a game, or a social site, on the whole, she will find simple observation of an experienced user engaging with the platform, or a video demonstration of someone performing in that digital environment, more helpful than reading an instruction set.

One could argue that a video demo is an archival format, but I claim that demo instruction is, in fact, a transmission of repertoire: a *showing-doing*. The learner of the repertoire learns by *watching-doing*, and then the learner *does* the actions that they have observed. One can *show-doing* and *watch-doing* on a screen as well as in physical space. (In fact, for the showing-doing and watching-doing of screen-based actions, a video recording that fills the frame with the screen activity may be more efficient than sitting beside someone and watching her manipulate the keyboard, although the ability to ask questions of the more experienced user "in person" has its own advantages.) One often, in fact, reverse-engineers the "doing," simply by noting how others comport themselves in networked spaces (for example, noticing that people append tag lines to their mobile phone and tablet messages, apologizing for any spelling or grammatical errors made because they are typing on a handheld device, may lead a user to append a similar tag line to his outgoing messages). There are, of course, many highly individualized repertoires, as each user has her preferences for arranging windows on her desktop, opening browser tabs in a certain order when she first "gets online" in the morning, using specific hotkeys to execute specific functions, and so on. But there is a growing shared digital repertoire also, one that current and future generations learn by observing others' doings.

Canon, as A. Assmann (2008) would say, is the content of a culture's repertoire because what is canonical is constantly reperformed, reused, restaged, reenacted. What is "in" the canon is shared through repertoire; the cultural canon is "done" again and again and again. Digital culture has built up a robust array of canonical movements and maneuvers, performed over and over again by individual bodies, and these canonical actions constitute the current digital repertoire. The widespread adoption of new categories of devices—motion sensor gaming consoles such as Kinect, wearable computers like the Apple Watch, virtual reality masks such as Oculus Rift, 3D printers, nanotechnology implants—will lead to the formation of new canonical moves and the incorporation of those moves into the digital repertoire. While there may also be a great deal of archival material about how to use computers and the Internet—how-to guides and lists of steps to take while working with various applications—these are not in the "working memory" of the current digital culture, but remain in the "passive memory," consulted only on occasion.

Print culture, too, has its repertoires (sitting in a chair to read a book, inserting bookmarks at stopping points in one's reading, conventions of correspondence, and so on). But where print culture privileged archival memory over embodied memory—for example, through large capital investments made in archival institutions such as museums and libraries—digital culture elevates repertoire. In three hundred years' time, owing to the high propensity of digital data to decay and disappear (as I described in chapter 1), it is uncertain whether any digital artifacts produced over the past twenty-five years will remain; but it is very likely that much of the current digital repertoire will still be in use, albeit modified to adapt to new device types.

Just as the contents of most telephone conversations have not been archived but the repertoire of conversing via telephone has persisted into the digital age, so too may much digital content be deleted over time even as digital repertoires endure. For example, not a single image macro from the 2000s may be retrievable in 2300—entire genres such as LOLcats and Ryan Gosling "Hey Girl" variants may vanish—but users will still engage in the practice of overlaying silly or adorable or remarkable pictures with humorous text and distributing the resulting visual assemblages online. Even if all the media texts distributed via the BitTorrent protocol are lost, and the BitTorrent protocol also falls into disuse, peer-to-peer file-sharing will still take place. If all of the documents released to the public by Wikileaks are forgotten, the techniques for leaking classified information by way of networked systems will be remembered, though updated and, probably, highly refined over the next few hundred years. Wikipedia may fold, but online crowdsourced encyclopedias will still be built.

While it may appear that new media have given rise to a preponderance of archives, it is really repertoire that is rising in the digital age. Digital archives must be labored on to survive, and who knows how many generations of labor each archive will attract? Every Internet archive that has opened may close down within three hundred years; the repertoires for digital archiving that are coalescing today will remain in play.

Repertoires of Archiving

I predict that many digital repertoires will outlast most digital archives. And thus, chapter 2, which I had originally intended to suggest a possible canon of digital archives, will offer instead a description of three canonical *styles* of digital archiving that I perceive as dominant. Because there can no longer be a single, consensus-based cultural canon for all of the reasons, and after all of the historical movements, described above, and because the coincidence of canon with repertoire is even clearer in digital culture than it was in print culture, I can only point to repertoires of archiving, rather than archives that contain canonical works or canonical archives.

The definitions of "canon" and "archive" so firmly established in the era of print have changed dramatically in a digital regime: "archive" is now an incredibly tenuous construct given the instability of digital data, and "canon" can be interpreted either as a concept that is infinitely multipliable (i.e., everyone has her or his own personal canon, but there is no shared canon) or as a concept that is fully aligned with repertoire, so that we can have canonical practices but not canonical objects. This impacts how we must think of digital archives, for we can only now conceive of arguing that certain archival styles will persist—that is, certain ways of constructing and designing archives, certain types of archives, certain tendencies in archival practice—rather than arguing that specific archives will endure.

2 Archival Styles: Universal, Community, and Alternative Digital Preservation Projects

The Proliferation Tradition

In this chapter, I will discuss three major digital archival *styles*, to which I assign the names "universal," "community," and "alternative." These archival styles have been the most frequently employed, most prominent and dominant styles employed in rogue digital archiving since this type of activity began four decades ago, but they cannot be said to be "canonical" methods of archiving—in fact, I will explain how each style is *anticanonical* in its way.

Rogue archives reject what Raymond Williams called "the selective tradition" of culture (Williams 2009, 47)—the custom by which a "minority" of experts chooses, from all cultural documents, the percentage that are put safely into repositories, and the even smaller fraction that comprise the cultural canon, which is the short list of visual, literary, and musical productions that every member of that culture *should* learn, appreciate, engage with deeply and repeatedly, and hold in common with every other member of the culture. (Pierre Nora [1984] argues that archives are often as selective as canons; he defines the work of "professionals of the archive" thus: "Professionals have learned that the secret of this trade is the art of controlled destruction" [xxvii].)

The selective tradition, so prevalent in the print era, already faced challenges before the rise of new media. Rogue archivists amplify the challenge to selectivity that began in the 1960s. Rogue archives operate according to a logic of proliferation rather than selection. What proliferates in a system of digital cultural memory is, first of all, the number and kinds of archives in existence, as the affordances built into digital technologies enable more and more people to undertake archival projects. And, with an increasing number of archives accessible to all Internet users (and this broad accessibility is a major difference from the archives of the print era, which erected strong barriers to use, if only by restricting use to those who could physically enter their structures), the process of canonization becomes severely monadic. Every individual user must make decisions about what to select and incorporate into her or his personal, unique canons from the wide range of cultural archives available to them. Digital cultural memory consists of an extreme multiplicity of archives, and a multitude of personal cultural canons derived from those archives—many millions of canons-of-one—a return to what Michel Foucault (1986) describes as the seventeenth-century mode of archiving, when "museums and libraries were the expression of an individual choice" (26). In the workings of digital cultural memory, the selective tradition gives way to a proliferation tradition.

Below, I will briefly gloss the universal, community, and alternative archival styles, and list a number of archives that I consider to be exemplars of each. The discussion of specific archives will, I think, allow the phenomenon of hacker/fan/amateur/pirate/volunteer archiving to take more concrete shape for the reader. Also, because I will name the founders of these archives and describe their contributions whenever possible, I hope that the reader will better grasp the immense amount of "techno-volunteer" labor that has been required to bring these online repositories into being and support them over time.

After guiding the reader through what I perceive to be the three main digital archival styles, I will introduce my primary case study of digital archives: Internet fan fiction archives. Fan fiction (also called "fanfic" or "fic") archives, built by fan archivists, store the creative output of fan communities, that output often taking the form of fictional stories that incorporate characters, plots, and settings from favored media texts (films, television programs, comic books, anime, popular music, and so on). I view fanfic archives as paradigmatic rogue digital archives, as they combine the key characteristics of all three archival styles: they are simultaneously universal, community, and alternative archives. A study of fanfic archives can therefore illustrate the motivations, methods, and challenges that have so far defined digital archiving.

My own long-term affiliation with online fan fiction communities and archives (dating from 1999) means that I have a deeper understanding of the work of fanfic archivists, and the workings of fanfic archives, than I do of other types of Internet archivists and archives. In addition, my history, and my research team members' histories, of involvement with fanfic archives enabled us to recruit fifty participants for an oral history project focused on the evolution of these archives, and the interviews that we collected have contributed greatly to my thinking on, and analysis of, fanfic archives as a specific instance of digital archiving, as well as digital archiving as a trending practice. Therefore, in the chapters that follow, I will make reference to the specific archives that I describe below, with most of my investigation centering on the archives constructed by and for media fans for their fiction production.

I will also discuss how all three core digital archival styles are anticanonical, in that they are attempting to do away with traditional, print-era notions of "canon," "canonization," and "canonicity." I have already reviewed the two major large anticanon movements that began in the United States in the 1960s: the movement to do away with distinctions between "high" and "low" culture and to incorporate low/popular/mass/commercial texts into the arenas of high art construction/exhibition and scholarly analysis/exegesis; and the movement to expand university curricula and research programs to include the study of ethnicities, genders, sexualities, and other categories of people that had long been marginalized by, or entirely excluded from, higher education. The digital archives that I will name here continue one or both of these attacks against the idea of a predominantly Global North, white-, and male-authored high-culture canon, and also battle the concept of canonicity in other ways.

Universal archives seek to replace canonicity and selective archiving—the process by which a small number of critics or experts choose which works are "worth" teaching and rereading generation after generation, and which works are sufficiently "valuable" to keep safe in protective store-houses—with comprehensive archiving, a process that strives to collect as many cultural texts as possible, to make all the texts equally accessible to the public, and to present all the texts as equally valuable.

Community archives support the canon-expansion work that was begun by university reformists, striving to assemble and preserve texts that originate from, or bear direct relevance to, cultures that have been historically marginalized in traditional memory institutions. Such archives stand as countercanons to the cultural canon dominated by the most privileged members of society, and encourage an understanding of cultural canonicity as always multiple (allowing for many canons representing many cultures), or as always specific (each canon representing a singular, specific culture, and never representing "everyone").

Alternative archives propose new canons, canons of new types of objects or objects that are ignored by traditional archives. These archives do not seek to replace print-era cultural canons, but are content to let their assemblies of odd, strange, controversial, nongeneric, or radically new texts stand alongside those older sets of privileged works. Alternative archives employ nonnormative criteria in assessing artistic value and historical importance, and, like community archives, call for an acceptance of multiple canons— at least one canon for every novel, degraded, or "forgotten" genre of cultural production.

I bring up the specter of canonicity in part to assert that what follows is not a suggested set of canonical archives, but simply a number of archives that, in my view, are interesting and important examples of the increasingly popular practice of digital archiving. I find these archives "good to think with," when considering what archiving is today, what it is becoming, whose efforts are making digital archives possible, and whose ideas of archiving are influencing all of our ideas about archiving. Digital archiving is deliberately opposed to the canonization of specific texts, and thus works to undo some of the core priorities of print-era cultural memory. Also, the chances that any of these particular archives will endure for more than one or two generations is minuscule—and many online archives built in the last quarter-century have already disappeared—but what is clearly ascendant, what is being enacted with increasing frequency and sophistication, is a repertoire of specific styles of archiving. In other words, what I describe in this chapter is *how* more and more people are *doing-archiving* using digital tools and networks, over and over again, regardless of *what* they are choosing to archive.

Traits of Rogue Digital Archives

Before I go into detail about what differentiates the three main digital archival styles, and describe specific archives that exemplify each style, I will offer the reader a list of the traits shared by all of these "rogue" archives:

• They are freely accessible online, that is, they are not hidden behind paywalls or institutional password-protected walls. Some of these archives, such as "Sly"[1] and Open Library, require users to register on the site and to maintain their "good standing" (as defined by the rules of each site) in order to access the archives' content, but membership is not fee based or predicated on any institutional affiliation. JSTOR and other academic archives that require either payment or a university ID login are therefore not among the archives that I am studying.

• They allow users to view or download cultural texts in their entirety. I do not consider encyclopedic projects such as Wikis to be archives, since they mostly offer factual information and commentary about cultural texts, and not the texts themselves.

• They are not restricted by copyright laws. Some archivists only upload texts that have entered the public domain (such Project Gutenberg), some archive texts to which they own the copyright (such as the FAMA Collection), some adhere to the copyright permissions used by public libraries (such as Open Library, many of whose texts readers can borrow, but not download permanently), some claim that their activities are permitted by fair use (such as Download Finished), and some simply contravene copyright laws that they feel hinder, rather than help, cultural preservation (such as the Eldritch Press and Sly). I am not studying YouTube because, in addition to being a for-profit, Google-owned platform and therefore driven by very different motivations than the archives I am investigating, YouTube "reserves the right to remove Content and User Submissions without prior notice," and most of its takedowns are motivated by suspicions of copyright infringement.[2] Though many users consider YouTube to be something *like* a media archive, the platform's position on copyright means that it cannot be relied upon to protect, or keep accessible, all of the content uploaded to it.

• They were founded outside of traditional memory institutions such as government- and university-supported libraries and archives and museums of physical artifacts. Thus, I am not including projects such as the Hemispheric Institute's Digital Video Library or Cornell University's Rose Goldsen Archive of New Media Art Archive, which were founded with the support of university libraries, even though they share many other traits with rogue archives. Although some of the rogue archives that I will describe below run on university servers and receive university support, they were not conceived by, or even in cooperation with, university LIS teams and are not extensions or subprojects of university libraries.

• They are dedicated to the persistent publication and long-term preservation of their contents.

• Their founders and workers are people who, for the most part, received no formal training in archiving or records management and are not LIS professionals.

• They are staffed primarily, or entirely, by volunteers.

Universal Digital Archives

What I call "universal" digital archives set for themselves missions of extreme breadth, and aim for all-inclusiveness. Project Gutenberg wishes to make every book in the public domain available online. The Rosetta Project aims to preserve all known human languages. Open Library hopes to one day host "a web page for every book ever published." Archive Team's informal motto is "We Are Going to Rescue Your Shit." Each universal archive strives to become the defining digital archive of its kind, or even, in the case of the Internet Archive, *the* preeminent digital archive. Their common goal of comprehensiveness matches Vannevar Bush's original aspiration for the memex. Everyone who works on these archives labors intensively to make the Internet fulfill Bush's (1945) dream of a machine-based system that will "encompass the great record" (sec. 8), even as the vast quantity of work they put into digital preservation underscores that the Internet falls far short of an automatic memory machine.

The adjective "universal" carries a certain historical weight, or "baggage." For centuries, Enlightenment language and thought defined the "universal" subject, the possessor of natural, innate "universal" rights, as a white (European-descended), heterosexual, able-bodied male of the bourgeois or propertied class in the Global North. I do not think it is a coincidence that all of the "universal" archives I will describe in this subsection were created by educated white American or European men, most of them computer programmers. I do not argue that these archives' goals of completism and comprehensiveness were wholly determined by the race, class, and gender of their founders, but there is some resonance between the founders' common status as "unmarked" persons[3] and their interest in creating "unmarked" archives, that is, archives that are not designated to be relevant to particular Internet users, but are intended for use by *all* people who have access to the Internet. These archives' organization, presentation, and content selection make no reference to identity differences—races/ethnicities, nationalities, geographies, physical abilities, genders, sexualities, political or class affiliations. These, more than any other rogue archives, could easily be taken for new expressions of the Enlightenment's affection for "'totalizing' and 'universal' representations which reject and obscure ... local knowledge and nuances" (Edney 1999, 167), and for "abstract and strictly functional systems for the factual ordering of phenomena in space" (Harvey 1989, 249).

Some universal archives are among the earliest online archives created (illustrating the fact that one specific race/gender/class of people gained network access, and the skills and opportunities to build new virtual spaces, earlier than others), and have become sufficiently sizeable and famous enough to warrant speculation that they could one day soon be promoted as important cultural resource repositories, like the Smithsonian or the Library of Congress, by schoolteachers to their students. They could join the ranks of many privately founded institutions that became public treasures, such as Benjamin Franklin's Library Company of Philadelphia (which inaugurated the free lending library system in the United States) and the Museum of Modern Art (MoMA). Something like a history of digital archiving could be agreed upon by new media scholars, and the story of universal archives that I tell below might be regarded as a draft of such a history. In other words, these archives' apparent disinterest in identity politics and their completist missions may make them prime candidates for incorporation into educational curricula and into mainstream cultural heritage and history practices in the near future.

Rather than operating in the "selective tradition" described above, universal digital archives are aligned with Raymond Williams's wish for a preservation of "documentary culture" which, "more clearly than anything else," can express the life of a past period "to us in direct terms, when the living witnesses are silent." The selective tradition causes much of the documentary record of a "lived culture" and its particular "structure of feeling," to be lost (Williams [1961] 2001, 65–66). Working against such loss, universal online archives strive to save and keep as much of the documentary culture as they can acquire and digitize, presumably for the benefit of future users who will be able to reconstruct "structures of feeling" of a past period with more ease and accuracy than they would have been able to do from the documents selected for preservation by print cultural memory.

Here is a list of some of the most well-trafficked universal digital archives in chronological order (organized by their founding dates).

Project Gutenberg was the first online archive of cultural material, founded in 1971 by Michael Hart while he was an undergraduate student at the University of Illinois. Hart was friends with the operators of the university's Materials Research Lab's Xerox Sigma V mainframe, and these friends, searching for uses for the mainframe, awarded Hart an operator's account and a "grant" of unlimited computer time. Hart decided to "repay the huge value of the computer time that he had been given" by facilitating "the storage, retrieval, and searching of what was stored in our libraries" (Hart 1992). Hart initially digitized and uploaded all of the books himself, averaging one book per month in 1991. In the 1990s, he began recruiting volunteers "from numerous nations to help type, scan, and/or proofread Project Gutenberg's 'eBooks,'" and by 2008, newly digitized books were being uploaded to Project Gutenberg at a rate of 340 per month, owing to the work of "tens of thousands of volunteers in various teams" (Lebert 2008).

Project Gutenberg initially ran on the ARPANET (Advanced Research Projects Agency Network), the precursor of the Internet, when few people had access to the network. When Hart opened Project Gutenberg, there were no hyperlinks, no websites, and no graphical user interfaces, and if Hart had tried to email his first 5K text file—a digital version of the US Declaration of Independence, which he uploaded on July 4, 1971, the 195th anniversary of the Declaration's signing—to the one hundred computers that were then linked to ARPANET, he "would have crashed the network" (Lebert 2008), so he stored the file in a directory and issued a message stating where others could find it. (Six users downloaded the Declaration file, indicating to Hart that Project Gutenberg could be a service that some found useful.) The system of networked computing had to become more robust, more popular, and more accessible before large-scale digital archiving could begin.

Digital archiving began in earnest in 1992, one year after the launch of the World Wide Web, which marked the beginning of what I call the "public Internet," that is, the Internet whose user group was not limited to employees and researchers at universities, research labs, and government institutions—the Internet that could be used by anyone who had access to, and knowledge of, computer hardware, network protocols, and an Internet service provider (ISP). In the early '90s, many people participated online at their workplaces, but early ISPs such as CompuServe and America Online (AOL) facilitated the growth of home-based networked computing.

In 1992, Judson Knott and Paul Jones designed and opened the SunSITE. unc.edu website. SunSITE was named for Sun Microsystems, the corporate donor whose grants made the site possible. It began, and is still housed, at the University of North Carolina, Chapel Hill, and was eventually mirrored at more than twenty other institutions. SunSITE, later known as MetaLab and now called ibiblio, started as "one of the first electronic repositories on the Internet to incorporate emerging networked information discovery and retrieval tools" (Knott and Jones 1996) such as Wide Area Information Server (or WAIS, a text searching system; WAIS was developed by Thinking Machines, Inc., a company that included Brewster Kahle, who later founded the Internet Archive) and Gopher (a pre–World Wide Web protocol for distributing, searching, and retrieving documents on the Internet). SunSITE's purpose was to build a library of content and make it searchable and readable by a large number of users; one of the first content collections hosted on the site were documents contributed by the 1992 Clinton Campaign (the Clinton White House went on to share a great deal of official presidential text documents with SunSITE).

Linux distributions were among SunSITE's most frequently downloaded content. The Linux kernel was developed by Linus Torvalds and released in October 1991 with the intention that the kernel would serve as the basis of free and open software development; Linux distributions, or "distros," are the multiple, varied operating systems built atop the Linux kernel. SunSITE archived not only the distros themselves, but also the guides created by the Linux Documentation Project, which is "an organization of volunteers authoring, reviewing and managing documents about the Linux operating system" (Garrels 2004). Garrels (2004) writes that between 1992 and 1996, "Sunsite (a famous server machine at the University of North Carolina) … was the first Web site offering information about Linux. Also, when you wanted to download Linux software, Sunsite.unc.edu was the place to go." Sunsite/Metalab/ibiblio thus started as an archive of archives, a database of databases, a "collection of collections": "It began as one of the world's first online libraries and as a way to share and support all kinds of free software. … From Project Gutenberg (the famous free book archive) to etree.org (where fans of tape-friendly bands share concert music), and from charities and non-profits both locally and worldwide … to video documentaries of folk practice, ibiblio.org hosts one of the largest collections of collections on the Internet" (ibiblio, "About"). On ibiblio's "People" page, one finds the header "Meet the people of ibiblio.org who, collectively, never sleep," followed by a list of four individuals, and a link to another page titled "Former ibiblio staff members" listing 79 people. These are, apparently, all of the people who have had a hand in managing and operating ibiblio's archiving efforts since 1992.

Another important online archive from the mid-1990s was Eldritch Press, now hosted by ibiblio. As related by Lawrence Lessig in *Free Culture*, in 1995, Eric Eldred, a retired disabled computer programmer, "was frustrated that his daughters didn't seem to like [the works of canonical American author Nathaniel] Hawthorne" and so "decided to put Hawthorne on the Web. An electronic version, Eldred thought, with links to pictures and explanatory text, would make this nineteenth-century author's work come alive" (Lessig 2004, 213). Eldred's experiment with digitizing Hawthorne motivated him to "build a library of public domain works by scanning these works and making them available for free" on the Internet, and not only copies of the works, but "derivative works from these public domain works" (213). The online library Eldritch Press was Eldred's variant on Project Gutenberg: rather than offering up "clean" digital copies of public domain books as Project Gutenberg did, Eldritch Press offered modified copies (with "pictures and explanatory text"). When the US Congress passed the Sonny Bono Copyright Term Extension Act (CTEA) in 1998, extending the terms of existing copyright "for the eleventh time in forty years" (Lessig 2004, 214), Eldred found he could not legally post Robert Frost's poetry collection *New Hampshire* online (*New Hampshire* was originally published in 1923, and because of the CTEA, the book will not enter public domain until 2019).

Eldred decided to wage a legal battle against the copyright extension, and Lessig represented him in the courts, eventually arguing Eldred's case—and the case against indefinite, unlimited copyright extensions and an apparent end to the notion of a public domain—before the US Supreme Court in 2002 in *Eldred v. Ashcroft*. The Court ruled against Eldred, and Lessig began crusading against unlimited copyright through his writing (*Free Culture* is dedicated to Eldred) and his participation in the nonprofit organization Creative Commons, whose licenses allow creators to place modified copyrights on their works, in order to give others the right to "share, use, and even build upon" those works (Creative Commons, "About"). In the lore of the copyright wars over digital remix, peer-to-peer file sharing, and "piracy" that began raging in the late-1990s and continue today, *Eldred v. Ashcroft*, Lessig's activism, and Creative Commons are all famous elements. Less well-remembered is that Eldritch Press, a free online archive of modified classic novels launched and operated by a single hobbyist, was at the heart of some of the most crucial early copyright battles involving digital technologies.

In 1997, Brewster Kahle published an essay in *Scientific American* called "Archiving the Internet," in which he announced that he had created a new organization, the Internet Archive, the year prior, which was "collecting the public materials on the Internet to construct a digital library. The first step is to preserve the contents of this new medium. This collection will include all publicly accessible World Wide Web pages, the Gopher hierarchy, the Netnews bulletin board system, and downloadable software." Kahle (1997) draws upon the "digital dark age" discourse, without employing the exact phrase:

While the Internet's World Wide Web is unprecedented in spreading the popular voice of millions that would never have been published before, no one recorded these documents and images from 1 year ago. The history of early materials of each medium is one of loss and eventual partial reconstruction through fragments. A group of entrepreneurs and engineers have determined to not let this happen to the early Internet.

Even though the documents on the Internet are the easy documents to collect and archive, the average lifetime of a document is 75 days and then it is gone. While the changing nature of the Internet brings a freshness and vitality, it also creates problems for historians and users alike. ...

Where we can read the 400 year-old books printed by Gutenberg, it is often difficult to read a 15 year-old computer disk. ...

Building the Internet Archive involves gathering, storing, and serving the tera-
bytes of information that at some point were publicly accessible on the Internet.

The Internet Archive officially made its online repositories public in 2001,
and today stores 16 petabytes of data. While the Archive is not staffed exclusively by volunteers (it employs approximately 200 people),[4] it depends on
a volunteer force for media migration, book scanning, and various day-to-
day operations such as event planning. Kahle himself is the public representative of the Archive and its Wayback Machine (described in chapter
1), promoting his project of "building the great library" and having the
Archive serve as a "home for the [cultural] commons" (Conrad 2014) in
numerous interviews and talks every year. It is ironic that, of the digital
cultural memory projects mentioned here, the most automated archive
(although the Internet Archive hosts far more content than that collected
by the Wayback Machine) probably has the most visible human face and
voice in the press.

The Long Now Foundation's Rosetta Project was launched by Alexander
Rose, Stewart Brand, and Doug Carlston (with input from Brewster Kahle)
around 2006. The Rosetta Project has archived text documentation and/
or multimedia recordings of over 2,500 languages, and intends to "build
a publicly accessible digital library of material on the nearly 7,000 known
human languages" (The Rosetta Project, "The Rosetta Project—Texts"). The
project is hosted at the Internet Archive.[5]

Open Library was founded in 2006 by famed Internet activist Aaron
Swartz and other collaborators. The library is primarily "an open, editable
library catalog, building towards a web page for every book ever published,"
but it also allows users to download and borrow full ebooks. It currently
offers more than one million out-of-copyright ("classic") ebooks for download, mostly through the Internet Archive's collection of digital texts (the
Internet Archive hosts Open Library), and hundreds of thousands of copyrighted ("modern") ebooks for borrowing, through cooperation with public
libraries all over the world. Open Library encourages registered readers to
contribute to, and correct, catalog information as well as to submit patches
to the Open Library API on a volunteer basis.

Archive Team was begun in 2009 by Jason Scott (an employee of the
Internet Archive) and a group of fellow self-described "rogue archivists,
programmers, writers and loudmouths dedicated to saving our digital heritage." The Team has downloaded a number of large websites and networks
that were facing permanent deletion. They also make copies of sites that are
not endangered, as a precaution against those sites' disappearance. Their

first massive archival download was the Web-hosting service GeoCities (on which many first-generation Internet users designed and ran their first websites in the 1990s). Wrote journalist Austin Modine in 2009, as Yahoo! (GeoCities' parent company) prepared to close the service, "Geocities is a resource worthy of preservation if there ever was one. Nearly two decades['] worth of blinking text, animated gifs, fanfiction, and broken links are at risk of disappearing with the blink of the eye. This is the personal internet young, raw and blemished—before big blogging services and social networking sites arrived to completely homogenize the space" (Modine 2009). Other sites saved by Archive Team just prior to their closures are FortuneCity, MobileMe, Posterous, Snapjoy, and GoogleReader; Archive Team also has saved a copy of FanFiction.net and selected streams/sections of Reddit, Facebook, and Twitter, all of which are (currently) thriving sites and services, "just in case." Users can download many of the sites preserved by Archive Team at their site or from their page at the Internet Archive. The Team is "100% composed of volunteers and interested parties" (Archive Team, "About"); a 2009 *TIME* article covering the Team's rescue of GeoCities' data reported that "30 people operating nearly 100 computers" worked for "nearly six months to download as many of the GeoCities pages as they could find" (Fletcher 2009).

Community Digital Archives

Not all digital archiving projects are informed or guided by universal thinking. Many online archives are of, for, and by highly specific communities, including communities defined by ethnic, national, geographic, linguistic, or temporal identities (or intersections of two or more of these) and communities of affinity. Stevens, Flinn, and Shepherd (2010) write that online "community archives" have been created in increasingly large numbers since 2000 by "historically marginalized groups for greater visibility for their histories."

I regard such archives and their archivists as participants in what Flinn (2007) calls the "community archives 'movement'" (152–153). Flinn traces the origins of this movement to the post–World War II period, when "local history became increasingly popular and respectable both as an academic discipline and at a non-professional grassroots level" (155). British local history groups were informed by "the developments in oral history, the History Workshop movement and public history in the 1970s and 1980s, all of which tended to be inspired by 'an allegiance to those whose lives are still excluded from historical practice and a commitment to praxis which places emphasis on what is being said rather than the status of who is saying it'" (155–156). This type of amateur and community archiving has only grown in the UK, the United States, and elsewhere over the past thirty years, with many "independent cultural heritage initiatives [emerging] directly out of a context of marginalization ... and struggle" (156–158). Archives created to house documents pertaining to the lives and cultures of working-class laborers, ethnic and religious minorities, LGBT and queer people, and women are among these (156–158).

Thus, born-digital archives, founded independently of traditional memory institutions, serve both extraordinarily generalist and highly particular aims. Amateur, volunteer, nonprofessional digital archiving has been undertaken both by white male hackers and engineers driven by motives similar to those of Bush—the safeguarding and transmission of enormous corpuses of information in order to perpetuate and augment human knowledge writ large—and by minoritarian communities that have exploited new media's democratizing potentials to launch archives for their own cultural artifacts, which were often ignored, excluded, or marginalized by the official state-sponsored brick-and-mortar archives of print and analog culture. What unites the two groups of Internet archivists is their archival labor: the time, effort, and skills that they have devoted to creating, and maintaining, sites of digital cultural memory.

Community digital archives resist notions of "canonicity." For example, designating some community archives "canonical" would be impossible. Such archives are designed for use by the members of specific groups, so that they may experience a sense of belonging and better understand different aspects of their shared identity; so none of these archives can be deemed "better" than others, only more or less relevant or pertinent to individual users. In addition, community archives are philosophically opposed to both the broad valorization of canonical cultural texts (as stated above, Williams argues that such valorization almost always reflects the tastes and interests of the dominant class, giving the impression that, for the most part, minority groups produce no cultural texts of importance), and to the canonization of specific items within their collections, as their goal is to gather and preserve as much material as possible pertaining to their members. Thus, a canon of community archives could never be proposed for use by a general audience, but each individual could point to a set of community archives that they find interesting and compelling for personal reasons.

Here is a short list of several specific online community archives that greatly interest me.

The FAMA Collection is a repository of creative works made by Sarajevo artists during the Bosnian War; one such artist, Suada Kapic, founded it in the mid-2000s and it remains operational today. The collection's mission is to "bring home the human scale of events, places and experiences of the Siege of Sarajevo '92–'96." "As a virtual Bank of Knowledge, it aims to bridge a digital divide between the Culture of Remembrance and the Real-Time Quest for knowledge" (http://www.famacollection.org/eng/). Throughout the war, FAMA's art projects, such as Kapic's dark parody of tourist pamphlets, the *Sarajevo Survival Guide*, disseminated crucial information about the human rights violations and daily horrors taking place in the former Yugoslavia to Western Europe and the United States. Therefore, the digital archiving of the FAMA works amounts to an effort to save valuable artworks that were also effectively weapons of antiwar. Although the FAMA Collection could also be considered an alternative archive (I describe alternative archives below), its major goal is to communicate the experiences of a people who lived under siege, who endured one of the most brutal ethnic conflicts in the post–World War II period, not to create an alternative canon to that found in art museums.

The South Asian American Digital Archive (SAADA) is a collection of ephemera (personal letters, flyers, magazine articles, photographs, and so on) that documents the experiences of South Asian immigrants to the United States. SAADA was created by Samip Mallick in 2008. Mallick states that SAADA is the only archive "working to systematically document and preserve the history of the South Asian American community. … We feared that this important history was in danger of being lost. Our mission is not just to preserve the history of our community, but also to ensure that these histories are more widely known to everyone, especially within our own community." Archive volunteer Manan Desai relates that SAADA's goal is "providing access to historical materials directly to the public without a great deal of mediation. Our goal is to allow the reader to confront and understand the material for her or himself" (Ganeshananthan 2011).

The Radfem Archive, a website that offers free downloadable texts of "radical feminist literature, writing and history," was launched in 2011 by anonymous archivists. The archivists state that they were driven to build Radfem by an awareness that "the popular books will get reprinted, while the unpopular, forgotten books will continue to stay out of print and out of the minds of future generations." For example, they argue, "Most of [anti-pornography activist] Andrea Dworkin's books are currently out of print, some for many years. … With this project, we hope that people will read and reread her work. We hope that her ideas will not be 'buried with her' and lost to future generations. We hope her anger, her voice and her ideas rediscovered will get us all that much closer to the days of liberation that she dreamed [of] and fought for" (Radical Content Collective 2011).

The Michigan/Trans Controversy Archive saves news articles, press releases, essays, open letters, petitions, and interviews about "the ongoing controversy over the exclusion of transsexual [people] (both male-to-female and female-to-male) at the annual Michigan Womyn's Music Festival [MWMF]" (http://eminism.org/michigan/). Emi Koyama has run the archive as a subsite of her personal website, eminism.org, since 2013. The policy of exclusion of trans people from the MWMF has been the subject of heated debate in feminist and LGBTQ communities since at least the early 1990s, when a group of women (trans and cis) began protesting the policy by organizing an annual event called Camp Trans that takes place at the border of the festival grounds, at the same time as the festival.

The projects I have described here are but a handful of a legion of online archives created by members of minority and marginalized communities over the past twenty-five years, intended to preserve the artifacts and cultural productions that are meaningful to them, in the hopes of conveying core information about their shared values, experiences, histories, identities, and affinities across their membership and across time, to their future membership, their constituents-to-come.

Alternative Digital Archives

What I call "alternative" digital archives take a markedly different approach to data collection than do universal and community archives. Rather than trying to acquire (or digitize, as Project Gutenberg, Open Library, and the Radfem Archive do) and safeguard as many cultural texts as possible, alternative and avant-garde archives limit their scope to targeted genres, and often serve as central repositories for emerging or degraded genres. They still may resemble universal archives in their aims; for instance, Sly states that it is building a "comprehensive library" of non-Hollywood films. But unlike universal archives, these are not generalist collections. Rather, alternative archivists seek to define new "universes" of art and media forms, forms that have not (yet) been granted significant status by traditional memory institutions. They are assembling diverse and robust collections of nonmainstream cultural genres.

These online collections facilitate the emergence of new canons by making accessible large collections of alternative material. In so doing, they question the supremacy and authority of traditional canons of art and media. Alternative archives fill a gap left by "high" art museums and film libraries' reluctance to recognize or incorporate certain genres; they function as the online museums/libraries of emerging, ignored, or derided genres. They do not seek acceptance by, or mergers with, what Lisa Lewis (1992) calls "official" culture, but operate alongside and independently of that culture. These are online archives of different cultures, other cultures, and subcultures.

Many art projects could fall into this category. I have decided to list only two projects by artists' collectives, Netbase and Download Finished, which are both still accessible by the public, even though they have been discontinued and are no longer adding new works. I am not including projects that have gone dark and are inaccessible, such as the HILUS Intermedia Project Research, "the first integrated reference system for media art, video, new media and art in Austria," which operated from 1992 to 1996 (Rhizome.org 1996). It appears that volunteers continue to maintain Netbase and Download Finished, despite their having ceased activity several years ago; as I have argued, only persistent human labor keeps online archives operational and usable, and when that labor ceases to be invested in an archive, the collapse of that archive inevitably follows, immediately or eventually.

Netbase, an "Institute for New Culture Technologies," was founded by Konrad Becker and Francisco de Sousa Webber in 1995 (as Public Netbase); in 2006, the right-wing Austrian government withdrew funding from the project and dismantled the Netbase organization, despite Netbase's having won prestigious awards such as the Prix Arts Electronica 1995 and the Prize of the City of Vienna 2000. Its archive hosts the websites, as well as text, image, and video documentation, of a number of political art events that took place in Western Europe during Netbase's active years. These events include "nikeground" (2003) in which the collective 0100101110101101. ORG temporarily rebranded Vienna's historic square, Karlsplatz, as "Nikeplatz," as a protest against the ubiquitous corporate branding of European cultural institutions; and "Free Bitflows," by exStream (a collaboration of five European media art organizations), which was a 2004 "digital culture event" in Vienna, consisting of a conference, an exhibition, and a series of workshops, that investigated the question of "'semiotic democracy,' that is[,] the ability of the largest number of people to create and share culture freely," while also seeking ways to ensure that "in the context of overabundance and heavy-hitting marketing machines, new, independent content can still find its audience" (Free Bitflows, "About"). Netbase also houses many documents pertaining to its own activities and its closure by the Austrian government.

The Rhizome ArtBase is the most prominent "online archive of new media art." Mark Tribe founded the ArtBase in 1999 with a handful of volunteers, who later became grant-funded employees (including Alexander Galloway, now a prominent new media theorist), at Tribe's digital arts platform Rhizome.org. ArtBase "provides an online home for works that employ materials such as software, code, websites, moving images, games and browsers towards aesthetic and critical ends." It now houses over 2,100 works, and regularly acquires new works through artist submissions (reviewed by the curatorial staff) as well as through invitations and commissions that it extends to artists. The ArtBase provides not only storage but technical support for the works in its collection: "As any artist who has worked with technology for more than a few years can verify— things break. ... We aim to ensure the longevity of these works, ... mitigating obsolescence while respecting artistic intent" (Rhizome.org, "About the Rhizome ArtBase").

The private file-sharing site Sly opened in 2005 (by my best estimate), which is building "a comprehensive library of Arthouse, Cult, Classic, Experimental and rare movies from all over the world," and currently hosts over 130,000 torrents. As is the case for most private peer-to-peer (p2p) file-sharing sites, the founders of Sly conceal their identities, but I assume that, like nearly all pirate sites, Sly is run by unpaid volunteers. In addition, all of the site's registered members are, in essence, volunteer workers for the site, since files can only be transferred between members with their active cooperation—some members must "seed" (continually upload) files in order for others to acquire (download) them. As Tim O'Reilly explains (using the BitTorrent p2p file-sharing protocol as an exemplar of Web 2.0 user participation), "the network of downloaders ... provide both bandwidth and data to other users. The more popular the file, in fact, the faster it can be served, as there are more users providing bandwidth and fragments of the complete file. ... Every BitTorrent consumer brings his [sic] own resources to the party. There's an implicit 'architecture of participation,' a built-in ethic of cooperation, in which the service acts primarily as an intelligent broker, ... harnessing the power of the users themselves" (O'Reilly 2005).

However, unlike the Pirate Bay and other p2p torrent sites, Sly is not only a network for content sharing, but a network for archive building: the site incentivizes members to upload new content, including not only film files but subtitles of films in as many languages as possible, and paratextual content such as descriptions and reviews of films, posters that accompanied the films' theatrical releases, factual information about the making of the films, and so on. Sly also rewards members for keeping films indexed on the site "seeded," or available for download, which also marks its difference from most p2p sites, which do not require persistent seeding.

Download Finished was created by Zurich- and London-based art collective !Mediengruppe Bitnik and "artist/entertainer/postmodernist" Sven König. Download Finished, which was active from 2006 through 2009, was a participatory art platform: the site instructs users to search for a popular film title of their choice, download that film file via a p2p protocol, transform the file into a pixelated, highly compressed version, append their name or pseudonym to the transformed file, and then watch "their" transformative artwork (a visitor to the site can still read all of these steps, but can no longer use the search, download, and transformation functions). Download Finished now serves primarily as an archive of hundreds of pixelated videos that people created using the sites' affordances: all strange and degraded replays of famous movies, all original appropriative artworks, executed entirely through the website's embedded software.

Fan Fiction Archives

In the following sections, I will draw on my research team's interviews with fan fiction archivists and users to explain how fanfic archives simultaneously exemplify the universal, community, and alternative archiving styles. Having access to the oral history testimonies of one category of archivists and archive users allows me—and will, I hope, allow the reader—to begin to comprehend the rich, textured, powerful emotional and intellectual experiences undergone by participants in rogue archival cultures. Oral history as a method aims not only to "fill gaps in written records" (Morrissey 2007, 161) and to compensate for the fact that the "written record simply ignore[s] so much of the daily life of so many people," but also to seek "to understand all forms of subjectivity, ... perceptions, and consciousness in all its multiple meanings" (Ronald J. Grele, cited in Morrissey 2007, 161). The "written record" so far left behind by amateur/hacker/volunteer/pirate/fan archivists is quite scarce; most archivists' motivations, attitudes, and thought processes have been documented in only a handful of interviews and "FAQ" or "About Us" sections on websites. The oral histories of fanfic archivists and archive users that my team and I collected enable me to present a more complete picture of digital archiving than I could have assembled had I only consulted the published traces of this cultural phenomenon.

Fan Fiction Archives as Universal Archives

Many fanfic archives are universal archives in the sense that their archivists work to collect all, or as many as possible, of the texts within the fandom, or subfandom, that they serve. The goal of comprehensiveness, of encompassing all known fanfic content produced for a given television series, film, or character pairing, guided the majority of archives from approximately 1995 through 2002. These years witnessed the first great wave of online fan fiction archiving, which many of our oral history participants called the period of the "central" or "centralized" fanfic archive. The Gossamer Project (figures 2.1 and 2.2) is the largest repository of fan fiction based on the sci-fi television series *The X-Files*, and one of the best-known single-fandom archives. Chael, one of the three lead archivists of Gossamer (Deirdre and Vera Heinau are the others), states in his oral history interview that the benefit of a central archive for a fandom is that fans can easily find the stories at one site: "If you can search [the Internet], you type in 'X-Files fan fiction' and Gossamer's going to come up. Because you know, 'Well, hey, I'm looking for fan fiction, and I want it to be associated with this TV show.' And now, you have 35,000 stories at your disposal. Have fun. That's more than an afternoon" (Chael 2012). Vincent Juodvalkis opened Gossamer in 1995, and Gossamer remains the unquestioned primary resource for *X-Files* fic. Even though many other smaller *X-Files* fic archives were active at the height of the series' popularity in the late 1990s, our oral history participants repeatedly mentioned Gossamer as *the* fanfic storehouse for *X-Files* fans. States Azure Lunatic (2012), "I discovered Gossamer pretty early [in its history], and I was all over that. And having discovered Gossamer, I didn't really need to look anywhere else, because there's all the fic, there."

Trekiverse (figures 2.3 and 2.4), an archive of *Star Trek*–related fic covering all television series and film installations of the *Trek* franchise (Constable Katie and Stephen Ratliff serve as its lead archivists today), and the Due South Archive (Figure 2.5), which contains stories by fans of the Canadian Mountie-in-Chicago detective show *Due South*, are two other famous central fic archives that launched in the mid-1990s and are still active as of this writing (Speranza is the current lead archivist of the Due South Archive). A variant of the idea of the centralized fanfic archive that focused on one fandom was the archive of all stories within a specific genre. For example, Francesca Coppa relates in her oral history interview that a fan named KS Nicholas, also known as KS Nick, ran a website called "Slash Fan Fiction on the Net" (figure 2.6), containing links to every slash (male/male pairing) fan fiction story and site online that she could find. Coppa recalls of KS

Nicholas's site, "That's where you lived" if you were a slash fan online in the late '90s. "It was just a plain list of, you know, 'Fairycat's *Highlander* Stories,' with a link. And just one after the other." Coppa means that KS Nicholas's slash archive was quite simple in appearance—stories were grouped by author name and fandom, and hyperlinks took readers to the authors' websites or to specific stories—but despite its lack of visual interest, the site served a crucial purpose for many fans. Coppa says, "[KS Nicholas's archive was] a fundamental kind of site for those of us who came in [to Internet fandom] at that period. You could look at two [web] pages and say, This was the whole world [of slash fic online]" (Coppa 2012).

Then, beginning in the early 2000s, with the rise of early social networks such as the blogging platform LiveJournal, which did not have robust archiving functionalities, many fandoms ceased to maintain central archives for fan fiction. Still, the impulse to create centralized fic archives persisted through the first crest of social media. Fans used social bookmarking sites such as Pinboard and Delicious to create more durable archives than could be reasonably created on LiveJournal blogs (for example, the BSG Femslash Archive [figure 2.7], which contains links to all of the female/ female fanfics based on the sci-fi series *Battlestar Galactica* that the lead archivist could gather, is located on Delicious).

In the late 1990s and early 2000s, fans began creating archives and archive software that allowed fan authors to format and post their own stories, rather than requiring "archive elves," as fan scholar Francesca Coppa calls early fanfic archivists, to code each story submission by hand; these included Fanfiction.net (FF.net) (figures 2.8 and 2.9), a multifandom database that opened in 2000 (founded by Xing Li), which is the largest fanfic archive today, and Automated Archive and eFiction, software with self-upload functions that many fans used to create their own customized archives. For example, my research team interviewed Liviapenn, one of the founding archivists of the Smallville Slash Archive (figure 2.10), dedicated to slash fic written for the Superman television series *Smallville*, which was built using Automated Archive software; Karen Hellekson, the current archivist of Warp 5 Complex (figure 2.11), a *Star Trek: Enterprise* fic archive, which was built with Automated Archive software and then migrated to eFiction; and Robin Nelson, one of the founding archivists of Gossip-Fic. net (figure 2.12), a *Gossip Girl* fic archive, which was also constructed with eFiction software.

Some fans created multifandom archives for specific genres rather than for specific source texts or pairings: oxoniensis opened an archive of the fics generated by her annual (or, in some years, semiannual) writing festival

The Porn Battle (figures 2.13 and 2.14) in 2006, and jinjurly launched the Audiofic Archive (figure 2.15), a repository for audiofic or "podfic"—recordings of fans reading fan fiction stories aloud, similar to "books on tape"—in 2006. Then, in the late 2000s, after fans began to sour on social media platforms as well as FF.net because of their censorial policies (which I will describe in more detail in chapter 3), a large body of fans gathered to found the volunteer-run Organization for Transformative Works, whose first major initiative was to build the Archive of Our Own (AO3) (figures 2.16 and 2.17), a multifandom database designed and coded by fans and hosted on OTW-owned (fan-owned) servers. AO3's mission is to act as a "noncommercial and nonprofit central hosting place for fanworks using open-source archiving software" (Archive of Our Own, "About the OTW").

AO3 is now second only to FF.net in size, and is growing at a faster rate than FF.net (see the conclusion for visualizations of both), and so is on track to become the largest fan fiction archive online. Many of the fans that we interviewed in 2012 regarded AO3 as already far superior to FF.net, regardless of the relative sizes of the archives, because FF.net is for-profit and AO3 is not-for-profit; because FF.net has a reputation for hosting fic primarily written by younger, "feral" fans; because AO3's user interface was built by fans for fans, and so offers better navigability and functionality (although AO3 is still in "beta," that is, many of its features are still under construction and being tested); and because FF.net has censored and deleted numerous fans' stories while AO3's policy is to never practice censorship or deletion. AO3 is thus currently building a strong reputation as *the* universal archive for fan fiction.

So, media fans seemed to transition from a phase of highly centralized archives (from the mid-1990s to the early 2000s) to a phase of decentralized archiving in the early rush of social media (during the 2000s), and around 2007, the concept of a central archive—which AO3 explicitly calls itself—became dominant in fandom once again. This trajectory of

Centralization   → Decentralization   → Centralization
(mid-1990s to early 2000s)   (early-to-mid-2000s)   (late 2000s to present)

over the years 1995 to 2012 certainly does not fit the history of every fandom, as fandom is not monolithic and each fandom has had its own history, but almost all of the fans interviewed by my research team perceived this to be the general arc of fan archiving. What comes through clearly from our interviewees is that the desire for archives for fan fiction has persisted over time, and that when the technologies and platforms have become popular with fans but have not offered affordances for archiving, fans have found complementary platforms and software or have designed new platforms and software to facilitate the construction of archives.

As my research team conducted interviews in 2012, before the platform Tumblr (which does not function as an archive) became such a prominent host for online fannish activity, it is difficult to say whether the current moment is one of centralization or decentralization for fan archivists. Coppa states that Tumblr, as a nonarchive, and AO3, as the result of decades of fans' experimentations with archival forms, serve fans quite well in combination: "Tumblr and the AO3 is becoming the new slash pairing of fandom. ... You post your link [to your fan fiction story] on Tumblr, and then you read [the story] at the AO3 and then you do your pictures [on Tumblr]. ... They complement each other in ways that are really interesting but we could not have imagined [at AO3]. There was no Tumblr when we started designing this thing. And I don't know that there will be a Tumblr in four years. But *we'll* [AO3 will] be around in four years, or ten years" (Coppa 2012).

The drive to digitally and publicly archive absolutely everything—at least, everything within certain parameters, everything within a specific genre—thus motivates fanfic archives as much as it does Project Gutenberg, the Internet Archive, the Rosetta Project, Open Library, and Archive Team; all universal archives and archivists demonstrate this impulse to acquire, contain, and offer all information that matches the archive's declared mission.

Universal archives appear to be highly disinterested in the question of canons. The idea of privileging some texts over others is alien to such repositories. Plenty of people may be invested in discriminating between the contents found in these capacious repositories: for example, in Internet fandom, individual fans' recommendation lists, usually containing titles and descriptions of their favorite fan fiction stories with links to those stories, is a popular type of fan site. Similarly, on the Internet Archive, the right margin of each category, such as "Texts," "Audio," and so on, contains a list of "Staff Picks." But such expressions of taste will always be highly personal, unique to each user, and the recommendations may change or rotate frequently, as they do in the case of the Internet Archive's "Staff Picks." Of course, taste leaders may establish themselves in any cultural arena—some fans' recommendation pages receive thousands of hits—but universal archives do not structurally, permanently prioritize any subgroup of texts over the remainder of their contents. There may be some algorithmic curation: the Internet Archive and Project Gutenberg both publish frequently updated lists of their most downloaded files, and many fan fiction archives allow readers to see the number of "hits" (views) and "reviews" (comments/ feedback) each story has received. Some users may choose to access certain files because of their popularity.

But rather than investing any resources into positioning themselves as the origin and ground for new, postprint "selective traditions," universal archives cultivate an image of impressive abundance. I think that universal archives are far more invested in performing plenitude than in servicing selection because so much selecting-out is already executed by the ephemeral properties of digital data and the proclivity for forgetting in digital culture. The propensity of data to disappear or to become unfindable, which stems simultaneously from technological affordances and information abundance, is so great that universal archives define victory as the accumulation of preserved data. The accumulation, the sheer quantity of files saved and kept retrievable, is what universal archivists desire to accomplish and to display. In volume lies their victory. There is no room for a selective tradition of any kind—no shuffling of less popular works to basement storage, no showcasing of special collections in the "best" room, no tacit cooperation with tastemakers or cultural critics who wish to erect cultural canons—in an archival repertoire so focused on fighting loss.

Fan Fiction Archives as Community Archives

The universal bent of early Internet fan fiction archives was simultaneously an impulse toward community archiving: a central archive typically operated in tandem with a single central mailing list, and together these comprised the online "infrastructure" of a fandom, according to Coppa: "Before [the 2000s], if you hit a new fandom [online], you knew what to do: you went to the archive, you joined the mailing list. You plugged yourself into the infrastructure" (Coppa 2012). Universal archives can thus help a community, especially a subcultural group such as a media fandom, to define itself and locate itself; a central archive that aims to corral all of the stories produced by a fandom in one site, like a central mailing list on which all discussions and arguments within a fandom take place, can help a community by providing stable and easily located gathering places.

In such a centralized system, the culture of an online community can be easily found, clearly identified, and quickly learned by every member of that community. Central archives thus facilitate the integration of new members. Many of our interviewees spoke about how they used central archives for this purpose, to "get up to speed," so to speak, with a fandom they had just joined. Te remembers that when she initially discovered slash fan fiction in 1997, "I read all of the slash that I could find that was online at the time, in fandoms like [*Star*] *Trek* [NBC, 1963–1969] and *X-Files* and *Highlander* [syndication, 1992–1998]" (Te 2012). Litotease says of her moment of discovery of *Sentinel* (UPN, 1996–1999) fan fiction, "I found this world and I could go crawl inside [it like] a book. ... I love the long fictions. I love the novel-like fictions. I like to go crawl inside a world and not come out. And I found one. And it was amazing. And I was following this path through all of these different—I've read all of the *Sentinel* stuff" (Litotease 2012). via_ostiense remembers that when she first found *Harry Potter* fanfic archives, "I didn't really know anything about fic, or who the good writers were or anything like that, so I started with the letter A, going by author listings, and tried to just work all the way through them" (via_ostiense 2012). From her first years in online fandom to the present, Kristina Busse has had a ritual of reading *every* story housed in the archives of each new fandom that she joins. For the *Sentinel*, *Due South*, and *X-Files* fandoms in the 1990s, and more recently, for the *Inception*, *X-Men: First Class*, and Bandom fandoms,[6] she would either read alphabetically by author, or "would start with the longest—you could sort them by length, and I would start with the longest story—and then just read all of them. ... And, of course, you encounter someone who can't write, and then, you know, you like throw out all the stories by them. But on the whole, I would really read every single story. And so ... I would always say something to people who're like, 'Well you can't know that,' and I was like, 'I've actually read the archive [of the fandom] comprehensively!'" (Busse 2012).

Rather than regarding these stories of intense usage of central fic archives as the behavior of media "addicts,"[7] I read these stories as illustrative of how deeply many media fans long for a sense of community, of not-being-alone, of membership in a group that they were not born into but to which they instantly feel they belong. Fan archives provide a sense of history and cultural memory to a fandom, and when newcomers join the fandom, they familiarize themselves with the storytelling conventions, major authors, popular tropes, rituals, and argot of their new community by immersing themselves all at once in the community's archive, and consuming its cultural texts until they deeply understand the fandom's workings and can rightly consider themselves *acculturated* to the group. The process of reading quickly through a central fic archive is a crucial step in making oneself into a member of that fandom. In fact, newcomers to a fandom who fail to take this step—who do not take the time to learn the culture of the community from its archives, and who contribute stories or participate in discussions without a knowledge of the past, the traditions, the customs of the group—are often despised and derided as "feral," a fannish term that con-notes childishness or immaturity, unsophistication, ignorance, and, most importantly, a not-(yet-)belonging.

Thus, fan fiction archives demonstrate that Internet community depends on infrastructure. The infrastructuring labor of fan archivists, and of techno-volunteers in similar support roles, makes possible the multiplication of affinity-based communities on digital networks. Early theorists of nascent Internet culture such as Janet Murray, Allucquére Rosanne Stone, and Howard Rheingold drew attention to how chatrooms, MUDs and MOOs, listservs and other platforms for discussion, debate, and storytelling could facilitate a sense of affiliation and connection between individuals who were not necessarily bonded by shared geographies, ethnicities, nationali-ties, age, or economic class;[8] Rheingold (1993) called these "virtual com-munities," and participation in these types of social networks has become a common practice for Internet users. But feelings of community are gener-ated by more than the everyday communications that transpire on social media sites. Archives, full of the cultural content produced by affinity-based online groups, and rich with those group's cultural traditions, very often serve as the mechanisms by which new members orient themselves to the groups' interpretive practices, expressive modalities, and preferred genres of production. Deep engagement with the archives of Internet subcultures gives newcomers the cultural knowledge they need to begin producing and sharing their own texts, and offering informed commentary on the textual production of others—in short, to begin participating fully in the subculture.

But a virtual community member does not need to generate content for an online community in order to fully feel invested in, and a member of, that community. Oral history participant Alexis Lothian (2012b) recalls that, upon discovering fan fiction for the first time through a *Harry Potter* fic archive, she experienced "a sense of belonging, even though I didn't, and never have actually, written much fiction. I still felt as if these were my people." In Lothian's remarks, we see how powerful a role online archives can play in Internet users' lives: archives can provide users with a feeling of having found a home and a "people" they can claim as their own (recall Coppa's phrase that KS Nicholas's slash archive was "where you lived" on the Internet during the years that it was active).

And having found this type of home on the Internet, new members may go on to add their own works to those communities' archives, or they may not; the immersion in the communities' cultural productions imbues them with the feeling of homecoming and community whether or not they become a cultural producer themselves. So-called lurkers in online fan groups, who read fan fiction stories and discussions but do not post their own stories or comments, may therefore feel the same degree of belonging to the group, simply through their uses of fanfic archives, as fan authors and fan reviewers feel. Lurkers and authors may not have the same *social* status in an online community, but they may have the same *cultural* status, in that they are both fully invested members of that community's culture, insofar as they are both deeply familiar with the community's archives of cultural production.

The importance that fans place on the feelings of belonging that they receive from their engagement with fan fiction archives stems largely from the fact that these archives are predominantly queer and female online spaces. Chapter 3 will explore fanfic archives as a queer, feminist archival tradition in detail. Here, to illustrate how fannish online communities and archives have enabled members' fuller exploration of, and identification with, queer and female perspectives, I will simply cite a few oral history participants' statements. Lothian says of her initial encounter with fanfic archives: "I was reading slash and I was reading, well, sexually explicit fictions, and so there was … something really amazing about this outpouring of sexuality and desire" (Lothian 2012b). Te recalls that when she initially discovered a *Star Trek* slash archive, she felt struck by lightning: "*Wham!* Here I am, finding authors like [redacted], and all of these other great, wonderful slash goddesses" (Te 2012). Te emailed feedback to the first author she read. "I was like, 'Holy crap! This [is] amazing! This is the best porn I have ever read. You're awesome!'" When the author replied to Te, Te began to understand that many women, not just the one author, were writing the kind of "porn" that Te wanted to read. "I realize[d], 'What the fuck? This is a community of incredibly perverse women" (Te 2012).

For many women, it is a powerfully validating experience to encounter storehouses of "pornography by women for women, with love" (as award-winning science fiction author Joanna Russ [1985] called slash fan fiction)—to find repositories of cultural production by female authors about nonheteronormative, or simply nonnormative scenarios of human interaction (nonnormative in that they are outside the bounds of what Gayle Rubin [1984] calls "the charmed circle" [280] of acceptable gender- and sex-related identities and acts for women, i.e., heterosexual marriage, monogamy, childbirth and child-rearing, and other forms of family care). The editors of *The Feminist Porn Book* argue, "The overwhelming popularity of women's erotic literature, illustrated by … the flourishing women's fan fiction community, … proves that there is great demand among women for explicit sexual representations. ... Women-authored erotica and pornography speaks to fantasies women actually have, fantasies that are located in a world where women must negotiate power constantly, including in their imaginations and desires" (Taormino et al. 2013, 14). Given how little the cultural industries cater to women's fantasies, and how rigidly mainstream media texts keep women characters' actions within the bounds of "normative and constricted sexualities" (14), it is unsurprising that female media users have turned to new media to assemble archives of their alternative versions of older media. Engaging with fanfic archives, queer and female subjects derive a sense of community belonging, for the sheer preponderance of alternative cultural production that they encounter in the archives informs them that, although they exist outside "the charmed circle," they are far from alone.

Like the FAMA Collection, SAADA, the Radfem Archive, and the Michigan/Trans Controversy Archive, fanfic archives work to save and "keep alive" the shared sensibilities, experiences, thoughts, ideas, and expressions of a group that does not find itself well represented in either mainstream culture or traditional memory institutions. The texts kept by a community archive have definite, often profound, relevance to that community's members, and are often viewed as irrelevant, unimportant, or simply not very interesting to nonmembers. However, most community archives welcome use by nonmembers who wish to gain a better understanding of the communities through engaging with their recorded cultures. Nonmembers thus educated can become *allies* of those communities, who support those communities' various struggles without identifying as one of them (as, for example, men can be allies of women's movements, though they do not identify as women, and as non–Asian/Pacific Islander Americans can be allies of API movements, though they do not identify as API). Also, nonmembers can become members of certain communities, such as fan fiction and radical feminist communities, through their use of those groups' online archives, by which they learn how to *be* members, and transform their identities through that learning (changing their identities from not-fan to fan, or from not-feminist to feminist).

The majority of community archives are politically opposed to the concept of "canonicity," as they typically refuse traditional notions of hierarchy, status, and privilege, and regimes organized according to vertical logics under which their members have suffered, or from which they have been systematically excluded from. Community archives encourage users to draw whatever they need from their stores—to construct their own personal canons from the collections, if they wish—and the archives themselves are not structured in ways that support the canonization of some items over others.

In addition, I predict that no community digital archive will become a dominant institution in the larger field of digital culture in the way that the Museum of Modern Art, the New York Public Library, or the Library of Congress are dominant cultural institutions founded in the print age, or even in the way that the Internet Archive strives to be a dominant cultural institution in the early digital age. New media have facilitated the assembly of communities, and the construction of community archives, that are small and specific, and that are "minor" in the sense proposed by Gilles Deleuze and Félix Guattari. These communities and their archives are minor not because their concerns, commitments, and contents are minor, but because their concerns, commitments, and contents are constructed within a major culture.[9] A single story about an individual that is written in a "minor" language is always political, argue Deleuze and Guattari (1986), because "a whole other story is vibrating within it" (17). That is, the story of the whole community, the whole story of a minor community, vibrates within one story of a lone member of that minority. Because a "minor" cultural production, within a "minor" culture's archive, contains multiple texts that each contain and, in some sense, represent the "whole," each text is equally valuable and each such minor archive is as important as any other. Or rather, each archive holds extraordinary importance, power, and significance for the minority that it serves. Thus, the community archival style refuses every permutation of canonicity.

Fan Fiction Archives as Alternative Archives

The question of quality often comes up when I present scholarly work on fan fiction. Nearly every time I have given a paper at an academic conference on the topic of fanfic, one or more audience members asks a variant of this query: "But is any of it *any good*?" My response is: Many fan fiction writers strive for a high degree of literary quality, not only mimicking styles learned from established print authors but producing new kinds of experimental fiction. At the same time, many fic writers do not aim for literariness in the slightest, but are trying to produce entirely different types of "quality" fiction.

In our interviews with fan fiction archivists, writers, and readers, we noted a wide range of comments on the topic of quality in fanfic. Some participants emphatically stated their preference for "literary" fic over poorly written fic. For example, Litotease states that when she first began reading online fic,

I was delighted by the stories. I don't know how I had the good luck to stumble across. ... My very first stories [that I read] were exquisitely written. I didn't trip over the twelve-year-old writing Mary Sue fanfic. I tripped over [renowned *Sentinel* and *Due South* fic authors] Francesca and astolat, at the very beginning. So, the world-building was phenomenal. The characterizations were true. One of the most amazing things about Francesca as a writer is that she'd write the characters one way, like [the reader will say], "Of course, that's exactly how they are," and then, just to play, she will switch them. And I'll read it and I'll go, "Well, of course. That's exactly how they are." (Litotease 2012)

Like Litotease, nightflier makes a strong distinction between badly written fic and literary fic, stating,

[The *X-Files* community was] the most amazing fic community I've ever seen. They produced so much quality of every level from the worst—I mean, barely writing in English, like, no grammar, no punctuation—I read stories that were like medieval manuscripts where all the words were written together and every other one was spelled wrongly. Like, I read fic written like that, and I read fic that was literature, that I will be quoting lines from those stories to my dying day. It was so poetic and beautiful and taught me so much about writing. (nightflier 2012)

We can derive nightflier and Litotease's criteria for distinguishing between "good" and "bad" fic. Good fanfic is defined by: solid "world-building" and "characterizations"; experimentations with form such as a single author writing the same characters completely differently in two different stories (both versions being convincing interpretations of the characters); "exquisite" and "beautiful" writing, which sometimes takes the form of "poetic" language, rich with memorable lines. Bad fanfic is defined by: immaturity or lack of sophistication in authorial voice ("twelve-year-old Mary Sue fanfic"); and poor grammar, punctuation, spelling, and formatting. Their standards for good fanfic seem to match widely accepted standards for good literary fiction.

But other interviewees defined "good" or "quality" fanfic differently, in ways that had little to do with literariness. Or rather, they acknowledged that much of the fanfic they enjoyed, or that found popularity in their fandoms, was not "quality" fic. Julie Levin Russo recalls that many or most femslash (female/female) fanfic writers in the late 1990s did not seem particularly interested in producing "literary" stories:

I think the stylistic emphasis of late-nineties [femslash] fanfic was very much influenced by romance novels. Or there are maybe two genres. So one was just straight-out porn, you know, ... like PWP [Plot-What-Plot]. Dirty fic. And then there were these whole romance novels that people would write. There was a real emphasis on the first-time story, like the saga of how two characters first got together. And even after you got past the first time, I think in the lesbian romance novel tradition, there would be constant obstacles that would come up in the relationship that the characters would then have to overcome. ... [It was fic] that was just very driven by the id, and fic that was really oriented toward producing certain feelings, and it didn't really matter if it was well written and if all the punctuation was right. But then also, I think, looking back at it now, you also have to cringe, too. Because a lot of it is so bad. So you can both really enjoy reading it, and get caught up in the story and the feelings and the erotic charge, and then also at the same time be really uncomfortable with how bad it is. So I think that's a unique pleasure of reading fic that's [more than] a decade old today.

And I think that [in] my later experiences [in the 2000s] in LiveJournal fanfic communities, there was a much bigger emphasis on literary writing, and on show-don't-tell, on carefully crafting prose. And on fan fiction as a sort of creative writing exercise. (Russo 2012)

Russo here acknowledges two kinds of "good" fanfic. One kind of "good" (or, we might say, effective) fanfic does not necessarily meet the standards of literariness that Litotease and nightflier lay out in their above quotes, but it succeeds with its readers because it delivers a certain affective experience, often a libidinal and/or romantic experience. The other category of "good" fanfic that Russo establishes is "literary": its authors adhere to the "show-don't-tell" rule, "carefully craft" their prose, and seem to engage in fanfic writing as a "creative writing exercise" rather than an exercise in conveying affect. Russo speaks of paradoxically holding both sets of criteria for "quality" in her mind when she rereads late-1990s femslash fic. She knows that some of what she can "really enjoy reading" and "get caught up in" is also "so bad," and calls this peculiar (re)reading experience "a unique pleasure."

Russo references the Freudian term "id" when she describes the category of effective/affective fanfic, and another participant, Kristina Busse, calls this category of fan writing "id fic." Busse says that when she first discovered fanfic, the first story that she read

was such—it was every cliché in the book. It was a Mary Sue, and it was ... just—I mean it was just horrible. However. However, I had never encountered this. ... I think one of the things I love about kind of, what we would usually call bad fic, is that it's real id fic and so it hits all of those things that, you know, you don't get in real literature. You don't even get [those things] in good fanfic. It hits all those, all those things where you lie in bed and dream up whom you want to pair with whom, and, you know, create these crazy scenarios. And that's exactly the stuff it was. (Busse 2012)

I underscore the difference between "literary" fanfic and "id fic" not because I wish to claim those as the only two definitions of "quality" fanfic that currently circulate in media fandoms—our interviewees spoke of an astoundingly diverse range of fanfic genres, writing styles, and tropes that they have found interesting, innovative, hilarious, compelling, entertaining, and otherwise "good"—but because I wish to illustrate that fanfic is an alternative system of cultural production that has not, so far, been systematically incorporated into either the world of "high" art or the commodity categories of the "mainstream" culture industries, and that this nonassimilation is divorced from questions of quality.

On the one hand, there is online fanfic that meets the standards that most literary critics would agree on for "quality" writing, and these stories have not been recognized as "literature." Fan fiction can be as "good" as good writing gets, and yet it is never a candidate for earning the designations of either "art" or "mainstream culture" because it is subcultural production, circulating in what John Fiske (1992) calls a "shadow cultural economy" (30). Fic is writing that originates from, and circulates in, volunteer-organized, affinity-based Internet communities rather than writing that comes to the public's attention through the funneling mechanisms of print publishing and mass media. On the other hand, much fanfic earns favor with fan readers precisely *because* it does not adhere to the definitions of "quality" established by the art/literary worlds and mainstream media. Busse says that the pleasures of "id fic" lie in its provision of content that "you don't get in real literature," and that "you don't even get in good fanfic" (Busse 2012). Readers and audiences do not often find the affective charge of which Russo speaks in the offerings of either mass culture or literary/high culture. And there are many other types of fanfic whose value, for appreciative readers, lie far outside the categories for aesthetic or conceptual achievement learned from what Lewis calls "official culture" or what Fiske calls "normal popular culture" (30).

Thus, fan fiction archives must be called "alternative" archives, even if a good deal of fanfic meets the bar of what the arbiters of "official" or "normal" culture would call "good" writing. The path of literary fanfic to realms of greater visibility and higher cultural capital remains "shadowy" at best. Fanfic archives store "bad" fic as well as "good" fic, or rather that they store fiction that might be received as "good" for any number of reasons—fiction that does not need to fulfill any requirements for "quality" writing set out by the print publishing industry—and thus facilitate the development of new reading tastes (such as Russo's "unique pleasure" in badly written but emotionally and affectively powerful fanfic), and the emergence of unexpected subgenres and styles.

Online fanfic archives thus resemble other alternative digital archives: fic archives collect and preserve a fairly new, fast-growing genre of digital culture, as does the ArtBase; fic archives collect users' digital derivations and appropriations of popular media that exist in a gray zone of legality, as does Download Finished; most fic archives collect both "bad" and "good" texts, as Sly collects both "badfilm" and "art film," under the overarching banner of nonmainstream film. As I will explore in chapter 6, fic archives also collect and document "events"—online writing festivals, contests, battles, exchanges, and other time-limited happenings designed to encourage fan production—as does the Netbase. All of these alternative and avant-garde archives are committed to corralling, preserving, and making broadly accessible digital material in new genres, "low" or derided genres, derivative (and therefore, questionably legal) genres, and genres that resist categorization.

The contents of alternative archives have not (or, again, not yet) entered into the canons of high or mass culture, and the archivists of these repositories do not seem deeply invested in forcing that entry. Rather, these archives serve as countercollections, storehouses of culture outside highly visible "official" cultures, from which users can construct their own canons employing curatorial tastes that deviate from the cultural norm. In fandom, "canon" has a specific meaning: it refers to the "source" texts on which fan works are based, so in a film fandom, the canonical text is the film itself, and in a television fandom, the canonical texts are the episodes of the TV series, and in a comic book fandom, the canonical texts are the comic book issues. Fan production is always noncanonical, by definition. This use of "canon" in media fandom parlance makes archives of fan works anticanonical, in the sense that these archives refuse to allow the source or canonical works to remain intact, untouched, complete in and of themselves—these archives refuse to let canonical works form inviolable, closed wholes. Fanfic archives record the multitude of ways that users open up canons, and revise, rework, interpret, and vary their contents.

And fanfic archives are also anticanonical in another, deeper way. Like other alternative online archives, they reject the "selective traditions" of both high art and mainstream media. They encompass marginal and emerging forms of digital making. They designate the deviant and subcultural worthy of preservation. If cultural canons are predicated on some common conceptions of artistic or literary "quality," alternative digital archives either utterly dismiss the question of quality or radically redefine quality.

The Repertoire of Archive Use

As cultural production, distribution, and consumption increasingly transpire on new media platforms, how does the seeker of culture proceed? How does the seeker of culture know where to look, what to look for, what to save and discard, and how to understand what networked society at large is saving and discarding? What seekers of culture must do now is begin to grasp the repertoire of archiving that has developed over the past forty years, and to take the initiative to create their own repertoires of archival use. Digital archives rise and fall, and all the ones I have named in this chapter may collapse in the next handful of years or decades. But the impulse to found cultural archives, to save small or large swaths of culture that one finds important, will continue and is only getting stronger in the Internet population, so that if one looks, one will always be able to find where culture is being "kept," and in turn, one must decide how to "keep" the texts, works, and artifacts that one finds in archives online. The digital reduces the "canon" to an individual's collection of material; the act of "canonization" becomes a constant, personal practice of searching, discovering, and consistently, actively preserving and reusing.

We will have universal archives long after the Internet Archive effort comes to an end; we will see more and more community archives built in the decades to come; and the tendency to create online spaces for emerging and alternative genres will not diminish. Seekers of culture in the digital age must be prepared to constantly quest for, and stumble upon, new archives of these types. They must also become accustomed to experiencing the frequent loss of archives—to watch archive after archive simply vanish from the Internet—archives to which they have become attached.

Thus, the general repertoire of archive use that develops in tandem with the repertoire of archive building is this:

1. Be on the lookout for, and actively search for, the *kinds* of digital archives you need.
2. Know that there are universal, community, and alternative archives—which of these are you seeking, and for what type(s) of content?
3. Be grateful when you find the sort of archive you wished to find. Be appreciative of the volunteers who labor to keep those archives functional and operational.
4. Decide what, of the contents you encounter from these archives, you want to save, and treasure. Copy these to your personal archive, your private storage. (You will necessarily develop many highly individualized

repertoires, of how to continually update and migrate and maintain your personal digital collection, following this step.) Anticipate that any service you use to manage your personal archive may fold, that any server on which you store your archive may degrade, and so you will likely have to migrate your data again and again, over the course of your life.

5. When your favorite Internet archives close, you will grieve, but you can also hope and even expect that new archives are likely in development, as long as new techno-volunteers are signing themselves up for archivists' duties. Return to step 1.

6. Also, during any of the above steps, know that you could become a volunteer archivist. You could support an existing archive, save a dying one, or found a new one. This is what repertoire means: all but the earliest volunteer archivists watched others do archiving before they opted to do it themselves, and they learned the "how" of rogue archive building partly by copying the actions, styles, methods, and designs they witnessed others performing and executing. So archive using can become archive building. The two repertoires not only repeat across multiple bodies, but sometimes merge in the same bodies.

The drive to archive has so far coalesced around these three styles—universal, community-based, and alternative—but more modes of digital preservation may become prominent in the near future. What all of these archival styles share is a quest to obliterate the "selective tradition" that served as a dominant cultural logic of the print era.

All figures are screenshots taken in May 2014.

Figure 2.1
The Gossamer Project, Main Page.

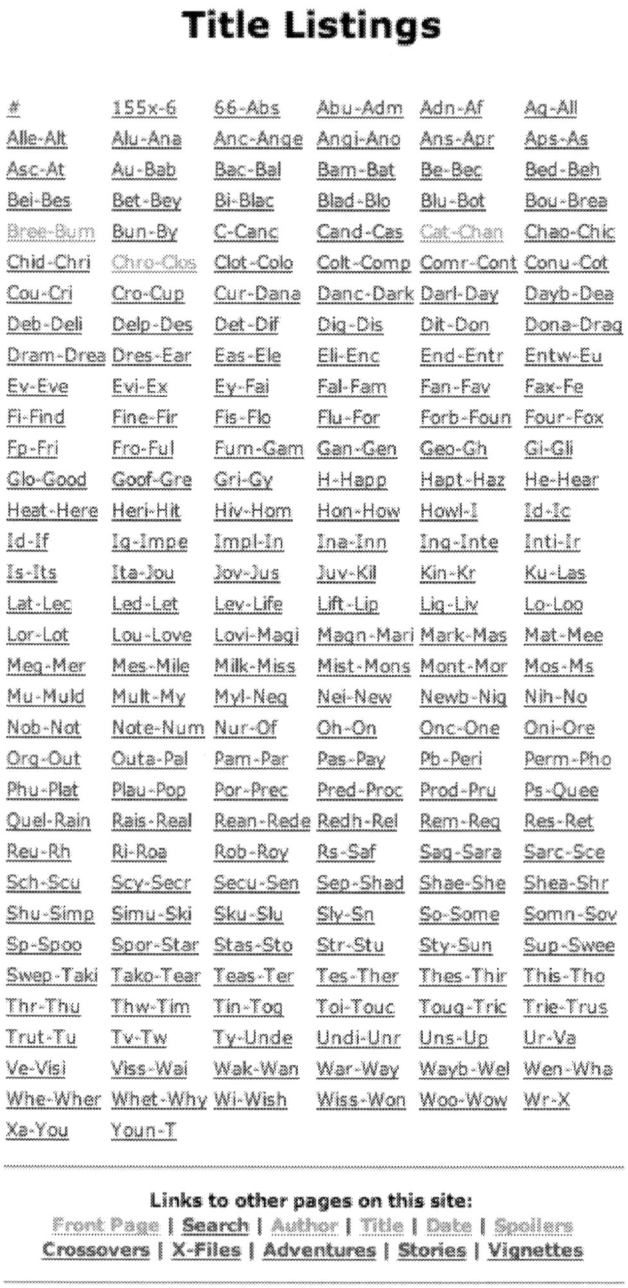

Title Listings

#	155x-6	66-Abs	Abu-Adm	Adn-Af	Ag-All
Alle-Alt	Alu-Ana	Anc-Ange	Angi-Ano	Ans-Apr	Aps-As
Asc-At	Au-Bab	Bac-Bal	Bam-Bat	Be-Bec	Bed-Beh
Bei-Bes	Bet-Bey	Bi-Blac	Blad-Blo	Blu-Bot	Bou-Brea
Bree-Bum	Bun-By	C-Canc	Cand-Cas	Cat-Chan	Chao-Chic
Chid-Chri	Chro-Clos	Clot-Colo	Colt-Comp	Comr-Cont	Conu-Cot
Cou-Cri	Cro-Cup	Cur-Dana	Danc-Dark	Darl-Day	Dayb-Dea
Deb-Deli	Delp-Des	Det-Dif	Dig-Dis	Dit-Don	Dona-Drag
Dram-Drea	Dres-Ear	Eas-Ele	Eli-Enc	End-Entr	Entw-Eu
Ev-Eve	Evi-Ex	Ey-Fai	Fal-Fam	Fan-Fav	Fax-Fe
Fi-Find	Fine-Fir	Fis-Flo	Flu-For	Forb-Foun	Four-Fox
Fp-Fri	Fro-Ful	Fum-Gam	Gan-Gen	Geo-Gh	Gi-Gli
Glo-Good	Goof-Gre	Gri-Gy	H-Happ	Hapt-Haz	He-Hear
Heat-Here	Heri-Hit	Hiv-Hom	Hon-How	Howl-I	Id-Ic
Id-If	Ig-Impe	Impl-In	Ina-Inn	Ing-Inte	Inti-Ir
Is-Its	Ita-Jou	Jov-Jus	Juv-Kil	Kin-Kr	Ku-Las
Lat-Lec	Led-Let	Lev-Life	Lift-Lip	Lig-Liv	Lo-Loo
Lor-Lot	Lou-Love	Lovi-Magi	Magn-Mari	Mark-Mas	Mat-Mee
Meg-Mer	Mes-Mile	Milk-Miss	Mist-Mons	Mont-Mor	Mos-Ms
Mu-Muld	Mult-My	Myl-Neg	Nei-New	Newb-Nig	Nih-No
Nob-Not	Note-Num	Nur-Of	Oh-On	Onc-One	Oni-Ore
Org-Out	Outa-Pal	Pam-Par	Pas-Pay	Pb-Peri	Perm-Pho
Phu-Plat	Plau-Pop	Por-Prec	Pred-Proc	Prod-Pru	Ps-Quee
Quel-Rain	Rais-Real	Rean-Rede	Redh-Rel	Rem-Req	Res-Ret
Reu-Rh	Ri-Roa	Rob-Roy	Rs-Saf	Sag-Sara	Sarc-Sce
Sch-Scu	Scy-Secr	Secu-Sen	Sep-Shad	Shae-She	Shea-Shr
Shu-Simp	Simu-Ski	Sku-Slu	Sly-Sn	So-Some	Somn-Sov
Sp-Spoo	Spor-Star	Stas-Sto	Str-Stu	Sty-Sun	Sup-Swee
Swep-Taki	Tako-Tear	Teas-Ter	Tes-Ther	Thes-Thir	This-Tho
Thr-Thu	Thw-Tim	Tin-Tog	Toi-Touc	Toug-Tric	Trie-Trus
Trut-Tu	Tv-Tw	Ty-Unde	Undi-Unr	Uns-Up	Ur-Va
Ve-Visi	Viss-Wai	Wak-Wan	War-Way	Wayb-Wel	Wen-Wha
Whe-Wher	Whet-Why	Wi-Wish	Wiss-Won	Woo-Wow	Wr-X
Xa-You	Youn-T				

Links to other pages on this site:
Front Page | **Search** | Author | Title | Date | Spoilers
Crossovers | **X-Files** | **Adventures** | **Stories** | **Vignettes**

Figure 2.2
The Gossamer Project, Titles Page (index of stories by title).

Figure 2.3
Trekiverse, Main Page. Art by Stephen Ratliff.

By Directory

All Original Series
Adult Original Series Restricted to Adults
General Original Series General Stories
Parody Original Series Humor or Parody
Original Series Drabbles 100 words of wisdom
Original Series Poems Poems and Filks

By Pairing

Kirk Spock Pairing
Kirk McCoy Pairing
Kirk Scott Pairing
Kirk Chekov Pairing
Kirk Uhura Pairing
Spock McCoy Pairing
Spock Scott Pairing
Spock Sulu Pairing
Spock Chekov Pairing
Spock Chapel Pairing
Spock Uhura Pairing
Spock Saavik Pairing
McCoy Scott Pairing
Sulu Chekov Pairing

Special Searches

2005 ASC Awards Searches
General Story
Kirk Spock Pairing
General Drabble
Kirk Drabble
Kirk Spock Drabble
Featuring Scotty
Spock Pairing
Featuring Kirk

Figure 2.4
Trekiverse, *Star Trek: The Original Series*, Categories Page (index of stories by category or pairing). Art by Stephen Ratliff.

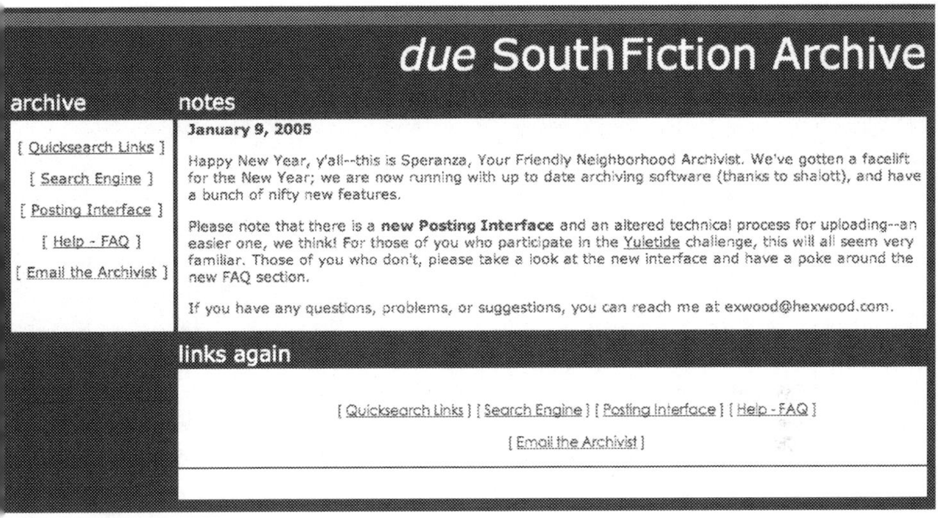

due SouthFiction Archive

archive   notes

January 9, 2005

[Quicksearch Links]   Happy New Year, y'all--this is Speranza, Your Friendly Neighborhood Archivist. We've gotten a facelift
[Search Engine]   for the New Year; we are now running with up to date archiving software (thanks to shalott), and have
                           a bunch of nifty new features.
[Posting Interface]
                           Please note that there is a **new Posting Interface** and an altered technical process for uploading--an
[Help - FAQ]   easier one, we think! For those of you who participate in the Yuletide challenge, this will all seem very
                           familiar. Those of you who don't, please take a look at the new interface and have a poke around the
[Email the Archivist]   new FAQ section.

                           If you have any questions, problems, or suggestions, you can reach me at exwood@hexwood.com.

links again

[Quicksearch Links] [Search Engine] [Posting Interface] [Help - FAQ]

[Email the Archivist]

Figure 2.5
Due South Fiction Archive, Main Page.

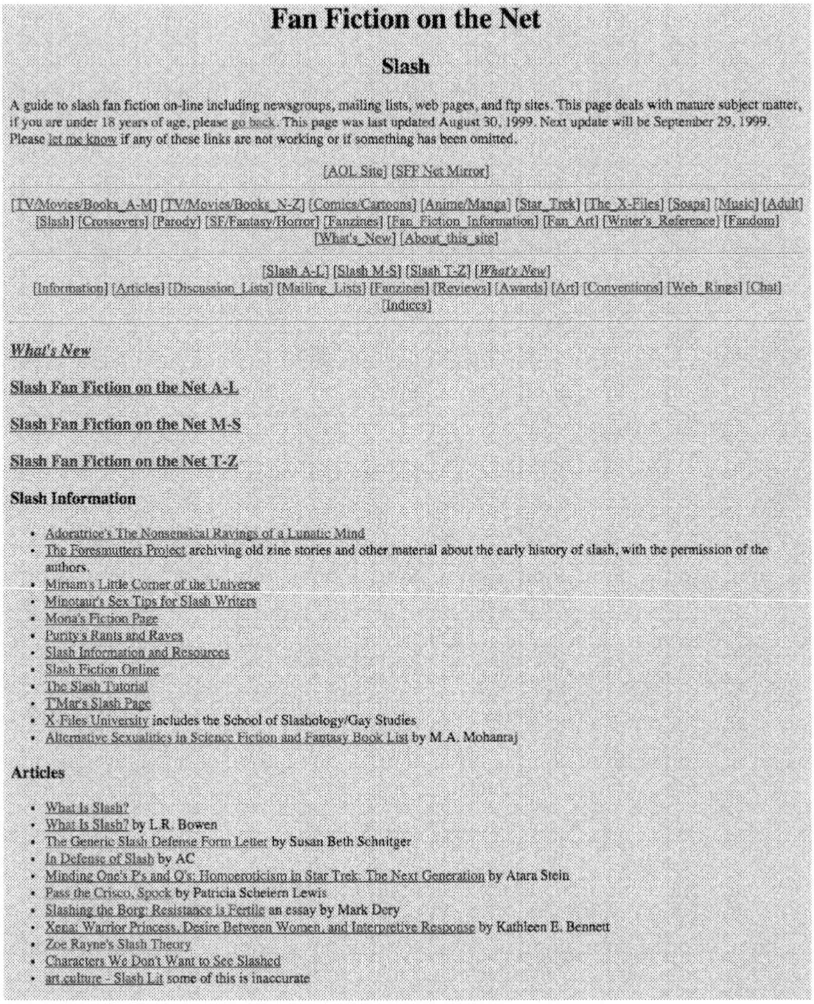

Fan Fiction on the Net

Slash

A guide to slash fan fiction on-line including newsgroups, mailing lists, web pages, and ftp sites. This page deals with mature subject matter, if you are under 18 years of age, please go back. This page was last updated August 30, 1999. Next update will be September 29, 1999. Please let me know if any of these links are not working or if something has been omitted.

[AOL Site] [SFF Net Mirror]

[TV/Movies/Books_A-M] [TV/Movies/Books_N-Z] [Comics/Cartoons] [Anime/Manga] [Star_Trek] [The_X-Files] [Soaps] [Music] [Adult] [Slash] [Crossovers] [Parody] [SF/Fantasy/Horror] [Fanzines] [Fan_Fiction_Information] [Fan_Art] [Writer's_Reference] [Fandom] [What's_New] [About_this_site]

[Slash A-L] [Slash M-S] [Slash T-Z] [*What's New*]
[Information] [Articles] [Discussion_Lists] [Mailing_Lists] [Fanzines] [Reviews] [Awards] [Art] [Conventions] [Web_Rings] [Chat] [Indices]

What's New

Slash Fan Fiction on the Net A-L

Slash Fan Fiction on the Net M-S

Slash Fan Fiction on the Net T-Z

Slash Information

- Adoratrice's The Nonsensical Ravings of a Lunatic Mind
- The Foresmutters Project archiving old zine stories and other material about the early history of slash, with the permission of the authors.
- Miriam's Little Corner of the Universe
- Minotaur's Sex Tips for Slash Writers
- Mona's Fiction Page
- Purity's Rants and Raves
- Slash Information and Resources
- Slash Fiction Online
- The Slash Tutorial
- TMar's Slash Page
- X-Files University includes the School of Slashology/Gay Studies
- Alternative Sexualities in Science Fiction and Fantasy Book List by M.A. Mohanraj

Articles

- What Is Slash?
- What Is Slash? by L.R. Bowen
- The Generic Slash Defense Form Letter by Susan Beth Schnitger
- In Defense of Slash by AC
- Minding One's Ps and Q's: Homoeroticism in Star Trek: The Next Generation by Atara Stein
- Pass the Crisco, Spock by Patricia Scheiern Lewis
- Slashing the Borg: Resistance is Fertile an essay by Mark Dery
- Xena: Warrior Princess, Desire Between Women, and Interpretive Response by Kathleen E. Bennett
- Zoe Rayne's Slash Theory
- Characters We Don't Want to See Slashed
- art.culture - Slash Lit some of this is inaccurate

Figure 2.6
Slash Fan Fiction on the Net, Main Page. Site closed. Image from http://web.archive .org/web/19991013054158/http://members.aol.com/KSNicholas/fanfic/slash.html.

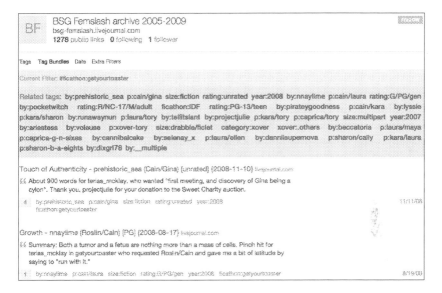

Figure 2.7
BSG Femslash Archive, Main Page.

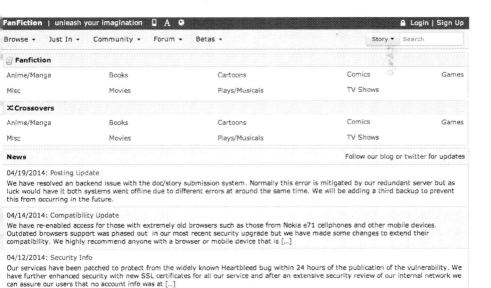

Figure 2.8
Fanfiction.net, Main Page.

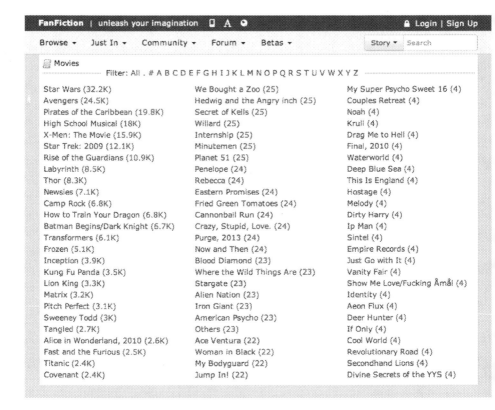

Figure 2.9

Fanfiction.net, top half of Movies Page (index of stories by source text [category: movies] on which they are based).

Figure 2.10
Smallville Slash Archive, Main Page.

Warp 5 Complex
Star Trek Enterprise fan fiction archive

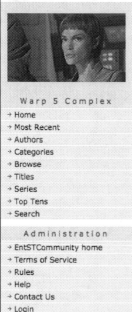

The Warp 5 Complex archives all kinds of *Enterprise*-related fiction—gen, het, and slash—of all ratings. All stories include headers that provide information about the story, such as warnings, so please read them to avoid surprises. We welcome all submissions, including crossovers. A click-through age statement is required to read explicit stories.

Warp 5 Complex

→ Home
→ Most Recent
→ Authors
→ Categories
→ Browse
→ Titles
→ Series
→ Top Tens
→ Search

Administration

→ EntSTCommunity home
→ Terms of Service
→ Rules
→ Help
→ Contact Us
→ Login

Categories

Gen [1169]
Het [1131]
Slash [2501]
Three And More [88]
Treksoap RPG [21]
Virtual Season [64]

We are the home of 502 authors from among our 11706 members. There have been 1555 reviews written about our 4857 stories consisting of 9796 chapters and 24743377 words. A special welcome to our newest member, xlqnqqcjv.

Most recent

A Meeting Of Mealtimes by Britpacker PG-13
Commander Tucker is curious about Enterprise's Armoury Officer. Where better...
Casualties Of War by Britpacker G
Set during 4.03 "Home". Not all the wounds of battle are visible to the naked...
Not Forgotten by Britpacker PG
A moment during 3.20 "The Forgotten". Jonathan sees a glimmer of hope.

Random story

Stand Alone Complex by Eri PG-13
Archer confesses to Trip about his relationship with Admiral Forrest. Forrest/Archer. (PG-13)

Figure 2.11
Warp 5 Complex, Main Page.

Figure 2.12
Gossip-Fic.net, Main Page.

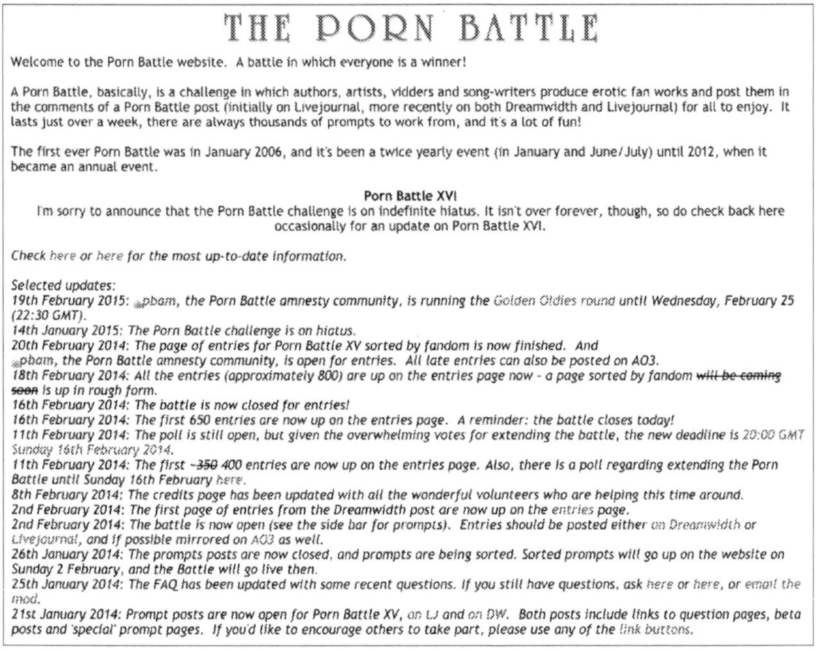

THE PORN BATTLE

Welcome to the Porn Battle website. A battle in which everyone is a winner!

A Porn Battle, basically, is a challenge in which authors, artists, vidders and song-writers produce erotic fan works and post them in the comments of a Porn Battle post (initially on Livejournal, more recently on both Dreamwidth and Livejournal) for all to enjoy. It lasts just over a week, there are always thousands of prompts to work from, and it's a lot of fun!

The first ever Porn Battle was in January 2006, and it's been a twice yearly event (in January and June/July) until 2012, when it became an annual event.

Porn Battle XVI
I'm sorry to announce that the Porn Battle challenge is on indefinite hiatus. It isn't over forever, though, so do check back here occasionally for an update on Porn Battle XVI.

Check here or here for the most up-to-date information.

Selected updates:
19th February 2015: ₚpbam, the Porn Battle amnesty community, is running the Golden Oldies round until Wednesday, February 25 (22:30 GMT).
14th January 2015: The Porn Battle challenge is on hiatus.
20th February 2014: The page of entries for Porn Battle XV sorted by fandom is now finished. And
ₚpbam, the Porn Battle amnesty community, is open for entries. All late entries can also be posted on AO3.
18th February 2014: All the entries (approximately 800) are up on the entries page now - a page sorted by fandom will be coming soon is up in rough form.
16th February 2014: The battle is now closed for entries!
16th February 2014: The first 650 entries are now up on the entries page. A reminder: the battle closes today!
11th February 2014: The poll is still open, but given the overwhelming votes for extending the battle, the new deadline is 20:00 GMT Sunday 16th February 2014.
11th February 2014: The first ~350 400 entries are now up on the entries page. Also, there is a poll regarding extending the Porn Battle until Sunday 16th February here.
8th February 2014: The credits page has been updated with all the wonderful volunteers who are helping this time around.
2nd February 2014: The first page of entries from the Dreamwidth post are now up on the entries page.
2nd February 2014: The battle is now open (see the side bar for prompts). Entries should be posted either on Dreamwidth or Livejournal, and if possible mirrored on AO3 as well.
26th January 2014: The prompts posts are now closed, and prompts are being sorted. Sorted prompts will go up on the website on Sunday 2 February, and the Battle will go live then.
25th January 2014: The FAQ has been updated with some recent questions. If you still have questions, ask here or here, or email the mod.
21st January 2014: Prompt posts are now open for Porn Battle XV, on LJ and on DW. Both posts include links to question pages, beta posts and 'special' prompt pages. If you'd like to encourage others to take part, please use any of the link buttons.

Figure 2.13
The Porn Battle, Main Page.

THE PORN BATTLE

Porn Battle XV - The Ides of Porn

Entries (sorted by fandom)

Last update: 20th February 2014.

10 Things I Hate About You (Movie)
Definitions by ᵦcaitfianna, Kat Stratford/Patrick Verona, curls, bed, smile, college, accent

2 Guns (2013)
Cheap Date by ᵦkat8cha, Bobby/Stig, grin, easy

28 Weeks Later
Daybreak by ᵦhiddencait, Doyle/Tammy, sunrise, together, age

A Civil Contract - Georgette Heyer
Daybreak by ᵦclaire1895, Adam/Jenny, life after heartache

A Song of Ice and Fire - George R. R. Martin
Knowledge by ᵦlion_heart, Jon Snow/Ygritte, forever, loss, fire, ice
Got down on my knees (and I pretend to pray) by ᵦfallingtowers, Brienne/Jaime, kneel, mouth, warm
minor victories by ᵦodyle, Sandor Clegane/Sansa Stark, scar, castle
Lay My Head Under The Sea by ᵦagirlnamedtruth, Asha Greyjoy/Theon Greyjoy, salt, ocean, comfort, family
Vermilion by ᵦskazka, Ramsay Bolton/Roose Bolton, garnet
Resetting the board by ᵦodyle, Sandor Clegane/Sansa Stark, Alayne
Honor Bound by ᵦlion_heart, Brienne of Tarth/Jaime Lannister
Snow Queen by ᵦdagonst, Sansa/Danerys, negotiation, alliance, treaty
Interlude in a War by ᵦria_oaks, Brienne of Tarth/Jaime Lannister, bath, dirty, first time
Don't you know... by ᵦagirlnamedtruth, Margaery Tyrwell/Sansa Stark, comfort, confide, letters, politics, masquerade
Mercy by ᵦdagonst, Sansa/Sandor, command, leashed, tempt
Left Without by ᵦgirlofgold, Joffrey/Myrcella, sin
Can't Train a Moth, I Guess by ᵦhalotolerant, Jon Snow/Robb Stark, modern

Ace Attorney
Mango Juice by ᵦsamuraiter, Apollo Justice/[Any], bicycle

Agents of S.H.I.E.L.D. (TV)
Keeping Score by ᵦdahlia_moon, Phil Coulson/Melinda May, [any], comfort, history, mats, past, warmth
For You by ᵦashen_key, Melinda May/Grant Ward, submission, trust, appreciation
Parachute by ᵦsalmon_pink, Jemma Simmons/Skye, awkward, cute, knees, quiet, insecure, privacy
The Documented Healing Properties of Kissing by ᵦtheleaveswant, Jemma Simmons/Skye, awkward, kissing, knees, science
realism and romance by ᵦmuselives, Melinda May/Phil Coulson, [any]
Penalties And Priorities by ᵦsalmon_pink, Melinda May/Victoria Hand, lessons, priorities
Hot Water by ᵦowlmoose, Melinda May/Natasha Romanoff, mission, together, hotel, relax
Purple Moss by ᵦiria4285, Jemma Simmons/Grant Ward, sex pollen

Figure 2.14
The Porn Battle, Entries Page for Battle 15.

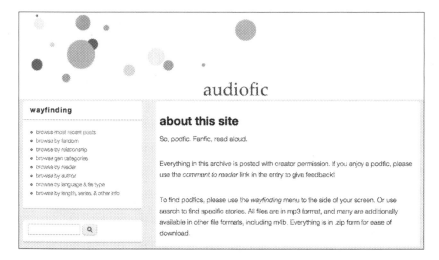

Figure 2.15
The Audiofic Archive, Main Page.

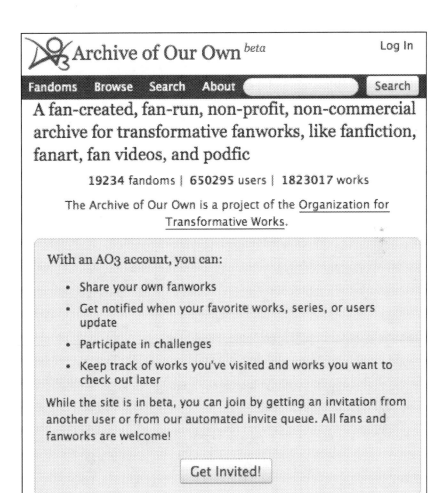

Figure 2.16
Archive of Our Own, Main Page.

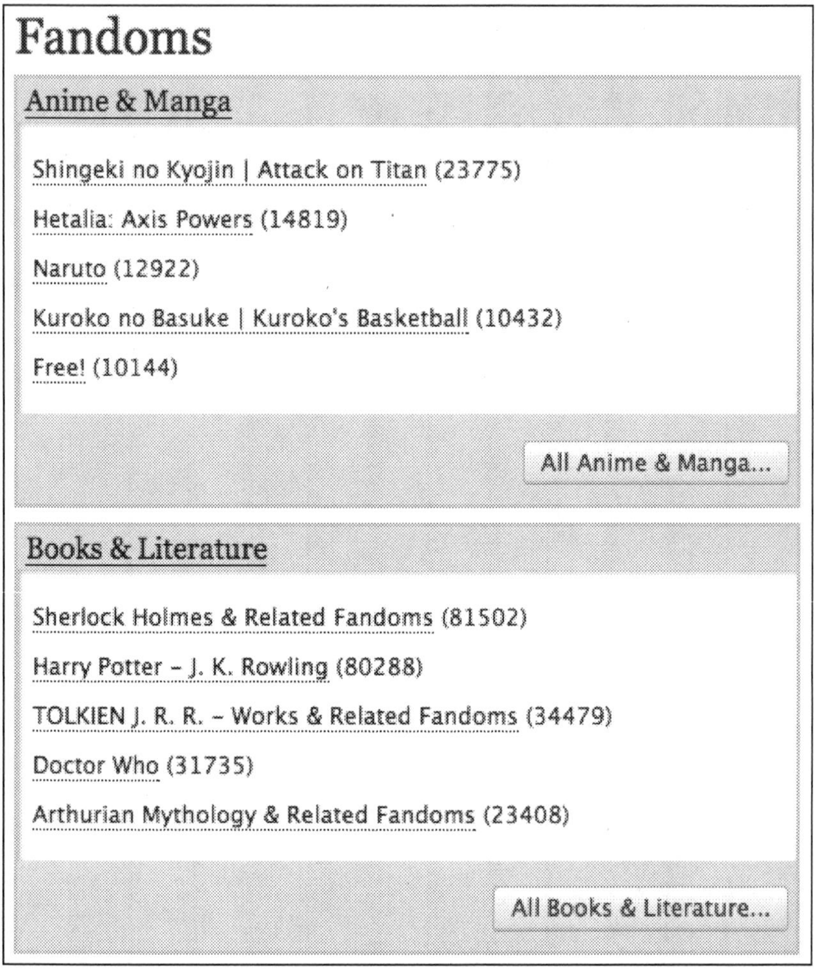

Fandoms

Anime & Manga

Shingeki no Kyojin | Attack on Titan (23775)

Hetalia: Axis Powers (14819)

Naruto (12922)

Kuroko no Basuke | Kuroko's Basketball (10432)

Free! (10144)

All Anime & Manga...

Books & Literature

Sherlock Holmes & Related Fandoms (81502)

Harry Potter - J. K. Rowling (80288)

TOLKIEN J. R. R. - Works & Related Fandoms (34479)

Doctor Who (31735)

Arthurian Mythology & Related Fandoms (23408)

All Books & Literature...

Figure 2.17
Archive of Our Own, "Fandoms" Page.

Break 2 Archive Elves

The repertoire of digital archival labor—the steps taken by each person or group who decides to construct an Internet archive from scratch—typically consists of the following (as described to my research team by our interviewees): getting sufficiently motivated to launch the project, which usually involves either feeling angry or scared that no archive exists for one's online community's materials; acquiring server space, and ensuring that the content one archives will not violate any of the server company's terms of service (which has led many archivists to purchase their own servers); designing the user interface; devising a system for intake that will keep up with the rate of submissions, which can be particularly difficult when one is archiving a "live" community, that is, an online community that is constantly producing new material; dealing with the public, which can mean handling cease-and-desist notices or other challenges from copyright holders if one is archiving appropriative or remix-based content—but more often means handling the queries and criticisms of archive users; managing growth, usually in the form of recruiting assistance (additional techno-volunteers) when necessary; redesigning the interface when it becomes technically or aesthetically outdated; and backing up the archive regularly, without fail.

This repertoire of archive building demands a great deal of archivists' skill, time, and, in many cases, money (some archivists must add "fundraising" to the above list), but tends to go unnoticed or misunderstood by archive users. Some users mistake hacker/pirate/amateur/fan-run archives for corporate-funded and corporate-developed sites—thinking there is no difference between, for instance, the Archive of Our Own (AO3) and Tumblr, both of which host enormous amounts of fan activity, but only one of which (Tumblr) is a for-profit business with engineers on staff—and they assume that a well-paid full-time team is constantly available to provide them with technical support and service. Some users know that teams of volunteers maintain some of the archives they use, and expect those volunteers to perform desired technical labor and fulfill user requests on demand. It is likely that a significant percentage of Internet users simply do not know for certain who or what creates or sustains the online platforms that they use every day, and do not know that there is a substantive difference between platforms owned and managed by corporations, governments, and endowed not-for-profit organizations, and platforms designed and run by hobbyists and not-for-profit organizations that must constantly solicit funds or pay out of pocket to stay operational.

Henry Jenkins suggests one reason that the work of networked infrastructure-building may seem opaque to the millions who regularly interact with the products of that labor: it is not online infrastructure, but online community, that excites and engages people. "The platform companies no doubt would love us to say that we are participating in their platforms; they talk about the Reddit community or the YouTube community. Yet I suspect in most cases, the participants do not understand themselves in these terms at all. The participants in the Archive of Our Own understand themselves as part of fandom" (Clark et al. 2014, 1465–1466), rather than as part of a platform, Jenkins argues. This viewpoint aligns with my description (in chapter 2) of the importance that "community archives" have to their members: such archives provide resources with which individuals can form and strengthen their understandings of their identities, and experience a sense of common identity with others. The details of infrastructure ownership and support may matter little to community archive users.

What looms large for users is that online resources allow them to find one another, and to feel a connection with one another. Archives provide this connection through giving members of a community a sense of shared culture. What makes those resources appear and what keeps them going are questions that may simply not occur to most people who take part in online communities. Even in the case of AO3, which was formed explicitly by fans to be a fan-owned platform, members and visitors who were not part of the early days of AO3's organization may be ignorant of the archive's origins and mission, and how deeply its founders felt the need to create an online space for fans over which no corporate interest could have control.

Other factors contribute to users' lack of awareness of network *work*. Sociologist Mauricio Lazzarato first proposed the term "immaterial labor" in 1996 (Michael Hardt and Antonio Negri [2000] adopted and popularized the term in their book *Empire*) to describe, Lazzarato states, "the changes taking place in workers' labor processes … where the skills involved in direct labor are increasingly skills involving cybernetics and computer control (and horizontal and vertical communication)" (Lazzarato 1996, 133). Lazzarato also glosses immaterial labor as "the activity that produces the 'cultural content' of the commodity," consisting of "a series of activities that are not normally recognized as 'work'—in other words, the kinds of activities involved in defining and fixing cultural and artistic standards, fashions, tastes, consumer norms, and, more strategically, public opinion" (133). By offering dual definitions of immaterial labor, Lazzarato attempts to account for both the apparent "immateriality" of digital work itself, the seeming nonphysicality (putting aside issues of hardware performance and ergonomics) of creating infrastructure and communicating with and via computers, and the "immateriality" of the Internet content created by cultural workers, most of whom produce this content voluntarily and during their "leisure" time, not under the rubric of "work." Part of Lazzarato's project is to emphasize that labor that appears to lack three-dimensional form or that seems largely divorced from physical expenditure is nevertheless *real* work. But the very "immateriality" of digital archival labor brackets it off from perception, making it seem either nonexistent (the user does not ask "Who or what makes this infrastructure possible?") or not-work (the user thinks that creating online cultural infrastructure is only fun and recreation for the creators).

A number of scholars in various fields—Lazzarato (1996), Tiziana Terranova (2004), and Trebor Scholz (2013) in new media studies; Shannon Jackson (2011) and Rebecca Schneider (2012) in performance studies; Hardt and Negri (2000) in philosophy; Saskia Sassen (1991) in urban studies; John Caldwell (2008) in media industry studies; Andrew Ross (2009) in cultural studies; and Gregory Sholette (2011) in art criticism, to name a few—have foregrounded the labor that produces the necessary infrastructure for creative endeavors, pointing out how often such work is downplayed or discounted. This scholarship makes plain how often those who do creative infrastructuring are depicted as invisible, even otherworldly, forces. In his analysis of digital effects designers working on major Hollywood blockbusters at shops such as Industrial Light and Magic (ILM) and Pixar, Caldwell (2008) highlights the frequency with which digital cultural labor is characterized not as effort, but as "magic": "No matter how complicated, intimidating, or overwhelming the behind-the-scenes picture of a studio back lot or a computer-generated imagery (CGI) effects department may appear in a making-of [video], the DVDs that include such things will typically explain or reduce the whole undertaking using fairly archaic notions linked, for example, to the persistence and playful 'magic' of artists and medieval alchemists" (21). Sholette similarly writes about the people who support the art world but are not famous or renowned artists; these people might teach in art schools, attend art shows, and purchase art journals and art equipment. Sholette (2011) calls them "dark matter" (1), an "army" (7, 16) of "invisibles" (3) who are "an essential component of the elite art world whose pyramidal structure looms over them"—they form an unseen base that props up the pyramid's peak (3).

Francesca Coppa, one of the founders of AO3, offers another way to think of those who work in support roles for digital creators and makers—behind-the-scenes and behind-the-screens, as it were—as magical entities. In my interview with Coppa, she recounted what it was like to interact with online fanfic archives in the mid-1990s, when a handful of workers had to labor intensively to keep those archives running smoothly:

Archives, the way you would do it is, you would literally [e]mail your copy [of your fan fiction story]—in other words, there was no automatic archive. You would have to send your copy to a person, and that person would put the story up, they would code—because nobody knew how to do HTML, you couldn't just put your stuff up, you didn't have a website, it was all so primitive, you know? But you could email your story to somebody, and they would put it on a website for you, and make it visible, and code it up in certain ways. And [we] called those people "archive elves." … And so, for instance, *Highlander* had an archive, and the archive elves would manually put the stories up. And often, they would fall behind, and people would complain. You know: "I sent you my story two days ago and it's not up yet." These [archive workers] are people with lives and jobs! They were doing it voluntarily. Putting [the stories] on the line like laundry for you, you know? (Coppa 2012)

Coppa here puns on the word "online," stating that early fanfic archivists put stories "on the line like laundry," and thus compares digital archival labor to routine, domestic, feminized labor that often goes unnoticed by those who benefit from the work. Coppa implies that just as residents of a household may think that freshly laundered clothes and linens miraculously appear, when laundering in fact requires someone's time and energy, so users of 1990s archives tended to think that their stories should simply appear online, without considering that archivists had to devote effort to marking up the stories in HTML before posting them.

One can detect a strong correlation between Caldwell's magic alchemists, Sholette's dark army of invisibles, and Coppa's archive elves: all three figurations of infrastructuring laborers relegate them to the status of unnatural, subhuman, or nonhuman actants, possessing impressive powers and necessary for the effectuation of important actions, but operating in the shadows of human creativity. The alchemists, invisibles, and elves are facilitators of more heroic archetypes: actors, artists, writers. The facilitators' creations make possible the creative work of others—but their supportive productivity is regarded as wand waving and spell casting—the manifesting of supernatural powers—rather than as ordinary human industriousness. Lazzarato's descriptor for digital and cultural labor, "immaterial," comes to apply to the laborers themselves, as they are discursively translated into disembodied forces and mystical, imperceptible beings.

In theater studies, a similar language is sometimes used to describe crew members who labor backstage: Alice Rayner (2006) calls these workers "the ghosts of theatre" (148) and "ghosts behind the curtains" (137), who make possible the "hallucinations of the onstage world" (142). Backstage theater work is far more material than digital infrastructuring labor in that it is more obviously physical and the output is a live embodied event. But there is something about digital archiving that invites comparison to a theater production's run crew. Something about the intangibility and invisibility of Internet infrastructuring calls to mind the image of crewmembers shuffling around in the near-dark; both kinds of workers create the conditions for entertainment without being seen. Digital archivists do much of their work at the "back end" of archives, as technical theater workers operate backstage; the public that interacts with the "front end" of archives does not, and is not meant to, see and understand all of what transpires at the back end, just as the public that watches a play unfold onstage does not, and is not meant to, see and understand all of what transpires backstage. Digital archivists want users' experiences of their archives to seem smooth and frictionless. Archivists think that it should be as easy for an online archive's visitor to dip into the database as it is for a play's audience to slip into the "hallucination of the onstage world" (for the moment, I am setting aside performance forms that strive to discomfort and disorient audiences rather than envelop and immerse them). The smoothness of platform use to which the majority of platform designers aspire requires the erasure of all traces of the designers' labor.

So, both archivists and users wish for digital archives to work *as if* by magic. It is no wonder, then, that the effort of archivists goes unnoticed by archive users: the nature of online infrastructuring is such that the infrastructure builders aim to make themselves and their work invisible, ghostly, and immaterial. If using a networked digital archive feels like using a magic memory machine, this is in part because both the server that stores data and serves it up on command, and the *servers* (archivists) who serve the archive users (on demand) and maintain the integrity of the archive, are concealed from the user's view.

From my perspective as a theater maker who has worked far more often backstage (or in the booth) than onstage, digital archivists seem much like a technical theater crew, who move set elements around between scenes, or operate sound, lighting, and video cues from somewhere behind the audience, clad in black, in low lighting so as to go as unnoticed as possible. Both digital archives and theatrical shows require a great deal of hidden human activity to produce seamless flows of onstage/front-end performance. Both bring into being virtual spaces with which the public expects to interact without suffering interruptions, delays, or barriers. In both cases, if the public can see you working hard to produce those effortless (in the public's eye) interactions, you're "doing it wrong." (Again, I am momentarily neglecting nontraditional performance forms that deliberately call attention to their technical and backstage workings.)

The comparison between digital labor and theatrical labor also helps to reveal what we might call the *nested* aspect of immaterial labor: performance artists and actors, like fan writers and other members of online communities who provide immaterial labor, most often at the fringes of mainstream society, themselves depend on large networks of people to allow their marginalized operations to transpire and come to fruition. Rayner (2006, ix–xxxv) refers to this nested aspect of immaterial work as the "double" of artmaking; Jackson (2011, 177), describing performance art events, states that however "immaterial" these events may seem, they "still need a certain kind of technical labor in order to exist." Fans who create digital works in (as John Fiske put it) the "shadow" of official cultural texts rely on teams of technically skilled people to publish, distribute, and preserve their creations, who operate in the shadow of the fan creators. Immaterial laborers do not work on their own, but within networks of production.

Like technical theater workers, rogue digital archivists do not typically labor in the hopes of generating tremendous profits, either for themselves individually or for the larger organization (the archive) that they support, so they are not quite the "netslaves" that Terranova (2004) discusses in *Network Culture*, the volunteer/intern moderators and Web designers recruited by large Internet companies whose free labor allows publicly traded firms to multiply their stock valuation (73–80). (At the same time, it must be acknowledged that all fans who generate online content indirectly add value to the media companies whose products they continually promote by extending those products' relevance.) Nevertheless, there can be a pernicious tendency for everyone who benefits from the creative and technical labor of back-end/backstage workers to *undervalue* that labor, by regarding the workers as simply part of the machinery of production, as robots who serve.

One fan, Morgan Dawn, spoke in her interview about the stresses that archive users can put upon volunteer archive workers:

There're these very weird preconceptions as to the people who are the drivers [of fan platforms and fan organizations]. There are very few people who get off their butts to do much of anything. And sometimes [the platform and organization builders] are not the easiest people to work with. I mean, usually they're not. But you have to admire the fact, and respect the fact, that they're getting shit done. And what you have to do is find a way to work with them and that is not happening. ...

It's more about the ability to drive away people who contribute, and I'm not talking about writers and vidders. I'm talking about people who do the infrastructure. A friend of mine is one of the people who works on the OTW [Organization of Transformative Works, parent organization of the Archive of Our Own] systems. So, ... this is the person who runs the servers, okay? And the pressures that they're being put under, with the criticisms all being heaped upon them, is wearing them down. And if you have individuals who are constantly under criticism, while they're doing, in my opinion, the most impossible shit, it's going to be very, very, very difficult [for those individuals] to maintain that kind of energy. (Dawn 2012)

Morgan Dawn points out that, in the case of AO3, a nonprofit fan-made archive whose early volunteers constantly struggled to bring online enough servers to handle the archive's rapidly rising demand, users sometimes treat the volunteers like servants, venting their impatience and dissatisfaction without recognizing the impact their complaints may have on workers' morale.

Chael, a lead archivist of the Gossamer Project (the major *X-Files* fan fiction archive), says that once, in response to users emailing to ask when the next update was coming, and to register their disappointment that "fresh stories" had not yet appeared on the site, he posted a testy message:

Hey, you guys always want to see the latest stories. We already have 10,000 great stories on the archive. And while you are waiting, I'd prefer you go read those stories rather than complaining. We are all volunteers. We don't ask anything from you to maintain this site. And we'll get the stories out as soon as we can get them out. (Chael 2012)

Soon afterward, Chael says, he posted a "more professional response," which stated that, going forward, the archivists would always announce a "Next Update Date" so that users could anticipate when new work would appear on the archive. Chael's follow-up message, which focuses on logistics rather than emotions, illustrates archivists' belief that, although they are volunteers, they should interact with their public as if they were professionals, present the archive as an efficient technical service, and resist any urge to gripe to users about their occasional struggles with intake. However, archivists' efforts to match or better the usability of commercial websites, and to maintain a professional demeanor at all times, likely encourages archive users to misinterpret their moments of being overwhelmed as technological glitches.

When users of digital archives conflate the mechanical servers and the human servers, they participate in what Georg Lukács called "reification" (which Christian Fuchs notes is "a reformulation of Marx's [1867] concept of fetishism" [Fuchs 2012a, 697]). In a process of reification, "a relation between people takes on the character of a thing and thus acquires 'phantom objectivity,' an autonomy that seems so strictly rational and all-embracing as to conceal every trace of its fundamental nature: the relation between people" (Lukács [1923] 1971, 83). The relation between users and archivists can take on the character of a thing—a memory machine—and the reification of the idea of fully automated digital cultural memory obscures the fact that digital cultural memory does not have any rational "objectivity," but is a nascent concept in flux, being unevenly realized through relations between people, in the work that archive builders do for archive users and the constant negotiating that takes place between the two groups.

The states and quasi-state entities that sponsored the founding of archives during the print era desired those archives' reification; they benefited from archives being taken for truth-collecting and truth-producing machines, for then narratives of state power, control, and hegemony were supported by the totality of documents preserved, and were therefore unquestionable. "It could never have been otherwise," announce archives of the state. But archiving in the digital era is not coupled with state power in the same way, and it does not need to reinforce existing hegemonic structures to the same degree. Therefore, the current generation would be remiss to reify archives, to mistake them for machines whose operations are concealed and secret to a large degree, and to again forget that humans in relation to one another produce cultural memory. If users can perceive the human labor that undergirds digital cultural memory, then they can continue to question what that memory is and what it should be, what narratives it does or should support, and what power structures it endorses, questions, or facilitates.

3 Queer and Feminist Archival Cultures: The Politics of Preserving Fan Works

I want us to own the goddamn servers.

—Speranza

Women Fans against Male-Dominated Tech

What motivates digital archivists to donate the labor and time required, often in vast quantities, to build and maintain their archives? Many archivists who spoke to my research team pointed to their fear of loss, their anxiety over digital ephemerality, and their suspicion that if they do *not* save a community's cultural works, those works will vanish entirely. For example, Deirdre, a lead archivist of the Gossamer Project (the main archive of *X-Files* fan fiction), recalls one prolific fandom from the 1990s whose works can no longer be found online:

The sad thing is, ... *Babylon 5* was *not* a rare fandom. *Babylon 5* was as popular [as a source text for fan fiction] in '97, '98 as *The X-Files* was. [But] the archives collapsed and vanished! ... Everything is gone. ... I *know* there was as much fiction being generated in that fandom [as in *X-Files* fandom], and it is all gone. ... One of the things that has always prompted me to keep on with Gossamer, and to try to keep it going and to try to keep it going the best [I] can, is because I watched a fandom disappear. (Deirdre 2012)

However, a different set of motivations led to the formation of the Organization of Transformative Works in 2007 and the Archive of Our Own (AO3) in 2009, which is currently the fastest-growing multifandom archive online. In the mid-2000s, a number of fans noted that significant transformations were taking place in the workings of the Web, a set of changes that gravely threatened the types of communities that fans had been forging online since the early 1990s. When "Web 2.0" discourse rose to prominence beginning in 2004 (O'Reilly 2005), technology firms and entrepreneurs began to show great interest in, and attention to, user-generated content and social networks, including Internet fandoms, which had pioneered many practices of online community, participation, and remix production that rapidly became standard on the "social Web."

On the one hand, social media corporations sought to impose restrictions on what types of content were permissible to share online, leading to events in which numerous users suffered takedowns of their content without warning. One such incident was "Strikethrough 2007," in which Six Apart, the company that owned the blogging platform LiveJournal, suddenly deleted hundreds of journals containing fan fiction and other fan works because they contained what was deemed offensive sexual content. Similarly, from the mid-2000s to the mid-2010s, the for-profit archive Fan-Fiction.net (FF.net) conducted multiple "purges," deleting thousands of stories that site moderators decided were too sexually explicit.[1] On the other hand, social media entrepreneurs aimed to build sites that would attract fan fiction writers and turn their productions into financial profit—for the site owners, not the fans and writers. The most notorious of these attempts to monetize fan fiction was the short-lived company FanLib (2007–2008),[2] but in the mid-to-late 2000s, there were signs that additional attempts might be made to corporatize fan fiction in ways that would not prove beneficial to fans.

In my interview with her, Francesca Coppa describes the feelings about Web 2.0 shared by many fans during this period:

[There was] a move away from a fan-owned, hacker's, primitive Internet to a more commercialized Internet. And that had repercussions, but nobody saw those until the second half of the [2000s]. And then it became clear that we were then being hosted on—like, *Who the hell owns this [site]? Wait, where are we sitting? Who owns this chair? I thought you owned this chair. No, I don't own this chair.* ... You just felt like every idiot who had [an idea that], *I'm gonna make a million dollars on the Internet! And I know what I'll do, I'll do something fannish and get all these fan girls working for me in some way.* ... Classic Web 2.0: *You make all the content, we'll take all the money.* ... Obviously, FanLib was the big one there. But there were others. You felt like there was always some—somebody's just gone and squatted on Fandom.com, somebody's gone and taken Fanfiction.com, Yourfanfiction.com—and you would think, *What the heck are they planning?* ...

And I have to say there was a gender piece of it, the sense that, like, some dude was going to come and make millions off of us. ... I remember some of us talking, and saying, "It's not even that they're gonna make millions and give us some great service." Like, our bigger fear was some idiot, who had really no sense of what he was doing or what the community was doing, was going to build something and get everybody on it, and collapse [it] in two years. *Ah, this isn't so profitable.* And just shut the thing down. And in fact, we were afraid that might [happen] already with some of the [social] networks that we were beholden to. And there was nothing—and there *is* nothing—to stop LiveJournal from saying, *You know, it just isn't that profitable.* And folding up the tent. And so we never really had a fannish infrastructure that was *so* dependent on people who didn't care at essence about the activity they were hosting.

And so when the Strikethrough issue [happened], and Fanfiction.net was purging adult fiction semiregularly, ... there was a whole sort of way in which you really felt that the infrastructure started to feel a little bit fragile. (Coppa 2012)

After Strikethrough and FanLib, the prominent fan Speranza (writing in her LiveJournal, cesperanza.livejournal.com) issued this "battle cry" to online fan communities: "I want us to own the goddamn servers" (Busse 2009). She and other fan leaders worked to raise awareness of the need for fans to own and manage their own Internet infrastructure, and to actively preserve their communities' works without interference from for-profit corporations unfamiliar with fans' community and cultural priorities. In response to these calls to action, a large group rallied to form the OTW as "a nonprofit organization established by fans to serve the interests of fans by providing access to and preserving the history of fanworks and fan culture in its myriad forms" (Organization for Transformative Works, "What We Believe"). The OTW developed AO3 to be "a noncommercial and nonprofit central hosting place for fanfiction and other transformative fanworks, using open-source archiving software." The OTW also founded Open Doors, another conservation effort that focuses on "at-risk fannish projects," such as fanzines and online fanfic archives that are in danger of disappearing because of hosting companies closing down, or archivists passing away (Organization for Transformative Works, "Our Projects").[3] The projects run on servers owned by OTW, purchased with funds donated by users (all news regarding the state of the Archive of Our Own's servers is tagged "servers of our own" on the AO3 site).

The majority of members of fan fiction communities are women, and reflecting and drawing upon their constituency, OTW and all of its projects, including AO3, have been brought into being by women coders. In 2009, Alex Skud Bayley delivered a keynote address at the O'Reilly Open Source Convention (OSCON) about the need for open source communities to recruit more women. The two majority-female open source projects to which she pointed, as examples to the rest of the open source field, were Dreamwidth, a blogging platform built by fans as an alternative to LiveJournal in the wake of Strikethrough, and AO3. Bayley related quotes from some of the women developers who had joined these efforts, who spoke of how welcoming of women contributors both projects were, and how willing they were to train beginners (Bayley 2009). One volunteer developer told Bayley, "Deep down, I had always assumed coding required this kind of special aptitude, something that I just didn't have and never would. It lost its forbidding mystique when I learned that people I had assumed to be super-coders (surely born with keyboard attached!) had only started training a year ago. People without any prior experience! Women! Like me! Jesus! It's like a barrier broke down in my mind." As a result of AO3's welcoming attitudes, writes fan scholar Kristina Busse, the archive offers not only "some of the things most of us would like to see in terms of accessibility, search functions, tagging, etc. but in the process teach[es] fans to code and to teach others to code" (Busse 2009). AO3 thus increases the likelihood of women having the skills to participate, voluntarily and/or professionally, in technical communities.[4]

AO3 emerged from a conscious effort on the part of women fans to open an archive that would be designed, operated, and managed at every level, from mission to code to interface, by members of their communities. While AO3 is singular in that it was deliberately founded as a reaction against the maneuvers of male-dominated corporate entities in the early years of Web 2.0 (in Coppa's [2012] phrasing, "there was a gendered piece" of the OTW effort, which was to prevent "some dude" from "com[ing] and mak[ing] millions off of us"), other fan archives, predating and postdating AO3, have shared AO3's mission of safeguarding women's cultural productions.

I argue that all fan-built fan fiction archives function as women's community archives. I also regard these archives as queer community archives, as I will explain below. In establishing AO3, female fans collectively made explicit their shared need to preserve the works that represent and express their common interests, experiences, and identities; but in my view, all fan fiction archives have been fueled by that need, even when it has gone unarticulated. These archival projects are motivated not only by a fear of losing content to digital ephemerality, but also by a need to reinforce a sense of collectivity among the women and LGBTQ-identifying people who populate fan fiction fandoms. Fan archiving is driven by a political longing: a longing to protect and sustain female and queer communities and cultures.

Archives as Counterinstitutions

In chapter 2, I explained that fan fiction archives fulfill the functions of all three major types of rogue digital archives: they are, at once, universal archives, community archives, and alternative archives. But my research team's interviews made clear that the community aspect has proved the most crucial to the people who have built, maintained, contributed to, and/ or used online fan fiction archives for many years.

One of the greatest political potentials of rogue digital archives is that groups that have occupied the margins of "mainstream" society, and have consequently been largely marginalized by traditional memory institutions, can build their own robust cultural memory sites, as something like counterinstitutions, akin to the "counternarratives" told by postcolonial, ethnic, and feminist writers who archontically rewrite the stories of dominant culture (I discuss this concept in more detail in chapter 7). Rogue archives transform "the museum," "the library," and "the archive," which have long supported, and been supported by, the state or private capitalists, into supportive infrastructure for groups whose histories and cultures are constantly in danger of being overwritten, forgotten, deleted, or relegated to dark corners by the guardians of "official" history and culture.

In myriad ways, Internet fan fiction archives serve as critically important community archives for female and queer cultural creativity. Because a great deal of fan fiction consists of sexually explicit content written by women for women, and because female sexual expression is heavily limited by sociocultural norms, fan fiction archives are sites in which women and girls can feel that they are participating in a tradition of female writing and reading, and can experience a sense of safety in numbers. In addition, fan archives are queer archives, in part because of the volume of stories located on these sites that are about male/male, female/female, and other romantic and sexual (and also, aromantic and asexual) pairings and groupings that diverge from the social norm of male/female coupling, and in part because of the large number of self-identified queer fans who use these sites, but also because fan archives facilitate numerous acts of representation and communication that exceed the bounds of heternonormativity.

The Moment of Discovery

One of the strongest themes that emerged in my research team's interviews with fans was their strong and positive affective response when they first found online fan fiction archives. I will call this initial encounter, described by so many interviewees, the *moment of discovery*. Alexis Lothian, remembering her moment of discovery, which took place in 2003 when she stumbled upon *Harry Potter* fan fiction, says, "I loved it. I was incredibly—it was exciting. ... Definitely it was a very visceral excitement" (Lothian 2012b). nightflier states that her moment of discovery, which was the first time she came across the Gossamer archive in the late 1990s, "was like a revelation. I'll never forget that day" (nightflier 2012). eruthros, using similar terminology as Lothian, recalls that she "sort of stumbled into some sort of online fandom, I think it might have been *Due South* first, and the *Due South* mailing list ... and archive," and says that "thirty seconds after I found the archive I found slash fandom and decided that was pretty awesome, and I wanted to be there" (eruthros and thingswithwings 2012). oxoniensis also employs the metaphor of "stumbling" to characterize her moment of discovery, with *Lord of the Rings* fan fiction, in 2002: "My first contact with fan fiction was an accident. I'd never heard of fan fiction, either by word of mouth or online, so it was all rather a surprise when I first stumbled across it. ... Some stories were moving, some funny, some incredibly hot, some utterly gripping. And to be able to find this all just by searching the Internet was wonderful" (oxoniensis 2012). oxoniensis says she feels "very nostalgic" about "those heady first days of discovery." Like Lothian, eruthros, and oxoniensis, Robin Nelson remembers her moment of discovery as happening by chance. "It was pure accident," says Nelson (2012) of finding a Usenet group dedicated to Anne Rice fan fiction in 1996 or 1997. "I didn't know that fanfic even existed at that point. ... I was actually thrilled. I was elated."

Participants gave a variety of reasons for their instantaneous affection for fan fiction archives, but a common theme was the feeling of being not-alone, of being suddenly a member of a community, at the moment of discovery. As indicated by the above quotations, many fans had never known of the existence of fan fiction before "stumbling" across a fic archive, and thus had always felt isolated in their acts of what I call archontic production—the appropriation and transformation of existing narrative worlds. These interviewees said that this feeling that they were alone in practicing transformative creativity was dissipated by their encounter with fan fiction archives. "I think the overarching emotion," Lothian (2012b) says of finding *Harry Potter* fan fiction, "was the sense of getting away with something. ... Because people are ... thinking of this stuff, and they're actually writing it down. And I know this is a common emotion among fans, this sense that you've ... been kind of telling these stories, or sort of expanding on universes that you've been reading about in your head, for your whole life, as I had, and then you discover that people are doing this and sharing it, and they're building a community around it."

Robin Nelson (2012) similarly recalls that one of the reasons that she was "thrilled" at discovering the Anne Rice fan fiction newsgroup was that "I did the same thing in my head. I had done that for years. Since I was a kid. I had always read books and then my favorite ones, I would make stories up about in my head." When she found the newsgroup, Nelson says, "I felt like for the first time, that it made sense. That other people did that, too. I always thought I was really weird." Victoria P. (2012) remembers that when she first found an archive of fic based on the television show *Homicide: Life on the Street*, "I read the first couple of stories I thought were good, and went, OKAY. I GET IT NOW. Because I had always made up stories about my favorite characters in my head—Mary Sue stuff,[5] sure, but also, just, what happened next and who got together, etc." Thus, one of the foremost pleasures experienced by fans upon first encountering Internet fan fiction archives was the pleasure of realizing that a solitary activity could be a group activity, that they were not alone in inventing original stories about borrowed characters. Lothian (2012b) describes feeling transgressive ("getting away with something") at her moment of discovery, and Nelson (2012) describes feeling relief ("I always thought I was really weird" before finding fanfic); these both suggest a transition from secrecy to nonsecrecy. The secret production of fan fiction, which had always been limited to the confines of their imaginations, turned out to be a secret that could be shared. Lothian reads this secret-sharing as an entrance into a kind of conspiracy, in which many fans were all "getting away with something" together, and Nelson reads this secret-sharing as a reassurance that she was more normal (less "weird") than she had previously thought.

The size of online fan fiction archives (which I explore in the conclusion)—the number of stories housed on these sites, and the number of authors who contributed them—gave Lothian, Nelson, Victoria P., and others a "sense of belonging," a feeling of recognition ("I GET IT"), and the security of knowing that they were not alone. In other words, if these sites had not been *archives*, had not immediately given the impression of being well-stocked repositories, trafficked by many writers and readers, then they may not have not have communicated to fans the same aura of safety— safety in numbers, safety in being among like-minded individuals, safety in standing with others.

One might say that any online community that one joins can give the same impression of being not-alone, and that it is not necessarily the archival format that creates a sense of safety. While that is true, there is a special attribute of archives that gives fans a feeling of being situated within something larger than themselves: archives allow users to access the documents that constitute the cultural tradition of a community. Archives allow users to develop an understanding of what cultural texts the archive's community has produced over time. In other words, archives are the bearers of the history and memory of a community.

The Emotional Power of Archives

One of the primary motives of community archivists, especially those that aim to collect, preserve, and make accessible the texts and ephemera of people who have been structurally denied social and/or political power, is to incite positive feelings in those who identify as members of those marginalized groups. Writes Joan Nestle (1990), a founder of the Lesbian Herstory Archives (LHA), "One of our battles was to change secrecy into disclosure, shame into memory" (90). Theorists of archives, taking into account the wave of community archiving that has grown steadily since the 1970s, also stress the importance of the feelings produced in those whose documents are archived, and those who access those documents through the archives. Achille Mbembe (2002) states that the archive "is supposed to belong to everyone. The community of time, the feeling according to which we would all be heirs to a time over which we might exercise the rights of collective ownership: this is the imaginary that the archive seeks to disseminate" (21). Jeanette Bastian (2003), in her study of the archives of the Virgin Islands, writes, "The development of bodies of records preserved and valued by communities over time suggests that the keeping of archives goes beyond the need to account for the past and speaks to other felt needs within the communities themselves, the primary one being that of a community (or national) identity." Bastian calls for "recognition of the profound emotional as well as historical value of records" to the identity-building of groups, such as former colonies, whose identity is in question (Bastian 2003, 6).

In *An Archive of Feelings* (2003), Ann Cvetkovich makes a strong case for the importance of archives' emotional effects, and for archives that store emotions. Cvetkovich (2003) describes "the profoundly affective power of a useful archive, especially an archive of sexuality and gay and lesbian life, which must preserve and produce not just knowledge but feeling" (241). Cvetkovich's concept of "an archive of feelings" refers to a multisited queer archive—one composed not just of brick-and-mortar community archives such as the LHA but also of cultural texts "as repositories of feelings and emotions, which are encoded not only in the content of the texts themselves but in the practices that surround their production and reception" (7)—and this broad archive, a version of which Cvetkovich assembles in her book, not only evokes feelings of identification and compassion in its users but serves to record and communicate queer feelings as well, that is, "the many forms of love, rage, intimacy, grief, shame, and more that are part of the vibrancy of queer cultures" (7).

Nestle, Mbembe, Bastian, and Cvetkovich all describe ways that community archives are heavily charged with affect, and that a successful archive, a "useful archive," in Cvetkovich's phrasing, incites powerful emotions in their users. The emotions that these theorists imagine community archives instilling include: the feeling that one belongs to a collective and is therefore not alone *in her feelings*, in whatever feelings that common positionality or identity incites in her; the feeling that the history of one's group warrants remembering, and that the social memory or collective memory of that group is deserving of being sustained and passed on; and the feeling that, if institutional and official archives ignore, or fail to recognize, the value of the group's documents, that the group itself does honor and treasure those documents. "The very existence of these independent archives provide evidence of just how much has been excluded [from official archives] and the professional practice [of archiving] that has been responsible for such exclusions," state Andrew Flinn and Mary Stevens (2009, 17).

The excitement, recognition, and belonging that fans feel when initially encountering fic archives are the very feelings that archivists and theorists claim are the intended affects imparted by community archives. Nestle writes about how the LHA has fought to "change secrecy into disclosure"; this phrase describes exceedingly well what Lothian and Nelson went through when they realized that their secret habits of archontic production did not have to be secret any longer, but could be shared with others—perhaps becoming a collective secret practice instead of a solitary one. The sheer number of stories contained in fic archives, and the number of people participating in those archives, communicates to fans that, even if fan fiction is rarely recognized as a proper literary or artistic genre by cultural gatekeepers (both industrial and academic), at least fans archive their own communities' cultural texts and, in doing so, assert that fans' productions have cultural value and are worth preserving.

The feelings of finding themselves not alone, but part of a community of fans, and part of a tradition of fan fiction writing, is part of what drives fans to immerse themselves in the fiction of the first archives they find. cofax7 (2012) states that immediately after she discovered *X-Files* fanfic on ATXC, Gossamer, and the Annex (an archive of novel-length *X-Files* fic), "I read an enormous amount of *X-Files* fan fiction in a *very* short period of time. I got totally overwhelmed by it." Gigi Morgan (2012) reflects on the period of time that she spent reading fanfic right after finding her first fic archive: "It does become much more consuming for that period. You really do want to read every fan fiction that strikes your interest and, you know, just kind of ... forget about everything else for a little while."

Why do fans tend to read archives so comprehensively upon initially discovering them? Most fans would probably say that they are simply desirous of consuming as much cultural production as possible that focused on an interest of theirs—that they are left "wanting more" by the source text, and are so pleased that to find that fellow fans have written stories to expand the story universe that they dive headlong into the fic, simply to get through as much of the longed-for storyworld as possible. Plenty of fans likely feel that the pleasure they take from immersing themselves in narrative worlds is what motivates them to plow through fan fiction archives at first: they enjoy committing themselves fully to source texts (commercially produced novels, films, television series, video games, manga, anime, and so on), for example, by reviewing these texts and closely analyzing them, learning the trivia pertaining to the texts, and so on; thus, fans might say, it is logical that when they initially come across fan texts, they find themselves committing fully to those, as well. By this line of reasoning, the internal proclivity for devoting what N. Katherine Hayles (2007) calls "deep attention" to cultural productions, which leads people to be fans of media, is what leads them to also be fans of fan fiction.

I perceive another motivation in fans' comprehensive reading of fic archives, which is fans' need to absorb, in a short amount of time, the cultural memory of a group—that is, a fandom—into which they were (in many cases) not born or raised, but with which they identify, and to which they feel they belong. Going through the backlog of stories housed in a fan fiction archive quickly confirms for fans the feelings that I discussed above, the feelings of being not-alone, of discovering a community that one instantly recognizes as, in some way, one's own. In other words, the experience described by fans is that of learning that a community exists to which one instinctively feels she is already a member. The process of immersing oneself in a fic archive all at once also enables the fan to instruct herself in a history, and a literacy, of archontic production for which she may feel an innate affinity, but of which she had no prior knowledge. Reading all of the stories that have already been written, prior to the fan's arrival, helps to educate her in the tropes and themes that are prevalent in a particular fandom's writing, which in turn informs the new fan about how the fandom has been processing the source text over time. New fans take in the cultural memory of the group in order to transform themselves into full members of the group, with some understanding of how the group engages with the source text and transforms it, and in order to continually reassure themselves, with each new story they read, that they have indeed found a group that is rich in the types of cultural production and practice that they formerly thought could only be done in secret and in solitude.

The fact that so many fans "stumble upon" fan fiction archives— that they never suspect the existence of fan fiction before finding these archives—indicates that fan fiction is missing from the archives of mainstream culture. Fans do not encounter printed books of fan fiction on the shelves of bookstores or of libraries; fan fiction is not regularly a part of school curricula and is not often the object of academic study. Therefore, when fans discover fan fiction archives, they respond to them and utilize them as community archives, as the repositories of the cultural memory of a group that has been largely ignored by institutional archives, by high culture or what Lisa Lewis (1992, 2–3) terms "official culture," and by commercial popular culture. The absence of fan fiction from what I am calling the archives of mainstream culture leaves people hungry for knowledge and training in the tradition of archontic production centered on media texts. Thus, they tend to rapidly consume all of the texts they find in the first archives they discover, because they long for exposure to, and education in, a tradition that they never knew from official cultural archives, but which they recognize as a tradition to which they are rightful heirs. (I acknowledge that these experiences of discovery described by our oral history participants may be historically specific. People who are now teens or younger may grow up with a high level of new media literacy and a deep, innate understanding of digital remix and online versioning, and therefore may regard fan fiction archives and communities as intrinsic components of their media landscape, not as new worlds to be discovered.)

Andrew Flinn (2007) defines community archiving as "the grassroots activities of documenting, recording and exploring community heritage in which community participation, control and ownership of the project is essential" (153). Flinn is interested in how digital network technologies have made possible new kinds of community heritage projects that "take place on the web with connections to ... shared identities made by a virtual community in a virtual space. Some of the digital material created ... might be artificial or ephemeral, but nonetheless it represents an important further source of material whose long-term preservations requirements need to be explored." Internet fan fiction archives fit Flinn's description of community archives in the digital age well: these archives are built by people who have a "shared focus ... [or] interest" (153), they are grassroots efforts that understand themselves to be solely beholden to their own members and not to any institutional archives, and they exist to house digital material, which challenges fan archivists to be inventive with their preservation strategies. But the term "community archives" carries connotations beyond Flinn's basic parameters.

Gender and Sexuality in Fandom

Above, I stated that community archives are often founded by and for subordinated groups that feel that their histories have been historically excluded from institutional archives. I propose that fan fiction archives are community archives that similarly safeguard the cultural memory of groups left out of the official archives of culture. Fan fiction archives are, de facto, archives of women's and girls' culture, as the majority of their contributors and users are female: in a 2003 survey of 1,000 participants in a slash fan fiction online community, only 26 people, or 2.6 percent, self-identified as male (rushlight75 2003); in a 2013 survey of 10,005 fan fiction writers and readers conducted by the Archive of Our Own, only 417 people, or 4 percent, self-identified as male (Lulu 2013); in the much smaller sample constituted by the participants in our oral history project, only 3 of 50 participants, or 6 percent, self-identified as male. Thus, fan archives definitely do the work of valuing and preserving a genre of gendered cultural production that is, for the most part, overlooked or derided by the male-dominated media industries. According to a 2013 *Celluloid Ceiling* study supported by the Center for the Study of Women in Television and Film, women working in the television and film industries in 2012 constituted 9 percent of directors, 15 percent of writers, 20 percent of editors, 2 percent of cinematographers, and 25 percent of producers; 38 percent of films employed 0 or 1 women in these roles (Lauzen [2013] and Newsom and Lauzen [2013]). Women are not the majority of authors of mass media texts, so they make themselves the authors of fan texts that rewrite and revise media texts.

I interpret female fan authorship as a response by women and girls to a media culture in which they rarely see their own narrative priorities and preferences play out, and so feel compelled to create their own versions and extensions of film, television, music, game, and comic culture. It is the very exclusion of female narrative desires from the archives of culture, in other words, that motivates women and girls to write fan fiction and to create their own archives for their archontic productions. As Francesca Coppa (2012) says in her interview, women are "just sort of accustomed … to watching movies for the middle. Or watching movies for particularly emotive parts. Because kind of inevitably, the arc of the [film] would be awful or disappointing or exclusionary" for, and to, women. "So you watched in this kind of selective way for the great bits in the middle. And I think fandom is all about the great bits in the middle. And we sort of trash the end. There's something female …, it's that we almost don't do endings. Or we end, we start again. And I think there's a suspicion the ending's not going to go well for us." Coppa offers the view that, because the majority of mainstream media's plot arcs and character development trajectories do not cater to women's interests, do not give female audiences what they would want, do not valorize female perspectives, and do not promote female-centric narratives, female fans must resource the "great bits in the middle" that they like, the parts that deliver what they desire from media, and use these bits to form female texts. The subset of archontic production that is fan fiction writing is largely driven by female imperatives. In this statement, I am echoing Adrienne Rich's 1979 statement on women's writing: "Re-vision—the act of looking back, of seeing with fresh eyes, of entering an old text from a new critical direction—is for women more than a chapter in cultural history; it is an act of survival" (Rich 1986, 33–49). For Rich, archontic production is a necessity for women; if women want to *see themselves* in the texts that they consume, they must *re-see*, that is, re-(en)vision, or re-vise, those texts. Fan fiction archives are thus archives of women's culture—of cultural products that women make, and of ways that women interact with the culture that surrounds them and yet often does not represent them in ways that women recognize or want.

Fic archives also have missions similar to queer archives, in several ways. Fic archives facilitate a "change [from] secrecy to disclosure," as described above, a process crucial to many members of queer communities. David Wojnarowicz (1991) writes, "Each public disclosure of a private reality becomes something of a magnet that can attract others with a similar frame of reference" (121–122), and fic archives help individuals who thought they were "really weird" (in the words of interviewee Robin Nelson) or all alone in their fannish proclivities realize that they can belong to, and participate in, publics (or semipublics) built around those very proclivities. Fic archives provide newcomers with access to cultural resources that help them orient themselves within a group with which they immediately identify. Fic archives reassure their members, through the numbers of stories and the number of people assembled on and in archival sites, that there is an entire culture that they can claim as their own.

But how is it possible to compare fan communities to queer communities, and fan archives to queer archives? Fans are, after all, not marginalized, oppressed, or targeted by laws or policies or prejudices in the same way that LGBTQ individuals and groups are; fans are not the victim of hate crimes or of structural sociocultural oppression. To be sure, there is a streak of fan discourse that employs the language of queer cultures. Some fans talk about being "closeted," that is, careful to conceal their fannish practices from others; some discuss their "coming out" to friends and family when they decide to publicly own their fannish identities and activities; some report "being outed" against their will by other fans, sometimes accidentally, and sometimes maliciously—their fannish pseudonyms exposed and their fan fiction stories circulated to their employers or coworkers or family members.

Queer scholars have not been uncritical of what can be perceived as fans' appropriation of queer frameworks. John Edward Campbell (Jenkins 2011a) has asked fan scholars "to be a bit more reflexive about comparisons of fans to sexual minorities," as the consequences for identifying publicly as a fan are typically far less severe than for identifying publicly as LGBTQ. "There is a way that sexual minorities growing up in this society must constantly police their behavior, their tastes, their gestures, even their subtlest glances to conceal their difference from mainstream society," Campbell writes; in contrast, fans do not have to police or conceal themselves in the same way, to the same degree, facing the same possibilities of ostracization and condemnation. In high school, Campbell states, "While I was very open about my love for all things *Star Wars* since seeing the first film, I was utterly silent about my love for men, even to myself. Being a fan of *Star Wars* was cool. Being different was dangerous" (Jenkins 2011a).

Next to Campbell's resistance to drawing an equivalence between "fan" and "queer," I will place Henry Jenkins's (HJ) and Cynthia Jenkins's (CJ) thoughts, shared in their joint interview, on the way that the fan identities and queer identities sometimes "parallel" one another:

HJ: I'm not unsympathetic to [Campbell's] critique. But I think it also doesn't acknowledge some of the very particular stories that I've run across through years in fandom where, in fact, the parallels are very, very strong. Because reading and writing fan fiction is so bound up with sexual fantasies and sexual identities for most hard-core fans. We hear stories of wives who don't dare tell their husbands they read and write stories, and end up lying about going to cons and deceiving them about that aspect of their lives. Or husbands who prohibited their wives from having their fan friends over when they're not there. I've heard of stories of parents who either destroyed all the zines or threw the kid out of the house because they found fan stories that had erotic content or just because they were fans.

CJ: Or the classic, "Oh my God, when I die, they're going to go through my stuff" stories.

HJ: Yeah, half the fans I know have stories of who's going to clear out their zines after they die before their parents or their husbands or their children go through and find what it is they read. And that stuff is bound up with ... To my mind, [the experiences of being queer and being a fan] are not so far removed. If all you mean is, there's a little social embarrassment because you like *Star Wars*, and half the planet likes *Star Wars*, then no, there's not a parallel. If your ability to conduct your personal life is directly affected by people's perceptions of your fantasy life, because of things they read in relation to your identity and desire, then that is a kind of queerness. (Jenkins and Jenkins 2012)

Henry and Cynthia Jenkins are here discussing zine- and con-based fannish practices ("cons," or fan conventions, are real-world events in which fans gather to discuss their favorite texts, sell and buy fannish products, potentially wear costumes related to their fandoms, and otherwise celebrate their fannish identities and communities), rather than practices based on the construction and use of online fan archives. But the stories they tell of fan lives bearing some resemblance to queer lives—of fans being secretive, guarded, or evasive about these practices for fear of their family members finding them out, or of being policed by family members as to whether and to what extent they can engage in these practices—were echoed by our oral history participants, all of whom are Internet fans. Many of the conflicts that fans experience either in their private domestic spheres, public spheres such as their workplaces and larger professional networks, or the "semipublic" (Michael Moon, quoted in Berlant 2008 and Cvetkovich 2003) spheres of Internet fandom, arise from fans' writing, or commenting on, fan fiction with sexual content. Above, I referred to the various "purges" that FF.net has initiated, including an especially deep purge in June 2012, which deleted approximately 8,000 stories containing textual descriptions of physical actions that FF.net's moderators judged to be too explicitly sexual or violent (Ellison 2012). Even fan fiction archives are not always the safe spaces that fan authors and readers hope they will be.

The disclosure of one's sexual fantasies, or of the relationships and acts that one enjoys eroticizing, or of the *degree* of eroticism (on the scale of "soft-core" to "hard-core" sexually explicit writing) that one favors, has led to censure and censorship, in the experiences of many fans. Not all Internet fan fiction contains sexual content, but because it is easier to find erotic fiction in fic archives than it is on the shelves of most bookstores and libraries, one of the aspects of online fic archives that fans value most is that they constitute a kind of female public sex culture. I am borrowing here from Cvetkovich (2003), who writes of a "lesbian public sex culture" being constituted by "a print culture of books about sex, consumer stores such as Good Vibrations and Toys in Babeland that are as much community centers as (thriving) businesses, performance cultures, and sexual subcultures organized around an increasing proliferation of sexual practices" (35). Fan fiction archives are analogues to many of the objects that Cvetkovich lists as constituting a lesbian public sex culture, as fic archives have an electronic publishing culture of stories about sex; are as much sites for communal activity as they are repositories to be accessed by individual users; are performance spaces and performance cultures (as I will discuss in chapter 6); and contain a great deal of content that explicitly describes sex acts, content that is informed by "an increasing proliferation of sexual practices." A number of fan scholars point to the liberatory potential, as well as the risks, that attend participation in female public sex cultures, and designate such cultures as both "female" and "queer."

Catherine Tosenberger (Jenkins 2011a), directly responding to Campbell, marks the difference between "affirmational fannish spaces" and "transformational fannish spaces." Affirmational fannish spaces, in which fans assemble trivia or facts, discuss minutiae pertaining to the source text, and otherwise investigate what the source text offers without seeking to alter or contradict it, are "often (not always, but often) majority male." "Transformational fannish spaces," such as fan fiction and fanvid communities and archives, in which fans collectively rewrite and revise the source text, "are more likely to be majority-female, and overtly queer or queer-friendly." "Transformational fans were also likely to be treated as an even more pathological form of the pathologized fan," writes Tosenbeger of early academic studies of media fans: "those fan boys fighting about the engines on the Enterprise might be hopeless geeks, but at least they're not perverts writing gay porn about Kirk and Spock!" Like Henry and Cynthia Jenkins, Tosenberger locates the queerness of fan fiction in its preponderance of sexual and erotic themes. "I think it's really important to point out that particularly in transformational fandom, sexuality, and fan production as a means of exploring and articulating sexuality, is a big deal—this is especially true for younger fans, whose expressions of sexuality are so heavily policed in institutional settings," Tosenberger states (Jenkins 2011a).

Tosenberger's highlighting of the "policing" of sex-related expression, particularly by young females, in public spaces, and of the routine derision by academics of transformational (i.e., "majority-female, and overtly queer or queer-friendly") fannish spaces, calls for an understanding of fan archives as spaces that offer fans shelter from censorship, mockery, and shaming (spaces in which it is the "norm" for female and queer people to share writing on diverse sexual themes with and for one another)—and at the same time, she implies that such spaces make fans perceptible to non-fans, and therefore render fans susceptible to ridicule and condemnation. Fan archives thus can function as explicitly queer spaces do, as simultaneously "safe spaces" and spaces of targeting.

Tosenberger also points out that many fan fiction authors and readers self-identify as queer. "In slash fandom, ... the majority of slashers identify as somewhere on the queer spectrum, myself included," Tosenberger writes (Jenkins 2011a). In 2010, a fan named melannen analyzed ten polls conducted over seven years on fan fiction sites (predominantly hosting slash content) that asked participants how they identified their sexuality. Counting as "straight" "any poll answer that was straight, heterosexual, primarily heterosexual, heteroflexible, or [the] direct equivalent," and counting as "queer" "everybody else, including people who identified as bi-leaning straight, questioning, and asexual," melannen found that between 37 percent and 84.5 percent of respondents to all ten polls self-identified on the queer spectrum; the median percent of queer respondents was 59.7 percent and the mean was 60.8 percent (melannen 2010). melannen's conclusion was that "the majority of slashers identify as queer," which she feels must be widely understood within fandom in order to advance fan discussion around "how straight women's sexuality interacts with queer sexuality," and other important topics around sexual identity and fan production.

The 2013 Archive of Our Own survey (analyzed by Lulu) mentioned above, which garnered responses from 5,709 slash readers and 2,765 creators (writers, vidders, etc.), similarly found that only 31.7 percent of respondents identified "solely as female" and "solely as heterosexual," with remaining respondents identifying either as "partially female," "partially heterosexual," or both; these results prompted numerous fans to affirm Tosenberger's and melannen's assertions that a significant portion of online fan fiction writers and readers self-identify as queer: "Evidence suggests that it is worth questioning the assumption that all or most M/M fans [fans who read and/or write fiction about male/male pairings, called "slash fiction"] are heterosexual women," wrote a fan named Lulu (2013), in a Tumblr post summarizing the AO3 survey results. "It boils down to this, *Slash fandom is a goddamn queer majority demographic*. ... Read it, breathe it, own it. Slash fandom is and always has been a queer community," wrote another fan, Suaine (quoted by sublimeglass 2013), also citing the AO3 poll. Among the participants in our oral history project, who were not all slash fiction writers or readers, 23 out of 50, or 46 percent, self-identified as queer (inclusive of terms such as "bisexual," "ambiguous," "hetero/queer," and "sapiosexual"). In addition, several of our interviewees said that they participate in fan fiction sites in part because they regard these sites as queer spaces. For example, eruthros states in her oral history interview, "The whole time I've been in fandom, I've been in fandom because I was queer. And because there wasn't a lot of queer fic or conversation or whatever happening in other spaces" (eruthros and thingswithwings 2012).

Thus, Internet fan fiction archives serve as queer spaces. I agree that, as Campbell points out, an individual who publicly claims the identity of "queer" is vulnerable to legal, medical, and sociocultural discrimination to an extent that an individual who declares him- or herself to be a "fan" is not (although, as the Jenkinses state, fans are not exempt from identity-based disciplining and repression). But even though "fan" is not equivalent to "queer" in legal/medical/sociocultural discourses, fan archives are queer archives. I make this assertion not only based on the counts of queer users of fan archives generated by the archives themselves (the Archive of Our Own 2013 survey and the ten polls analyzed by melannen) and by my own study, but also based on the ways that fan archives "count" in the lives of fans, both straight and queer. Here I am building on the work of Alexis Lothian, Kristina Busse, and Robin Anne Reid, who deem online slash fandom "queer female space," on Alexander Doty's idea of "queer reception," and on Jack Halberstam's and Cvetkovich's thinking on queer archives.

Fan scholars Lothian, Busse, and Reid (2007) write, "For us, slash fandom has become a place where a young urban dyke shares erotic space with a straight married mom in the American heartland, and where women whose identity markers suggest they would find few points of agreement have forged erotic, emotional, and political alliances." While asserting that slash fandoms are usually "dominated by middle-class, educated, liberal, English-speaking, white North American women," the authors declare that their personal experiences in slash fan fiction communities, and the testimonies of the slash fans that they quote in their essay, "suggest there is something interesting, and queer, going on here" (Lothian, Busse, and Reid 2007, 104). They contend that online slash fan fiction sites facilitate "forms of radical intersubjective contact" (105), bringing women of diverse sexual identities, geographic locations, and family constructions into intimate connections with one another.

One fan, Cat, quoted by Lothian, Busse, and Reid states, "For me, what's interesting about the eroticism of fandom isn't the erotic content in general but its communal nature and the way sexual activities and proclivities on the fringes of ordinary acceptability are considered quite normal" (106). It is not just male/male or female/female sex acts being depicted in fan fiction that makes fan fiction archives queer female spaces, in other words; it is the communal play with boundaries and borders that fannish sites permit, which Cat describes as "a continual negotiation of who we are and how we constrict ourselves" (108). Lothian, Busse, and Reid quote a number of fans who are uneasy with the expansion of the term "queer" to include such play, which can be interpreted as a shallow "playing-at" being queer that blithely appropriates a sexual minority's scripts, and they also cite fans who imagine that some fans who self-identify as straight might "be involved in a queer community/queer writing and object strenuously to being described by that term" (109). Nevertheless, because fans, queer and straight, congregate in online fan sites in order to collectively produce and consume "slash products that ... can be queer in their content ...—many of them in ways more profoundly transgressive than simply containing m/m or f/f relationships," states a fan named T., this type of Internet space "provides room for people to queer their identities. Queerness isn't a mandate here—it's an open possibility" (109).

What comes across clearly from the group of fans that participated in Lothian, Busse, and Reid's study is that online slash fan fiction spaces have real-life, real-world consequences for their participants, whether or not those participants identify as queer, because in these spaces, fans can question and defy prohibitions and policing on their own imaginations, identifications, and intimacies. It is fan sites' actual effects on fans themselves, rather than the virtualized fictions of same-sex encounters, that make these queer female spaces. Lothian, Busse, and Reid again cite T., who says, "When I think of the exuberance I felt participating in fandom, I think it was at seeing women stepping forward to describe their own erotics, because our culture silences female desire as effectively as it silences queer desire" (106). In his oral history interview, Henry Jenkins speaks to this silencing: "In my mind, the whole point of queerness is to talk about nonnormative sexualities" (Jenkins and Jenkins 2012). If we consider how thoroughly most females' fantasy lives are constrained by heteronormative imperatives, then we can see how necessary and enjoyable queer spaces, such as Internet fan fiction archives, might be for many women and girls, as they offer the opportunity to explore concepts of sexuality, romance, friendship, and other types of connections that fall outside of dominant social regulation and policing, in numbers that provide participants with a sense of safety for their creative practices.

But while Lothian, Busse, and Reid write specifically about online slash fandom as a "queer female space," I propose that all Internet fan fiction archives—which I define broadly as sites where users can access multiple fan fiction stories, including individuals' online journals—are queer female spaces, regardless of whether they contain same-sex content. Female expressions, articulations, preferences, priorities and desires are lacking in public discourse generally, and in mass media texts specifically—particularly highly erotic and sexualized expressions. Female fans "queer the [source] text" in specifically sexual ways when they write stories about intercourse between two male characters or two female characters, or stories about nonnormative erotics such as BDSM (bondage, domination, sadism, and masochism), incest, polyamory, and nonconsensual sex. As Jack Halberstam writes, many male/female sexual scenarios can be read as queer. Writing about the interplay between superhero Batman and antiheroine Catwoman in the 1992 Tim Burton film *Batman Returns*, Halberstam (1992) states, "When they [Batman and Catwoman] encounter each other in costume, something much sexier [than what Halberstam, earlier in the essay, calls "vanilla sex"] happens. ... To me their flirtation in capes looked queer precisely because it was not heterosexual: they were not man and woman, they were bat and cat, or latex and rubber, or feminist and vigilante. ... Just because Batman is male and Catwoman is female does not make their interactions heterosexual. Think about it. There is nothing straight about two people getting it on in rubber and latex costumes, wearing eyemasks, and carrying whips and other accouterments" (11).

Similar to Halberstam's argument that male/female character pairings can "look queer" is Alexander Doty's (1993) claim that users of cultural texts need not identify as queer in order to engage in what he calls "queer reception": "Queer positions, queer readings, and queer pleasures are part of a reception space that stands simultaneously beside and within that created by heterosexual and straight positions. ... Queer reception is often a place beyond the audience's conscious 'real-life' definition of their sexual identities and cultural positions—often, but not always, beyond such sexual identities and identity politics, that is" (15). Doty states that he doesn't "want to suggest that there is a queer utopia that unproblematically and apolitically unites straights and queers (or even all queers) in some mass culture reception area," because "queer reception (and production) practices can include everything from the reactionary to the radical to the indeterminate" (15). Following Doty, I assert that queer-identifying *and* straight-identifying fans often interpret mass media texts queerly, and create queer versions and variants of the texts they use—and rather than thinking that these interpretations and versionings take place in a purely theoretical "reception space" or "in some [hypothetical] mass culture reception area," I can state definitively that these actions of queering take place, with great frequency and in high volume, on specific fan websites and online archives. I do not regard the "areas" in which fans collectively queer texts as "utopic," "unproblematic," or "apolitical." Rather, fan websites and online archives are real queer spaces populated by people who identify across a broad range of genders and sexualities, which, like all real queer spaces, are rife with internal and external conflicts and are highly political.

In addition to engaging in what Doty calls "queer positions, queer readings, and queer pleasures," female fans *queer themselves* when they identify with male characters in heterosexual narratives, writing and reading about male heroes' feelings of romantic affection for female characters. Female fans *queer female characters* each time they depict a specific fictional woman or girl as more empowered, more self-determining, more dominant than she is in the source text—in short, placing her in the position of centrality and mastery typically assigned to male characters. Female fans *engage in queer relations* by writing sexual or romantic fiction specifically for fellow female fans, for the purpose of intentionally turning other women on, or at the least, fulfilling those women's desires to be temporarily transported into an imaginary that is highly charged with libidinal energies. Whichever of these acts women and girls perform when they make and consume fan fiction, they are *all acts of queering.*

Thus, Internet fan fiction archives are queer female spaces, because they are spaces in which women explore myriad alternative ways of feeling, being, sexing, doing, and communicating, and thereby resist or defy or transgress what Adrienne Rich (1986) called "compulsory heterosexuality." Internet fan archives facilitate multiple genres of female narrative interpretation and creation, multiple modes of female relation, and multiple registers of female affect, desire, and sexual identification, all of which exceed the boundaries of compulsory heterosexuality.

The Work of Queer Archives

Halberstam (2005) and Cvetkovich (2003) detail the significant work that queer archives do. Halberstam states that "the notion of a [queer subcultural] archive has to extend beyond the image of a place to collect material or hold documents, and it has to become a floating signifier for the kinds of lives implied" by the archive's contents. "The archive is not simply a repository; it is also a theory of cultural relevance, a construction of collective memory, and a complex record of queer activity." The queer subcultural archive, in other words, is a record of "queer history in the making"

(169–170). Halberstam allows us to perceive fan archives as sites that not only store fan productions, but also record the transformations of fan groups' "cultural relevance" and "queer activity"—their impact on mainstream media and nonfannish media users, and their ways of communicating and creating that mark their differences from the mainstream—over time. These archives testify to the various "kinds of lives" lived by members of these queer subcultures in different historical periods, and enable a larger understanding of fans as actors in "queer history."

Cvetkovich characterizes queer archives as focused on preserving the "intimate and personal," and consisting of objects "collected according to sentiment and emotion," "materials that archive emotion and feeling," "in contrast to institutionalized cultural memory" (269). "In the absence of institutionalized documentation or in opposition to official histories, memory becomes a valuable historical resource, and ephemeral and personal collections of objects stand alongside the documents of the dominant culture in order to offer alternative modes of knowledge" (8), Cvetkovich writes. This privileging of feeling and sentiment in queer archives also takes place in fan archives, as fans are often defined (primarily by their detractors) by the strength of their emotional responses, positive or negative, to source texts. Also, fan fiction stories are themselves "materials that archive emotion and feeling"—each story bearing traces of what its author felt about a particular mass media production. Affective experiences and investments that are excluded from traditional cultural memory institutions—powerful feelings that, when publicly manifested by queer individuals or by individual fans, can be interpreted as "too much" emotional demonstration—are prioritized and carefully preserved by alternative cultural memory institutions. Cvetkovich implies that queer groups have a felt need for the expressions of their feelings to be acknowledged *as* culture, *as* valuable productions worthy of saving, if only by their own members for their own members; I argue that fan groups feel the same. Both groups would claim that their preservationist efforts are rooted in "the fierce conviction of how meaningful and palpable these alternative life worlds can be," and are motivated by "the fear that they will remain invisible or be lost" owing to their ephemerality (166).

Cvetkovich also explicitly brings queer archiving and fan archiving into alignment when she discusses the importance of popular culture "reception and fandom" among queer communities. She writes (in alignment with Doty) that, for decades, the "ostensible heteronormativity" of celebrity culture and pulp fiction has been "queered by the machinations of reception and fandom" (252–253), and that therefore, films and pulp novels, and processes of viewing and interpreting and "camping up" popular culture that are documented in queer art and performance works, must be included in the lesbian archive of feelings. In assembling archives of transformative acts of media reception, Cvetkovich states that fan archivists lead the way for queer archivists to follow:

I take the fan as a model for the archivist. The archivist of queer culture must proceed like the fan or the collector whose attachment to objects is often fetishistic, idiosyncratic, or obsessional. The archive of lesbian fandom and fantasy would need to include, for example, pinup photos, gossip, film clips, and other memorabilia that serve as the material evidence of fan culture. The fan cultures that queer certain stars or the use of pulp novels as an indication of the existence of homosexuality are historical practices whose story is not wholly told by the objects and persons in and around which these forms of reception take place. ... In the archive of lesbian feeling, objects are not inherently meaningful but are made so through their significance to an audience. (253–254)

Cvetkovich views the fan "as a model for the [queer] archivist" because fans have collectively generated deep knowledges around how objects are *made* meaningful by audiences' interpretations and attachments, how to collect objects that come to have fetishistic or deeply emotional significance for individuals and groups, and how to build and sustain such collections. I stated above that despite the fact that "fan" and "queer" are not equivalent, fan archives *are* queer archives. Viewing the link between queerness and fandom through Cvetkovich's lens, we can rephrase my earlier statement: queer archives are frequently, at least partially, fan archives. Both queer and fan groups grasp the power of appropriating and transforming received cultural texts, and therefore, any archive that hopes to adequately represent either queer or fan sensibilities must archive queer and fannish archontic productions.

Necessary Archives

Fan archives must be regarded as having consequence and relevance for both fans and for larger society, in the way that community archives—particularly queer archives—do, because they are "safe spaces" for nonheteronormative practices, and because they safeguard fans' histories of affective experiences and transformative productions, which are histories of explorations of, and experimentations with, possibilities (including possibilities of sexual identifications, desires, and fantasies) that are not recorded or documented anywhere else. As many queer archivists, fan archivists, and community archivists would argue, society benefits when, rather than seeking to suppress or eliminate minoritarian, marginalized, and nonmainstream cultures, it strives to perpetuate these cultures; according to the logic of inclusiveness, the importance of these groups' cultural memory institutions must be acknowledged.

At the same time, the cultural productions of queer and marginalized groups, when archived, can lead these groups to be clearly marked, identified, and targeted for various types of exploitation and repression—and the same is true of the archived productions of fans. People who identify as fans are exposed to different risks by their participation in fan archives than nonfans who identify as ethnic or sexual minorities and who take part in building archives specific to their communities. I would never claim that fans are subjected to the same mechanisms of control, or are disciplined in the same ways, as these structurally disempowered groups. But fans, most of whom identify as female, and many of whom identify as queer, are vulnerable to attacks by corporate and legal entities, and fan archives can be undermined by a wide range of censorial forces that oppose female and queer expressivity, especially in the realm of explicit sexuality. A desire to protect their communities against these threats motivates fan archivists, whether they manage small, single-fandom databases or volunteer for the enormous, and rapidly expanding, multifandom repository of AO3. Fans' archival labor is crucial preservationist work in the contemporary digital media space, for if we admit that a diverse and open society needs women's archives and LGBTQ archives, then we must count fan fiction archives among our vital cultural memory institutions.

Break 3   Fan Time versus Media Time

Time and Performance in the Global Theater

In *Acting Out*, Bernard Stiegler ([2003] 2009) expresses anxiety over the mass *synchronization* of individual consciousnesses by media: "[Media audiences] end up being so well synchronized that they have lost their *diachrony*, that is, their singularity, which is to say their liberty, which always means their liberty *to think*" (55). This break will investigate time and media consumption, opposing *fan time* to *media time*, and will address a concern that several theorists in addition to Stiegler have raised, which is that fans make themselves captive to the temporalities of mass media by producing many online performances (I am here drawing on Marshall McLuhan's idea of the "global theater," which posits that computer-mediated communication facilitates new forms of everyday performance, as I explained in break 0). I posit that archives of fan works serve as an infrastructure that allows fans to keep to an alternative, even oppositional, temporality to media time.

In *Audiences*, Nicholas Abercrombie and Brian Longhurst (1998) characterize mass media audiences as "diffused," meaning that "in contemporary society, everyone becomes an audience all the time. Being a member of an audience is no longer an exceptional event. ... Rather it is constitutive of everyday life" (68–69). And when everyone is an audience member, everyone is also a performer: "People simultaneously feel [that they are] members of an audience and that they are performers; they are simultaneously watchers and being watched" (75). Abercrombie and Longhurst explicitly state that their thinking is informed by the blurring of boundaries between "art and life," "intermedia and performance art," and "arts and non-arts" promoted by postmodern performance artists and theorists,[1] and along these lines, they cite Erving Goffman as an important early articulator of the idea "that performance is entirely pervasive in everyday life" (74). But they also criticize what they regard as Goffman's failure to historicize this phenomenon.

In Abercrombie and Longhurst's analysis, the combination of "spectacle and narcissism" that leads to everyone performing for everyone else, and constantly serving as audiences for everyone else's performances, has not existed in every period of human society, but is specific to the era of mass media: "One of the reasons that modern societies are more performative is that the media of mass communications provide an important resource for everyday performance" (74). The "resource" that telecommunications provides would seem to be that of a stage, a theater so capacious that, as McLuhan (1970) says, it encompasses the globe, in which billions can perform in ways that are perceptible, accessible, and consumable by others.

Although Abercrombie and Longhurst never mention the Internet, their conception of mass-media-as-stage echoes the "global theater" theory of new media that McLuhan inaugurated and which I am developing throughout this book: the Internet is a stage that allows all users to perform to other users, through text posts or images or videos or songs, through sharing playlists or liking others' posts or publishing remixes or founding digital archives. Building on Abercrombie and Longhurst's arguments, Matt Hills's *Fan Cultures* (2002) also reads fannish audiences as performers and takes a critical view of such performances—he does not deride fans for performing online, but argues that by performing, fans turn themselves, as a group, into a disciplined extension of the culture industries. Hills (2002, 177) writes that when fans participate in an online newsgroup related to a television series, this segment of the "'audience' can be approached as a mediated product or performance itself," with fans' online posts collectively constituting a secondary consumable media text, made up of their aggregated "self-representation[s] and self-performance[s]."

Fans' "speculations, observations and commentaries," gathered together in large online communities, present "the audience-as-text" to fellow fans and interested lurkers, and this audience-text gets consumed alongside "the originating commodity-text" (Hill 2002, 177) (for example, a television program that serves as the primary object of interest of an online fandom). Hills reads the "just-in-time" (178) temporality of online fan performances as rigidly determined by the television broadcasting schedule: "Practices of fandom have become increasingly enmeshed within the rhythms and temporalities of broadcasting, so that fans now go online to discuss new episodes immediately after the episode's transmission time—or even during ad-breaks—perhaps in order to demonstrate the 'timeliness' and responsiveness of their devotion" (178). Here, Hills echoes Stiegler's fears of mass synchronization. (I wonder if Hills would interpret forms of Internet fan performance that are even more "just-in-time," such as live blogging and live tweeting—posting reactions on social media platforms as a television program or sports event is airing—as contemporary exemplifications of what he calls "the colonizing spatiotemporal processes of timely and information-saturated commodity exchange" [177].) Hills unfavorably contrasts the timeliness required of online fan performance with the more relaxed temporality of pre-Internet, print-based fan participation. He writes, "Describing the temporality of just-in-time fandom as a techno-evolution towards fuller 'interactivity,' which is deemed superior to the prior 'time-lag' involved in writing to and reading niche magazines' letters pages, ... neglects the extent to which this eradication of the 'time-lag' works ever more insistently to discipline and regulate the opportunities for temporally-licensed 'feedback,' and the very horizons of the fan experience" (179).

I will put aside for the moment the question of what has happened to the temporal structuring of online fan performance in the postnetwork era, when television content is consumed in a less regularized way (owing to time-shifting technologies and the increase of the practice of all-at-once— "marathon" or "binge"—viewing of television seasons and series). What remains relevant from Hills's writing is his suggestion that mediated fan performances might be giving rise to new kinds of temporalities, or new perceptions of time. Hills's distaste for what he reads as an increasing conflation of the temporalities of online fan performance and those of television broadcasting lead me to suggest that we establish a concept of "fan time" as distinct from "media time."

Wishing for Alternative Temporalities

I define "media time" as consisting of the schedules mandated by the culture industries' production and sales cycles: the time of broadcasting in the network television industry, the time of "drop dates" or release dates in the music industry and in the online streaming industry, the time of premieres in the film industry. We can read in Hills a wish for fan time to be different from media time, for fans to have their own performance times, that is, their own schedules for making and sharing performances, that are not so tightly pinned to media time. Hills writes almost nostalgically of the way that print time, and postal time, were structurally, technically slower than electronic media time, and so print- and postal-based fan activities (and, I would add, convention or "con"-based fan activities) de facto took place on a divergent time frame than media releases. But in an age of digital networks, when fan time *can* be (and, Hills would say, is *compelled* to be) coincident with media time, can fan time also still sometimes be different from media time?

Online fan archiving is one way that fans can assert and defend their ability to determine the temporality of their engagements with media texts. Fan archivists, and all contributors to and users of fan archives, manifest a wish to delay and/or repeat their consumption of fan performances (in the case of fan fiction archives, fan performances take the form of fan-authored stories), so that the instant that a fan performance appears online is not the *only* time that that performance can be consumed and appreciated. In addition, Internet fan archives maintain the possibility of individuals joining fandoms, and creating fan performances, long after a media text has ceased to air on television and can only be found on a streaming site, or after it has left the movie theaters and is only circulating on home media.

In other words, just as Jacques Derrida (1995, 24) says all archives open onto the future, fan archives keep open their doors to fan performances that do not coincide with media time, and in doing so—in giving fans a way to join fandoms belatedly, in offering fans sites and content repositories where fans can locate and engage with fan performances made earlier—fan archives tacitly encourage fans to perform, and to make public their performances, in their own time, on their own schedule, whenever they first discover a favorite media text or years after they first become fans of a text, irrespective of when the text was initially released. Thus, in addition to preserving fan works themselves, fan archives also preserve fan time itself, allowing fan time to be variant and undecided—in fact, allowing it to be decided entirely by individual fans—even as market forces work (if we follow Hills's and Stiegler's arguments) to bring fan time and media time into as close a bind as possible.

Time Feminized and Queered

The word "bind" in relation to temporality brings to mind Elizabeth Freeman's (2010) landmark work *Time Binds: Queer Temporalities, Queer Histories*, and I find many resonances between my idea of "fan time" and Freeman's and Jack Halberstam's (2005) idea of "queer time." Freeman coins the word "chrononormativity" to describe "the use of time to organize individual human bodies toward maximum productivity," which results in a sense of normal or regular time being implanted in individuals; she states that chrononormativity is "a technique by which institutional forces come to seem like somatic facts." She gives the example of industrial wage work enacting a "violent retemporalization of bodies once tuned to the seasonal rhythms of agricultural labor" (Freeman 2010, 3), and Halberstam discusses the "time of reproduction," and other timetables governing conception, childbirth, and childrearing, as fictions governed by "strict bourgeois rules of respectability" and believed by many to be "natural and desirable" (Halberstam 2005, 5). "Factory time" and "family time" are therefore two temporalities that arose in Western nations owing to a sedimentation, in the modern period, of certain social, economic, and cultural norms, but "queer time," for both Freeman and Halberstam, throws these chrononormativities into question.

"Fan time" similarly casts doubt on a range of dominant temporalities—not only on "media time," but on what I would call "work/leisure time," "linear time," and "self/other time." Fan time is usually time spent on pleasure rather than on productivity (or, when it is productive time—as when fans invent their own performances—it is a productivity driven by pleasure seeking rather than by an imperative to do wage work); it is time spent in repetition rather than in progression (or rather, time spent consuming multiple works related to one source text, rather than time spent consuming successive, distinct media products); it is time spent on one's self rather than on one's family or work customers/colleagues (although one can argue that fan time is also usually time spent with other fans, in online spaces, and so it is not exclusively time spent on the self—but it is typically time spent *not* on economic or domestic obligations).

The time that women spend on recreational, media-related pursuits, such as reading romance novels and viewing soap operas, has long been suspect in Western cultures, as indicated by the popular stereotypes of the romance- or soap-"addicted" housewife as delusional, lazy, and/or unintelligent, and by women's commonly affixing the label "guilty pleasure" to women-centric reality television shows and melodramas that they regularly view. But feminist scholars such as Janice Radway (1991), Tania Modleski (2007), and Lauren Berlant (2008) have argued that women's time is usually subjected to so many diverse demands that many women experience moments of private reading and viewing as periods of relief from others' requirements, of self-restoration, and of escape from workplace and domestic labor. Fan time can therefore be seen as countering the ways that women's time is typically structured and routinized.

We might also think of how "fan time" and "queer time" overlap, as when fans "queer a text," producing online performances (which, again, can be stories, videos, animated GIFs, commentary/reviews, and so on) that foreground homoerotic or homosexual relations, or any nonheteronormative romantic and sexual relations, between characters. Same-sex fiction or "slash" fiction is an extraordinarily popular genre of fan fiction, as evinced by the fact that most early scholarly research on fan fiction focused exclusively on slash fan communities and slash fic. The sheer quantity of slash, polyamorous ("threesome" or "moresome"), BDSM (bondage-domination-sadomasochism), and other nonheteronormative fics produced suggests that a considerable percentage of fan time is queer time. The fact that the majority of fic writers and readers are women and girls suggests that the majority of fan time is women's time, or what we might call alternative women's time, since that aligns better with my earlier statement that women's time is largely defined by external demands related to work and domestic duties. With these readings of fan time in mind, I argue that Internet fan archives not only help fans to refuse any temporal regulation of their performances by media time and the culture industries; fan archives also aid fans' refusal of chrononormativities linked to gender and sexual orientation.

4 Repertoire Fills the Archive: Race, Sexuality, and Social Justice in Fandom

Wanted: Content

Traditional memory institutions are built by professional archivists, who acquire new entries either by purchase or other forms of active search and collection, or by donation. Rogue archivists also use these acquisition methods (search-and-collect or donation), but they also actively solicit the submission—and sometimes the creation—of content. Just as computing communities and corporations occasionally organize "hackathons" to inspire participants to write new code or brainstorm innovative projects in short, defined periods of time, many rogue archivists run challenges, drives, exchanges, and other time-constrained events to expressly encourage the contribution of new materials to their repositories. In many cases, archivists structure these events to attract or generate specific types of content, if they notice that certain categories of their archives are lacking and need to grow.

In this chapter, I will describe how communities of volunteer/amateur/fan/pirate archivists and archive users stage events for digital content creation and storage. In other sections of this book, I ask the reader to consider the repertoires of archive building and archive use, as well as the repertoire of another kind of memory work, the work of versioning, of which fan authorship is but one genre. Here, I will present another type of repertoire: the repertoire of archive contribution. I will show how archivists seek to motivate the enactment of this repertoire, combined with the repertoire of versioning, not only to assist them in growing their archives quantitatively, but to *qualitatively* change the nature of their archives. In other words, by urging archive users to become archive contributors, archivists seek to realize, at least partially, the promise of democratization and difference inherent in rogue digital archives.

Thus, the uses that archivists make of repertoire—the ends to which they put their audiences' repertoires—are not only practical but political. Rogue archivists not only want to grow their archives by inviting and facilitating crowdsourced contributions, they also wish to fulfill the potential of digital archives to allow anyone (in theory) to make deposits, and in doing so, to expand the archives' possible purposes and significations. The repertoire of archive contribution is a *carnival* repertoire, for the digital archivists that stage online events to promote a flurry of contribution activity often seek to imbue these events with an air of festivity and fun, demarcating the event times and spaces (the spaces are the digital archives themselves) as special and extraordinary in the lives of their communities. To explore the operations and effects of the carnival repertoire that plays out on digital archives, I will delve into the large body of theoretical writing that has taken up Mikhail Bakhtin's (1984) analysis of carnival in medieval Europe, as "a second world and a second life outside officialdom, a world in which all medieval people participated more or less, in which they lived during a given time of the year" (6). I will argue that the carnival-like events organized by digital archivists to encourage contributions are intended to influence broader society and culture, and to serve as unofficial, idealized spaces that make imaginable, conceivable, and graspable new modes of living, being, identifying, and communicating. I claim that rogue archivists who run archive-donation events are as concerned with shaping a collective future as they are interested in memorializing or preserving a collective past.

Archive Events

Sly,[1] a file-sharing site that aspires to be "more than just a regular BitTorrent tracker for movies," and defines itself as "a comprehensive library of Arthouse, Cult, Classic, Experimental and rare movies from all over the world," runs a Master of the Month (MoM) uploading event every month. Moderators announce a new MoM theme at the start of the month, and "ask our users [to] share everything related to each Master of the Month and get a fat bonus in the process" (bonuses take the form of share ratio—the ratio of bytes uploaded to bytes downloaded—and the higher a member's ratio, the more files they can download from the site). Past MoM themes include: Iranian films, stop-motion animation, blaxploitation, Kay Francis, Hammer films, Kaiju-eiga, the golden age of serials (1929–1956), Polish animation, Marguerite Duras, Otar Iosseliani and Georgian cinema, ethnographic cinema, twenty-first-century video art, Spanish cinema under

Franco, European sovereign-debt crisis, Ida Lupino, Chinese cinema under Mao, Israel, Palestine, queer cinema(s), and many others.

The moderators of Sly use MoM events to bulk up categories of their archive that they deem to be undersized. Sly need not encourage uploads of well-known art-house classics such as Chris Marker's *La Jetée* (of which three versions of differing resolutions are currently available on the site) or of camp/cult classics such as Russ Meyer's *Beyond the Valley of the Dolls* (of which Sly offers two versions). Rather, as evinced by the heterogeneous list of MoM themes, it seems that the Sly moderators feel they must actively solicit users' contributions of films from overlooked historical periods; films made under restrictive political regimes that were rarely distributed internationally; films from non-Western nations; films about ethnic and sexual minorities; films in "minor" genres (nonfiction, serials, video, and animation); and films starring, directed by, or adapted from the works of important women artists who may not be as well known to contemporary audiences as they deserve. From the MoM themes, we can deduce what Sly's moderators have perceived to be gaps or deficiencies in their archive.

Looking through the "collections" generated by the MoM events, we can see that the Sly archive successfully expands its holdings through these monthly community events: the average number of films uploaded for each of the MoM themes listed above is 405. The least generative MoM theme was Marguerite Duras (41 films), and the most generative MoM was queer cinema(s) (2,770 films). Through incentivizing members to contribute specific types of content at specific times, the archive fills in its weak areas, and also exposes users to bodies of work with which many are likely unfamiliar. Thus, the MoM events allow Sly to more robustly fulfill its mission of becoming a "comprehensive library" of nonmainstream cinema. Without the themed MoMs, if the Sly moderators simply allowed its members to upload whatever they chose to, the Sly archive might only contain the most popular, most often-watched "art-house, cult, classic, experimental and rare movies," and smaller categories might be left underpopulated indefinitely.

Sly is not the only digital archive to organize contribution drives. Archive Team constantly recruits volunteers to help download and save certain websites, online communities, and social networks. Their deadlines for each project are determined by the site owners' intention to shut down, or "sunset," their sites at specified times (for example, as of this writing in July 2014, Archive Team is operating a project focused on "Saving Verizon customer pages, shutting down September 2014"). The South Asian American Digital Archive (SAADA) is currently running the First Days Project, which invites archive users to submit their personal stories of their first day in the United States, formatted as video, audio, or text (South Asian American Digital Archive, "First Days Project"). Rhizome commissions digital artworks for its ArtBase through its annual commissions cycle (which makes some awards based on the decisions of a jury and other awards based on the votes of the online public), its Rhizome|Tumblr Internet Art Grant program (for artists working in and with the Tumblr blogging platform), and its Internet Microgrant program (which funds proposals that attract the most online votes in the amount of $500). In 2013, the Internet Archive (IA) solicited proposals for a yearlong Tumblr residency program; the archivists-in-residence each curated content from the IA and showcased their mini-collections on the Internet Archive's official Tumblr for one week in 2014 ("Commissions").

Some of these archive events attract contributions of content that users already possess; for example, members of Sly may have saved digital files of rare films on their drives or servers, and respond to the MoM's call-to-upload whenever they see an appropriate theme pop up. Other archive events are intended to inspire archive users to create new content; SAADA's First Days Project, Rhizome's commissions programs, and the IA's Tumblr residencies all incite users to generate new digital material for the enlargement of these archives' stores and, hopefully, of the archives' audience base as well (it is a truism of website operation that if a site that wishes to increase its traffic, it must constantly publish new content). Another way that we might think of these archive events is as drivers of transmediation: for the Sly MoMs, users might "rip" (make digital files of) their hard-copy versions of films; for the First Days Project, SAADA users must transform stories that exist in their memories, which they may have only told orally, into text/audio/video recordings; for the IA Tumblr residencies, IA users must select a body of items already contained in the IA and fashion them into a collection with a visual style of presentation suitable for the Tumblr platform. We might say, then, that archive events motivate users to either donate digital content that they already have, make new digital material that they can contribute to an archive, or make new (digital) versions of material that already exists, either in their personal memories/collections or in the archives themselves.

From the preponderance of archive events, we see that digital archivists have the same goal as traditional archivists—that of preserving existing material—and take on the additional objective of inciting users to deliver fresh material to the archives. To the repertoires of archive use and archive building, which I discussed in earlier sections, we must therefore add another repertoire: the repertoire of archive contribution, which is practiced by both digital archivists (who must organize and run the content-driving events) and their audiences (who, hopefully, fulfill the requests for new content issued by the archivists). Through the repeated enactment of the repertoire of archive contribution, digital archives grow.

Battles, Bingos, and Bangs

Internet fan fiction communities and archives have frequently designed and hosted content-generating events, such as kink_bingo, Amplificathon, and the Porn Battle, which were/are all moderated, rule-governed, and time-based writing challenges, similar to National Novel Writing Month or Wikipedia's Open Barn Raising (a kind of hackathon at which volunteer members of WikiProject Open gather "online and in person to improve Wikipedia articles related to openness in education"; see Wikipedia 2014).

Many fanfic communities and archives organize these types of events in order to fill perceived gaps in the archives, like the Master of the Month drives on Sly, or to inspire the creation of more of the kinds of content desired by archivists, like Rhizome's commissions programs and SAADA's First Days Project. In addition to the fan writing challenges listed above, there are several other popular genres of fan content drives. For example, Big Bang challenges require participants to produce novel-length stories in a stated period of time (the original Big Bangs, in the Harry Potter fandom, set a 50,000-word minimum, but more recent Bangs have lowered the mandatory word count), upon completion of which fan authors are rewarded with fan art created specifically for their stories.[2] Currently, the AO3 hosts 1,799 Big Bang works written for a diverse set of fandoms (Archive of Our Own, "Big Bang Challenge").

Another challenge called Remix Redux invites fan authors to "remix" other fan authors' works, for instance, by rewriting the earlier story from a different character's point of view. The challenge is in its eleventh year, and AO3 now holds 1,320 Remix Redux stories spanning 413 fandoms (Archive of Our Own, "We Invented the Remix ... Redux"). Trope Bingo, another multifandom challenge, "uses common and well-known fandom tropes as squares" on bingo cards that are sent to all "players" (fans who sign up to participate), and asks players to make "bingo" by creating one fan fiction story, of 500 words or more, for each of five contiguous squares on their card (so, each player creates a minimum of five works over the course of the challenge) (Dreamwidth, "Trope Bingo"). The list of possible tropes includes amnesia, forced to marry, mistletoe kiss, poker/strip poker, presumed dead, road trip, secret twin/doppelganger, sharing a bed, snowed in, and time travel (trope_bingo 2013)—all scenarios and situations that frequently recur in most fandoms' fan fiction. At present, the AO3 contains 1,768 Trope Bingo works in 613 fandoms (Dreamwidth, "Trope Bingo").

Probably the most famous fan works exchange is Yuletide, an annual winter holiday event dedicated to small or "rare" fandoms (that is, fandoms with few fan fiction stories written for them), in which fans nominate rare fandoms for which they want stories written, and/or sign up to write stories in rare fandoms; based on their preferences, fan writers are then given assignments to write stories of at least 1,000 words for specific fandoms, and have four weeks to complete their assignments before December 25, when all stories are "revealed," or posted online, at the AO3 (Archive of Our Own 2009). The eleventh year of Yuletide took place in 2013, and the AO3 now holds 23,826 Yuletide works written for 5,421 fandoms (Archive of Our Own, "Yuletide").[3]

dark_agenda Challenges

Of special interest to me are fan events that aim to increase the racial, ethnic, national, and sexual diversity of fan works. A fan activist group called dark_agenda, founded in 2009, states its mission to be "offer[ing] resources [to fans] in order to increase the representation of international, non-English and non-Western fandoms in multi-fandom fanwork exchanges and festivals, as well as promote the responsible portrayal of characters of colo(u)r" (Dreamwidth 2014). The group's members have so far run a number of ficathons focused on "chromatic" characters—"chromatic" being the term selected by dark_agenda's leaders as "an umbrella definition for 'person of colo(ur),' 'non-white,' 'multiracial,' 'indigenous,' 'sourcelander,' 'hyphenate,' 'diasporian,' etc."

In 2009 and 2010, dark_agenda ran Chromatic Yuletide, a "subchallenge" of Yuletide, which operates according to the same rules as Yuletide but focuses on "increas[ing] the representation of chromatic sources and characters in rare fandoms." Over those two years, 279 Chromatic Yuletide works in 298 fandoms were archived on the AO3 (Archive of Our Own, "Chromatic Yuletide 2009," "Chromatic Yuletide 2010").[4] In 2010, the group also launched the Racebending Revenge Challenge "as a protest against whitewashing in Western media and in particular *The Last Airbender*" (dark_administrator 2011b).[5] Participants in the challenge were asked to "Re-write one or more white characters in the fandom(s) of your choice as chromatic/non-white/PoC [people of color], in a story of at least 500 words, with some acknowledgment of how the racial difference would make a difference to the story being told." The master list of challenge submissions on Dreamwidth contains 48 works in 36 fandoms (Dreamwidth 2013).

In addition, dark_agenda organized Chromatic Remix Redux in 2011, which operated alongside the main Remix Redux challenge, and asked participants to feature a chromatic character in their remixes. The Chromatic Remix Redux archive on the AO3 now holds 1,320 works in 413 fandoms (Archive of Our Own, "Chromatic Remix Redux"). In 2011, the founder and moderator of the Porn Battle, oxoniensis, invited dark_ agenda to run a Chromatic subchallenge for Porn Battle XI. In her oral history interview, oxoniensis (2012) states, "The Chromatic side to the Battle was inspired by the Chromatic Yuletide. I wanted to do something to help encourage more entries that included people of color. Actually making a separate list of all the Chromatic prompts had two purposes: to put the idea of writing/drawing etc. a person of color in people's minds and make it easier for them to do so." The Porn Battle archive shows that the Chromatic Porn Battle resulted in approximately 1,957 prompts (The Porn Battle, "Chromatic Prompts") and 218 fills (The Porn Battle, "Chromatic Entries") in 115 fandoms. Also in 2011, dark_agenda ran the Kaleidoscope Fanwork Exchange, "a multimedia fanwork exchange … open to all sources with chromatic characters or people and by chromatic creators," welcoming all genres of fan productions in all languages, "particularly in English dialects and non-English languages associated with chromatic cultures." The Kaleidoscope archive on the AO3 holds 64 works in 61 fandoms (dark_administrator 2011a).

The above is not a comprehensive listing of dark_agenda's activities, but the events described are the group's highest-profile projects.

A Darker Archive

The first way that I will "read" the online activities organized by dark_ agenda—the Chromatic Yuletides, Racebending Revenge, Chromatic Remix Redux, Chromatic Porn Battle, and Kaleidoscope—is as a series of responses to, and protests of, the notorious underrepresentation of racial and ethnic minorities in mass media productions. In my view, the primary intention driving the dark_agenda was similar to the intention behind Sly's MoMs and SAADA's First Days Project: to incite the crowdsourced creation of new content, content of a specific category and type that was perceived to be lacking from an archive. In the case of the chromatic fanworks challenges, the "archive" whose gaps were being filled was not an individual online fan fiction archive; it was the enormous metaphorical archive constituted by studio films and broadcast and cable television programs.

For decades, media scholars and watchdog groups have accused mass media of offering predominantly "negative and/or stereotyped images of many groups," as well as of "providing too few images of certain groups" (Klein and Shiffman 2009, 56). On this last point—that films and television programs contain "too few images" of certain groups, particularly nonwhite characters—every study of media content ever published is in agreement. The 2014 Hollywood Diversity Report issued by the Ralph J. Bunche Center for African American Studies at UCLA, for example, shows that "minorities claimed only 10.5 percent of the lead roles" in Hollywood films made in 2011 (Ralph J. Bunche Center for African American Studies at UCLA 2014, 6), and that "minority actors claimed just 5.1 percent of the lead roles in broadcast comedies and dramas" in the 2011–12 season (8). Minority performers fared better in cable comedies and dramas, playing 14.7 percent of the lead roles (8–9). The report's analysis of "minority cast share," or the percentage of the total cast of the media text consisting of minority characters, showed that there were more minority actors in supporting positions, but only 26.7 percent of films (6–7), 25.3 percent of broadcast television programs (11–12), and 27.2 percent of cable television programs (12) had casts that were at least as diverse as the US population (which is 36.3 percent minority). In both lead and supporting roles, therefore, nonwhites are dramatically underrepresented in the mass media.

Gaye Tuchman (1978), Debra Merskin (1998), Bonnie Y. Ohye and Jessica Henderson Daniels (1999), and Hugh Klein and Kenneth Shiffman (2009) refer to the media's underrepresentation of specific groups as "symbolic annihilation." Merskin defines symbolic annihilation "as the way cultural production and media representations ignore, exclude, marginalize, or trivialize a particular group" (1998, 335). I choose to think of the media's symbolic annihilation of minorities as an annihilation from an archive of images and sounds and narratives—an archive of recorded storytelling media. When Klein and Shiffman point to the "near-total absence" of certain groups from mass media (2009, 56), I think of this absence as an archival absence, that is, as the exclusion of those groups' documents and texts from an archive. When Klein and Shiffman state that "the absence of a particular group in the media instructs people, albeit tacitly, about how one should or should not act, and about what one should or should not look like" (57), I consider Eric Ketelaar's (2001) arguments that all archives contain "tacit narratives of power and knowledge" (132), that "social, cultural, political, economic and religious contexts determine the tacit narratives of an archive" (136–137), and that the analyst of an archive "should make these contexts transparent, maybe even visible" (137). Like an archive, the corpus of mass media texts is replete with tacit narratives that reflect the power structures of the society and culture in which the text is made, and mass media scholars like Klein and Shiffman make visible the media archive's tacit narratives.

dark_agenda's project, therefore, is at least in part the construction of a parallel archive to the archive of mass media, an archive of fan-produced storytelling media that features characters of color as the lead characters, and that symbolically annihilates not white *characters* (who may still, after all, feature—as supporting players—in the works created for dark_agenda's "chromatic" challenges), but white dominance and white privilege in media representations. dark_agenda, in other words, sets an *agenda* for fandom, as a collective, to answer the erasure, exclusion, and diminishment of characters of color from the archive of media by collectively constructing a *darker archive*, an archive full of the stories of the darker characters found in filmic and televisual source texts, who most often "prop" and "pedestal" the white characters. Another way that we could conceive of this darker archive is as an addition, an insertion, a forced entry, of stories about people of color into the total archive of media, which we might call the Mediascape. By calling into being a darker archive, dark_agenda has attempted to transform the Western Mediascape, or cultural imaginary, as a whole—has tried to make the giant Media Archive more inclusive and more representative of the actual racial and ethnic diversity of human existence than it would be if the culture industries' productions were allowed to proliferate unanswered.

Touring through the "dark archive" that was called into being by dark_ agenda, one finds that the only stories about "Disney Princesses" feature Tiana, the African-American heroine of *The Princess and the Frog*, and Mulan, the Chinese warrior heroine of the eponymous film; Cinderella, Aurora (*Sleeping Beauty*), Ariel (*The Little Mermaid*), and Belle (*Beauty and the Beast*) do not figure in this archive, except to serve as foils to the princesses of color. One encounters a story in which the Kryptonians in the Superman universe, including Kal-El/Clark Kent/Superman himself, are black (written for the Racebending Revenge challenge), and young Clark must deal with rampant racism in Smallville growing up. One notes that all of the stories taking place in the universe of the CBS award-winning television program *The Good Wife* "star" Kalinda Sharma, the British Indian investigator, rather than the series' actual lead character, Anglo-American attorney Alicia Florrick. Chromatic characters are always the lead characters, with white characters either absent, "cast" (or rather, recast) in supporting roles, or acting as villains and obstacles. In her analysis of Ernest Hemingway's fiction, Toni Morrison notes that Hemingway's white American male heroes are often surrounded by black African male nurses: "Tontos all," Morrison calls the nurses, "whose role is to do everything possible to serve the Lone Ranger without disturbing his indulgent delusion that he is indeed alone" (Morrison 1992, 82). Morrison here could well be describing the relation between characters of color and white characters in most US media fictions: chromatic characters "do everything possible to serve" the white heroes without disturbing the illusion that *they* are the sole heroes/protagonists/ stars/leads. The stories generated by dark_agenda's challenges reverse this historical relation, putting chromatic characters in the heroic and dominant positions, and white characters in the positions of support.

I realize that "dark archive" has another meaning, that of an archive that functions but is closed to the public, whereas here I use the phrase to refer to a metaphorical archive full of stories about nonwhite characters. Similarly, the phrase "dark agenda" usually refers to a group (real or fictional) having a concealed, nefarious plan—a conspiracy plot—but the fan collective dark_agenda undertakes schemes to correct (in some small degree) an injustice, which is mass media's historically, consistently, foregrounding and focusing on white characters and marginalizing characters of color. The name "dark_agenda" is therefore somewhat ironic, as it implies that media audiences must engage in conspiracy tactics in order to bring about even a minor revolution in media representations of nonwhite peoples—that is, only an unofficial, largely unnoticed, series of writing and media production events, taking place in the "shadow economy" (Fiske 1992) of fandom, and making no difference to the casting processes of films or television series, can hope to create archives in which every text is primarily about a person, or people, of color. My term "dark archive" is also ironic, as it hints that the only archive that can effectively feature characters of "darker" skin color than the characters who dominate cinema and television is one that will go largely unseen and unused by Hollywood media producers and the vast majority of media consumers—the archive is dark not because its archivists intend it to be inaccessible, but because so few media makers and audiences are interested in the question of where to find versions of media texts that are predominantly populated by nonwhite characters.

In break 2, I cited Gregory Sholette's characterization of amateur artists, whose labor and purchases support those at the pinnacle of the professional art world, as "dark matter" and as an "army" of "invisibles" (Sholette 2011, 1, 3, 7, 16). Those who participate in dark_agenda's events constitute a different kind of dark army of invisibles: one that does not support the top of the media industry pyramid, but tries to undermine its racist worldview from below, from the unseen base. The "agenda" of this army is to combat mass media's symbolic annihilation of darker-skinned peoples by constructing a parallel "dark archive"—or, we could say, by "darkening" the total Media Archive—through staging events that prompt the production of a plethora of stories about characters that usually exist only in the shadows of whiteness.

The Vernacular Creativity of Archivists

Rogue digital archives are therefore often filled through events, that is, through archivists demarcating specific objectives for archive users, special places (sections of the archives, or subarchives), and/or particular times (the durations of the challenges) in which users must make their deposits. In the collective excitement and sense of group fun that they elicit, these online content drives resemble real-world event genres such as community theater/amateur dramatics, local fairs, quilting bees, and craft competitions—all forms of what Tim Edensor et al. (2010) call "vernacular creativity," which they contrast with "state-led spectacular flagship projects" (5) such as art biennials, high-profile music festivals, and the development (read: gentrification) of "distinctive cultural quarters" within urban centers (5–6). With their idea of vernacular creativity, Edensor et al. seek to expand the definition of cultural creativity beyond long-standing notions of "the uniquely creative individual" (8) or the "cool city" (5), to include creativity that "is located in everyday, popular, vernacular culture" (9).

Evoking the earlier work of British cultural studies scholars such as Dick Hebdige (1983), Raymond Williams ([1958] 2002), and Paul Willis (1997), Edensor et al. argue for greater recognition of what Willis calls "common culture," that is, the "vibrant symbolic life and symbolic creativity in everyday life" (Willis 1997, 206) and "the necessariness of everyday symbolic and communicative work" (208). Vernacular creativity, for Edensor et al., is a term that honors the "sensation, fun, desire and festivity" in common culture. I regard digital archives' content drives as a recently inaugurated category of vernacular creativity, though this category bears close relation to far older vernacular traditions. Like barnraisings (a term that, as I stated above, Wikipedia sometimes uses for their page editing events), bake sales, fundraising races, charity auctions, craft competitions, and other live local practices already mentioned, online archive-contribution events encourage members of a community to come together and share their creative and productive energies, in designated spaces and at specified times. Digital archivists import a long-standing repertoire of community activity—the repertoire of festival organization and local event management—from physical into virtual space. They use this repertoire of community activity to literally enlarge a "common culture," that is, the cultural texts held in common by a group. Edensor et al. permit us to perceive the creativity of digital archivists in appropriating older, real-world traditions as the bases of new kinds of online festivals. Edensor et al. write: "Creativity should ... be conceived as an improvisation quality that, across all forms of cultural activity, requires people to adapt to particular circumstances. Even in apparently repetitive practices, regeneration actually takes place under circumstances that are always different. ... This means that there 'is creativity even and especially in the maintenance of an established tradition'" (Edensor et al. 2010, 8; citing Hallam and Ingold 2007, 5–6). By translating real-world traditions into virtual sites, and ensuring that ancient repertoires of communal fun-making and collective content production survive through continual online reenactment, digital archivists increase the quantities of data stored and saved in their servers. Thus, a repertoire of vernacular creativity fills archives of crowdsourced content. In this, as in so many other ways, the memory modes of repertoire and archive are shown to be mutually and inextricably dependent on one another in the digital age. By "remembering" and renewing traditional event structures that inspire a group to take enthusiastic and timely action, rogue archivists fill their communities' networked memory banks.

"'Carnival' Is an IP Address"

A closely related repertoire to that of the "vernacular" and "everyday" creative practices lionized by Edensor et al. is the repertoire of carnival. If we can see how the baking competition and the book drive are translated into Internet events, how does carnival take place online? One might say that the Internet itself is a carnival; Bakhtin eases the path for such a definition by describing medieval carnival in similar terms to those that Marshall McLuhan uses to describe global networked telecommunications. Where McLuhan and Nevitt (1972) state that in the "global theater," "all men become actors and there are few spectators" (145), Bakhtin ([1965] 1984) writes, "Carnival does not know footlights, in the sense that it does not acknowledge any distinction between actors and spectators. ... Carnival is not a spectacle seen by the people; they live in it, and everyone participates because its very idea embraces all the people" (7). Donald Theall explicitly compares the Internet to carnival as defined by Bakhtin, stating that the Internet and the Web in the 1990s challenged "those accustomed to the comfort of the hierarchical control of the state, corporation, and church" by inaugurating "anarchic freedom [within] an essentially non-hierarchical entity permitting powerful exchange and communication"; an entity that serves as "a site of personal freedom as an extension of [the user's] home, common room, or watering place" and that offers "great potential for car- nivalesque unmaskings" (Theall 1999, 158). In this framework, the Inter- net seems quite analogous to the "second world and second life" (Bakhtin [1965] 1984, 6) incarnated by the medieval carnival, and the virtual world and the physical world could be regarded as constituting a new "two-world condition" (6).

But of course, the Internet only has the *potential* to be carnivalesque. It *can* serve as a site of "anarchic, personal freedom," but it is also, writes Theall, "a serious source of communication, information and data," oper- ating as a crucial platform for business and government: "[The Internet] intertwines the manipulative promotion of commercial ... interests with the indulgent leisure of transgression and playfulness" (Theall 1999, 159). And there is a persistent danger, Theall argues, of corporate forces seeking to close down certain types of play that transpire online, just as the eigh- teenth and nineteenth centuries witnessed "the sanitization of traditional carnival and other transgressive spaces" (159). So, if we make the case that we can find a new version of carnival online, we must find it in spaces and events that are, in some way, directly or indirectly, opposed to what Bakhtin calls "officialdom" and what Theall calls "serious" enterprises. And we must acknowledge that carnival does not take place all year round, but is confined to special times; "carnival time," as Bakhtin says, is different from other times of the year, and it is only "during carnival time [that] life is subject only to its own laws, that is, the laws of its own freedom" ([1965] 1984, 7). So, while I do not think it can be said that the Internet as a whole is a constant manifestation of carnival, I think we can discover carnival tak- ing place on the network, and that one group of sites where carnival thrives is fan fiction archives. The "doing" of carnival, the repertoire of carnival, has been imported from physical to virtual reality. As my colleague at the Berkeley Center for New Media, Professor Greg Niemeyer, hearing me talk about the carnivalesque in online fan communities, remarked, "'Carnival' is now an IP address."

I perceive the spirit of carnival to suffuse dark_agenda's challenges. The challenges are time specific, and, like Bakhtin's medieval carnival, their pri- mary purpose is to upend an existing hierarchy: the racial/ethnic hierarchy of media representation. "Carnival shakes up the authoritative version of language and values, making room for a multiplicity of voices and meanings," writes Shanti Elliot (1999, 129). "Carnival reversal implies a change from principles of stability and closure to constant possibility" (130). Elliot derives the idea of "carnival reversal" from Bakhtin, who argues that carnival demonstrates "the peculiar logic of the 'inside out' (*à l'envers*), of the 'turnabout,' of a continual shifting from top to bottom, from front to rear, of numerous parodies and travesties, humiliations, profanations, comic crownings and uncrownings" (Bakhtin [1965] 1984, 11). dark_agenda's fanworks exchanges effectuate a reversal, an inside-out, a turnabout, of mass media's all-too-stable principles, which favor white heroes and their narratives above all. dark_agenda brings about times and spaces in which, only briefly and only through what Elliot calls Bakhtinian "'unofficial' language" (Elliot 1999, 130), the media world's habitual privileging of whiteness is transformed, and the prominence of nonwhite characters and their stories becomes possible.

Other fan challenges, such as kink_bingo and Amplificathon, also are carnivalesque, perhaps even more so than dark_agenda in their emphases on (what some might deem) bodily excesses. Although many "kinks" included in kink_bingo's cards[6] are not sexual acts, the moderators, eruthros and thingswithwings, always include sexual kinks that are not common in fan writing, such as watersports, enemas, "plushie" or furry kink, blood play, and medical play. "I think we've done some good work to help make kinky fic more acceptable and less shadowy and locked away," says thingswithwings (eruthros and thingswithwings 2012) in her interview. Amplificathon, the challenge run by jinjurly (founder of the Audiofic Archive), invites fans to record themselves reading fan fiction stories aloud and to share those recordings ("audiofics"), which jinjurly (2012) says are often perceived as "*very* strange" and "very intimate," in that "you are basically sharing a part of your body with people in a way that, yeah, sometimes people find really creepy." jinjurly describes how some audioficcers express regret for their vocal performances: "The number [of audioficcers] I've seen apologize for having Southern accents is really pretty dismaying, or German accents, or whatever your unpopular accent-of-the-month is. ... I mean, you see people self-castigating for accents *all* the time. ... [People say] 'Oh, I talk too fast, or I talk too slow, or my voice isn't pretty enough, or oh, my accent.' You know what? Who cares? It's your voice. It's your voice, and because you're a person, your voice is important" (jinjurly 2012). For jinjurly, the uniqueness and distinctiveness of each reader's speech is precisely what should be celebrated, as every individual voice matters, and deserves to be heard, literally and metaphorically, in fandom and in larger society. She says,

That diversity is—that's what I want the world to be, that's what I want fandom to be. And so that's what I want the [Audiofic] archive to be. I want it to include as many things as possible and I want to not curate. I don't want to pass judgment on anything. ... I want to say, "Hey look, we're [fandom is] big and we're [all] different and isn't it cool that we're this giant tapestry that you're too close to see it, but I'm sure there's a picture there somehow." ... The fact [is] that I approach this fairly politically and that I definitely have an agenda there—I mean, the agenda is sort of, broadly stated, is that every voice be valued and that everybody's contribution be valued. ... So yeah, that's why we solicit [for the Audiofic Archive through Amplificathon and other mechanisms]. (jinjurly 2012)

Both kink_bingo and Amplificathon ask fans to bring into being representations and performances that may strike some as "too much." Some of the kink_bingo prompts may strike a portion of the players as too perverse; some of the audiofics produced for Amplificathon may sound to listeners as too accented. But this too-much-ness in the productions of composed and default bodies (defined in chapter 6), which both challenges not only welcome but actively call for, is a mainstay of the carnival repertoire.

Bakhtin makes clear that carnival, as a form or style or action, does not only transpire in the lived world, but is also evident in a wide range of artistic genres. In *Problems of Dostoevsky's Poetics*, Bakhtin ([1963] 1993) focuses on the carnivalesque in literature; he writes, "Carnivalization, once it has penetrated and to a certain extent determined the structure of a genre, can be used by various movements and creative methods. ... In fact, every movement and creative method interprets and renews it in its own way" (160). Bakhtin argues that the translation of live carnival into the realm of literature is evident in the genre of "grotesque realism," exemplified by Miguel Cervantes's *Don Quixote* and the body of Sancho Panza: "Sancho's fat belly (*panza*), his appetite and thirst still convey a powerful carnivalesque spirit. ... Sancho's materialism, his potbelly, appetite, his abundant defecation, are on the absolutely lower level of grotesque realism" (Bakhtin [1965] 1984, 22). I read kink_bingo and Amplificathon as allied with Cervantes's project to import carnival into the format of written text—to transmute the physical event of carnival onto the page (or screen)—and, in doing so, to reverse, challenge, and unsettle Western modernity's idealization and normalization of the body. Writes Bakhtin, "The Renaissance saw the body in quite a different light than the Middle Ages. ... As conceived by these [Renaissance] canons, the body was first of all a strictly completed, finished product. ... All signs of its unfinished character, of its growth and proliferation were eliminated; its protuberances and offshoots were removed, its convexities (signs of new sprouts and buds) smoothed out, its apertures closed. ... The inner processes of absorbing and ejecting were not revealed. The individual body was presented apart from its relation to the ancestral body of the people" ([1965] 1984, 29). Kink_bingo and Amplificathon ask participants to join them in staging carnivals online, carnivals that take place through written words and spoken stories, as do Cervantes's novel and Quixote's tales. These networked fan carnivals, like medieval carnivals and the carnivalesque literature studied by Bakhtin, revel in all permutations of bodily desire and all possible accents of speech. They open up the metaphorical archives constituted by source texts and the actual archives located on Dreamwidth and the AO3 and the Audiofic Archive, and they urge fans to add their stories of piss and blood and fecal matter, and their voices of diaspora and transnationalism and regionalism and immigration, to those archives. The stories produced for and through kink_bingo and Amplificathon not only enlarge archives quantitatively, they also transform them qualitatively, demonstrating that the archives can hold more than anyone thought them capable of, stretching the capacity of the archives beyond all conventional limits of appropriateness and normality.

"The body of grotesque realism was hideous and formless. It did not fit the framework of the 'aesthetics of the beautiful' as conceived by the Renaissance," writes Bakhtin ([1965] 1984, 29). The fanworks challenges that I have described all refute dominant "aesthetics," as established and reified by mass media. Aesthetics that privilege the white body, that shun "deviant" forms of pleasure and connection, and that designate a small spectrum of American and British accents to be the "norm" in spoken English—all come under attack by the proliferation of stories generated by those who accept the challenges set forth by dark_agenda, kink_bingo, and Amplificathon. Bakhtin states that carnival has political ramifications, in that "its joy at change and its joyful relativity, is opposed to that one-sided and gloomy official seriousness which is dogmatic and hostile to evolution and change, which seeks to absolutize a given condition of existence or a given social order" (Bakhtin [1963] 1993, 160). Carnival reminds its participants that the future is open, that existing social structures and divides are more fluid, and more subject to transformation, than they appear. The carnival of Internet fan production events urges media consumers to realize the transmutability of mass media's representational logics, and to take the initiative themselves to invert and broaden the culture industries' definitions of "acceptable," "beautiful," or "legible" bodies, voices, and physical acts.

Elliot interprets Bakhtin's emphasis on the physicality of the carnivalesque—Bakhtin's fascination with the constant openness of mouths and other bodily orifices in carnival literature—as indicative of Bakhtin's belief in the "constant possibility" of change. Elliot writes that "nothing is fixed in Bakhtin's carnival world, and everything is in a state of becoming. ... By paying close attention to the relationships between objects (mouths, anuses, food, excrement), Bakhtin reveals a hidden network of values. The image of becoming expresses hope for the future, which Bakhtin contrasts to the 'official' preoccupation with the past that renders life pre-determined and unchangeable. ... [Bakhtin] understands interest in the open orifices of the human body as an artistic way of shaping the future by passing the material of the world through them" (Elliot 1999, 130). Elliot gives us yet another way to understand archontic production: as a digestion of the past, as an embodied transformation of received matter into new substance, as a way of opening oneself to archival material and feeding on it, then using that nourishment to project a future that little resembles the raw input. Rather than carnival time being marked by its being a temporary but short-lived exception from "regular" time, we can see carnival time as a critical time when change occurs, or becomes imaginable. A carnival may be brief in duration—even in carnival literature, the experience of reading *Quixote* or a Dostoevsky novel, or a kink_bingo story, or a chromatic challenge story, or any carnivalesque piece will not last very long—but it can infuse its participants with a conviction that the prevailing social and cultural order and structure need not always prevail.

Fictions for Real Change

But by what mechanisms will the writing of fictional stories, and the building of fan archives, lead to radical social and cultural change? Scholars on "fan activism" have demonstrated that media texts serve as powerful shared archives of symbols, narratives, slogans, and characters that millions of citizens have used in demonstrations and other public actions. In a special issue of *Transformative Works and Cultures* on "Transformative Works and Fan Activism" (vol. 10), Henry Jenkins (2012) writes about the Harry Potter Alliance's numerous campaigns for human rights, marriage equality, labor rights, net neutrality, and other liberal causes; Jonathan Gray (2012) describes protestors of the Wisconsin union-busting Budget Repair Bill in 2011 using iconography and narratives from *Star Wars*, *South Park*, and *The Simpsons* in their clothing and signage; and Melissa M. Brough and Sangita Shresthova (2012) analyze the decision of Palestinian West Bank activists, in December 2010, to cosplay (costume-play) as the blue Nav'i from James Cameron's film *Avatar*, identifying their cause with that of the fictional Nav'i, who are forcibly evicted from their land by invaders in the movie, in order to draw mass media attention to their grievances.

As Rebecca Schneider documents, numerous Occupy Wall Street (OWS) participants and supporters wore costumes based on mass media archives, including the Wachowski Siblings' *V for Vendetta* (many who took part in OWS wore Guy Fawkes masks, with their "white-face grin," used by the protagonist of the film) and zombie texts such as George A. Romero's classic cult movie *Dawn of the Dead* and the popular comic and television series *The Walking Dead* ("In a 3 October 2011 protest action, OWS protesters representing the 99% bloodied themselves, munched on Monopoly money, and marched on Wall Street as zombies," writes Schneider [2012, 154]). Louisa Ellen Stein describes how, in the wake of the 9/11 attacks, members of an online community dedicated to the television series *Roswell* "drew on *Roswell* fan repertoires to manage disagreements and debates, to organize community actions and charity drives, to create memorial art images and to share their experiences and feelings" (Stein 2002, 473).

Clearly, participants in media fandoms often use their "fan repertoires" of communal discussion and collective action for real-world, political, and even revolutionary causes and goals. Stephen Duncombe (2012) argues that in fact, fandom is a necessary, or at least highly generative, groundwork from which activism springs: "Scratch an activist and you're apt to find a fan. It's no mystery why: fandom provides a space to explore fabricated worlds that operate according to different norms, laws, and structures than those we experience in our 'real' lives. Fandom also necessitates relationships with others: fellow fans with whom to share interests, develop institutions, and create a common culture. This ability to imagine alternatives and build community, not coincidentally, is a basic prerequisite for political activism" (sec. 1).

In her interview, Tari talks about fans' ability to collectively conceive of political and social change in language similar to Duncombe's. Commenting on the allegation that participation in fandom is mere escapism, she says: "[Fandom] is escaping [reality], but I think there's a lot of benefit in fantasizing and dreaming of things that are not necessarily realistic, you know?" (Tari 2012). Fans, having cultivated the skill of immersing themselves in, and expanding, unreal worlds, can create elaborate fantasies of utopian ways of being, and to construct activist performances, demonstrations, and campaigns that try to bring the real world closer to those utopias.

Change Within

Another means by which fans' politically oriented stories can affect or influence lived reality is through the internal changes that such stories might effect in fans themselves. We might think of the carnivalesque challenges run by dark_agenda, kink_bingo, and Amplificathon as "tactical media," defined by Rita Raley (2009) in her book of that name. Under the umbrella term "tactical media," Raley discusses leftist Internet-based appropriations, takeovers, and interventions by digital artists and political hackers. She writes, "'Tactical media' is a mutable category that is not meant to be fixed or exclusive. ... In its most expansive articulation, tactical media signifies the intervention and disruption of a dominant semiotic regime, the temporary creation of a situation in which signs, messages, and narratives are set into play and critical thinking becomes possible. Tactical media operates in the field of the symbolic, the site of power in the postindustrial society" (Raley 2009, 6). While leftist (or antineoliberal) video games, network maps, and "hacktivist" actions constitute the bulk of Raley's examples of tactical media, I regard political fan fiction as belonging to this category of cultural production. Like Raley's chosen objects, politically charged fanfic "operates in the field of the symbolic," "signifies the intervention and disruption of a dominant semiotic regime," and constitutes a "parasitic media response" (9)—that is, "the substitution of one message for another, the imposition of an alternative set of signs in the place of the dominant" (6). But in one respect especially, political fic works as tactical media does: the change it is most likely to manifest is in the minds and hearts of its audience.

Raley states that tactical media "engage in a micropolitics of disruption, intervention, and education" (2009, 1). It is the possibility of *education* that I wish to stress—by this, Raley means the education of those who view, consume, play, or participate in, tactical media. Raley writes that she prefers to think of tactical media pieces as "performances" rather than as "objects" specifically because the rubric of performance contains (in Raley's view) an implicit acknowledgment that the point of the work is how its audience perceives it. She writes,

To articulate tactical media in terms of performance rather than as static art object emphasizes viewer experience and engagement. ... To conceive of tactical media in terms of performance is to point to a fluidity of its actants, to emphasize its ephemerality, and to shift the weight of emphasis slightly to the audience, which does not simply complete the signifying field of the work but records a memory of the performance. ... Tactical media is performance for which a consumable product is not the primary endgame; it foregrounds the experiential over the physical. ... As the action comes to an end, what is left is primarily living memory. (12–13)

These statements allow me to perceive a direct alignment between Raley's idea of tactical media and Aleida Assmann's concept of "working memory," which is synonymous with cultural repertoire, as I discussed in break 1. I asserted that there is little reason to try to define a contemporary cultural canon, or repertoire—after the onset of postmodernism and the "canon wars" over university curricula, there is no body of works that presumably everyone in a given culture knows, and collectively rereads or reperforms. Rather, each of us, individually, now forms our own canons, curates our own repertoires, and decides what will enter our working memory, or what Raley calls our "living memory." It is the private individual's canon/repertoire/working memory/living memory that tactical media can change. The greatest "victories" that tactical media can achieve, Raley posits, are not "any systemic change" (2009, 9), but rather consist in revolutionary transformation that takes place at the level of the "micropolitical," that is, within the personal perspectives of the people who engage with tactical media projects.

In foregrounding nonwhite and non-Western characters and making them the heroes and protagonists of familiar narratives, drawing attention to nonnormative sexual practices, and encouraging the multiaccented voices of fans to be recorded and heard, dark_agenda, kink_bingo, and Amplificathon try to disrupt the individual fan reader's private belief systems, which are likely heavily shaped by the racial/sexual/national/regional hierarchies of mass media representation. Reading these fanworks challenges through Raley's lens, we should measure dark_agenda's success not by whether the group ever influences Hollywood studios and networks to be more inclusive in their casting and writing practices (although, as fan-organized boycotts of *The Last Airbender* show, fan activism can garner public attention and influence the culture industries' revenues), but by whether dark_agenda raises individual fans' awareness of the systemic racism of media representations, and inspires them to become critical of, and opposed to, the ideology of white privilege that informs most mass-marketed narratives.

Raley thinks that tactical media consumption can turn their audiences into tactical media makers/producers/coders/hackers, and that this multiplied resistance to networked power structures can, and must, occur primarily in the network. dark_agenda, kink_bingo, and Amplificathon also have this goal: to turn fan consumers into fan producers, to encourage fans who read stories about chromatic characters or who listen to an accented person's podcast to then write about chromatic characters and record their own podcasts, in their unique voices. However fleeting, momentary, and ephemeral (like performances) such resistances may be, they may also, Raley hopes, amount to something like constant, distributed, networked critique, which may be the most effective way to disturb, and pose an ongoing challenge to, networked power. Raley writes, "If we have only a 'plurality of resistances,' a 'being-against,' always and everywhere (with echoes of Trotsky's Permanent Revolution and Snowball's continual rebellions difficult to overlook), then in fact the teleology of revolutionary organization is itself disrupted. Instead of a single, spectacular disruption, we have a 'multiplicity of discontinuous sites of enunciation'" (2009, 25; citing Arditi 2007, 104).

But some fans feel that even if the majority of effects engendered by fanworks challenges transpire in the minds and memories of individual readers, just that change in people's private worldviews is a change in the world. jinjurly states, "I think that reading and reacting to things, or even just reading silently and never talking to anybody about them, that's a role, and that's a really important role, and I think that enjoying fanworks, and …—'consuming' them—is a fanwork in itself. I think that you're doing work inside your head if you're pulling together ideas, you're synthesizing stuff. That's work, … and it is changing the way that you're reacting to the world, the way that you're interacting" (jinjurly 2012). The most important network effects of politically oriented fan writing events may manifest in the form of one-to-one interpersonal exchanges, in the ways that people think and speak about race, ethnicity, sexuality, and nationality in their day-to-day lives, and in the actions that people take as private citizens— even in the seemingly simple decisions that they make about whether or not to buy a ticket to a certain film, or to add to the audience of a television program; that is, whether or not to be a fan of a given product. If the "personal is political," as the New Left espoused (Duncombe 2003, 237), then the alteration of people's personal fannish perspectives, commitments, and investments may have a political result. The "cumulative effect" of fans' "parasitic media responses," Raley states (2009, 9), "may not be immediately perceptible" or discernible as revolutionary at all, but may nevertheless constitute a "cultural critique … invested with a transformative power … in which one must place a certain belief" (14).

"RaceFail '09" and Social Justice Fandom

In fact, fans seeking to change the minds of fans, especially fans' views and opinions of race, ethnicity, sexuality, and nationality, has been a major movement within Internet fandom since at least 2009, when an event widely referred as "RaceFail" took place, initially on the blogging network LiveJournal and then spiraling out to many other platforms that hosted fan discussion and publication. RaceFail '09 began with a post by professional science fiction/fantasy author Elizabeth Bear (2009) on her LiveJournal (LJ) entitled "whatever you're doing, you're probably wrong," in which she gave advice to fiction authors about "writing The Other"—meaning, characters of a different ethnic, gender, national, or cultural identity than the author's own—"without being a dick." The post was widely linked to and quoted on other people's LJs, and some of the responses to Bear's piece also attracted a great deal of attention and popularity. These included posts by people of color and people originating from the Global South who pointed out the prevalent biases in sci-fi/fantasy representations of "the Other," including in Bear's own books. Numerous professional authors, as well as readers and viewers—fans—of sci-fi/fantasy texts then began engaging in debates over racism and other prejudices in both mass-marketed works and in fan works, these debates occurring through hundreds, if not thousands, of online posts addressing how people of color, and difference in general, are depicted in popular media, and how fans of color often feel silenced and marginalized by these portrayals, as well as by fannish discourses and practices that reproduce many of mass media's biases and hierarchies.[7]

From 2009 onward, many Internet fans, fan discussions, fan productions, and fan organizations have committed themselves to a broad movement that many call "social justice fandom." Social justice fandom does not have an obvious set of leaders and does not take place on a specific set of websites. We might think of it in the terms that Manuel Castells uses to describe recent political movements in which social media has played a large role, such as the Egyptian revolution, the "Arab Spring," and Occupy Wall Street. Castells (2012) calls these "leaderless movements" (224), and states, "Because they are a network of networks, [they] can afford not to have an identifiable centre, and yet ensure coordination functions, as well as deliberation, by interaction between multiple nodes" (221). Some of the "nodes" that make up social justice fandom include fans who post critical reflections on how they process the racism, sexism, and jingoism inherent in so many texts of which they are fans;[8] fans who document and comment on the resistance to discussions of difference, and to the points of view expressed by people of color, that they witness in Internet fandom;[9] and fanworks exchanges and challenges that explicitly strive to increase fandom's inclusivity and diversity, such as kink_bingo, Amplificathon, and the chromatic events organized by dark_agenda. Of course, each of these actions is not entire leaderless—Christian Fuchs prefers the term "soft leaders" (Fuchs 2012b, 783)—but the authors and coordinators of these online posts and events are not setting any long-range plans or objectives for social justice fandom to accomplish as a whole; rather, they are "moving and networking, keeping the energy flowing," in Castells's (2012, 144) words. That is, their actions sustain fans' constant critique of prejudice in mass media and in fan discussions, and disseminate to a broad spectrum of fans the feeling that such critique is worthwhile and significant.

Many fans who participated in our oral history project consider political fanworks challenges to be part of social justice fandom. Alexis Lothian speaks of kink_bingo as

a kind of formation that comes from pan-fandom social justice ... but [is] also really very much about pleasure, you know. So kink_bingo ... is all about, like, writing fic about weird sex, ... out-of-the-ordinary sex, nonvanilla sex. ... But the whole framework and the way that it's organized is about—it is explicitly political in the broadest sense, you know. It says, well, you've gotta understand, ... your kink is—one kink is not better than another, ... but at the same time, like, we really don't want to see stories that are using kink in a really oppressive and horrible way. ... A lot of the discussion on the community is about ... how kink intersects with social justice and with people's personal politics, or people's personal experiences. So for example there's a lot of stuff about disability, ... and then, you know, there's a kind of implicit thing which is that a lot of disability kink is very dehumanizing to people who actually have disabilities, but how do you engage the intersection of kink and disability in a way that's actually both sexy and respectful. (Lothian 2012b)

Tari, who is one of the organizers of Kaleidoscope, a dark_agenda challenge, recalls that she was inspired to volunteer for the Chromatic Yuletides, and to help plan Kaleidoscope, after RaceFail. She says that before RaceFail, public discussions of race were often disturbing to her, as a person of color:

People would ... say really problematic things, like, "Oh but black people are racist against white people, too." And, "Why are they so sensitive?" and blah, blah, blah. And I'd listen to all of this and I wouldn't speak out, you know? I'd just keep my mouth shut and felt really uncomfortable. And then RaceFail happened. And ... when I got wind of it and I started following these links, I saw people describe exactly the sort of language that I'd been hearing offline and explaining why that was not right. And I was just like, "Oh, *that's* what I was looking for. That articulates all these—why that [kind of discourse] made me feel uncomfortable." You know, I'd be like, "Oh it's not really racism because no one's threatening to kill me or beat me up or something." But why this counted as violent speech, and why this was harmful—all of those articulations were *really* helpful to me. And then RaceFail entered this point where it started getting really racist, and [there were people] saying some really, *really* horrible things, ... comparing people of color to animals and things like that. ... But ... there was this real mobilization of fans of color to support each other and be support networks for each other. ... And I think that was what got me interested in these fandom challenges that do have a social justice theme. Because for me, it's—*that's* what it's about—it's about that decolonization process. In actively trying to encourage and also to consume fannish works that are about people like me that have positive messages about people like me. (Tari 2012)

Tari subscribes more to Raley's theory that tactical media's greatest impact and legacy are to be found in the "living memory" of its audiences and participants than to a Castellian idea that online fan activism will one day spark revolutionary action. She states, "I don't even really think of [Kaleidoscope] as 'advancing the cause of social justice in the world at large'—that's not how I think of it. I think of it as like this personal project of dismantling those thought cycles and internalized stereotypes and harmful messages that you've gotten from your socialization growing up. That's what I see it as. And I think telling stories about female characters, characters of color, ... LGBT characters. All of these are basically serving that function, to rewrite those messages that you've internalized" (Tari 2012).

Fans we interviewed averred that RaceFail and the subsequent rise of social justice fandom have, indeed, altered their perspectives, actions, and speech on issues of difference and diversity in cultural texts. For example, Starlady, who identifies as white American, recounts that RaceFail "changed my understanding of science fiction and ... catalyzed my becoming more knowledgeable about social justice issues. ... I was like, 'Well okay, there's these people on this one side who are claiming that there's no problem [with depictions of nonwhite characters] here,' and I'm like, 'That's clearly not true, so I'm going to identify with the other side. Count me in with them! There's a line, and I want to be on that side of it!'" (Starlady 2012). Starlady began tracking the books she reads in a spreadsheet, and taking note of how many characters in those books, and authors of those books, are people of color. "I have definitely made an effort to read more books by women and by nonwhite authors. ... And I can post about [these books] and alert people that, 'Hey, this cool thing exists.' I've also become much more conscious about issues of race and representation in fanfic and [in other fiction] writing" (Starlady 2012).

Lothian has noticed that professional sci-fi/fantasy writers, particularly those who attend WisCon (a feminist sci-fi convention held annually in Madison, Wisconsin), in the wake of debates around representations of nonwhite, non-Western characters and cultures in fiction, are "either stepping back from" discussing how they are depicting "the Other" in their writing, "or really stepping into it and saying, 'Well, okay. This is what I'm writing; I want to think about the implications of what I'm writing,' and seeking, for example, beta readers [who volunteer to read and edit fics before they are published], who will hopefully, you know, help them [writers] to understand when something, if something is problematic." eruthros and thingswithwings feel that, with kink_bingo, they have accomplished a greater acceptance and acknowledgment of diverse kinks in fandom generally. Says thingswithwings, "What we see in fandom now as opposed to even five years ago or ten years ago is kinky fic being integrated … into fandom space where one of the first things people do with a new fandom now is find the kink meme. … The point of kink_bingo is to challenge people to engage with things that they don't think about very much, or maybe they even have a squick for, and there's obviously a big difference between a squick and a trigger. … We want to make as much space as we can for people with triggers while also … providing this challenge and helping people to move themselves out of their comfort zones when they want to" (eruthros and thingswithwings 2012). eruthros adds, "And also safer spaces for people whose kinks these are" (eruthros and thingswithwings 2012).

Though social justice fandom discussions and fanworks challenges have influenced many fans and professional authors to work at what Tari calls "decolonization" and the "dismantling [of] thought cycles," they have also attracted a great deal of criticism and backlash. Several of our oral history participants said that they see a kind of bandwagon or "dog-piling" effect happening in many social justice discussions, with people tending to hurl insults at fellow fans for being racist or otherwise prejudiced in ways that seem to do more harm (by "bullying" the offender) than good (by, for example, educating the offender about their missteps). What is generally called "call-out culture" on the Internet is described by some as "the act of drawing attention to problematic behavior," which can "involve discussion and forgiveness" (Uprichard 2013), but is dismissed by others as "toxic" and "a tool to legitimate aggression and rhetoric[al] violence" (Dzodan 2011). One of our interviewees, Arduinna, describes how many fans deride what they perceive to be social justice fandom's call-out culture: "They [people who are critical of social justice fandom online] call the dog-pile-y people 'social justice warriors,' SJW, as people who aren't really—who are less interested in real social justice [than] in waving the flag of social justice. As people who just want to talk the talk and look really good and get points for being attack-y and dog-pile-y: 'Oh, I dump on everybody, therefore I'm awesome'" (Arduinna 2012).

Tari talks about how some of the critics of Kaleidoscope, and of dark_ agenda generally, seemed to perceive the chromatic challenges as somehow "calling out" white fans for not being sufficiently concerned with social justice: "A lot of the criticism that is raised about dark_agenda is that it makes people feel guilty for not participating in it. … I think people miss out on [the point of the challenges] because I think they interpret it as being, 'Oh, this is for white people writing about people of color.' No, I mean, if that happens, that's great, but that's not the point. If you don't participate in the challenge, I don't care. I don't judge your social justice cred or whatever. I—the point of the challenge is for people who want to write about characters that look like themselves. And to find fic for characters that look like themselves" (Tari 2012).

The fact that some fans strongly oppose or mock social justice fans while others eagerly identify with it makes me optimistic that, at the least, issues of inclusion and difference, and how fans should or should not handle them, are being openly debated on fan sites—as long as these debates continue, questions about race/ethnicity, disability, nonnormative sexualities, and nationality are not being ignored, sidelined, or repressed in fandom. In my view, the disagreements and attacks, misreadings and misunderstandings, that have arisen around the theme of social justice in fandom show that both internal, highly personal political work (in individual fans' "living memory," as Raley [2009] would say) and external, highly communal political work (in fan networks, as Castells might say) are currently taking place in Internet fandom. The online carnivalesque events that fans stage, in the form of fanworks challenges, are generating change, not only by filling fan archives with diverse content, but by transforming how fans, privately and collectively, think and talk about diversity.

Break 4   "Works" or "Performances"?

What Counts as a "Work"?

This break will explore, and question, the prioritization of "works" over "performances," and of the logics of "archive" over "repertoire," in Internet fan cultures.

In *Dissonant Identities*, Barry Shank writes on the circle of fandom and performance that endlessly loops in music scenes: "Spectators become fans, fans become musicians, musicians are always already fans, all constructing the nonobjects of identification through their performances" (1994, 131). Such a scene is thus "an overproductive signifying community; that is, far more semiotic information is produced than can be rationally parsed" (122). Applying this framework to Internet fan archives, we can see that not everything, not every performance, produced by the "signifying communities" of online fandoms, can be archived; there is simply too much production to effectively save. The vast majority of online fan archives were designed to save *fan works*, not *fan performances*—that is, the archives assumed a clear distinction between the online output of fans considered "works" rather than "performances," and have preserved works rather than performances. Fan fiction stories, fan art, and fanvids have always counted as "works." But what of fan dialogues and discussions? Reviews and comments? What about fan theories and encyclopedias? Episode reviews and clips? Links to interviews with actors, directors, writers, and producers? What about pic-spams and icons?[1] What about "meta"?[2] What separates fan productions deemed "archive worthy" from those that are not?

From Usenet to Databases to Social Media

The history of the technological infrastructure that has supported fan archives shows that how fandom has regarded works versus performances has evolved over time. When I first read the discussions on early (1990s) online fan fiction communities, such as Usenet newsgroups, I noticed many posts asking for a complete list of the fan fiction stories that had been previously posted to the group. Such lists would presumably help fans know whether or not they had missed any stories, and might help them locate the posts corresponding to those stories they had not yet read. The emergence of fan fiction archives to exclusively house stories seems related to fans' demand for stories to be separated from other kinds of posts, to be easily located, and to be preserved over time so that fans joining a newsgroup months or years after its founding could still access all of the stories that the group's members had produced. Many digital archives attempt to separate "signal" from "noise," but first, archivists must decide what is signal and what is noise; for early fan archivists, it was apparently a simple distinction made along the lines of "story" versus "nonstory."

But with the evolution of Internet technologies and the incredible growth of online fandom between the year 2000 and the present, distinctions between "fan works" and "fan performances," between "stories to be archived" and "nonstories to be excluded from archives" have become less rigid. 1990s fan archives were mostly custom-built single-fandom databases and individual fans' websites containing links to recommended stories, both of which aimed to save fan fiction stories and to make these stories accessible to later readers. But the rise of social media in the early 2000s, including blogging platforms such as LiveJournal and Dreamwidth, and microblogging platforms such as Tumblr and Twitter, led to archiving formats that combined stories and nonstories (commentaries, debates, reviews, and so on), that mixed fannish and nonfannish content, and that facilitated interactivity and collaborative performance between authors and readers (for example, readers can request that specific plotlines be written, and writers can volunteer to "fill" particular requests). Readers on these sites are not merely visitors to an already fixed archive of stories, whose responses to finished works have no bearing on the works themselves; rather, readers' prompts and comments are integral to the creation of fan works, and readers and writers perceive themselves to be coperformers in what Ernst (2013, 82) would call a "dynarchive," an archival scene that is dynamic and evolving rather than static.

"Digital Performances" and "Stone Soup"

Internet fan fiction has almost always been produced in the context of lively fan communities. Although fan writers can certainly contribute new stories to the archives of "dead" fandoms (inactive fandoms, in which no discussions are taking place and no new stories are being posted), it is far more often the case that fan writers feel inspired to write fresh works by an active fandom's multiplicity of shared performances, ranging from debates over the source text's meanings to screenshots to vids to fanmixes.[3] The broad spectrum of fan performances, in other words, feeds fan works, and under the definition of Internet performance suggested by the "global theater" school of theorists, fan works are themselves a part of the fan performance spectrum. So, hard distinctions drawn between fan works and fan performances have always been dubious: many fan fiction stories can only be comprehended by readers who are familiar with other fan performances that circulated at the time that the stories were conceived and written.

Fan scholar Alexis Lothian, who applies the term "performance" to online communications in a way that aligns her with the "global theater" school, points out that when fan works are archived separately from the discussions and other fan performances that give rise to them, important "affective elements" are lost. Lothian writes, "Residues of *digital performances* might include blog comments, IM messages, and the cached versions of postings taken down by their producers or rights holders. ... [A fan] archive framed as deposit library cannot account for the traces, glimmers, and residues that give subcultural art its meanings and its feelings. Fictions may be the traces of lived experience, but, when deposited in the archive, they will be framed as art—the 'thing itself'—with the politics and urgencies of the *performance* it once embodied slipping out of memory" (Lothian 2012a, 11; emphasis added). Social media–based fan archives may acknowledge the interplay between readers and writers and make more visible the performances that inspire and inform fan fiction, but databases that separate out fiction from other types of fan performances are the largest and most heavily trafficked types of Internet fan archives today. As a result, large segments of the activities of fan communities—the "fast-flowing" performances that are, by convention, not framed as art—are "constantly vanishing" and "incompletely archived" (Lothian 2012a, 10–11).

Social media fan sites and fan databases are not always enemies. Increasingly, fan communities are using social media platforms in tandem with fan databases, encouraging members to collaboratively perform on the social platforms, then cross-posting or porting all resulting fan works to a database for long-term preservation (fan fiction authors, for example, often use Tumblr and AO3 as complementary sites, using the first for "marketing" their stories, and the second for publishing and archiving them). I do not argue that fan archives should merge database functions and social media functions. Fan databases that resemble older cultural institutions such as libraries for print publications and museums for plastic arts—which distinguish between works and social performances, and preserve the former but not the latter—serve fandoms in crucial ways that no other format does, and are highly valued by fans. What I wish to suggest, following Lothian, is that databases' design and features mask the extent to which fan works always depend on fan performances, always emerge from and respond to a broad range of fan performances, and are, in and of themselves, only one of many kinds of fan performances. In other words, archival systems, such as fan fiction databases, cover over the important fact that performance undergirds the creation of works, that works are constituted in and as performance, and that even the category of "work" itself, as wholly separate from performance, is something of a fiction.

It would be interesting to speculate about a future fan archive structure that could preserve a fan community's totality of performances and not only fan works, that could serve as an archival record (with tags, indexes by date and author, keyword search, and other navigation and retrieval features) of commentaries, interpretations, reviews, flame wars, and requests, as well as fan fiction stories. Such an archive might allow a fuller, richer grasp of the meanings of individual fan fiction works, as readers would ideally be able to recover more of the communal activity that spurred a given author to write a particular story.

Such an archive might even pose a challenge to traditional definitions of authorship. Legal scholar Rebecca Tushnet (2013) argues that copyright law defines "authorship" quite narrowly, even though many cultural productions today are constructed collaboratively. Tushnet states that contemporary creative works "often resemble the soup in the fable of 'Stone Soup,' in which a sharp operator convinces a village that he can make soup out of stones—as long as each of the villagers contributes a little bit of meat, vegetables, spices, etc. The resulting dish is delicious, and the stones are a but-for cause of the soup" (1019). Copyright law's restricted definition of authorship is a bit like "say[ing] that the stranger with the stones is the true owner and proprietor of the soup" (1019), Tushnet argues.

Applying the stone soup analogy to fan fiction, we might think of the appropriated source text elements as just one category of ingredients that goes into the "soup" (the fanfic story), with additional ingredients consisting of fans' speculations, wishes, interpretations, videos, fanmixes, icons, GIFs, and art—a fan writer might derive inspiration and ideas from all of these for a new story, just as any author or artist is influenced by the culture and society in which she or he is immersed. A fan archive that defined its objects as the complete range of an performances taking place within a given fandom might make possible a far wider conception of authorship or "makership" of fan works, in which the "sources" from which a fan author archontically selects for incorporation into a fan fiction story include not only mainstream media texts but also fan performances. All fan works might be said to then be communally authored, although there would always be individuals identifiable and nameable as the writers/assemblers/documentors/distillers/archontic producers of fan stories, just as there is always an identifiable director and writer of a collaboratively made film, and an identifiable producer and singer of a collaboratively made musical recording. A fan archive that stores an expansive array of a fandom's performances, rather than only its works, would not do away with the category of the fan author, but might usefully complicate and broaden current understandings of how, and by whom, cultural works are created.

But any attempt to actually archive even one subcultural scene in its entirety would likely end in failure, if only because, as Shank says, "more semiotic information is produced" in a fandom "than can be rationally parsed." The privileging of "works" over "performance" will continue to be a useful fiction for the foreseeable future in digital cultural memory, even as more and more participants on global networks recognize that performance is the stuff that digital culture is made of.

5 Print Fans versus Net Fans: Women's Cultural Memory at the Threshold of New Media

Women's Anxiety about Digital Archives

Let us visit a scene of fan cultural memory at a moment before digital archives, or rather, at the moment when fandom's cultural memory transitioned from print media and face-to-face interaction to digital networks. Between approximately 1989 and 1998, as the Internet became an increasingly popular locus for fan activity, fans began to wonder if their history and culture would survive their mass migration to digital networks. This question was directly linked to the gender of fandom: women fans experienced discrimination and harassment in their early forays into online communities, and in the print-to-digital period, there was a strong public discourse, or "cultural imaginary," that identified women as the repositories (living archives) and conveyers (enactors of repertoires) of humanness, who would preserve the essence of humanity against the encroaching wave of cyborgism and computing culture. This chapter documents female fan communities' initial resistance to, and mistrust of, the prospect of relocating to virtual online space. In the late 1980s and most of the 1990s, women fans expressed strong feelings about the imminent digitization of their entire culture.

I wish to record this moment of women's anxiety about digital archives in part because, without it, the history of digital archiving would appear extraordinarily masculine, as the founders of the most prominent universal archives, such as Project Gutenberg, SunSITE/ibiblio, the Internet Archive, the Rosetta Project, Open Library, and Archive Team, are men, and many cooperate with one another or have a history of working together. ibiblio used database searching software WAIS, developed in part by Brewster Kahle, when it opened, and today ibiblio hosts Project Gutenberg. Kahle, founder of the Internet Archive, is involved with the Long Now Foundation, which directs the Rosetta Project (it was Kahle who initially suggested the "hard copy" format of the Rosetta Project's collection of human languages, a three-inch nickel disk with an estimated 2,000-year lifespan [Kelly 2008]), and the Internet Archive hosts the Rosetta Project Archive as a special collection. Aaron Swartz, architect of Open Library, worked at the Internet Archive, and Kahle convened a memorial for Swartz at the Internet Archive after Swartz's death (Kahle 2013). Jason Scott, founder of Archive Team, is the software curator at the Internet Archive (Scott 2013). (It is thus Kahle who serves as the primary connector for this "boys' network" of archivists.) This group could easily be written up as the heroes of the rogue memory movement, and such a narrative would feature their heroic declarations regarding the promise of digital archiving, such as Kahle's statement: "This is our chance to one-up the Greeks! It is really possible with the technology of today, not tomorrow. We can provide all the works of humankind to all the people of the world. It will be an achievement remembered for all time, like putting a man on the moon" (Kelly 2006).

While Kahle's network deserves credit and praise for launching and growing their important archival initiatives, a history of digital archives that focused exclusively on them would ignore what it meant for women's communities to enter into digital archiving. In a history of Internet archiving primarily centered on women's cultures, fan communities become the clear object of interest: 1980s and 1990s media fandoms were populated by women who were early adopters of digital networks—as well as women who resisted the move to new technological platforms, and so many battles that constituted the print-to-digital transition played out in those communities. The print-to-digital transition, as regards cultural memory, must be understood as a repertoire-to-archive transition for female fans, as what was at stake for them in this period was, as we shall see, the potential loss of their individual bodies and the loss of their collective body and embodied memory to new media.

Women fans did not begin digital archiving from a position of Enlightenment triumphalism, touting the possibilities of new technologies to make tremendous advances in preserving the great project of human knowledge, as Kahle and other male programmers did (though, as I discussed in chapter 2, Kahle and others also immediately recognized digital content's proclivity for disappearance and loss). Instead, the entry of women's fan communities into the digital age was fraught with internal debates and doubts about new media's ability to capture, and sustain, their collective culture and memory.

"Half-digital, half-not"

Between 1989 and 1998, fandom as it was practiced prior to the advent of the Internet came into contact, and often clashed with, fandom as it began to form online. Media fandom, the branch of popular-culture-based fandom that began in the mid-1960s with the first airing of NBC's *Star Trek* (and quickly expanded to include other television and film properties), consisted for several decades of conventions, face-to-face meetings, telephone chats, and the in-person or postal-based trade or purchase of "zines," which were printed publications containing fan works. From 1966 to 1989, fan fiction circulated primarily in zines that were curated and collated by fan editors, and sold at prices that were intended to cover the editors' costs. The practice of making and selling printed fan fiction zines did not end in 1989, but starting around that time, fans increasingly published their own fan fiction on Internet sites.

It is too simplistic to state that there were two "camps" in media fandom through the 1990s, but two terms, referring to different mentalities or practices—two ways of "doing" fandom—were repeatedly utilized in this period: "print fans" and "Net fans." An individual could be both a print fan and a Net fan; if she joined fandom in the '60s, '70s, or early '80s, participated in cons and bought zines, but then began accessing the Internet in the late '80s or early '90s and became equally "fluent" in online fan practices as she was in offline practices, then she was both a print fan and a Net fan. But while many fans were interested in having and using both offline and online literacies of fannish production and engagement, many other fans were literate in either print or Net fandom, and resisted or disdained the other mode. Although the two groups were not only or always opposed to one another, tensions between the two cultures of fandom— "print fandom" and "Net fandom"—ran high throughout the first decade of widespread Internet usage. What was at stake in fan debates during this period was the question of which set of fannish practices would be primary, and which would be secondary.

Henry and Cynthia Jenkins (HJ and CJ) gave a joint interview for our Fan Fiction and Internet Memory oral history project, and shared their memories of the print fandom versus Net fandom era. Henry and Cynthia were highly active in fandom before the Internet: they both contributed to APAs;[1] Cynthia participated in the famous *Professionals* Circuit;[2] and they regularly met face to face with other fans in small and large gatherings, ranging from get-togethers with a few fans in someone's home to large sci-fi conventions. Then, in 1989, when Henry got Internet access through the university where he worked, he began "staying after work an extra hour or two" and reading fan discussions that were taking place online (Jenkins and Jenkins 2012). That same year, he connected with a local fan group dedicated to the CBS television fantasy series *Beauty and the Beast*, and began attending their monthly meetings as part of his research for his landmark fan studies book *Textual Poachers*. He was "the only guy who went to those meetings, between it [the *Beauty and the Beast* fandom] being fan-fiction driven and a fandom noted for being overwhelmingly female" (Jenkins and Jenkins 2012). And at those meetings in 1989 and 1990, he recalls that some of the members were informing other members about online *Beauty and the Beast* fandom via printouts:

HJ: When I'd go to those meetings, there were two or three people there who were using the Internet at that point at work, and who were printing out … those discussions around *Beauty and the Beast* on long dot-matrix paper and bringing it in notebooks to the club meetings and passing them around. … Every month, people would bring in—they'd read highlights [out loud], people would sit around the whole meeting, and flip through, and read the discussions, and so forth. But it was moving from the digital back to the physical because most of those people didn't have access to networked computers. … There wasn't a lot of fiction online at that point, but they probably did print out some fiction. (Jenkins and Jenkins 2012)

This moment of in-person fan meetings being places and times where some fans learned about the Internet from other fans, and gained partial, belated, transmediated access to the network through their fellow fans' efforts, reminds Henry of "the stories you hear of factory workers who hire one person to read aloud to them while they're working. This was particularly [frequent in the case] of Lower East Side Jewish factory workers at the turn of the century, that they would pool their money to have someone at work who read [aloud to the other workers]. And one of them would have access to literacies the others benefited from. And this [1989–90] is that transitional moment where the half-digital, half-not phenomenon really comes in" (Jenkins and Jenkins 2012).

"Half-digital, half-not": Henry here is describing the relatively small body of *Beauty and the Beast* fans who held regular meetings, at which some who had Internet access passed around printouts of online fan activity to those who did not. But "half-digital, half-not" also describes the larger body of media fandom. I am using "body" here deliberately, to draw a parallel between the collective, social body of media fans in 1989–90, and a fictional body frequently found in science fiction "cyberpunk" novels, television series, and films that were in vogue at that time: the body of the cyborg. Both the body of fandom and the body of the cyborg in the '80s and '90s were sites of overlapping technologies: in the collective fan body, it was technologies of print and face-to-face interactions that intersected with network technologies; in the fictional cyborg body, it was advanced mechanical and digital technologies that fused with human flesh and blood. In other words, the "half-digital, half-not phenomenon" that Henry Jenkins describes arising at "that transitional moment" of the late 1980s and early 1990s, the cusp of the transition between print culture and digital culture, was not limited to the group of fellow *Beauty and the Beast* viewers in his university town, but was a phenomenon experienced viscerally by thousands of media fans across the United States, and experienced conceptually by millions of media consumers who read cyberpunk novels or watched cyberpunk television programs and films. Fandom as a whole was two halves at this historical moment. Partly print- and flesh-based, partly digital, and majority women, fandom was a female cyborg entity.

Bionic Women or the Borg?

Henry and Cynthia Jenkins recall that the *Beauty and the Beast* fan group welcomed the information about the digital sphere that their members circulated at their periodic meetings. Here is Henry and Cynthia's exchange about that group's attitudes:

HJ: The *Beauty and the Beast* women were [saying], "This is really cool. This is access to more information. Our community just expanded."

CJ: … People were not feeling threatened [by online conversations] and feeling like they were being cut out.

HJ: No, it [Internet fandom] was something exotic, and an extra.

CJ: And that was because the center of gravity was still face-to-face. And there was just peripheral added richness [from the Internet], as opposed to the center of gravity shifting away from the face-to-face and onto the digital.

(Jenkins and Jenkins 2012)

Other oral history participants also recall early online fandom as being harmonious with print-based and in-person fan practices, and as supplementary to those "real-world" practices rather than displacing them. Arduinna (2012) states that the online fan communities that she joined in 1994–95 facilitated zine exchanges and meet-ups at conventions. She recalls, "If someone had zines to sell, you would talk to them privately. I met a few people that way, where we just got chatting [online] about 'I want to borrow from your zines,' or 'Let's trade zines,' and we would wind up in these gigantic conversations for weeks or months just talking about the zines and whatever." Arduinna and five or six of her fellow fans on the *Forever Knight* mailing list often conversed in a private IRC (Internet Relay Chat) chatroom, and Arduinna says that those fans "came to visit me, we had a great—We would meet at the cons. We had a great time. It was some really good friends. And I'm still in touch with a couple of them" (Arduinna 2012).

Arduinna talks about fans using online sites to arrange for the exchange of videotapes as well as zines, and those exchanges serving to inaugurate friendships: "If you were willing to write to someone [online] and say, 'Do you have a tape of this episode?' Well that—Anything could be an opening to an actual conversation and a friendship. It could be something as simple as, 'I missed taping my show—the show last night. Does anyone have a tape they can send me?' So, lots of trading stuff back and forth. Lots of physical material went back and forth then" (Arduinna 2012). In Arduinna's telling, it seems that the back-and-forthing of physical material sometimes led to the back-and-forthing of physical bodies, as fans who "met" online agreed to meet in person at fan conventions and at one another's homes.

In this timeframe of 1989 to 1998, then, some fans looked to the Internet as a supplement to, or facilitator of, what could be called "in-person" fandom. As the Jenkinses say, the Internet was "exotic, and an extra" component of fandom, but "the center of gravity" of media fandom was still physical, manifesting in the form of in-person gatherings as well as in the trade of material artifacts such as zines and videotapes. Fans like those in the *Beauty and the Beast* group, and on the *Forever Knight* mailing list to which Arduinna subscribed, were cyborgs, but only just: they were humans first and foremost, who enjoyed Internet fandom because it aided, or added a new dimension to, their real-world exchanges and interactions. In their experiences, the body of fandom was a human body with digital prosthetics or extensions—a mostly human cyborg.

But other fans in this period felt differently about the Internet, perceiving the new media as threatening to their decades-old traditions of practicing fandom through embodied interactions and physical objects. To these print fans, the Internet was an alien entity that sought to incorporate all fans into its vast, immaterial streams, and they resisted total assimilation. I am borrowing the terms "resistance" and "assimilation" from a major villain featured in the series *Star Trek: The Next Generation*, *Star Trek: Deep Space Nine*, and *Star Trek: Voyager*: the hive-minded Borg, who attempt to forcefully assimilate all species that they encounter in their space travels into their biotechnological Collective. The Borg typically begin their assimilatory processes with an announcement to the species-to-be-incorporated that "Resistance is futile." I am inspired to invoke the Borg by my student Lisa Cronin's (LC) oral history interview with the fan archivist Morgan Dawn (MD) (2012). In the interview, Morgan Dawn remembers the fierce antipathy toward the Internet that many print fans expressed in the early 1990s:

MD: That interaction, that negative or "Oh my God. What's going on?" [attitude] only lasted for two or three years, before literally everybody was overrun by the Internet. So, it didn't really matter whether we liked it or not. [Laughing]

LC: Yeah, the Internet was kind of assimilating.

MD: Yes.

(Dawn 2012)

In this short dialogue, I think that Lisa and Morgan Dawn draw a clear parallel between the Borg and the Internet. Morgan Dawn describes print fans' attempting to fight incorporation into the network for a handful of years before this resistance proved futile, as "everybody was overrun by the Internet," regardless of print fans' wishes ("it didn't really matter whether we liked it or not"), and Lisa more directly frames that takeover as a Borgian assimilation (Dawn 2012).

In the universe of *Star Trek: The Next Generation*, *Star Trek: Deep Space Nine*, and *Star Trek: Voyager*, the complete text of the Borg's proclamation to a species informing it of impending assimilation is as follows: "We are the Borg. Lower your shields and surrender your ships. We will add your biological and technological distinctiveness to our own. Your culture will adapt to service us. Resistance is futile."[3] The Borg absorb all physical abilities and technical achievements of a particular species into their own unified complex, robbing those species of a distinct future for their culture. "Your culture will adapt to service us," the Borg declare, rather than the culture being allowed to remain independent and to develop on its own terms, in its own time, following the trajectories that it was already following before the encounter with the assimilating Borg hive. This horizon of cultural death—the possible assumption of the entirety of print fan culture into digital fan culture, or the imposition of a networked monoculture onto fandom that would obliterate all traces of the face-to-face and physical practices that preexisted the network—loomed large in many print fans' minds in the 1989–98 period and informed the tone of their responses to the Internet.

While some fans perceived themselves to be mostly human cyborgs, other fans feared that they, or all of fandom, were facing impending assimilation into the collective cyborg entity of the Internet. The *Star Trek* Borg are a very different sort of cyborg than, say, the Bionic Woman (the protagonist of a popular 1970s television series of the same name, starring Lindsay Wagner). The Bionic Woman is a human being who has machine parts surgically fused with her bones and muscles to make her far stronger, faster, and more perceptive than the average person; the Borg comprise a collective technological complex that requires all who enter its field of surveillance to wholly merge with it, such that their organic matter and creativity are instrumentalized to keep the Borg entity alive and growing. While *Beauty and the Beast* fans, and Arduinna and her fellow *Forever Knight* fans, saw the Internet as an enhancement technology, making them (as Net users) akin to the Bionic Woman, other fans feared that the Internet would operate like the Borg, as a master technology with extensive control over human operations, to which humans and all their output would be mere fuel.

The Failings of Net Fandom

Reading through fans' submissions to the letterzine *Comlink* in 1992 and 1993, one finds fans highlighting what they perceive to be three main failings of the Internet: it is elitist, it encourages bad writing and poor communication, and it is not an archival medium. The writers frame the elitism of the Internet as class based. They imply that only relatively wealthy fans will be able to afford computers, and thus Net fandom will exclude fans who are less well-off, whereas print fandom is not restricted to the upper classes. The writers attribute the low quality of Internet prose, in both fan fiction and discussion, to the speed with which networked communication takes place: "the immediacy" of the Internet "encourage[s] off-the-cuff writing," and conversations that take place over the course of a year in a zine last "only a week" online, encouraging people to post without first "consider[ing] the words that one leaves behind in a public arena." A separate issue from the poor use of written language is the speed with which people leap into heated arguments on the Internet. The writers attribute the frequency of online "flame wars" to Net fans not knowing one another personally; Net fans are therefore not able to decode one another's intentions (Fanlore, "Fandom and the Internet").

The fact that the Internet is not an archival medium (the "ephemerality" of Net fandom) is framed as a problem for newcomers in the *Comlink* comments: "It may be possible to download and save BBS discussions but apparently, it's rarely done, and few newcomers have access to what has gone before ... a sort of a background which gives people a sense of Group Identity" (Fanlore, "Fandom and the Internet"). This argument resonates with one I made in chapter 3, about the importance of new members of a fandom having access to that fandom's archives for their own enculturation, in order to gain a sense of belonging to the group. To some print fans, the absence of any reliable way to conserve online activity apparently promised a future for media fandom that had no past, or no way to access the past. Thus, Net fans would suffer from a lack of "Group Identity" and an "absence of tradition." Also, print's superiority to the Internet as a medium for textual preservation means that zine fan fiction is of a higher quality than online fic: "Fanzine writers have at least an eye on the possibility that people ten years in the future may be reading what they're writing now."

But for each of these arguments for the advantages of print fandom over Net fandom in the late 1980s and early 1990s, there were counterarguments. With regard to economic elitism, Jacqueline (2012) states in her interview that the Internet created a "level playing field [of] interaction" between fans, in part because it

made reading fanfic free. Back in the days when we could only get [fan fiction] in dead tree fandom ["dead tree fandom" being a tongue-in-cheek nickname for print fandom], you were talking about a $30-per-zine investment. And this is in the early '80s when $30 was probably a lot closer to the buying power of $60 now. And that meant either you were dealing crack on the side or all of your money was going into zines. And even if all of your money went into zines, and even if you were making a five-figure income, at some point you couldn't keep up. You couldn't read all the important stories in the fandom. You couldn't do the interaction with the people. Essentially, for your financial health and well-being, you had to pick a fandom. Or four. (Jacqueline 2012)

Computer equipment, from the 1980s through the present, has always required a significant financial investment and has never been affordable by all, but Jacqueline's comments show that class-based exclusions in media fandom did not begin with Net fandom, as print fandom also erected financial barriers to participation. What print fans' allegations of elitism covered over was a fear that the "center of gravity" (as Cynthia Jenkins put it) was shifting away from print fandom to Net fandom in these years. The tradition of fandom that had been founded in the 1960s was threatened with disappearance in the 1990s owing to the rise of new media.

In their oral history interview, Henry and Cynthia Jenkins describe the tensions that suffused print fans' discourse during this period:

HJ: The original community felt they lost control as this stuff expanded. So one friction is, "These people aren't doing fandom right. They're doing fandom by a different set of rules. ... These people are interacting online with each other all the time, despite geographic distances." Whereas the other group got together a handful of times a year, it was really special, there was an enormous bond that grew out of going to cons together over time. And those who couldn't be there [online] every day got more and more left out of the social interactions of the community.

CJ: By the time the con came around, those conversations they wanted to have were just so old hat, everybody was bored with it.

HJ: They couldn't participate at the same level. Their community was damaged, because there was this new thing that was closer, more intense, more real-time, more evolving, that formed its own norms and consensuses. ... I think people thought very hard that this was just going to exist alongside the old fandom, not that it would become fandom.

(Jenkins and Jenkins 2012)

Henry remembers that Net fans offered fans who were not yet online "peer-to-peer mentorship of technical skills." He also remembers other systems that fans put in place to help them get online or otherwise learn about online fandom: "Fans donating equipment to fans who didn't have [access to computers or the Internet] through work or couldn't afford it. The systems of printing things out and bringing them to meetings. ... In a lot of ways, fandom dealt *better* with the digital divide than many other segments of the population." However, despite some early Net fans' concerted efforts to close the digital divide that some of their ranks were experiencing in the early-to-mid-'90s, the divide was real for a significant number of print fans.

Print fans thus voiced a range of opinions on a number of issues regarding the ascendance of Net fandom from 1989 to 1998. I argue that a single thread tied together all of their concerns: a preoccupation with the absence of human female bodies from the virtual network.

Missing Female Bodies

How would the female body inhabit the Internet? Conspicuously, as a target? Or as a conspicuous absence, a structurally excluded other to digital culture? (These two scenarios are tied together—targeting can easily lead to exclusion.) These questions undergirded print fans' criticisms of Internet fandom.

Fans' concept of a digital network that would prove inhospitable to human female life drew from, and contributed to, the "cultural imaginary" of cyberpunk that circulated widely in US media from the 1970s through the 1990s. A plethora of cyberpunk novels, television series, and films depicted a near-future in which human bodies, especially women's bodies, were extraneous and disposable owing to the preponderance of advanced technologies, such as intelligent machines waging outright war on the human race, and sophisticated digital networks that make bodies unnecessary for action. In *The Closed World*, Paul N. Edwards (1996) uses the term "cyborg discourse" as an umbrella descriptor for this pervasive set of narratives. "Cyborg discourse," writes Edwards, includes "practices of computer use," "experiences of intimacy of with computers and of connection to other people through computers" (Edwards references Sherry Turkle's work here), and "fictions and fantasies about cyborgs, robots, and intelligent machines, increasingly prominent in science fiction and popular culture" (20–21). Many works of cyborg discourse envision a near-future of human–machine relations (ranging from complete merging to entrenched warfare between the two parties) in which "human" is equated with femaleness.

In its summer 1989 issue, the *Whole Earth Review* published a forum on the question, "Is the body obsolete?" with contributions from artists, scientists, academics, and fiction writers. Cultural historian Fred Turner describes the *Whole Earth Review* as a key part of entrepreneur Stewart Brand's efforts to bring together "the residual countercultural and the flourishing technical" and to provide "the conditions within which a network of conversations could move fluidly between the online and off-line worlds" (Turner 2006, 132), by bringing news from the "electronic frontier" to curious nontechnical readers, and by fostering debates about new technologies among a multidisciplinary set of thinkers. Throughout its 1985–2002 run, the *Review*, which was a successor to Brand's earlier publication the *Whole Earth Catalog*, served as a central node for nationwide discourses and activities concerning new media: it popularized the term "hacker ethic";[4] it published Howard Rheingold's article coining the term "virtual community" in 1987 (Turner 2006, 159); and the *Review*'s editor, Kevin Kelly, would go on to become the founding executive editor of *Wired* magazine, one of the most influential periodicals on the global tech industry since its 1993 launch. The *Review* in large part determined what people thought was important to know, and ponder, in the sphere of technology, and what it thought was important in 1989 was what Claudia Springer (1996) calls the possibility of "deleting the body" (16).

Some contributors to the *Review*'s 1989 forum respond affirmatively to the magazine's question: if the body is not yet obsolete, it is getting there. Artificial intelligence (AI) pioneer Marvin Minsky shares that "If it was possible, I would have myself downloaded. Why not?" and opines that "evolution seems to be leading us to a machine consciousness" (Carstensen and Kadrey 1989, 37). Author William Burroughs recommends that humans prepare themselves for "biologic alterations," for a radical reconfiguration of the human body that will ensure the survival of the species (Carstensen and Kadrey 1989, 54). Other contributors oppose this dream of "bodiless immortality" (Springer 1996, 27): author Kathy Acker writes, "I don't think I can even conceive of the body being obsolete unless I start thinking about suicide" (Carstensen and Kadrey 1989, 51); environmental author Stephanie Mills states, "Bodies are holy, right down to the asshole" (45); and feminist porn actress Nina Hartley declares, "Anyone who has regular orgasms can tell you the absurdity of saying the body is obsolete" (41). While there are male contributors in this issue of the *Review* who argue against "downloading" the human mind into a machine construct, it is notable that all of the women contributors are staunch defenders of the body, its utter necessity and its sacred profanity. In response to the question, "Is the body obsolete?," the female respondents are the guardians of embodiment, the ones who remember that bodies matter, the preservers of the "natural." This is a persistent trope in visions of the future that circulated during the 1980s and 1990s: as the flesh appears ever weaker and decreasingly mandatory in the face of technology's galloping developments, women become the "natural preserve" of human embodiment, the memory-keepers of, and advocates for, the importance and significance of physicality.

This association between women and embodiment permeates cyberpunk fictions from the 1980s and 1990s. Cyberpunk is a genre of science fiction that was founded by William Gibson's novel *Neuromancer* (1984) and gained global popularity through blockbuster Hollywood films such as James Cameron's *Terminator* films and the Wachowskis' *Matrix* franchise. Cyberpunk fictions usually depict a dystopian near-future in which, as Sherryl Vint puts it, "humanity and its technology now share the narrative foreground" (Vint 2007, 103); cyberpunk stories often take place largely or wholly in cyberspace, and concern human–tech relations. Whether these relations are too intimate or frighteningly adversarial, they are always depicted as fraught.

Vint writes that the "appeal of cyberspace is linked directly to the repression of the material body in cyberpunk fiction. … The world of cyberspace is the consummate world of the Cartesian dualist: in cyberspace, one *is* the mind, effortlessly moving beyond the limitations of the human body. In cyberpunk fiction, the prison of the 'meat' [*Neuromancer* characters' derogatory term for the human body] is left behind" (103–114). But, Vint argues, just as Cartesian dualism "has a misogynistic heritage" (for many

Enlightenment thinkers, only the male subject may achieve "the transcendence of pure mind," while "the female subject must remain immanent, absorbing all the limits of materiality that man has cast off" [104]),[5] so the gender politics of cyberpunk often award to male characters the ability to leave the body behind for the limitless range of motion of cyberspace, and relegate women to what we now, following Gibson's nomenclature, call "meatspace" (the real world, the other of cyberspace). In *Neuromancer*, the female character Molly is much physically stronger in the real world than the male protagonist, Case, but Case is far more capable in cyberspace—a difference that becomes painfully clear to Molly when she breaks her leg, and Case, temporarily "jacked in" to her consciousness, "is able to simply switch away from the pain" (Gibson 1984, 105). N. Katherine Hayles (1996) states that in this sequence in the novel, "the character immersed in her physicality is a woman and the character who can escape it is a man" (118), a gendered division of embodiment–disembodiment familiar from Enlightenment philosophy.

Cameron's *Terminator* movies and the Wachowskis' *Matrix* trilogy seem to make a similar argument for the superiority of the nontechnological but physically strong woman over male figures who are fully merged with technology, as both texts feature female characters who are alienated from technology, and/but are responsible for saving humans against the encroaching power of machines (Sarah Connor in the *Terminator* franchise and Zee in the later *Matrix* films). In *Digitizing Race*, Lisa Nakamura (2008) explicitly makes a connection between the Matrix's visual representation as overwhelmingly white and male and the Internet as a dominating force. Nakamura states that the problem at the heart of the *Matrix* movies is "the problem of fractious machines, machines that we know are machines because they are identical to each other, infinitely replicable, and spread in a viral fashion. So too do we know that they are inhuman because they are represented by white men, the 'agents' ... who embody the uniformity of white male culture and equate it to machine culture. This is how the films portray their strong critique of information society ... machine culture is viral, oppressive, and assimilative" (Nakamura 2008, 100).

Like the Borg in *Star Trek: Voyager*, the AIs in the *Matrix* films are an assimilating force; the Borg and the Matrix machines seek to denude humans of their individuality and capacity for independent action, and in doing so, they strive for the elimination of humanity, that is, of the most human aspects of humans. All three antagonists are totalizing forces seeking total control over the Earth (or in the Borg's case, over the universe). And in the fictions in which these techno-villains appear, the antidote to hypertrophic technologization is femaleness. Edwards offers an interpretation of the *Terminator* movies' uses of gender: in the *Terminator* universe, Edwards writes, "Women are the final defense against the apotheosis of high-technology, militaristic masculinity represented by the Terminator—not only because they harbor connections to emotion and love, as in more traditional imagery, but because they are a source of strength, toughness, and endurance" (Edwards 1996, 25).

Thus, speculative debates about the future of high-tech, as well as cyberpunk fictions, in the 1980s and '90s suggested that women would somehow stand outside of technologies that aimed to either "delete" or co-opt the human body. These texts posit that, among humans, it will be women that fight for an embodied future, and for the future of embodiment writ large. According to this logic, it is to women's—and indeed all of humankind's—advantage that women's bodies will be missing from the absorptive technological entities that will threaten human existence. This equation of women with the "natural," nontechnological human body is enormously problematic, as it mirrors and reproduces the male mind–female body split that, as I argued above, has been a large part of widespread misogynistic tropes from the Enlightenment onward. But it is important to note that a number of massively popular cyberdystopian visions of the '80s and '90s "privileged" embodiment, and especially female embodiment, over and against the looming prospect of a large-scale merger of humans with machines.

The Cultural Imaginary of Cyberdystopianism

For print fans, the Internet of the '80s and '90s was a destabilizing technological entity that promised to overwhelm or incorporate their community, analogous to the threatening supertechnologies that were hypothesized during those decades, such as Skynet (the technological system that attempts to extinguish humans in the *Terminator* films), the Matrix, and the Borg. As soon as fans began populating the Internet and conducting fannish business there ("conversing" about favorite media properties, posting and reviewing fan fiction stories), print fans perceived Net fandom as threatening to obviate their bodies.

I do not claim that print fans were projecting fears inculcated in them by fictional representations onto the actual Internet, but rather that print fans' reality and cyberpunk's fantasies both partook of, and contributed to, the same "cultural imaginary" of advanced networked technologies that circulated in the last two decades of the twentieth century.

I am using the concept of "cultural imaginary" that was formulated by literary theorist Winfried Fluck in his book *Das kulturelle Imaginäre* (1997). Susanne Hamscha (2013) summarizes Fluck's concept: "Fluck employs the notion of the 'cultural imaginary' to describe the 'inventory,' as he calls it, of images, affects, and desires that both determines and challenges one's perception of reality" (44, citing Fluck 1997, 21). Hamscha points out that Fluck's "cultural imaginary" functions much like Jan Assmann's "cultural memory." Writes Hamscha, "Assmann describes cultural memory as 'that body of reusable texts, images, and rituals specific to each society in each epoch, whose "cultivation" serves to stabilize and convey that society's self image,' and introduces the notion of an 'inventory' or 'archive' in which legitimate performances, articulations, and cultural texts are stored for reactivation" (Hamscha 2013, 47; citing Assmann 1995, 132). Fluck's "cultural imaginary" and Assmann's "cultural memory," as interpreted and brought into correspondence by Hamscha, function much like my notion of the archontic in fiction. Fluck and Assmann see "archives" of "texts, images, and rituals" being used by social actors to give shape, character, and meaning to the events transpiring around them, and I see similar "archives" of textual elements (characters, settings, storylines) being used by media fans to generate interpretations and new versions of favorite narratives. What is common to all of these theories is a view that cultural artifacts and performances do not directly impose their logics on their audiences; rather, mass cultural productions are raw materials for ordinary individuals' transformations, reenactments, and alterations. People engage with culture *as archive* because cultural productions and discourses provide resources for meaning-making activities. Fluck and Assmann propose that reality and fiction often feed into one another to give definition, a kind of "identity," to a society in a specific era or "epoch." That is, the operation of "fanficcing"—extracting specific elements of circulating discourses and renewing them through repetition and translation—is a method by which people reinforce and extend certain perceptions of reality, not only fictional worlds.

Moreover, as with my idea of archontic production, when people enter the archive of a cultural imaginary and transform its elements, their productions add to and expand that cultural imaginary. Hamscha describes the perpetuation of the American cultural imaginary through individual and collective embodied practices as "performances." Americans, Hamscha claims, constantly reenact "foundational scenarios" that "produce fantasies of national unity and integration, fantasies of an indivisible 'America'" (2013, 43). Hamscha takes up Lauren Berlant's work on how the American flag, Uncle Sam, Mount Rushmore, the Pledge of Allegiance and other "aesthetic and discursive 'national' objects" form an "archive of hiero-glyphic images" that works to "create a national 'public'" (Berlant 1997, 103); in other words, this archive of images, places, and words holds out a promise of national wholeness for Americans. Hamscha wishes to con-sider how, in addition to nationalistic symbols, "literature and popular cul-ture" are also used as archives that people plunder for the "construction of national identities" (Hamscha 2013, 44).

The identity of "fan," like the identity of "American," is a collective iden-tity that must be perpetuated through archontic uses of a shared cultural imaginary; the archive of a cultural imaginary consists largely of "foun-dational scenarios" that must be constantly reperformed in order to give definition and a sense of cohesion to the group. Media fans' cultural imagi-nary from the 1960s through the 1980s drew on utopian sci-fi discourses, such as those promulgated by *Star Trek: The Original Series*, that emphasized fellowship and friendship among individuals from diverse backgrounds who found themselves sharing common spaces in the joint pursuit of one enterprise—fannish enjoyment, pleasure, and community. Fans' traditions, as described in the testimonies of the Jenkinses and the *Comlink* contribu-tors above, included many varieties of in-person meet-ups, ranging from local fan group sessions to conventions, and they also included participa-tion in print publications, such as zines, APAs, and letterzines. However, as the Internet became an increasingly prominent site of fandom in the 1990s, print fans started to draw on, translate, and augment a different cul-tural imaginary: the cyberdystopian scenarios of the '80s and '90s, which depicted computer networks as oppressive to humankind in general, and alienating of women in particular (an alienation that, as stated above, was not always viewed by fans as an exclusion, but sometimes as an advantage).

References to Net fandom taking place on a different time scale than print fandom—Henry and Cynthia Jenkins (2012) compare the "interact-ing … all the time" of online fandom to the "[getting] together a handful of times a year" of print fandom, and one letter in *Comlink* notes that "a conversation that, in *Comlink*, for example, spans a year, lasts only a week on the bulletin board" (Fanlore, "Fandom and the Internet")—call to mind the moments in the *Matrix* films when the AIs in the Matrix move at "bul-let time" speeds, much more rapidly than the human protagonists' avatars (only Neo, the only human who seemingly has the ability to manipulate the Matrix, can match the machines' speed).

For print fans, as for the human characters in 1990s science fictions, faster was not better. The Internet seemed to operate on machinic time rather than on human time, but machinic time seemed inimical to human modes of movement, expression, and relating. In (what they perceived to be) the poor quality of online discourse, print fans found evidence that humans could not communicate at the speed of machines without their communication suffering. The Internet not only compressed the temporality of fannish interactions, it also collapsed the space that used to separate fans. Henry Jenkins points out that the "real-time" interactions of Net fans took place "despite geographic distances" (Jenkins and Jenkins 2012). In her oral history interview, Rachael Sabotini (2012) describes print fandom, or "early fandom," as "like a giant house party. Since you tended to participate together either at cons, or in local gatherings, you know, or in writing letters and stuff. ... Extraversion was required for that initial stuff ...; there was a lot of activity that required you to go outside of yourself." New media changed that spatial relation of the individual fan to other fans, and to fandom at large, says Sabotini. "The technology of having your phone, ... having the computer, just brings a different aspect. ... It's much more— you're carrying fandom in your head all the time now. ... It's in your head, it's in your pocket, it's—you're constantly immersed. Whereas there was much more space in that original environment. And other people tended to fill that space, and it wasn't so much in your head" (Sabotini 2012). The language that Sabotini uses characterizes the onset of Net fandom as a transition that individual fans made from body to mind, from physicality to virtuality. Sabotini herself was a full participant in both print fandom and online fandom during these transitional years—hence her unwillingness to establish a hierarchy between them—but she acknowledges that other print fans had difficulty with the shift to Net fandom. "It [was] a little unsettling to the very early fans, because it [was] so different from what they were used to and how they were used to thinking of fandom," she states.

I argue that the sweeping change that was "unsettling" to print fans in the 1990s was, in essence, the same sweeping change that was unsettling to readers and viewers of dystopian cyberpunk fictions in the same time period: the change from the body to the mind as the primary agent for meaningful interaction, as the Internet and other new media became increasingly integrated into millions of people's lives. Cyberpunk announced and articulated, in exaggerated visual, sonic, and narrative vocabularies, the frightening consequences of digital technologies' relegation of the body to the status of insignificant, irrelevant "meat."

Against the threat that humans would soon become immaterial (meaning both nonmaterial or virtual beings and not mattering or being irrelevant to machinic processing), cyberpunk posited women as the repositories and guardians of the human body and of the defining essence of human society. Rather than characterizing female fans as resistant to new technologies because of some irrational inertia and distrust of the new, or as excluded from online participation purely because of economic circumstances,[6] I perceive print fans as a group that experienced, in a visceral way that had direct ramifications for their communities, the dread of bodily "deletion" that permeated US culture in the last decades of the twentieth century.

The Female Body Always Remains

One reason that print fans may have resisted networked "connection" was that they understood, or rapidly learned either from their own or other fans' initial engagements with the Internet, that the female body does not actually ever go unmarked, even in purely text-based virtual encounters. Morgan Dawn (2012) recalls, in her oral history interview, that in the early '90s, women were frequently harassed online. Morgan Dawn states, "We [female fans] were concerned with what was happening to women who were online in the early '90s. Which were, 'Hi! I'm a woman.' 'Hey, wanna have sex with me?' You know, literally, that's what we were constantly getting hit with, when you identified yourself as a woman. And God forbid you identified yourself as a geek woman, because you would get hit on even harder" (Dawn 2012). This accords with Rose Allucquère Stone's assertion in 1991 that online communications "maintain the preexisting codes" (14) of gender: "Bodies in cyberspace are ... constituted by descriptive codes that 'embody' expectations of appearance. Many of the engineers currently debating the form and nature of cyberspace are the young turks of computer engineering, men in their late teens and twenties, and they are preoccupied with the things with which postpubescent men have always been preoccupied. This rather steamy group will generate the codes and descriptors by which bodies in cyberspace are represented" (Stone 1991, 14–15). In other words, given that the majority of computer scientists in the early years of the public Internet were (and are today) male, bodies in cyberspace will be described, represented, and recognized—and, one can extrapolate, *addressed*—according to "the preexisting codes for body" (14), that is, for gendered bodies, that proliferate in real-world spaces.

The alienation from the Internet that female fans experienced when they began to take part in online fan discussions had to do not only with their *being* women, but with their *reading* and *interpreting* source texts in ways that are frequently gendered as female. In their oral history interview, the Jenkinses share recollections that echo Morgan Dawn's, discussing how, on

the Internet in the late '80s and early '90s, "women [were] feeling unsafe ...
going into a space [where] they were going to be picked on, harassed" (Jenkins and Jenkins 2012). They locate the cause of women's "feeling unsafe,"
being "picked on" and "harassed," in the clash between how men tended
to define fandom and how women tended to define fandom, a clash that
took place openly for the first time on the Internet.

HJ: You had all these different fandoms. If you go back to my fandom as a male
experience versus Cynthia's experience, those conversations [between male and
female fans] hadn't happened before. So to be a ... male *Star Trek* fan [meant that
you] lived in a world where you knew how to read *Star Trek*, what to talk about, what
episodes mattered. And women lived in a totally different world. And you created a
discussion list, and you brought them together, and, "*What?!*"

CJ: You knew a male *Star Trek* fan who could tell you specs on every kind of ship. It
[male fandom] is, like, totally hardware centered.

HJ: [Male fans] knew the command structures, the uniforms and the badges, the
ships and the technology. And had a totally different sense of what episodes were
good and bad than those [female fans] who were into the characters. And so flame
wars were *everywhere*. ... Flame wars that were leaving women unwilling to talk
online.

(Jenkins and Jenkins 2012)

Morgan Dawn also has memories of the content of female fans' interests—
in "characters" rather than "hardware"—making them feel targeted when
they tried to participate in early online fan communities: "There we were
talking about slash [fanfic], or wanting to talk about slash, which was not
very well accepted in fandom at the time, or at least online. And so we had
all this vulnerability." The Jenkinses and Morgan Dawn recall that female
fans, in order protect themselves from the "flame wars," "feeling unsafe,"
feeling "vulnerable," being "picked on" and "harassed" in mixed-gender
Internet communities, founded majority-female and exclusively female
online groups. Morgan Dawn (2012) recalls that in order to sign up for
Virgule-L, which was likely the first slash mailing list opened and "was all
run for women, by women," a newcomer had to "give them your real full
name," had to "sign a statement that no one but you would be reading your
email," and had to "promise not to advertise or talk about the mailing list
in open areas." Says Morgan Dawn, "You couldn't even mention [Virgule-L]
online. [...] It was extremely restrictive, but ultimately, [that was] what we
needed to get [it] off the ground." Eventually, as "more and more people
were joining online—in various CompuServe and AOL and GEnie communities," Morgan Dawn remembers, "it became less of an issue to be open

and talking online about slash." But the opening years of the Internet were difficult for, and sometimes openly hostile to, women fans and their interests in slash fan fiction.

Morgan Dawn successfully overcame the barriers to online participation that female fans faced at the start of the 1990s; other women in fandom either could not or did not want to fight to push past those barriers of shaming and flaming. Women's bodies as objects of male desire, women's bodies as targets of men's sexual come-ons, women fans as preoccupied with men's bodies and overly invested in fantasies of male/male sexual intercourse: these were the stereotypes and predominant conceptions of female bodies that, as Stone argues, "generated the codes" of male fans' interactions with female fans in the opening years of Net fandom. As stated above, many cyberpunk fictions and nonfictions establish an unbreakable link of femaleness to flesh, even in worlds dominated by digital environments; this equation of "woman" with "body" is also highlighted in the recollections of early Net fans. The fact that female fans could not be decoupled from female embodiment as they ventured online did not invite their mass migration to the Internet in the late 1980s and early 1990s.

Fan Cultural Memory as Repertoire

What weighed even more heavily against the prospect of "going online" than the targeting of female bodies online in this timeframe was the expectation that print fandom's collective memory would be erased if Net fandom became dominant. For print fans, the fear of the body's "deletion" that numerous cyberdystopianists expressed was more than a vague anxiety for humankind's future—fans quickly became pessimistic about their own culture's future. A transition of fandom from the body to the network meant that the institutional memory modalities that fans had developed would possibly dissolve. These memory modalities were embodied: print fans' cultural memory was constituted through repertoire rather than through archive. In the quotations above, one can sense the great significance that print fans placed on meet-ups, and the idea that face-to-face connections among fans might be replaced by virtual interactions haunted print fans. If fans' bodies never occupied the same spaces, and if the timescale of fan interactions sped up to match machine time rather than human time, how would generations of fans understand one another, and how would the traditions, rituals, and concepts of fandom be passed down from one generation to another?

Practices such as new fans seeking out more experienced fans at conventions, talking zine dealers into showing their fanfic zines (which many kept separate from general content zines), and exchanging videocassettes with fan friends by mail constituted the repertoire of print fandom. Through experienced fans' acts of initiating and guiding newcomers, acts that were primarily performed face to face, print fandom perpetuated itself. Before the Internet, fans preserved and transmitted their shared cultural memory through a well-established repertoire that was not written down in a manual or widely publicized in any press, even the zine press.

The lack of documentation of fandom and its repertoire—that fact that nowhere could new fans find written instructions that spelled out how to acquire fanfic—is attributable to fans' strong desire to not draw attention to themselves and their activities, particularly the writing and dissemination of fan fiction. Fans wished to escape the notice of copyright holders of the source texts on which fans based their unauthorized fiction, as they felt that copyright holders could claim that fanfic was infringement and issue cease-and-desist orders, or even sue fans who published zines. Fans also sought to avoid pinging the radar of "mainstream" society, which fans suspected would mock and condemn fanfic and its writers. By limiting knowledge of its customs, traditions, and transactional methods to face-to-face encounters (or requiring some face-to-face, personal, full-real-name familiarity as the basis for the transmission of fannish knowledge), fandom was able to keep its workings relatively secret; at the least, fandom was able to believe that its workings remained secret. Fandom chose repertoire—that is, it chose embodied methods for keeping its culture alive and growing—in the years before the Internet, as a defense against discovery. But once fandom entered the arena of the Internet, and the majority of fannish meetings and transactions began to take place online rather than in-person at conventions, print fans forecasted that the "deletion" of the body from fandom might mean the deletion of the entirety of fandom. Fan culture had endured only through repertoire; if the repertoire was forgotten and left unrepeated by Net fans, would the culture as a whole perish?

The thread of continuity that had run through media fandom and connected different generations of fans since the mid-1960s, comprising fannish customs and rituals that was handed over from fan to fan via embodied practices, appeared to breaking in the face of Net fandom's rising popularity in the 1990s. When print fans tried to peer into the future of Net fandom, past the breaking of their thread of tradition, they could see ... nothing. If Net fandom did not care to archive itself, and if it did not require new fans to know anything about its past, then it would be a fandom that might endure for many years, but it would be a collective without memory.

The Body + the Book

But how can I claim that the primary memory modality of print fandom was repertoire rather than archive, when *print* fandom defined itself largely by its archival component—printed zines, which were compiled, edited, reproduced, and sold by fans? It is clear that print fans regarded zines as artifacts of cultural memory that held the promise of duration, in contrast to online fan fiction, which they perceived to be extremely ephemeral. For example, one fan, the-other-sandy, posted a piece on her LiveJournal in 2007 called "No More Zines? :-(" in which she compares the short life of online fic with the endurance of zine-published fic, stating, "Electronic fic is highly perishable. ... Yet, no matter how old my zines get (and some of them are over twenty-five years old), I've never opened one up and gotten a 404 File Not Found error."

Print fans conceived of their embodied routines and rituals as constitutive of what Aleida Assmann (2008), in her essay "Canon and Archive," calls "working memory," which she defines as the "active dimension of cultural memory" (100), which operates through "repeated performance," attracting "continued individual and public attention" (101) to the religion, art, and history of a society. The Catholic church's "continuously and periodically repeated liturgical rites and practices" (100) are an example of working memory; another example can be found in the Western world's "canon of classical texts" being "performed on the stages of theaters and in the concert halls" (101). Assmann makes direct reference to Diana Taylor's writings on indigenous performance as "nonarchival system[s] of transfer" (Taylor 2003, xvii) and links her own concept of working memory to Taylor's idea of repertoire, equating "active cultural memory" with "embodied repertoires that are performed in festive rites and repeated practices" (Assmann 2008, 105).

Fans coming together in real-world spaces to celebrate their "canonical" texts, in local groups and at large conventions; experienced fans tutoring new fans one on one; fans physically exchanging treasured goods: these formed the repertoire, the working cultural memory, of print fandom. Zines served a different function in the worldview of print fandom, the function of what Assmann calls "passive memory," which is made up of the "objects in the historical archive" (103) of a society. The written documents of a nation or a community are "not trashed, because they are considered to be of historical or scholarly interest" (103); therefore they are "stored in the archive" as "inert" and "potentially available" knowledge, giving them "the chance of a second life that considerably prolongs their existence" (103). The embodied modes for the passing-on of fannish knowledge were print fandom's working memory, or repertoire, and zines were print fandom's passive memory, or archive.

But there is another way to view the role of zines in print fandom. In the published remarks of print fans who sought to defend their way of fandom from being decimated or swallowed up by the growing Internet in the 1980s and 1990s, as well as the statements of print fans in the 2000s who wished to keep alive the memory of print fandom, I find that printed zines are discussed more as repertoire than as archive. In other words, at the historical moment when printed matter began to be threatened with obsolescence, fans started to characterize their material publications as important because they gave onto specific *acts of reading*. Here are some descriptions by print fans of zine reading, as a meaningful *experience*, published in zines and online between the 1984 and 2010:

First, I just sit a minute with the zine in my lap and feel its weight. I turn [to] the table of contents and read that, plus any comments, notes, etc. that the editors might have put in. Then I page through the entire zine, not reading any of the stories, but just looking at the illos [illustrations] and imagining the stories that they are illustrating. Only then comes the serious business: THE FIRST READING. I read right through each page in order from the first to the last. I like to get the feel of a zine, the momentum, because I feel that every editor puts a lot of thought and energy into the distribution and order of the material. (from the letterzine *Not Tonight, Spock!*, Issue 2, March 1984; Fanlore, "Zines and the Internet")

There is something very tactile about holding [a zine] in your hands that cannot be duplicated by downloading fiction off the 'Net. (from the editorial of the *Starsky & Hutch* printed slash anthology *Leave a Light On for Me*, October 2002; Fanlore, "Leave a Light On for Me")

If you were "raised" on zines, even with all the great things to enjoy on the web, on the Kindle or other ebook reader, there's still nothing quite like holding a zine in your hands. Especially a zine that has the tactile pleasure of fine papers, interesting textures. That was one of my favorite things about the early B7 Complexes[7]—portfolios were printed on lovely parchment paper that not only looked great, they were a treat to touch and hold. (Walsh 2010)

These odes to zine culture contain numerous references to the human body's contact and interaction with the printed zine: the "tactile pleasure" of feeling the textures of the paper on which a zine is printed; the physical and durational act of plucking a new zine out of a mailbox, sitting down with it, weighing it in one's hands, and flipping through its pages twice, first speedily and then carefully; the ritual of ensconcing oneself on one's couch or in one's bed, preparing to read a zine intensively, in the same manner that one reads novels. In these fans' accounts, the zine is not valued as a textual repository or archival document; it is not defined as a printed form intended to preserve fans' cultural productions for posterity. Rather, for these fans, the zine is a prop that is integral to (what were in the heyday of print fandom) routine experiences of physical joy. The zine is the fetish object for the print fan, and the fan's engagement with that object is a highly pleasurable and personal embodied performance. Let us also recall Henry Jenkins's observations of the *Beauty and the Beast* fan club passing around printouts of Internet discussions and fan fiction in 1989, which show that even when printed matter was not fetishized for its rich textures or fine illustrations, or for the difficulty of its acquisition, printed text was still a prop for ritual—and in this case, social—experiences. Printed material played a crucial part in fans' repertoires.

Thus, the repertoire of print fandom, the working cultural memory of pre-Internet fandom, consisted of both body and book. There were many physical practices through which fans communicated their specialized knowledges to one another, and there were also embodied rituals that centered on printed artifacts, such as zines and printouts of online communications. These rituals of finding, buying, trading, touching, handling, holding, sitting with, scanning, passing around, reading quietly in private, reading aloud to a group, and other physical interactions with zines were highly affectively charged for fans, and became even more meaningful when fans had cause to mourn their fading away, as zine culture became displaced by Internet culture. Although zines did fulfill the function of passive memory in print fandom, fixing the textual productions of fans in an archival format that would allow them to be accessed long after their initial printing, at the close of print fandom it was clear that the more significant function of zines was as a key component of print fandom's working memory. In the end, what print fans *did* with zines loomed larger in their cultural memory than the printed matter itself.

Uncertain Surrogacy

At the heart of these widespread anxieties about sophisticated digital technologies in the last decades of the twentieth century, I perceive a deep concern with replacement and uncanny repetition, or what performance theorist Joseph Roach calls "surrogation." In *Cities of the Dead*, Roach (1996) explores "the three-sided relationship of memory, performance, and substitution," and proposes that "culture reproduces and re-creates itself by a process that can be best described by the word *surrogation*" (2). Surrogates step into roles vacated, by death or other kinds of attrition, attempting to perform those roles in ways that imitate the departed predecessors. However, Roach claims, "because collective memory works selectively, imaginatively, and often perversely, surrogation rarely if ever succeeds" (2). Roach offers a number of scenarios in which substitutes are found wanting or are rejected outright, such as the surrogate either failing expectations ("creating a deficit") or exceeding expectations ("creating a surplus"); the surrogate polarizing their audience and causing the group to divide into camps; or the surrogate tapping into fears of "uncanniness," which "may provoke many unbidden emotions, ranging from mildly incontinent sentimentalism to raging paranoia" (2).

Although Roach's examples of surrogates in *Cities of the Dead* do not include cyborgs or automata, they do include other categories of objects that breach the life–nonlife divide, such as effigies and puppets, and it is the question of whether these objects should be accepted *as if* they were living that disturbs audiences and interlocutors: the puppet, automaton, or cyborg is not—or not fully—a living human, but should it be *taken for* a fully alive person? *Is the cyborg an acceptable substitute for a human?* As I have argued, this question is especially fraught when the cyborg purports to be a substitute for the female body, as Western epistemologies from the Enlightenment through cyberdystopianism have so closely tethered femaleness and human embodiment. From E. T. A. Hoffmann's Olympia to *Metropolis*'s Robot Maria to the operating system vocalized by Scarlett Johanssen in *Her*, the hypothetical female mechanical surrogate is repeatedly presented as a deeply unsettling figure. Fans, as a majority-female subculture—a subculture that learned when they first went online in the 1980s and '90s that their gender would not be forgotten, overlooked, or made welcome in the new media but would bear the weight of many of the same stereotypes and subject positions in cyberspace that it did in meatspace—had much to consider as they found themselves transitioning into a female collective sited primarily in digital networks.

Could a fan culture that was digitally embodied be an effective surrogate for a fan culture lived through human bodies? This was the question for fandom in the late years of the twentieth century, the early years of the Internet. Were human transactions and interactions that transpired online, through avatars and marionettes (defined in chapter 6), acceptable substitutes for the embodied human practices that they were attempting to replace? A core function of "in-person fandom" was the transmission of fannish culture, comprising traditions, knowledge, and cultural objects such as zines. If cyborg, networked fans—fans who were "half-digital, half-not," and who "lived" and "talked" and "met" online, but never or rarely in person—were not going to transmit their culture through techniques of repertoire, would they do it through technologies of archive? To some print fans in the 1990s, it seemed that the cyborg version of themselves would have neither repertoire nor archive. The cyborg would have no memory. Print fandom feared that Net fandom would become a substitute for print fandom without any knowledge of its predigital past, and would also be devoid of any capacity for recording its own digital history as it unfolded.

The Other Cyborg

At precisely the same time that the cyberdystopian thinkers, writers, and producers developed the cyborg as the totem of a possible future, a future of frenzied networked production taking place in compressed machinic time, in limitless virtual space, without human physicality to restrain it or cultural memory to track it, feminist theorist Donna Haraway generated a very different cyborg figure. Haraway's 1985 "Cyborg Manifesto" posited the cyborg as "an ironic political myth faithful to feminism, socialism, and materialism" (Haraway [1985] 2000, 291), a hybrid being "resolutely committed to partiality, irony, intimacy, and perversity" (293). Breaking with feminists (and antifeminists) invested in equating women with the human body and with nature and in dividing womanhood from technology and from machines, Haraway calls for a new, cyborg feminism, a feminism that aligns itself with "the breached boundary," "the leaky distinction." Haraway's cyborg "would not recognize the Garden of Eden" and is "wary of holism" (Haraway [1985] 2000, 293). At the point where body and machine touch and merge; where nature and culture fuse or become confused for and with one another; where genders and sexualities multiply and binaristic identities and relations dissolve; where "the boundary between physical and non-physical" becomes "imprecise" (294)—there, Haraway's feminist cyborg arises.

Anne Balsamo, in her history of postmodern feminist thought, reads Haraway's cyborg feminism as "based on affinities rather than essentialist identities" and "rooted in fragmented identities" (Balsamo 1987, 68–69). She emphasizes Haraway's recognition that technoscientific postindustrialism is a "matrix of complex dominations," but that that matrix is also "a polymorphous information system" that is a "possible means of great human satisfaction" (68). As interpreted by Balsamo, Haraway acknowledges and affirms Jean Baudrillard's, Frederic Jameson's, and Jean-François Lyotard's observations about the shifting conditions of cultural production in the information age, but reserves a space for the birth of a new feminism amid the traffic of massive technocultural change, a feminism rooted in "fragmented identities" and "permanent partiality" (69). Balsamo quotes Haraway: "We do not need a totality in order to work well" (69). Haraway suggests that at the millennial moment, as new media shift relations and flows between global actors, feminists have the opportunity to declare themselves cyborg, to use the technoscientific "matrix" for their own "satisfaction" even as they understand that matrix tries to absorb and control them, and to form alliances that cross all previously established boundaries associated with body-based identifiers.

My position is that one instantiation of Haraway's mythical cyborg is the female fan online. Women fans blurred the boundaries between the body and the digital, not only individually but in the thousands, then the millions. They organized and formed associations based on voluntary affinities, and in doing so, they created spaces for the circulation and exchange of female and queer information and production. Internet fandom is irreverent and ironic, intimate and perverse, revealing of the multiplicity of female desire and uncovering the lie of "natural" gender-specific preferences. Online fandom brings women into close communion with new technologies, as fans function as users, writers, beta readers, moderators, list owners, archivists, coders, site designers, recommenders, historians, vidders, editors, challenge organizers, fundraisers, and other roles covering the entire producer–consumer spectrum. Fans created a digital surrogate for print fandom on the Internet, and went to great lengths to endow online fandom with cultural memory, as well as community, rituals, routines, and the other meaningful components of print fandom's repertoire. Fans have built a culture of both archive and repertoire on the Internet, a collective project that has often had political aims—in sum, a project that, in many ways, has proven print fandom's most cyberdystopian fears to be fictions.

And yet, even as online fans have attempted to realize the potential of cyborg feminism, the power and force of the cultural imaginary of cyberdystopianism cannot be discounted, not just in fandom but in Western culture more broadly. Print fandom's pessimistic prognostications that the Internet would marginalize the human body, would force humans to ramp up the volume and speed of their production to match the instantaneity and ceaselessness of machines, would reduce humans' physical contact (and as a result, the depth of their connections) with one another, would attempt to assimilate all forms of labor and recreation, and would threaten to extinguish printed matter—all seem like early expressions of anxieties about digital culture that are widespread today. The darkest fantasies of the 1980s and '90s about cyborg culture cast a shadow that is currently growing, not diminishing. The two cyborg figures from the dawn of the Internet era—the cyborg that annihilates and the cyborg that liberates—remain operative metaphors in fandom and beyond.

Break 5　A Femslash Parable of the Print-to-Digital Transition

Femslash as Reconciliation Fic

Between the extremes of the dystopian and utopian cyborg myths that I explained in the previous chapter, fan fiction in the late 1990s suggested a third fantasy, one of a loving union between a human female and a cyborg female. One of the most popular character pairings in fan fiction from this period was the "femslash" (female/female) pairing of *Star Trek: Voyager*'s Captain Janeway, a human, and Seven of Nine, who was born human but is, in the timeframe of the series, a de-assimilated Borg drone that retains some Borg characteristics (nanoprobes and various cybernetic implants); Seven, as she is called, is permanently part machine. Janeway/Seven stories are about a romantic and/or sexual relationship between an middle-aged woman and a twenty-something cyborg, and many Janeway/Seven fics from the late '90s are of the "first-time" genre, in which Janeway and Seven have their first sexual encounter and Janeway must teach Seven about human communication and emotional and physical intimacy. Janeway helps Seven understand how to express her own desires and guides Seven in how to be sensitive and responsive to Janeway's desires.

Janeway/Seven fics are about two different generations of powerful females coming together, the older woman drawing on her leadership abilities and years of experience to mentor, teach, coach, and nurture the younger woman, while the younger one is able to excite and arouse the older woman's interest—in every possible way—with her machine-enhanced strength, intellect, and self-assuredness.

I argue that one reason for the popularity of Janeway/Seven femslash fan fiction at the turn of the twenty-first century was Janeway/Seven's usefulness as an analogue for the reconciliation of print fandom and Net fandom after 1998. While one might readily agree with oral history participant Morgan Dawn (2012) that after 1998, "literally everybody was overrun by the Internet," and can easily interpret the history of fandom as being completely dominated by net fans beginning in the late 1990s, the surge in fannish interest in Janeway/Seven, following Seven of Nine's 1998 introduction on *Star Trek: Voyager*, inspires me to read what occurred in fandom at the turn of the millennium differently.

Janeway/Seven fic is about "crossing the line": the generational line and the technological line. In the diegesis of *Star Trek: Voyager*, Janeway and Seven not only differ in age, they also occupy different places on the human–machine spectrum (Janeway is a human who is proficient at using technology, but who wars against the Borg that seek to wholly assimilate humankind; Seven was assimilated by the Borg at age six, and after Janeway effectively severs her connection to the Borg collective, Seven must learn to exist as a human–machine hybrid). Janeway/Seven fic, then, is concerned with the question of how two such different women can join together.

Cyborg–Human Connection

Most J/7 (as Janeway/Seven is often abbreviated) fic begins with the premise that the two women want one another—their felt *need* to join is not in question. But how the two can bridge their differences, and create unity out of apparent disparity, is at issue. Although I am sure some J/7 fanfic includes descriptions of the techno-erotics of a human woman coupling with a cyborg woman, it is not the mechanics, so to speak, of J/7 sex that seems to interest most J/7 authors; rather, the main question at the heart of many J/7 stories is how the two females manage to connect with one another despite each being deeply intimidated by the other. In other words, the coming-together of two extremely powerful women, who mutually desire, respect, and even fear one another, drives much J/7 storytelling. Here is an excerpt from a 1998 J/7 fic, "Just Between Us" by G. L. Dartt, which was the first of a fifty-story series, one of the most highly recommended bodies of work in the J/7 fanfic corpus.[1] In this scene, Janeway and Seven are on the brink of their first sexual encounter, Seven lying naked on Janeway's bed:

Oh my, Janeway considered as she slipped the robe from her shoulders, letting it drop to the floor. This might be more difficult than she had originally thought. Somehow, in her fantasies, everything had been rose petals and soft touches, straightforward with an instinctive knowledge of what to do. No hesitation, no confusion and certainly not the six foot reality of powerful Borg in full, splendidly healthy womanhood. It occurred to her suddenly that there might be a certain amount of logistics to this. ... *She'll expect a lot more than any man would, you know.* ...

Seven of Nine watched as Janeway slid onto the bed beside her. ... It was hard for her to think clearly. She wondered if there were something wrong with her implants, a feedback loop perhaps. She was also confused by how swiftly and easily Janeway had taken complete command of the situation, and now Seven found that she could only follow the older woman's lead. (Dartt 1998)

In this scene, Janeway and Seven appear equally uncertain of themselves. Each is simultaneously impressed and daunted by the other's confidence. Janeway is awed by the alluring hybrid female before her, as indicated by Janeway's (mental) description of Seven: "the six foot reality of powerful Borg in full, splendidly healthy womanhood" (the combination of "Borg" and "full womanhood" seems to double Seven's appeal to Janeway, rather than making Janeway uneasy at the uncanniness of a cyborg body). Seven is *more* than a woman, being part machine, and therefore, Janeway predicts, Seven will expect "more than any man would." Seven is literally a superhuman being, a more-than-human cyborg, and Janeway infers that this means that Seven will place superhuman demands on Janeway as a lover, as a partner. For her part, Seven is stunned—unable to "think clearly," "confused," wondering if there is a technical failing in her Borg neural implants—by Janeway's quickly "taking complete command" of their lovemaking session, such that Seven can "only follow the older woman's lead." Janeway is the commanding officer of the *Voyager*, so Seven may be intimidated by Janeway's standing and authority as much as by anything that Janeway does as a lover, but Janeway's innate leadership skills are such that she may be asserting them just as strongly in her bed as she does on the bridge of her ship.

In my reading, Janeway is an incarnation, in the figure of a single character, of print fandom, while Seven represents Net fandom. Print fandom in the '90s was made up of an older generation of female fans, women who regarded the Internet as a supplement to embodied fannish practices and print-based fannish objects, but not as a primary or central site and medium of fannish communication and publishing. Janeway can be seen as a highly positive symbol of print fandom, as her accumulated years of experience, her willingness to use advanced technologies combined with a firm resistance to being incorporated by a networked collective, and her history of command are all portrayed as strengths, for both herself and her crew, in both the television series and in fan fiction based on that series.

Net fandom in the '90s had younger female fans as members, women who regarded the Internet as the core arena of fannish being and doing, women who readily "merged" with networking technologies and did not necessarily regard in-person or print fandom as more special or more important than Internet fandom. Seven positively represents this group in her advanced technical knowledge and her sophisticated capacity to interface with, and manipulate, complex machine-based systems, her supreme air of self-confidence (arising from her youthful beauty in addition to her technological skills), and in her ability to repeatedly demonstrate to the noncyborg crew members of *Voyager* the advantages of being "half-digital." The pairing of Janeway/Seven therefore is a fantasy about print fandom and Net fandom joining and combining, not exactly easily, but in a way that brings pleasure and excitement to both parties. In both the text of *Voyager* and the "Just Between Us" fan story, Janeway is impressed with Seven's more-than-humanness, but is not afraid to lead and teach the younger cyborg; Seven is overwhelmed by Janeway's surety and authority, but that does not stop her from being assertive, forthright, and direct with Janeway in their ordinary communications and in their lovemaking.

Understanding Janeway as an incarnation of print fandom and Seven as a stand-in for Net fandom, we can read Janeway/Seven fanfics as expressive of a strong wish in late-1990s fandom that print fans and Net fans, older female fans and younger female fans, will respect and learn from one another's skills and abilities, each one bringing their own unique attitudes toward human/machine identities and practices to their relationship. This female and queer bond between Janeway and Seven is a romanticization of the possible unity among different categories of female and queer fans, which has the potential to deliver to women fans "more than any man would," or, at least, something very different than any man can: the continuity, the perpetuation, of a female and queer tradition across generations, even as new media radically alter how that tradition is routinely performed.

Janeway/Seven fic reframes "print fandom versus net fandom" as "print fandom/net fandom," the slash, as always in fandom, signifying pairing, partnership, eroticism, longing, lust. Janeway loving Seven is a fantasy of print fans loving Net fans for their easy relationship with the technical, their understanding of the human–technological relation as fluid and dynamic and not as a strict opposition; this love of Net fans can overlook or forgive Net fans' impoliteness (most *Voyager* crewmembers find Seven to be quite rude), brashness, and occasional disdain for the "purely" human. Seven loving Janeway is a fantasy of Net fans loving print fans for their maturity, their experience, their authoritative knowledge, and their passionate defense of human being and human doing, despite print fans' inability to fully understand the benefits of human–technical hybridity, and their stubborn prioritization of all things human over anything cyborg. To my thinking, Janeway/Seven fic rose to popularity in the late 1990s because fans wanted reassurance that print fandom and Net fandom were uniting of their own volition, motivated by mutual admiration and desire, rather than because the Internet "assimilated" all of fandom into its totalizing collective.

Cyborg versus Human Cultural Memory

In the *Voyager* series, though Janeway and Seven's relationship never takes an explicitly sexual turn, the two characters develop a warm friendship and deep trust. Janeway and Seven's bond may have stood for a rapprochement between those who resisted the invasion of everyday life by digital technologies, and those who welcomed the wave of new media, for many of *Voyager*'s viewers in the late '90s and early '00s, not only for fanfic writers and readers. But, however close Janeway and Seven became in the series and in fan fiction, they remained complete opposites in one respect: their preferences with regard to practices of cultural memory. On *Voyager*, Janeway's memory modes are embodied. She verbally narrates her "Captain's Log," presumably recording entries regularly (the viewer hears excerpts from Janeway's log as the framing narration of each episode), and on one memorable occasion, at the close of episode 4.01, in which *Voyager* tangles with both the Borg and another highly technologically advanced race, Janeway opts to situate herself in a holodeck simulation of Renaissance-era Italy, and to handwrite her log entry with an inked quill on parchment paper, by candlelight. When her First Officer finds her in the holodeck, hunched over a fifteenth-century desk, he remarks that she is writing her log "the old-fashioned way." Janeway explains, "I wanted to get as far away from bio-implants and fluidic space and … and this feels more human, somehow." Janeway, like print fans, thinks of memory as an embodied practice (her logs are either spoken aloud or handwritten). For Janeway, the physical performance of record-keeping is a reinforcement of human culture, and a refusal of machine culture.

Seven, on the other hand, relates to memory very differently than Janeway. Seven is proud of the fact that all the memories of her early life have been uploaded to, and stored in, the Borg's cloud-like shared memory, and that therefore a part of her will live forever. She frequently shows that she possesses a remarkably wide-ranging, detailed, digitally enhanced, eidetic memory—she can access all of the Borg's knowledge that she "downloaded" before she was disconnected from the collective, and she informs her fellow crewmates that she "requires only seconds to commit what I see to memory" (episode 4.20). Seven's interest in her own past, and in the past of Earth and of Starfleet, is selective. She understands that voluminous records are stored in *Voyager*'s central computer, but she does not delve into them as deeply or as often as she is advised to. For example, when Janeway discovers some data on Seven's birth parents, and suggests that Seven scan the information, Seven replies that she "may do that someday" (episode 4.06); in another episode, when Seven is asked if she is familiar with the Earth event known as World War II, Seven answers that she "knows nothing" about it (episode 4.18).

Seven, like Net fans, assumes that any and all cultural memory will be available to her when she requires it, and thus she is not overly concerned with making an effort to record new memories or to recover older memories. Seven, the cyborg, seems to absolutely trust that the complex technological structures that have always surrounded and supported her—the Borg collective, *Voyager*'s intranet, and her own neural implants—are constantly, consistently, keeping perfect records of everything that she, the human race, and many other species have experienced. For this reason, she takes an almost casual approach to cultural memory, not valuing it very highly, and only utilizing archives when she has a pressing need, rather than to learn about any traditions that preceded her. In the matter of cultural memory, then, Seven is an excellent representative of the fan who relies entirely on digital cultural memory, trusting that its infrastructure can be relied upon to fill in any gaps, whenever necessary.

6 The Default Body and the Composed Body: Performance through New Media

The Body in New Media

Digital networked culture is intensely concerned with bodies and embodiment. In this chapter, I will characterize fan fiction as a *body medium*, that is, a means of porting bodies from one medium to another. The bodies with which online fandom works are what I call *composed bodies*, that is, bodies that online users make and maneuver in networked spaces. In some cases, composed bodies are avatars of their makers/users, but in many fan practices, composed bodies are appropriated from media culture, and are marionettes rather than avatars—that is, rather than representing users' selves, composed bodies often represent characters.

Composed bodies are used by fans to interact with one another, and to enact narratives for one another, in the "global theater" (McLuhan 1970). I will build on the avatar theories of B. Coleman, E. Gordon Craig's concept of the "über-marionette," Diana Taylor's idea of repertoire as "downloading media," and articulations of the collaborative and performative nature of fan production by Francesca Coppa, Karen Hellekson, and Rebecca Tushnet. I will also analyze both texts and paratexts of fan fiction stories, and cite a number of fan participants in my oral history project, in order to think about how writing and embodiment are reconfigured by new media.

A Mystery of Paratext

Throughout this chapter, I will be discussing a mystery that arose for me recently, concerning the paratext of a fan fiction story.

Searching for a story that I could include in this chapter as a representative work of fan fiction, I read through a portion of my own archives of fan fiction, collected over the past decade and a half, culled from a variety of fic archives, representing a wide array of fandoms. My eye was drawn to an *X-Files* fic from June 2000, "Night Giving Off Flames," by Jesemie's Evil Twin (JET). I consider JET to be one of the towering authors of the *X-Files* fandom, and many of her stories to be classic *X-Files* fics. I have read "Night" several times, but when I reviewed it for this book, I was surprised to realize that there was a portion of the text, or rather, the paratext, that I had never seen before, a section that I overlooked during all my previous readings.

"Night" is a mournful tale that takes place in an alternative universe (AU) to the universe of the *X-Files* television show, an AU in which the Earth has been colonized by hostile aliens, some of them shape shifters.[1] The premise of "Night" is that the series' protagonists, FBI agents Dana Scully and Fox Mulder, partners and close friends, have been separated in the colonization and Scully has been taken prisoner by the shifters. At the start of the story, Mulder rescues Scully from captivity and takes her to a lakeside cabin to recover from her trauma. We learn that, during her imprisonment, Scully was convinced by the aliens that Mulder was killed; then she was subjected to a nonstop series of interrogations and torture sessions by numerous shifters who all chose to take the form and voice of Mulder, in order to maximize her psychological anguish. Scully learned to hate the face of the man she most trusted. Thus, when she is alone with the real Mulder in the cabin, she is convinced that Mulder is simply another shifter, and that he will turn on her at any moment and dispel what she thinks is the illusion of having been freed—that the entire scenario of her escape from captivity is a cruel joke designed to deepen her pain.

Mulder, who has been searching for Scully since the start of colonization, is devastated to see that Scully does not believe he is himself. Scully thinks of Mulder as "it" (a shifter) rather than "him" (a person), avoids "it" as much as possible, and continually expresses her wish to run from the cabin. All Mulder wants is to reconnect with Scully, and to revive their friendship and partnership, but he cannot penetrate Scully's thick defenses of disbelief and doubt. One night, after several weeks of cohabitating in the cabin but barely speaking to one another, the standoff between Mulder and Scully comes to a head when Scully chooses to briefly speak with "it" about Mulder as they sit before the fireplace. Scully is nostalgic and reminisces about her partner, talking to Mulder as if he is a stranger who did not participate in the original conversation she is recalling, but since Mulder is Mulder, he remembers the conversation she references and supplies his line in the dialogue, which sends Scully into a rage, as she thinks the shifter is using Mulder's appropriated memories to imitate him:

"We had a discussion once, he and I," she says. It nods for her to continue. "I asked him what divination by flame was called."

"Lampadomany," it replies flatly.

"Do you have all his memories? Is that one of the things you can do? Did you steal _everything_?" she asks, feeling breathless and hysterical and missing Mulder so much she's almost weeping.

It shakes its head feebly, and its eyes are bright and sorrowful. "No," it whispers. "No."

"Why should I believe you're him? Tell me. Give me some definitive proof. Give me something they couldn't have tainted."

But it shakes its head again, and closes its eyes, and takes a shuddering breath. "I can't," it says. As it stands and pushes in the table chair, it says, softly, "But he loved you more than you will ever know. I can't pervert that. Nothing can."

Scully does not sleep this night. And she doesn't think it does either. (JET 2000)

Mulder confesses his deepest feelings for Scully at the moment when he realizes that even his love will not break through her wall of disbelief; in that instant, he knows that, tragically, he has found her only to lose her again. Scully leaves the cabin the morning after their fireside confrontation, intending to strike out on her own. Mulder sinks into despair. He allows the fire to go out and sits on the floor in darkness, utterly lost. But that evening, Scully decides to return to the cabin. When she finds Mulder hunched into himself on the floor, she touches him on the shoulder and looks into his eyes. The fear and sadness she sees there prompts her to think, for the first time, that maybe he *is* Mulder:

Oh God, she thinks. Oh my God.

He whispers, over and over, "It's me, Scully. It's _me_," and his voice is so soft and frightened the words seem dissolved by tears. ...

"Mulder, it's me," she whispers brokenly. "It's me, too." (JET 2000)

JET concludes "Night" here, with the words, "An end," the same line with which she closes all of her stories.

But, when I reread "Night" a few weeks ago, the mystery arose: after reaching "An end," I noticed for the first time that there was additional text, at the foot of the web page. Here is that additional text, which I had ignored in all my previous encounters with this story:

Improv Elements (Thanks, guys. <g>)

* Mulder losing his gun (again) on a case somewhere snowy, and defending himself with snowballs instead. From: Lori Daul
* A tango. From: Ambress
* Scully wearing a pair of Frohike's fingerless gloves. From: Maria Nicole

* Scully having a call waiting and it turns out to be Richard Gere who she met while on set. From: X-File_Addict
* Mulder getting a pedicure. From: Prianka Nandy
* Mulder, Scully and Skinner in a hot tub. Suits are optional. From: dksm
(Hey, they said I could use the elements any way I chose. ::blinking innocently::)
(JET 2000)

What this list of "Improv Elements" told me is that "Night Giving Off Flames" was specifically written in response to a writing challenge put forth by some *X-Files* fan friends of JET's. Evidently, the challenge was for JET to write a story, as an "improv" or "improvisation," incorporating a number of seemingly random story elements, each suggested by a different fan. After seeing the "Improv Elements" items, I glanced up to the story "headers," the text that precedes the story, at the top of the web page; in the headers, authors usually place all information that they think is relevant to orienting the reader. I quickly scanned the headers for "Night," which read as follows:

Night Giving Off Flames
By Jesemie's Evil Twin
[JET's email addresses]
Summary: "Yet from those flames no light, but rather darkness visible."
—John Milton
Disclaimer:[2] Not mine. Grr.
Category: Angst, Oddness, M/S [Mulder/Scully].
Quasi-Post-Colonization AU that occurs sometime after "Hollywood AD." Oddness. One wee-tiny spoiler for "HAD" and hardly any others whatsoever. Did I mention it's Odd?
Thank You: Shari and Liza. Mwa! You rock.
Feedback: Would be lovely, please and thank you. [author's email addresses] (JET 2000)

Then I read the final lines of the headers:

Scullyfic Improv (elements given at end)
June 2000 (JET 2000)

I had never before read these lines in the headers for "Night," just as I had never read the list of "Improv Elements" at the foot of the story. The words "Scullyfic Improv" refer to an event that occurred weekly on Scullyfic, a popular mailing list focusing on the Dana Scully character, founded in 1998 by renowned *X-Files* fan author Jill Selby (Fanlore, "Scullyfic"). Because I had overlooked the last line of the headers and the entire last section of text of "Night Giving Off Flames," I had never realized that the story was written when JET was selected as the Scullyfic Improv author-of-the-week, a selection that came with the task of weaving the story elements suggested by other mailing list members into a new story, to be completed and posted the following week.

It surprised me greatly to learn that "Night" was a Scullyfic Improv story, for three reasons. First, "Night" seems so well-crafted to me that I find it hard to believe that JET composed the piece in a single week. Of course, many fan authors write quickly, but it is difficult for most writers to achieve the refinement and depth that I think JET achieves in "Night" in seven days. Second, the list of Improv Elements that JET received from other fans, and which she had to place somewhere in her story, seem either comical (Mulder defending himself with snowballs, Richard Gere calling Scully) or kinky (Mulder and Scully in a hot tub with their supervisor, Agent Skinner), and thus completely antithetical to the tone of "Night," which is a somber story about wartime captivity, psychological torture, post-traumatic stress, and grief.

The final reason that I was shocked to read that "Night" was written as an Improv is that I cannot believe how thoroughly I ignored the author's clear indications, in the story headers and "footers," that this was the case. Why did I never attend to these sections of paratext before? Gerard Genette (1997) argues that "the main issue for the paratext is … to ensure for the text a destiny consistent with the author's purpose" (407), this purpose being "to ensure that the text is read properly" (197), however the author would define a "proper" reading. And thus, by overlooking all references to the improvisatory nature of "Night" contained in JET's preface and postface, I have to acknowledge the likelihood that for many years, I have read this story improperly. I must not have correctly or adequately understood what "Night Giving Off Flames" *is*, which is a story that emerged from a structured, regularly recurring group writing ritual in a fan community, a ritual that its founders chose to name after a type of live performance: *improvisation*. JET marks the story, in two places, as bearing a specific relation to improvisational theater, and so to read the story "properly" would mean to take this relation to theater, to embodied performance, into account.

What would it mean to *take into account*, that is, to take seriously, to count as noteworthy and significant, that this fan fiction story links itself to improv theater? It would mean, first of all, recognizing that some key characteristics of improvised performance can be found in the online improv challenge that gave rise to "Night." Hazel Smith and Roger Dean (1997) state, "Improvisation … provides a tool for collaboration between several individuals, be they creators, performers or audience/participants" (4). In a live improv show, there is typically collaboration between the performers and the audience when audience members call out themes, phrases, characters, or scenarios to the stage, and the improv artists work to spontaneously weave these suggestions into their sketches.[3] Similarly, JET received suggestions from her fellow *X-Files* fans and incorporated all of them into the fic she wrote in one week. Although the seven days that JET was given to write "Night" makes her experience far different than that of a stage improv performance troupe, which must respond to audiences' prompts within minutes, the fact that the Scullyfic site chose to title its time-limited writing assignments "Improv Challenges" speaks to the desire of online fans to create group experiences of immediacy, spontaneity, and urgency, experiences similar to live and in-person improvisatory performances.

Many of the "Improv Elements" given for "Night" make their appearances in the story as flashbacks, when Scully or Mulder recall the adventures they had, before the alien colonization, investigating weird and strange phenomena as FBI agents. At one point in the story, Scully remembers "Mulder defending himself with snowballs" as they were both being chased by vampires in Vermont; at another point, Mulder flips through his old journal and finds a note that was once passed to Scully in a meeting, stating "Richard Gere's on line two," which was a coded message informing her that their supervisor, Skinner, was calling regarding an urgent matter. In the same journal, Mulder spies a photograph taken of him, Scully, and Skinner standing (clothed) in an empty hot tub in the middle of a showroom, all three examining a huge cocoon containing an unknown creature hanging from the ceiling. Thus, by liberally using the device of flashbacks, JET managed to integrate the highly disparate, and mostly very lighthearted, elements provided to her by her "audience"—the fans who were eager to read the story that she would create from their suggestions—into her fic, relegating these humorous moments to Mulder and Scully's past, while the narrative present, the time in which "Night" takes place, is permeated by sorrow and despair for the protagonists.

Another characteristic of improvisational performance, according to Smith and Dean (1997, 4), is that "an audience can often recognise that improvisation is taking place. This knowledge … encourages an enthusiastic response which is otherwise sometimes lacking. An audience sympathetic to the risk-taking of performers is a supportive one." Here, too, a relation between improvisational theater and JET's writing "Night" as an "improv fic" can be inferred: we can assume that the Scullyfic mailing list members, those who contributed story suggestions to JET and those who simply read the improv challenge as it was launched on the mailing list, understood the "risk" that JET undertook when she accepted the challenge. JET did not know what elements would be suggested to her, and so she did not know what she would have to incorporate into her story. Like the audience of a live improv performance, JET's readers were probably highly appreciative of JET's willingness to have story requirements imposed on her by others, and of her attempt to write a viable story under strict time constraints.

The Scullyfic mailing list is no longer accessible, so I have no evidence as to whether JET's improvisational effort met with "an enthusiastic response" from a "sympathetic" and "supportive" audience. However, we do have evidence that the author felt a connection with the fans who gave her suggestions (requirements) for her improv, as she addresses them with gratitude (which may or may not be sarcastic) and a grin ("Thanks guys. <g>") in her postface. She also addresses members of her audience who were not a part of the group that proposed the "Improv Elements": "Hey, they said I could use the elements any way I chose. ::blinking innocently::". And she thanks a pair of individuals ("Shari and Liza") who may have helped her in some way with the story, perhaps by beta reading;[4] she blows them a kiss in text: "Mwa!"

Thus, in addition to the structural resemblances between live improv and the online Scullyfic Improv challenge (the artist/audience collaboration and the enthusiasm of the audience for the improviser), we have analogues of physical gestures included in the paratexts of "Night"—the author *grins* and *blinks* and *blows kisses* at her readers. She also growls at them, in humorously expressing her unhappiness at not being the legal owner of *The X-Files* in her disclaimer: "Not mine. Grr." There is thus a reference to a body in these paratexts, the author's body, or rather, the author's *face*, a face that communicates the author's feelings, intentions, and moods to the reader through economical combinations of text and punctuation.

What are we to make of these allusions to, and explicit invocations of, live performance and physical expression in the paratexts surrounding this Internet fan fiction story? Should we think of JET's, and her fellow fans', collaborative participation in the Scullyfic Improv challenge as *like* improv theater, but *not really* improv theater, since obviously JET's story consists of HTML read as words by her geospatially diffused readers on their screens, and not a set of physical and vocal actions executed in front of her audience's seated bodies? Should we discount the *expressions* communicated by JET's virtual face because the grin and kiss and growl are not made by a mouth that readers can see or hear, and the blinking is not performed by eyes that readers can meet with their own gazes?

It is probable that the body of the Internet fan author and the bodies of her readers do not physically interact in an event such as an improv writing challenge like the Scullyfic Improv. Nevertheless, I am certain that there is *embodied interaction* between the writer and the readers. In fact, I would say that Internet fan fiction, a genre comprising narrative texts distributed via digital networks and accessed on computer screens, is a *body medium*. A *body medium* mediates between physical bodies that are remote from one another. My thinking on body mediums/media builds on Beth Coleman's (2011) theory of avatar communication in "X-reality."

The Body in X-Reality

"My assessment is that networked media, as a whole, simulates presence. … Being here does not rely exclusively on a physical instantiation. In other words, neither geographic territory nor corporeal embodiment stand as the exclusive indication of being somewhere, or being present. I am not arguing for an equivalence of lived, bodily experience with our experience of being filtered through an avatar (our networked proxies). I am arguing for recognition of porous spheres of engagement that meet across a continuum of the actual" (Coleman 2011, 36). In this quote, Beth Coleman lays out the major claim of her book, *Hello Avatar*: that "reality," inclusive of phenomena bearing names such as the "real world," "real life," and "really there," is now mixed.[5] Since at least the advent of networked computing, humans have become accustomed to repeatedly having "the sense of being in two places at once," experiencing "an interlacing of virtual and real experiences" (19). Coleman calls the crossing between virtual and real presence, and the uncertainty of what is produced at that crossing, "X-reality." She writes, "X-reality describes a world that is no longer distinctly virtual or real but, instead, representative of a diversity of network combinations. … With the concept of X-reality, I see … an end of the binary logic of virtual and real. What has emerged from our collective use of networked technologies is an engagement that moves across sites that are real, simulated, and variously augmented" (19–20).

Many of Coleman's examples of "the sensation of being together across lines of mediation, which is called 'copresence'" (25), consist of real-time, avatar-based interactions, such as two Second Life users waving to one another through their designated digital forms. But I extend "X-reality" to instances that are asynchronous, and not avatar-based in the way that Second Life is. I argue that online improvisatory writing challenges, such as the weekly Scullyfic Improvs from the late 1990s and early 2000s, were just as much examples of people coming together, *being* together, and *doing* together, as any event that transpired in Second Life. In fact, given Second Life's clunkiness, its frequent lag times, and its plastic-looking avatars with their jerky motions, I would say that the networked text-based collaborations of the 1990s, beginning with collaborative text-based game spaces such as MUDs (multi-user dungeons) and MOOs (MUDs, object oriented) and ending with online fan fiction communities such as Scullyfic, were equally or more convincing to users *as* a mixed reality than Second Life and other visually rendered, real-time virtual spaces from the early-to-mid-2000s.

Coleman acknowledges that, while she, as a Second Life participant, could ignore that platform's "hitches and glitches" (22) and feel immersed in the communities that sprung up there, "perfect simulation is not a baseline requirement for meaningful communication" (31). Even when Internet users have been limited to quite slow and low-resolution forms of networked communication, they have "seize[d] upon the opportunities to extend sites of connectivity and bring, with all manner of resourcefulness, a great capacity to weed through the noisiness of a media signal to find the message being sent" (31). On the one hand, we can interpret JET's laconic "facial" expressions, her <g> and her ::blinking innocently::, as digital gestures that her readers did not need any visual cues to comprehend— JET found a way to send visual, physical messages through a nonvisual medium, and her readers figured out how to decode, how to "see," the faces that JET was making. On the other hand, I would say JET's delivering a facial performance through text in 2000 was a faster, crisper way of communicating "physically" than most of today's synchronous video-based applications permit—there is an ease and speed of expressiveness, even physical expressiveness, that text can achieve that networked video still cannot. Until Skype, Google Hangout, FaceTime, and other video chat software can represent human faces and bodies to one another with a clarity and instantaneity that replicates that experienced in the "real world," where people are "face to face" with one another, networked text (or voice—let us not forget the benefits of clear telephonic connections) may be preferable to video as a *body medium*.

Networked text functions as a body medium in that it brings bodies together in a mixed reality (X-reality) space and represents them to one another. JET's grinning and blinking to her readers is an example of one user communicating bodily gestures to many users. Another, more contemporary example is the use of emoticons and "emoji" (the Japanese term for ideograms of "smileys" or smiley faces) in SMS (Short Message Service) or mobile texting, in which users convey their feelings to one another using digital faces or other body-representing icons. Through abbreviations such as "LOL," "LMAO," and "ROTFL," commonly used in email and texting and first popularized in early online Usenet newsgroups, users indicate to one another that they are laughing, perhaps loudly, perhaps so loudly that the force of their laughter has sent them proverbially tumbling to the floor, where they are still rolling around, laughing. The mental images of bodily movements and actions conjured by electronic text are crucial to networked communication; body representations permeate all manner of Internet writing.

When a person *"is* online," or *"on* email," or *"on* their phone," she is experiencing what it is to *be* in X-reality. What defines this mode of being is the simultaneous use of two bodies. In the "real" world, the user has a visible, physical body that is largely un(der)utilized, used only for the purpose of remaining still, often reduced to eyes, wrists, thumbs, and fingers, which we might call her *default* body. In the "virtual" world, the user has a body composed of letters, punctuation marks, icons, photos, animations, graphically rendered humanoid figures, or video of physical bodies, which we might call her *composed* body.

I choose the term "default" for the physical human body for an intuitive reason: the body into which each person is born is the body that they cannot escape, and into that body, no one else can enter; it is hers, and hers alone, by default. My use of "default" also stems from Bernard Stiegler's (1998) use of "default" in his essay "The Fault of Epimetheus" (in *Technics and Time*, vol. 1). The essay focuses on the myth of Prometheus, the Greek Titan who brought fire from the realm of the gods to humankind and was severely punished by for this crime. Stiegler, interpreting Plato's *Protagoras*, which offers one version of the Prometheus story, relates that, at the dawn of creation, Prometheus (meaning: forethought) had to give humans the gift of fire to remedy a mistake made by his brother, Epimetheus (meaning: afterthought): Epimetheus had been charged with distributing all possible talents and abilities to all of the creatures of the world, but after Epimetheus had given out all powers to the various animals, he realized he had forgotten to save anything to give to humans. Writes Stiegler (1998, 114), "Man arrives because of something forgotten by Epimetheus, who had distributed 'all the qualities,' leaving man naked, in default of being, having yet to begin being: his condition will be to supplement this default of origin by procuring for himself prostheses, instruments." Stiegler regards the state of human being as a state of inherent default, of always needing technics, of never being sufficient without tools, without prostheses, without instruments. The "originary default" that humans have always perceived in themselves (mythologized in the Prometheus/Epimetheus story of creation, in which humans must "steal," or have stolen for them, fire from the gods in order to begin to *be* human) has driven humans to be technical, to produce and hybridize with technics from the start of human history.

Thus, by calling the physical human body "the default body," I mean that the human body is always, and has always been, searching for technological supplements, augmentations, alternate incarnations, mediations. The default body yearns for composed bodies. Humans require both bodies of nature and bodies of *techne* for their being human. This is in opposition to a view of human being that rejects the necessity of mediation, which was thoroughly articulated by Jean-Jacques Rousseau and still thrives today: "Rousseau, precisely, wants to show that there is no originary default, no prostheses, that the claws missing in man ... [are] not inscribed in any process of mediation. The man of nature, without prostheses, is robust, as robust as man can be—and it is civilization that will weaken him" (Stiegler 1998, 115). If humans are not in default, then technics only weaken them; but by conceptualizing the sense of being-in-default as the defining feature of human being, we can embrace the drive for technical augmentation and transformation that humans have always sought.

Just prior to the rise of digital technologies, John Fiske took note of humans' enthusiasm for the multiplication of their bodies via media: observing a 1994 live televised news event featuring massive crowds of people,[6] Fiske (1996) wrote, "On seeing themselves on their own TVs, they waved to themselves, for postmodern people have no problem in being simultaneously and indistinguishably livepeople and mediapeople" (264). Composed bodies are not exclusive to television or digital media, but in electronic media spaces, composed bodies proliferate, and the plurality of embodiment becomes a norm.

Even though only "mediapeople," that is, users' composed bodies, meet in X-reality, they do meet, often, and do things together, such as prod one another to write fan fiction stories at certain times, and demand that certain semiabsurd and seemingly incompatible elements be incorporated into them. And who, or what body, performs these tasks put to them in the electronic spaces and events where composed bodies gather and hang out? The default bodies must apply fingers to keyboards and actually write the stories, but it is the composed bodies that "present" the finished stories to their comrades and followers—their audiences—on the mailing list or in the archive. It is JET's composed body that announces, in the preface to "Night," that "Night" is the result of an improv writing challenge, and it is JET's composed body that, in the postface to the story, expresses thanks, and grins, and blinks innocently. It is the composed body that rolls on the floor, laughing out loud. The default body may be sitting, expressionless, while the composed body guffaws, howls, and tumbles about in such a way that its addressees in X-reality can "hear" and "see" it.

Sometimes, the composed body strongly evokes and echoes the default body: legions of posts on social media sites, blogs, and vlogs describe, sometimes in great detail, physical bodily events such as a baby's diaper disasters, a cancer victim's illness, or a transgender person's pre- and post-op experiences. Internet readers and viewers of these posts feel that they become familiar with the default bodies of the posters by coming into contact with their electronic representations, their composed bodies (which again, are pixels on screens, whether the pixels form texts or images, whether the pixels are taken from life or not). As I mentioned in break 0, a great deal of scholarly literature on performance and new media concentrates on the many ways that users "perform the self" online, through first-person postings or references to real-world events, and even though many of these self-presentations can be quite far from the "reality" of posters' default bodies (both Stone [1991] and Waskul [2005] give examples of men "passing" as women in online chat rooms), they can make other users believe in their reality.

But the composed body that LOLs or blinks innocently at its readers often does not evoke, in the imaginations of its audience, any body at all. If the reader of an email personally knows the individual who includes an LOL in their message, then perhaps he imagines the face of the sender breaking out into laughter. But in the case of a fan author grinning at her fellow fans, I imagine a blank face, something like a mask. And even in the case of reading LOLs in messages from people whose faces I know well, I do not imagine their default bodies laughing; I imagine that it is their online persona who laughs, some face that exists only as a representation of their mental state, or their moods, that is showing itself to me.

Or, a composed body may reference something that has actually taken place in the default body, but in online communication, it is what happens to the composed body that holds significance for its interlocutors. For example, in her interview, fan author Jacqueline (2012) recalls when she wrote a fanfic for an online friend who asked Jacqueline to "stop bothering me with all of this *Stargate* stuff, because I'm into *House*." (*Stargate* refers to a science fiction franchise about time-and-space travel that includes three films, three live-action television series, and one animated television series; *House* is a US television medical drama.) In response to this request, Jacqueline says, "I paid her back. I wrote a *House*/*Stargate* crossover with porn in it and turned her bright red, which I can tell over the Internet" (2012). Jacqueline here indicates that she did not see her friend's facial or bodily reactions, but that she "can tell over the Internet," despite the absence of visual data, that Jacqueline's erotic fiction turned her friend "bright red." I suspect that even though this blushing may have actually taken place in Jacqueline's friend's physical body, what matters to Jacqueline is that it definitely took place in her composed body. In other words, the friend likely gave some information to Jacqueline, through text or emoticons, that expressed a degree of embarrassment that Jacqueline interpreted as blushing, and this "facial" reaction is what so pleased Jacqueline.

Coleman declares that, given the proliferation of "new practices around media engagement," we must begin "trying to fathom what it means to come face-to-face by way of mediation" (Coleman 2011, 28). Jacqueline's interaction with her friend is, to me, an instance of mediated face-to-face communication. Jacqueline and her friend *are* "face to face," but in a media space, not in a physical space. Jacqueline "can tell over the Internet" that her friend has turned "bright red" after reading a pornographic fanfic that Jacqueline wrote for her, because the friend's composed body makes this reddening clear. And it was not important to Jacqueline whether or not the physical body blushed; she did not need to see a photo of the friend's face. Jacqueline triumphed because she made her friend's composed body, the body she knows and comes into contact with, blush.

Then, there are many composed bodies that have little or nothing to do with posters' "real," physical, default bodies at all. The fantastical creatures of MMORPGs (massively multiplayer online role-playing games) such as World of Warcraft come to mind. Any photos or icons of purely imaginary beings, symbols, or animals used as online avatars are immediately understood by those who view them as being nonidentical to the users' actual embodied forms and appearances. And into this category of nonidentical avatars I place Internet fans' appropriations of bodies that are well-known to them through mass media texts. I do not think that JET, or any fan author, means for the fan reader to conflate the bodies of Gillian Anderson or David Duchovny, the actors who portrayed Scully and Mulder in the *X-Files* television series and films, with their own default bodies, even when they write from Scully's and/or Mulder's point of view. Fans' appropriations of performers' bodies as composed bodies are not executed for the purpose of self-presentation, but for another purpose. I call it *marionetting*.

Marionette versus Avatar

In break 0, I discussed a number of early new media theorists who framed global communications networks and computer use as "global theater," including Marshall McLuhan, Brenda Laurel, Allucquére Rosanne Stone, and Sherry Turkle. I also cited two theorists of fan practices, Kurt Lancaster and Francesca Coppa, who propose that writing fan fiction is akin more to producing performances than to producing literary texts. Coppa uses the phrase "writing bodies in space" to describe what fans are undertaking when they create fan fiction stories, which is the "appropriation and use of existing characters." Coppa defines fan fiction "as a textual attempt to make certain characters 'perform' according to different behavioral strips" (Coppa 2006b, 230), citing Richard Schechner's argument that "living behavior[s]" are "strips of behavior" that, like film strips, "can be rearranged or reconstructed; they are independent of the casual systems (personal, social political, technological) that brought them into existence. They have a life of their own" [Schechner 2013, 34]). Coppa takes up Schechner's notion that embodied behaviors have a "life of their own" and applies it to fictional characters: "Perhaps the characters who populate fan fiction are themselves the behavioral strips, able to walk out of one story and into another, acting independently of the works of art that brought them into existence. … Characters are able to 'walk' not only from one artwork into another, but from one genre into another; fan fiction articulates that characters are neither constructed nor owned, but have, to use Schechner's phrase, a life of their own" (Coppa 2006b, 230).

McLuhan's theory of the global theater invites us to conceive of online content as performance. McLuhan and Nevitt (1972) postulate that electronic networks constitute a world-spanning site in which a "perpetual happening" takes place, in which all users can take advantage of the affordances of network technology to be "actors." Some of the performances by users/actors are presentations of self, in a Goffmanian sense. Self-presentations online consist of users creating virtual selves to represent them, which can take the form of an avatar, or what I call a composed body, in textual, visual, or audiovisual form; in some cases, as I mentioned above, users' performances of self through their composed bodies need not bear any resemblance to their default bodies or real-world personas.

But a different type of online performance is the performance of others, the presentation of composed bodies that represent not users' "selves," but characters. Fans and other remix artists appropriate the appearances, voices, manners of speech, gestures, ways of walking and moving through space, and ways of making contact with other bodies, from characters whose performances they see in films, television programs, music videos, animated films and anime, and other audiovisual media. Schechner states that "strips of behavior" can be extracted from their sources and "rearranged and reconstructed" like film strips, and fans do exactly this: they treat media recordings as archives of bodies moving, and then "copy" those bodies and extend their movements into spaces of their own design, following scripts of their own devising.

Schechner anticipated Internet fan culture and remix culture when he compared restored behavior in performance to film strips, for fan and remix practices highlight human performance as the most crucial and usable parts of film and other recorded media. Whether in fan fiction and fan videos, or in image macros, GIFs, or memes such as rickrolling[7] in which Internet users deploy images or clips of actors, singers, and other performers (in or out of character) to make a joke, express a feeling, or advocate for a social or political cause, human performance is the important element in film, TV, and video that gets ported into digital networks.

In the mixed reality of online communication, fans create a "mix" of extracted behaviors with original scenarios, turning the actual bodies of performers into composed bodies that act out the stories fans direct them to, similar to the manner in which children use virtual action figures, dolls, or puppets to "enact" (through the children's manipulations) a wide scope of adventures. One reason that I now call fans' processes of extraction and transformation *archontic production* (instead of *archontic literature*, a term I used earlier) is because the content that fans produce for the Internet is as much theater as it is literature, and fan authors are producers and directors as much as they are writers. *Marionetting* is another term that can point to the ways that performers' bodies are virtualized and translated into networks; appropriated, replicated, and altered by multiple users in the network; and then made to play out a range of narratives for other users' entertainment. While online users can perform themselves through digital avatars, they can also make characters perform through digital marionettes.

My basis for the term "marionetting" is theater director E. Gordon Craig's idea of the "über-marionette," which he proposed in a 1907 essay. New media performance artist Christopher Maraffi states that Craig, influenced by the stylized movements of his contemporaries, such as actor Henry Irving and dancer Isadora Duncan, argued that for acting to move completely to a language of symbolic gesture, "all live actors should be replaced by autonomous puppets" (Maraffi 2011, 1). In "The Actor and The Über-Marionette," Craig ([1907] 2002) writes, "The actor must go, and in his place comes the inanimate figure—the Über-marionette we may call him, until he has won for himself a better name" (159). Craig's objection to live actors was their unreliability: live actors are inconsistent from performance to performance, and therefore subject the audience to "emotional confessions of weakness"—uncertainty, forgetfulness, and other human foibles that manifest as missteps in theatrical performances—"which are nightly witnessed by the people" (161). In contrast, the puppet, wholly controllable by the puppet master and therefore capable of delivering identical performances night after night, may "become the faithful medium for the beautiful thoughts of the artist"; that is, the puppet can be entirely devoted to the controller's artistic vision, and can execute that vision perfectly, while a live actor can never be perfect in their execution. Craig foresaw the emergence of something more than a puppet, some performing agent that would be realized through a new technology that he could not predict: "No longer content with a puppet, we must create an über-marionette. The über-marionette will not compete with life—rather will it go beyond it" (161).

Paul M. Malone's historical research reveals that Craig borrowed the term "über-marionette" from Heinrich von Kleist and Friedrich Nietzsche, both of whom saw the marionette as "the symbol of an epiphany both aesthetic and spiritual," an entity capable of enacting "the perfect relationship between director and actor—or rather, artist and implement performing subject and performing object" (Malone 2000, 58). The composed bodies that fans use in X-reality achieve the relationship of which Craig dreamed, the unity of artist and implement. The bodies visible in the mass media archive, over which fans have little to no control, are transformed by fans into bodies that they can script and direct as they choose. Fans' appropriation of bodies from the archive of mass culture is often born of frustration with the quality of the media industries' products, or rather frustration at the often-unrealized potential (whether for character/plot complexity, emotional depth, or explicit sexuality) that fans perceive in these products, and this frustration is akin to Craig's ire with the unreliable, imperfect actor, the live actor who can never deliver exactly what the director wants. The digital marionette can do what the live actor cannot: enact precisely the scenario that the fan creator desires. Through the marionette, the audience member seizes power over the media properties that the media industries sell to her, and customizes the mass-manufactured product into an "implement" that she, as artist, can use to make entertainment for herself and others—forms of entertainment she longs for, but never receives from official media.

The Workings of Digital Marionettes

Marionetting depends on its audiences being well situated in, and already oriented to, the source texts that get "reconstructed" into new intertexts— already familiar with the source bodies that get translated into new composed bodies, in the network. This is what Coppa means when she states that "we know who these [mass media] characters are because we know the actors who play them, and we bring our memories of their physicality to the text, so the reader is precharged" to encounter the characters again in fan fiction (Coppa 2006b, 235–236). In JET's "Night Giving Off Flames," as in all fan fiction stories, it is necessary for the reader to have prior knowledge of the performances of Anderson-as-Scully and Duchovny-as-Mulder, individually and together. Without knowing how the characters interrelate, verbally and physically—what conversations they have repeatedly, what conflicts continually arise between them, how they stand and walk together, how they address one another—it is impossible to decipher "Night," to understand how it works.

To grasp "Night," one must first know that a core feature of *The X-Files*, reenacted over and over in the majority of the series' episodes, is the divide between Scully and Mulder along the lines of doubt and belief: Scully is a medical doctor, a forensic specialist, and a skeptic about anything outside the bounds of science; Mulder is a psychologist, a researcher of paranormal and occult phenomena, and someone who takes seriously reports of alien abduction. Most episodes contain at least one scene in which Scully balks at the notion that the underlying cause for a mystery she and Mulder are attempting to solve has anything to do with supernatural or alien phenomena, and at least one scene in which Mulder fervently tries to convince Scully to believe that beneath the mystery-of-the-week are real aliens, ghosts, magic, vampires, golems, or some other strange being or force. "Belief" is one term that comes up again and again in Mulder and Scully's debates; Mulder has a poster of a UFO behind his desk with the phrase "I Want to Believe" printed in bold white letters on it, and Scully doggedly refuses to believe in extraterrestrial life. But, while the partners disagree about whether or not to "believe," they agree on another term: "trust." Trust also comes up repeatedly in Mulder and Scully's talks, as they uncover the invasion conspiracy piece by piece and reiterate to one another that they can "trust no one," and that the only person each can trust is the other.

JET's "Night" is thus a fan fiction story about the core axes on which Mulder and Scully's partnership and relationship turns: they are opposites in matters of "belief" (Mulder believes and Scully does not), and united in matters of "trust" (they trust only each other). JET takes these two principles and plays them out to an extreme: What if Scully were definitively stripped of her trust in Mulder? What if her innate skepticism were greatly amplified by a terror-inducing period of captivity, and her disbelief coupled with radical distrust of her partner? In all of Scully's declarations of refusing to believe that Mulder is who he says he is in "Night," we hear the echo of Scully saying, "That's impossible," or "There's no science to back that up" to Mulder in the episodes of the series. And in all of Scully's avowals in "Night" that she cannot trust Mulder, not for a moment, we can "see," in our mind's eye, Mulder's pain at losing the one person whom he trusted.

Our ability to envision Scully and Mulder's suffering as they experience a seemingly unbridgeable rift also depends on our having already seen, on the television series and in the *X-Files* feature films, Scully and Mulder's occasional forced separations, reunions, and reaffirmations of their bond. One of the series' recurring plot devices is that Mulder and Scully are often "taken" from one another. Scully and Mulder are each abducted, presumably by aliens and/or their human conspirators, over the course of the series, and the psychological and physical well-being of each is often endangered. Images of the protagonists running frantically when they have been separated, searching for one another in the corridors of an alien spaceship, the backyard of an abandoned tract house, the hallways of a hospital's cancer unit, and a vast cornfield in Iowa fill the screens and memories of *X-Files* viewers. "You're the only one I trust," and "You are my touchstone" are phrases the partners tell one another earnestly, in soft voices, their gazes locked onto one another's, each time that they reconnect after rescuing one another from some harrowing predicament. Scully and Mulder rarely touch, but they do when one is physically injured or otherwise in distress, usually just a brief clasping of hands or a touch on the shoulder. Typically, they sit vigil at each other's bedside when one is in the hospital. All of these physicalized gestures of urgency, desperation, anxiety, and need when they are apart, and of closeness, friendship, and emotional intimacy when they are reunited, are recorded in viewers' memories. JET calls up these visual and emotional tropes in "Night," distilling the entire relationship of Mulder and Scully down to their greatest fear, and the apparent realization of that fear: their seemingly irrevocable loss of one another.

He slips into her bedroom and tiptoes to her bedside. He brushes the inside of her wrist with his fingers, feels the sweet-slow hot pulse there. He touches her only once, and only for a second.

He tries not to think that he may lose her yet again, and permanently. His eyes are dry and stinging. He is awake until dawn, her heat echoing across the nerves in his palms as though he's been scalded. (JET 2000)

These short paragraphs are poignant for the fan reader, as they invoke many scenes that have played out in the series. These paragraphs' effectiveness depend on the reader previously having seen similar sequences of abduction, rescue, trauma, and the threat of separation and death played out multiple times in the source text. And yet the scenario of threatened division between the partners that JET delivers is far more dire than anything the television show or films depict—after all, *The X-Files* is fundamentally an action/adventure/mystery series, not a series about aliens colonizing the Earth, imprisoning and torturing law enforcement officers, and those individuals subsequently plummeting into post-traumatic stress disorder. An alien invasion facilitated by human conspirators is the presumptive future that Mulder and Scully work frantically to forestall, but the premise of the series is that the heroes can and will succeed in exposing the conspiracy and preventing this future from coming to pass. By resetting the show in a fundamentally darker universe, JET is able to stage already familiar characters in a scenario in which they must play out what they most dread: an alternate reality in which their quest to stop the conspiracy has failed, the world is colonized by a hostile extraterrestrial force, Scully has been horribly victimized, and the bone-deep connection of Scully and Mulder is broken.

At the end of the story, however, JET inserts a happy ending, when Scully's realizes that "it," whom she believes is a clone keeping her captive, is actually Mulder, who has rescued her from captivity. When Scully returns to the cabin and Mulder avers, "It's me, Scully," Scully responds, "Mulder, it's me. It's me, too." Here, JET invokes one of the most often-repeated, and most mundane, exchanges of dialogue between the partners from the series: anytime Mulder or Scully call one another on their mobile phones, they announce their identity without stating their names, Scully usually saying "Mulder, it's me," and Mulder saying, "It's me, Scully." JET knows that these simple lines, heard so often in the source text, will resonate for her readers when the readers come to them at the end of "Night Giving Off Flames." The "It's me" that both characters speak at the end of "Night" serve not as simple perfunctory telephone greetings but as a spoken solution to the mystery of the entire fan fiction story, which is: Will Scully ever believe, and trust, that "it" is Mulder? "It's me" has tethered them, simply and effectively, when they have been physically remote from each other in the "past," and at the end of the events of "Night," "It's me" binds them together again, after a time when they have been close in physical proximity, yet distant and divided from one another emotionally.

Thus, the fan author translates or ports the embodied speech and actions of the characters of an audiovisual source text into virtualized, composed bodies that she can control and maneuver. The performances of Anderson and Duchovny as Scully and Mulder, their voices and gestures, how they stand and sit in physical proximity to one another, how they look at one another, their repeated—Schechner would say "restored"—behavior in recurring situations, for example, situations of abduction/separation and reunion/rescue, are all crucial to the fan author's writing of the story, and to the fan reader's ability to make sense of the story. The fan author deliberately echoes dialogue and actions from the source text so that the reader can understand the particular torque she is putting on the familiar characters and the universe in which they dwell. Without any prior knowledge of the physicality and aurality of Mulder and Scully, as well as of the common themes and narrative arcs of the series, a reader of "Night Giving Off Flames" could not grasp that the story actualizes two of the most terrifying potential futures hinted at in the series—devastating global colonization by aliens, and a rupturing of the Scully and Mulder partnership—to their logical but harrowing ends. (Is the story compromised by the sudden reunion of the partners, which seems to pander to most fans' refusal to tolerate any permanent rift between the heroes? In my opinion, JET's transformation of the usually quotidian "It's me" lines into magical, healing speech saves the ending from being maudlin or incredulous, but other fan readers may disagree.)

Fan fiction is therefore a body medium and a form of marionetting, in that fan authors, in textual fictions, translate recorded performances by live bodies into composed bodies represented by text, and stage new performances by those bodies. The network is the site of these virtual enactments; it is the performance space, a "global theater," in which shows are put on and received by any user who wishes to participate in the "perpetual happening."

Archival Bodies

Fan fiction, like theatrical restagings, incorporates translations and echoes of the physicality and aurality of previous performers. The gestures, blocking, and manner of verbal delivery used in early stage productions of any given play inform later productions of that play; these become the *conventional* ways of staging the play, and even if later productions defy the conventions established by the initial productions, they still must contend with them. Similarly, the bodies and voices of actors who appear in mass media texts are the models for the composed bodies placed by fan authors in the global theater. This influence on, modeling of, and *remembering* of, bodies by bodies is what Diana Taylor calls *repertoire*.

Taylor does not strictly oppose *repertoire* to *archive*. "The archive and the repertoire exist in a constant of interaction," Taylor writes. "They usually work in tandem, and they work alongside other systems of transmission—the digital and the visual, to name two" (2003, 21). One example that Taylor gives of archive and repertoire interacting is based on media scholar Jesús Martín-Barbero's research on Latin American soap opera fan cultures: Taylor writes that Barbero "illustrates the uses that viewers make of mass media, say, the soap opera. It's not simply that the media impose structures of desire and appropriate behavior. How populations develop ways of viewing, living with, and retelling or recycling the materials allows for a broad range of responses. Mediations, he argues, not the media, provide the key to understanding social behaviors. Those responses and behaviors, in turn, are taken up and appropriated by the mass media in a dialogic, rather than one-way, manner" (Taylor 2003, 21). Barbero's essay, published in English in 1995 (in Robert C. Allen's influential edited essay collection *To Be Continued ...: Soap Operas around the World*) makes arguments about media fans being active participants in their receptions of mass texts, arguments that resonate with those made by Stuart Hall, John Fiske, Dick Hebdige, and other prominent US and UK media and cultural studies scholars at that time. What Taylor adds to the "active audience" line of thinking is her focus on embodiment. Taylor claims that embodied behaviors (repertoire) and mass media (archive) engage in mutual appropriations, relating "in a dialogic, rather than one-way, manner." Taylor draws on Barbero to advance the idea that repertoires emerge from audiences' consumptions of "archival"—that is, recorded—media, such as film and television.

Applying Taylor's insights to fan fiction culture, I would say that fans plunder archival media for bodies they can use. Fans appropriate the repertoires of bodily performances that they see on screens, and reenact those repertoires in different spaces. One perceives, in fans' stories of the myriad ways that they have converted mass media archive into repertoires both embodied and textual, a fluidity of travel between the real world and X-reality. This fluidity indicates that repertoire lends itself readily to transmediation. Repertoire migrates freely from medium to medium, from physical space to media space and back again. Fans copy performers' bodies over and over again, using clothes and makeup and voices as well as text and icons and videos. Repertoire is manifested through both default bodies and composed bodies.

Writing is certainly a major component of fan fiction creation, but when we seek to understand how a piece of fanfic works and how it should be judged in terms of success or failure, virtuosity or banality, we would do better to look to performance cultures rather than literary cultures for models. One question that a fan reader might ask in evaluating a fan fiction story, for example, is, Did the new incarnations of the familiar characters seem both true to their sources, and yet revelatory, showing some dimensions of the characters that we never before suspected but that felt utterly believable when we witnessed those previously unseen aspects displayed? This is a question that theatergoers would ask of a contemporary production of any classic play, any widely known cultural source material. Does the new Clytemnestra, Lady Macbeth, Hedda Gabler, Song Liling, or Walter Younger— the one who appears before me now, at this moment, in this version—seem recognizable as the one I know from the written texts of Aeschylus (1984), Shakespeare (1997), Ibsen (2013), Hwang (1993), or Hansberry (1994), and/ or from prior productions of the source material, and yet also seem very different? Does the new version take the character, and perhaps the entire production, in an unexpected direction, unearthing buried facets that may have lain dormant in the source, or adding surprising twists that make of the originary piece something entirely fresh? In other words, does the new version make good use of the archive of source text elements, and does it also make an interesting, unique, or otherwise valuable contribution to that archive?

Global Media, Local Uses

Composed bodies based on fictional characters are not the only bodies that perform fan repertoires. Fans also perform their constructed selves in the global theater. We can elaborate on Taylor's argument that fans build repertoire from their receptions of archival media, and propose that founding and participating in fan communities are among the forms of repertoire that emerge from active audiences' interactions with mass media texts. Taylor writes that the media event of Princess Diana's funeral in 1997 sparked a number of appropriations by Latin Americans, South Americans, and people of color in the United States, including murals that depicted Diana as a "saint, victim, and media object"; Taylor (2003) asks, "How did these global images get downloaded onto these neighborhood walls?" (135). Taylor expresses surprise at how quickly, and how widely, the "downloading" of images of the much-photographed and much-televised UK princess occurred after her death; Taylor is especially struck by how many minorities in the United States and people in the Global South identified with, and mourned, Diana. But the "downloading" of useful iconography from the archive of images and sounds constituted by mass media is the exemplary operation of repertoire on the Internet. In other words, it is appropriate that Taylor uses a networking metaphor ("downloading") in her discussion of Diana's fans' appropriating Diana's image and porting it from their television screens into their own wall murals, for this creation of repertoire from archive is precisely what Internet fans do when they appropriate the images and voices of any performer who appears in a media text and transmediate it into fan fiction, video, or art.

Acts of "downloading" popular media culture can be seen as instances of *repertoire* partly because they are made for specific local audiences. These downloadings are responses to global media by members of the global media audience *for one another*. Although the Diana wall mural artists may have enjoyed the opportunity to have their art "taken up and appropriated by the mass media in a dialogic manner" (Taylor 2003, 21), their murals were repertoire rather than archive (or rather, were archive-based repertoire) because they were communications by fans to fellow fans, by mourners to fellow mourners. These murals were not broadcasts, but "narrowcasts," community-casts. And the majority of people who saw the murals and understood them, their meanings, and crucially, their *affective power*—that is, the people who were *affected* by the murals as the artists intended—were the people who had been *affected* by Diana's death in the same or similar ways as the artists. Taylor offers a powerful analysis of how the repertoire of mural making, and other mourning rituals, in the wake of Diana's death was, in some ways, mandated by the ubiquity of global media, and in other ways, manifested the capacity of active audiences to make their own meanings from media events:

Because we are all caught in transnational economic and iconographic systems, we have no choice, it seems, but to participate in the circulation of capital, symbolic as well as economic. How we download these images and engage with them, however, reflects the power of the local community in framing the terms of the debates. ... If we must engage, as it seems we must, these muralists show that people will establish the terms of the conversation. Rather than constitute one more space for a downloading of the global, it opens one more strategic site for the negotiation of the local. (2003, 157–158)

Taylor's claims here strongly resonate with McLuhan's understanding of global telecommunications: we are all now encompassed in a single theater, meaning that we cannot escape the media networks that span the world. However, unlike in a broadcast model, no group of users is permanently relegated to the position of receiver; any user can put out their own signals for other users to receive. Taylor suggests that the global theater can be made to function like a community theater. Fan "downloadings," appropriations and transmediations of performers and performances found in mass media are practices by which media users make global archives into "local," that is, community-specific, repertoires.

The Event-ness of Fan Fiction

At the beginning of this chapter, I related that I was surprised when I realized that JET had written the fanfic story "Night Giving Off Flames" in response to a Scullyfic Improv challenge in 2000. As soon as I read the paratexts that indicated the story's emergence from a structured challenge, I haphazardly opened a number of other fanfics stored in my personal archives, and noticed that many stories had comparable paratexts, marking them as having resulted from specific structured interactions between authors and readers. For example, a *Firefly* fic in my collection, "Not One to Settle" by Jedi Buttercup (2006), begins with an author note: "This was written for spacesantafic a couple of weeks ago; when I found this community today, I knew I had to post it here as well." "spacesantafic," or "SpaceSanta," was the name of a LiveJournal community active in the mid-2000s that organized a *Firefly*-themed holiday fanfic exchange, in which fan authors were secretly assigned to one another (as in a Secret Santa gift exchange) and each wrote stories about *Firefly* characters to please their designated recipients. I found "Not One" on a different LJ community dedicated to *Firefly* fic, when Jedi Buttercup cross-posted it there, and had never before noticed that it had been written for SpaceSanta. Another story, a *Battlestar Galactica* fanfic, "The Way It Should Be" by embolalia (2014), contains the following author's notes: "Written for workerbee73 for the song prompt 'Box Full of Letters' and the lyrics *I wish I had a lotta answers/'Cause that's the way it should be/All these questions/Being directed at me* … Also for the comment that you don't mind AUs [alternative universe stories]." So, this story, like "Not One," was a fanfic created as a gift for a particular reader. Yet another story in my personal archives, a 2005 *X-Men* fanfic by brynnmck called "Brightly Shone the Moon," is a birthday wish: "Happiest of birthdays to the sweet, adorable bandgeek. […] Also, since you requested 'holiday-ish

Logan/Rogue' for Christmas, I thought it would work out well to have it done by today ... I know it's uncool to do the combo birthday/Christmas present, so just consider this a Christmas present that *happened* to arrive on your birthday." Here was another fanfic-as-gift.

I also noticed stories in my archives that had been written for the Porn Battle, an annual fan fiction challenge founded by oxoniensis in 2006 in which fans post prompts (content that they wish to see in a fanfic), and authors write stories that "fill" those prompts (incorporating the requested content elements), within a specified time frame—a somewhat similar format to that of the Scullyfic Improv challenge. For example, a 2013 *Dark Knight Rises* fanfic in my collection, "Identity" by purple_cube, includes an author's note that reads, "Written for Porn Battle XIV, for the prompt 'start over.'" I also found stories written for prompts but in a less structured way, such as one of the *Doctor Who* fics that I saved, "Incense and Peppermints" by Skylar (2007). "Incense" tells the tale of what happened when the time-traveling Tenth Doctor (or "Ten") and his companion Martha Jones were trapped for several months in 1969, an event that was alluded to on *Doctor Who* but never shown. The author's note at the top of "Incense" states, "I so love Ten/Martha/1969 stories but there aren't many of them, and at smith_n_jones [a LiveJournal community for fans of Ten and Martha] someone suggested there should be a 'what happens in 69 stays in 69' prompt. So this is an answer to that ghost prompt." In this case, there was no time-sensitive "challenge" or "battle" to motivate the author, nor did a friendship with the prompt-giver inspire Skylar to write the fic, as was the case for other authors who wrote fics as gifts. Skylar states that she has written in response to "someone" posting that there "should" be this prompt, and so she is filling this hypothetical prompt, which she calls a "ghost prompt."

Another prompt-driven format I found among my archived fanfics was the "comment ficathon," such as "At the Close," a *Harry Potter* Comment Ficathon organized by anythingbutgrey to coincide with the July 2011 release of the seventh and final *Harry Potter* film. The directions are as follows:

How do I prompt?
Prompts should contain the following format:
Characters/Ship (optional)—Timeline (optional)—Prompt (which may be a song lyric, quote, etc., but is *not* optional. ...

How do I respond?
There are no restrictions in terms of word count, format, tense, point of view, etc.
Please title all of your response fics as such in the comment title box:
Title—Character/Ship—Timeline. ...

You can fill prompts that have already been filled. If something speaks to you, as it were, it doesn't matter if there's already fic for it. You can write your own. (anythingbutgrey 2011)

"At the Close" consists of over 2,500 comments; some of these are prompts, others are fanfics written in response to those prompts, and others are reviews of those fanfics. Although there was no closing date announced for the ficathon, "At the Close" appears to have taken place over the course of three and a half months, from July 16, 2011, when anythingbutgrey launched it, through October 29, 2011, when the 2,572nd comment was posted.

I certainly recognized that "At the Close" was a comment ficathon when I first came across it in 2011, but what I did not realize until this recent scan of my archives was that "At the Close" was *typical* of the fics that I had collected. Rather than being the exception in my archives—the one ficathon that I had saved in its entirety—"At the Close" was simply one of many *writing events* that I had stored over the past fifteen years. In reviewing my favorite stories, the abundance of references to specific readers and specific prompts, to rule-based and time-limited challenges—to writing within given parameters for particular audiences—that I found foregrounded for me how fan writing takes place so often in the context of an *event*. Of course one might say that the production of any piece of fictional writing is an event, in the life of its author if for no one else; but digging into my own archives taught me that, in many or even most cases, the production of a piece of fan fiction is definitively an event in the lives of more than just its author. Online fan fiction is frequently produced *in and as* a specific moment, for a designated readership that is, in some form or other, asking for that production to occur. A fan author writes because and when a friend, a challenge, or a prompt compels, requires, inspires, or requests her to write. A fan writes for an audience—of at least one (the person who requests a birthday fic, whom the fan author presumably knows; or the person who posts a prompt, whom the fan author may or may not know). I want to emphasize that the demands placed by a fan community on a fan author are not necessarily personal or explicit in nature, they can be implicitly made. For example, a discussion about an aspect of a relationship, the importance of a supporting character, or a narrative trope might take place in a mailing list, a Previously.tv forum, or a Tumblr tag, and fan fiction will begin to appear in those communities or related archives that takes up those issues and renders them into story form. The inception of the *Doctor Who* fic created on the basis of a "ghost prompt" is an example of a fic being asked for and delivered in the absence of any preexisting relationship between the prompt giver and the prompt filler.

Thus, the repertoire of fans comprises at least two kinds of performances: those performed by composed bodies based on appropriated media characters, of new narratives created by fans; and those performed by composed bodies that represent actual fans, which are the rituals and routines by which fan readers demand that fiction be written, and by which fan authors fulfill those demands. Both performances take place whenever fan fiction is produced, and it is the combination of these performances that constitutes the *event-ness* of fanfic. Events such as going to the theater and attending festivals, or spectating at sports events, are similar: they consist of the central attraction being played or executed *and* the attendant performances of spectators/fans buying tickets, entering the arena or festival area or playhouse, reading programs or schedules, applauding and cheering for the "main" performers, and discussing and reviewing the proceedings when they are completed. The performances of the main players and of the audience members are both necessary—the *interaction* of the main players and the audience is especially crucial—to make the event happen. In an event, players and audiences each have their repertoire (the portion of the proceedings that they regularly enact), and the rapport between them (the alchemy that takes place when performers and audiences connect) is what gives life to an event and makes it special to all who take part in it. Fan fiction is produced under much the same conditions as sports events and festivals, with fan authors and readers enacting repertoires akin to those of players and spectators. It is because fan fiction emerges from the exchange of ideas, desires, and energies between the two groups that it feels significant and relevant to fans (and let us keep in mind that many readers *are* writers; fans switch positions in the producer–consumer, actor–audience relationship constantly—this is the defining feature of McLuhan's concept of global theater).

My thinking on fan-production-as-event builds on the philosophical distinction between "events" and "objects"/"things" (see D. Hugh Mellor [1980], "On Things and Causes in Spacetime"), but it is important to note how the field of performance studies has complicated this distinction. Richard Schechner, for example, acknowledges that media artifacts, such as films, are "things," but he argues that each separate act of media

reception is a unique "event": "It may be that a film or a digitized performance art piece will be the same at each showing. But the context of
every reception makes each instance different. Even though every 'thing'
is exactly the same, each event in which the 'thing' participates is different. The uniqueness of an event does not depend on its materiality solely
but also on its interactivity—and the interactivity is always in flux. If this
is so with regard to film and digitized media, how much more so for live
performance, where both production and reception vary from instance to
instance. Or in daily life, where context cannot be perfectly controlled"
(Schechner 2013, 30). I appreciate Schechner's opening the possibility of thinking of media reception as event, which draws the entirety of
fandom—which consists largely of intensive and attentive media reception—within the bounds of performance studies. But in arguing that fan
productions are events, I am less interested in Schechner's claims about
media reception than what he is saying about live performance and daily
life as events: fan fiction is produced from interactivity, and new stories
emerge from new interactions all the time; each new story then gives
onto more interactivity between fan authors and fan readers. Fan fiction
is thus an event not only because fans consume media and moments of
media consumption are events, but because fans produce in moments of
direct interaction with other fans. Although a fan fiction story has the
appearance of a textual "thing," its ontology is closer to that of a live performance or an occurrence in daily life as far as how much "flux," "interactivity," and "variation from instance to instance" informs and shapes it.
Clearly, as the creation of fan fiction occurs in X-reality and not in physical reality, fanfic-as-event is *not* a live performance, as might take place in
a physical theater, or an occurrence in face-to-face life; however, as I have
argued, new forms of copresence and "face-to-face-ness" have emerged in
the mixed reality of the Internet, and so Schechner's characterization of
how events transpire in live environments can, I think, be transposed into
the environments of digital networks.

A fan fiction story cannot be viewed as a wholly self-contained object,
a text delimited by the first and last words that appear on the screen, the
way that readers of novels and other genres of print culture conventionally read books as bounded by their covers. In fact, as the survey of my
archives showed me, the headers of a fan story often announce that story to
be inextricably linked to people other than the author, to fan sites other
than the web page on which the story is published, and to ideas or components that originated outside of the story itself. When print was the

dominant technology for textual publication and distribution, critical theorists labored to argue that texts are not crafted in isolation, and that authorial intent does not circumscribe a text's possible significations; reception theory, theories of intertextuality, poststructuralist theories, and new historicism all are attempts to unseat the individual author as the sole origin and locus of a printed text's meaning. But Internet culture is not print culture, and online fans have always understood that there is no "sole" author of a fan work, no exclusive origin of the meaning of a fan fiction story. By the customs of online fan fiction culture, fan authors often make clear in their paratextual notes that their stories arise from interdependencies and flows of information between fan authors and readers. Even when fan authors do not declare their stories to be entrants into some specific writing challenge, the context and subtext of their fictions are most legible to the fan communities in which they participate at the moment in which they write and post the stories.

This does not mean that fan stories are altogether indecipherable to people who discover and read them in archives, long after they are written, nor does it foreclose the possibility of fan authors writing for inactive fandoms, or writing exclusively for their own enjoyment (rather than for an audience of fellow fans, with whom they have regular contact in online communities). But to most fans, reading a fan fiction story at the moment when it is created and shared, and participating in the fan community that gave rise to that story when that emergence occurred, feels different than reading it afterward, because an event is experienced differently by those who learn about it after its occurrence, who read its documentation or view its recording or handle the artifacts generated through it, than by those who "were there when it happened."

Fans Thinking and Making Events

Using different frameworks, fan scholars before me have argued that Internet fan culture generates events rather than objects. Karen Hellekson writes of the "gift culture" of Internet fandom, referring to online fans' persistent practice of creating fanworks for one another, such as the "birthday/holiday gift" fic mentioned above.[8] Hellekson states that "the items exchanged have no value outside their fannish context," and that fan works-as-gifts "have value within the fannish economy in that they are designed to create and cement a social structure, but they themselves are not meaningful outside their context" (Hellekson 2009, 115). I read this to mean that fan "gifts" derive their meaning from the circumstances of their exchange: any significance that fan works have for their givers and receivers is tied to the time of gifting, or more precisely, to the themes and memes circulating in the fandom at the time a gift is made and to which the gift relates; such a gift is also a part of the bond between the giver and receiver (where a social bond between them already exists or arises from the gift exchange). Even when a friendship does not precede the gift giving, a fan author's giving of a piece of fan fiction to a challenge or battle strengthens the fan author's bond to that community, and also reinforces that community's cohesiveness. So, fan works do not signify, and do not hold value, outside of, or apart from, their event-ness, their arising from a specific set of relations (between one fan and another fan, or between one fan and a fan community) at a specific moment in time.

Rebecca Tushnet also alludes to the event-ness of fan fiction when she advocates, from a critical legal studies perspective, for an understanding of fan and other transformative works as multiauthored rather than single-authored. As I mentioned in break 4, Tushnet draws an analogy between "multi-contributor productions" and the fable of "stone soup," the soup that results from many villagers donating their meat, vegetables, and spices to the person who claims that he only needs stones to make delicious-tasting soup (Tushnet 2013, 1019). Through her use of this fable, Tushnet articulates that fan creation is a matter of collaborative process, of communal preparation, of many contributors coming together and throwing elements into a pot, so to speak. The case of the Scullyfic Improv challenge that produced "Night Giving Off Flames," in which half a dozen fans gave JET a set of diverse required elements to be woven into her story, immediately comes to mind as an example of how multiple fans' ideas get incorporated into what appear to be single-authored works. And in calling fan fiction stories "events" rather than "objects," I am attempting to argue that all fan fiction, not only the percentage of stories written explicitly for challenges or lists of prompts, emerges from contributions by multiple fans.

Many of our oral history interviewees discussed their writing and reading of fan fiction using vocabulary that emphasized fanfic's event-ness. For example, multiple authors made the point that they were motivated to write, and influenced in their writing, by their connections to fan readers, and to the collaboratively constructed "traditions" of the fandoms in which they write. Jacqueline (2012) remembers that she wrote some fan fiction before she started participating in online fandom, and that the stuff I wrote before I was fannishly interacting was non-identical to the stuff I wrote after I was fannishly interacting. When you're [writing] non-fannish interacting stuff, you're just writing it because you think, "Oh my God, this character is so hot. I must have more of that." You're writing for yourself. Period. You're not writing for anybody else's reaction. When you're in fandom, and then writing among fans and with the expectation that your work is going to be seen by other fans, you're at least partly writing to achieve a response from them. And you're writing in context of the tradition. [...] You're writing *at* other people to an extent, and you're writing imagining their reaction. And that does, to a certain extent, change what you're going to write. (Jacqueline 2012)

Jacqueline went on to name some tropes in the *Stargate: Atlantis* (*SGA*) fandom about which she wrote fanfic, tropes that were the subjects of "wank" (heated debates, or "flame wars") in the *SGA* fan communities, which would not be decipherable to people who did not participate in, or later learned about, these intense discussions. Jacqueline wrote about topics that rose to prominence in her fandom's debates, topics that she knew would be relevant to her readers, as they were raised *by* the readers. In one sense, Jacqueline wrote her fan fiction stories, but in another sense, the entire fandom generated the subject matter of Jacqueline's fic. I read Jacqueline's statements as revealing the collective authorship and time-specificity of fan fiction: the fan author writes differently for herself alone than for a fan readership, and when she writes for a fan readership, she is really writing *with* them and *for* them, writing about issues and themes that they have, by consensus or dissensus, declared to be important, and writing about those themes *at the time* when they are focal points of the fandom. This is the "fannish context" that Hellekson writes of, and the stone-soup-like multiauthorship that Tushnet discusses. Each fan fiction story arises at a certain moment in a fandom's history, out of the "tradition" built by the discussions and disputes of fans, crafted by its author for an audience that is known to that author. This audience is, in some sense, waiting to receive the fiction and is able, by virtue of being well-versed in the group's shared tradition, to decipher the meanings of the stories. Jacqueline's stories in the *SGA* fandom arose from, and responded to, events in that community's history, and thus were themselves events in that history.

Fan writing challenges are events in the literal sense, as they have beginning dates and (in most cases) end dates, and parameters, rules, and guidelines that all participants must follow. Many oral history participants spoke of how important challenges have been in motivating their own writing. Several of the interviewees are organizers of fan writing challenges, and

derived the names of their challenges from live events that usually transpire in physical space. jinjurly, founder of the Audiofic Archive, states in
her interview that she created "Amplificathon," an annual challenge that
"is all about getting fandoms and podficcers into the archive who aren't
already there" (jinjurly 2012). The challenge's name is thus a clever play on
"amplification," meaning an increase in volume (meaning sonic loudness),
as jinjurly is attempting to amplify, or increase the volume (meaning size)
of, the Audiofic Archive, a site hosting an oral/aural format of fan fiction.
jinjurly says that she created Amplificathon "both as a festival, which is
entirely to feed the archive, ... and as a community" (jinjurly 2012).

Amplificathon is only one of many fan fiction challenges with
"ficathon" in the title, a term that seems clearly related to "marathon"
races and endurance-based contests such as "dance-a-thons." oxoniensis
(2012) says that she got the idea for naming the Porn Battle "from dance
battles, where dancers take it in turns to dance as hard and brilliantly as
they can. Dance battles are just so full of life, and such fun, and although
they're called battles, there's generally no such thing as losers. [...] More
than anything they're just about going for it, giving your all. So I thought
the fannish equivalent could be a porn battle, where writers all get their
chance to write as hard and brilliantly as they can!" eruthros and thingswithwings founded the kink_bingo challenge with the goal of making it
game-like:

eruthros: So I think we were spitballing all of these random—like, "We could do a
challenge that was like"—and then we would name a game. "It's like Monopoly!" But
how could you do a challenge that's like Monopoly? [Laughs]

thingswithwings: Monopoly always ends in tears, as well.

eruthros: Right.

thingswithwings: So you want something that ends in "Hurrah!" like Bingo.

(eruthros and thingswithwings 2012)

Festivals, marathons/dance-a-thons, dance battles, and parlor games—
these are the activities from which fans borrowed the names, and, in the
case of kink_bingo, the structure, for their fan fiction challenges. With fan
writing challenges, as with fan fiction, we find default bodies modeling
action for composed bodies. The attitudes, the atmospheres, the levels of
excitement and energy with which fan organizers hope to imbue their
events, they appropriate from real-world events, translating these attitudes
and atmospheres for the mixed reality of the Internet, motivating real bodies to get to work making new productions of composed bodies for the

global theater. By delimiting special times and sites for fan production, by marking out a kind of Bakhtinian ([1965] 1984) "carnival time" from the "perpetual happening" of the Internet, fan challenge organizers are able to incentivize fans to take their turns on the global theater stage.

My Gutenberg Mistake

And now, I will briefly to return to the mystery with which I opened this chapter: How is it that I overlooked the paratexts in JET's "Night Giving Off Flames," as well as in a good number of stories in my personal fan fiction archives, that indicated that these stories were written in response to challenges, as gifts, for prompts, and so on? In other words, how could I have ignored, for many years, the fact that these stories were not free-standing stories but were events in the lives of their fandoms, and entries into those fandoms' histories?

I think the answer is that I acquired literacy in the last period of print culture's dominance. Having been born very near to the close of what Tom Pettitt (2007) and L. O. Sauerberg (2009) call the "Gutenberg Parenthesis," and having opted to complete a BA in modern thought and literature, an MA in humanities, and a PhD in comparative literary studies, I was thoroughly trained to read print. Any digital literacy skills that I possess today, I acquired on my own rather through any institutional education, as is the case with (I think) most of the humanities scholars of my generation. And while I have flattered myself in the past as to my degree of new media literacy, this exercise of rummaging through my own archives and being surprised by them has held up a mirror to my self-image as a digital literate and shattered my self-perception.

The reason that I never before noticed that "Night Giving Off Flames" was an improv challenge fic, or that any of the rest of my collection of fanfic were stories written for various other writing challenges and exchanges, is simple: I was reading fan fiction as print culture in electronic form, rather than as digital culture. Even though I was aware that fan fiction concerns borrowed characters rather than wholly original ones, I still applied the same frameworks, the same modalities of reception, the same criteria for evaluation, to digital fiction as I did to print fiction. As Pettitt says, "The difference between the world within the Gutenberg Parenthesis [i.e., the world of print culture's dominance] and the world without (be it before or after) is in the first instance the significance accorded to the composition of a given work as opposed to its performance, and in the second instance

Pre-Parenthetical	Gutenberg Parenthesis	Post-Parenthesis
re-creative	original	sampling
collective	individual	remixing
con-textual	autonomous	borrowing
unstable	stable	reshaping
traditional	canonical	appropriating
		recontextualizing
Performance	**Composition**	

Figure 6.1

Pettitt's diagram of the history of human culture, from the "Pre-Parenthetical" (i.e., culture before the rise of printing), to the "Gutenberg Parenthesis" (when print is the cultural dominant), to the "Post-Parenthetical" (the time after print's dominance). Pettitt equates "post-parenthetic" culture with "digital internet culture" (2007, 2).

the degree to which either process involves the introduction of material from other works/performances" (Pettitt 2007, 5). So, those locked into the Gutenberg Parenthesis look for compositions by single authors and judge them on their originality and uniqueness, and those who lived before the print era and who now, after the print era or at the cusp of that era's ending, are acquiring as many or more digital literacies as print literacies, and look for performances of works that "introduce material from other works/ performances." Inside the Gutenberg Parenthesis, states Pettitt, are criteria for valuation such as "original," "individual, "autonomous," "stable," "canonical," "COMPOSITION." Outside the parenthesis: "re-creative," "collective," "con-textual," "unstable," "traditional," "sampling," "remixing," "borrowing," "reshaping," "appropriating," "recontextualizing," "PERFORMANCE" (2) (see figure 6.1).

Let us take note of Pettitt's deliberate typography here: "composition" and "performance" are clearly marked as the master terms of print-analog culture and digital culture, respectively, by their bold letters.

When first encountering fan fiction, collecting it, and rereading it over the years, I perhaps understood the "sampling," "remixing," "borrowing," and "appropriating" aspects of digital culture, but I did not thoroughly grasp it as "collective," "con-textual," "unstable," "PERFORMANCE." I still, for the most part, saw "COMPOSITION" when I read online fanfic. And because my print-based literacy was much more developed than my digital literacy, or what Gregory Ulmer (2005) calls "electracy," I was blind to the many paratexts in my fanfic collection which announced that a new form of reading, of receiving, culture had begun in my lifetime. I was using an old lens, COMPOSITION, to view this new phenomenon launching on digital networks: PERFORMANCE.

My attempt to expand and strengthen my own media literacy skills, by seeing, interpreting, and analyzing the objects of my study for *what they were*—as events, as PERFORMANCE—constitutes the chapter that you have just finished reading.

Break 6 Body and Voice in Fan Production

There are many ways that media fans translate mediated bodies into written texts, or reenact them through their own bodies, or imagine bodies for nonembodied characters. This break will explore a few of the varied ways that fans connect embodiment, media, and textuality through their archontic productions.

Real-World Performances

So far, I have focused on how fans perform the repertoires of favorite characters in written stories. But fans also perform these repertoires in real-world spaces: when they dress in costumes and role-play as their favorite characters at conventions, LARP (live-action role playing) events, or other fan gatherings; when young fans "play pretend" together, each player assuming the identity of a different media character, such as Iron Man or Wonder Woman; or when they play with action figures or dolls representing media characters and enact new challenges and adventures with the figurines.

In interviews with fans, my research team heard many instances of fans combining embodied play with the writing of fan fiction, especially in their childhood and adolescent years. For example, Henry Jenkins and his friends, at eleven years old or so, regularly spent their free time afterschool in Henry's backyard, pretending to be movie monsters in full character makeup that they learned to apply from reading the fan magazine *Famous Monsters of Filmland*; Henry wrote scripts for the monster movies that he was convinced the group would one day make together based on their enactments of Dracula and Frankenstein (Jenkins and Jenkins 2012). Cynthia Jenkins recalls that as an adolescent, she and a friend would have sleepovers during which they would collaboratively make up stories about Neil Armstrong, Captain America, Alexander the Great, and other fictional and nonfictional personages who interested them at the time; after their storytelling sessions, Cynthia would document their stories in written out-lines (Jenkins and Jenkins 2012). When Francesca Coppa was twelve or thirteen years old, she met a girl who was writing what she called a *Star Wars* "soap opera," which she was staging using *Star Wars* figurines in a dollhouse; Coppa and a few other tweens joined in and both playacted and scripted the ongoing *Star Wars* narrative, using a different color of marker to write the lines for each character and then regular pen to denote stage directions. When Tari (2012) was thirteen, one girl in her circle discovered fanfic based on Anne Rice's *Vampire Chronicles* online, and started printing out her favorite stories and reading them aloud to friends, which was how Tari discovered fanfic: "I would just really listen to [my friends] reading fanfic that they found on the Internet, but I didn't actually look for fan fiction myself" (Tari 2012). All of these fans experienced fan fiction in their youth as both written and performed; in Tari's case, fan fiction was initially an exclusively oral literature.

Other interviewees talked about performing as media characters in the real world. Many mentioned cosplay, or costume-play, which is usually lim-ited to fan conventions, but one fan, Louisa Stein (2012), talked about a way that fans can also imitate characters' physical appearances subtly, on a daily basis. Stein participated in a *Roswell* fan website called Roswell Beauty Divas, on which fans shared where the clothes and makeup products fea-tured on the show could be acquired, so that fans could incorporate ele-ments of the characters' styles into their everyday wardrobes and "looks." "If you love a character that has particular qualities and these qualities are expressed through their styling, how do you channel that styling? ... And it's a sort of personalization, but not through fan fiction, not through discussion, [but] through performing it in your everyday life," says Stein (2012). She recalls that one of the major projects of the fans on the site was to share advice on how to replicate characters' style affordably, for example by hand-sewing certain clothing items and accessories, or buying approxi-mations of them at Walmart. "And then there was a real sort of joy and celebration in that, and in the characters through their aesthetics." Stein worked as a temp at Citibank during *Roswell*'s run, and recalls that "it was a corporate context, ... and at first I was dressing very conservatively, ... but also browsing [the Divas site], and by the end of it, I was like, inflecting all my corporate outfits with Maria-inspired clothing" (Stein 2012) (Maria DeLuca was one of *Roswell*'s main female characters). Although Stein does not frame this stylistic "inflection" explicitly as a resistance to the corpo-rate dress code of her workplace, it is amusing to think of a minor form of *Roswell* cosplay being performed regularly in that environment.

Audiofic Performances

Another form of embodiment that fans give to textual fan practice is "audiofic," or "podfic." Audiofics are audio recordings of fans reading aloud works of fan fiction; they are analogous to audiobooks, which are audio recordings of performers reading aloud published fiction or nonfiction books. As with audiobooks, the majority of audiofics are read or recorded not by their authors, but by fan readers. In her oral history interview, jinjurly (2012), who founded and maintains the Audiofic Archive, the largest online archive of podfic, describes podfic as a physicalization of fan fiction, which she acknowledges some fans find distasteful or off-putting. When a fan becomes a "podficcer," or someone who records a podfic, says jinjurly,

You are basically sharing a part of your body with people in a way that, yeah, sometimes people find really creepy. Usually, one of the objections that authors sometimes have, and fans in general sometimes have, to podfic, that they have a really hard time putting into words, [is] basically ... that sort of, 'I think it's creepy." Yeah, okay, that's valid. If you find it creepy, that's fine. It is a very physical thing that someone is doing that has this physical result with your story that you wrote, and it does change it. ... Odds are ..., it's not going to be what the author heard in their head, and it also demonstrates very very strongly that we all have different interpretations. (jinjurly 2012)

Though jinjurly is here addressing what she perceives to be a widespread objection to podfic, there were many fans of podfic among our interviewees, such as Rebecca Tushnet (2012), who says that "a lot of my comfort consumption is podfic, which I really like," in large part for "the emotional tone of someone's voice," and Kristina Busse (2012), who says that "podfic does a lot for me. ... That's actually become kind of my comfort thing, more than story reading these days, because I just, you know, I lie in bed, and close my eyes, and just have someone read me a story." However, the idea of podfic being "creepy" to some fans, perhaps particularly fan authors whose works are transformed by being read aloud, interests me because fan fiction incites the same kneejerk response in many authors and producers, as well as fans, of source texts. Bestselling science fiction and fantasy novelists George R. R. Martin, Anne Rice, Ursula K. Le Guin, and Diana Gabaldon have all been vocal in their opposition to fan fiction, Le Guin stating that fanfic is "not sharing but an invasion, literally—strangers coming in and taking over the country I live in, my heartland," and Martin saying, "My characters are my children ... I don't want people making off with them, thank you" (Goofusgallant 2012). While some authors have difficulty with fanfic because of potential copyright infringement, Le Guin's and Martin's comments speak more to an instinctual conviction that some authors have that only they can compose the bodies of their characters (Martin's "children"), and only they can dwell in the mixed realities they create (Le Guin's "heartland"). I think that these authors' deeply felt resistance to fan fiction is echoed in fan authors' finding podfic "creepy." Beyond any arguments that I, or any of fan fiction's proponents, may make about culture being inherently shareable and prone to interpretation, adaptation, and remix, there is a deep irony in *fans'* disliking a transformative use of fan-made transformative works.

jinjurly defends podfic by comparing it to stage performance. In chapter 6, I argued that fan fiction is a translation of default bodies into composed bodies, and jinjurly's perspective leads me to think of podfic as a translation of composed bodies back into default bodies—the default bodies of fan readers. States jinjurly:

> Podfic is a transformative work in its relationship to the original source. Is podfic a transformation from a transformative work in relationship to the story? No. It could be. ... What it is is generally derivative, but that doesn't mean that it doesn't have a lot of creativity behind it. Its relationship to the actual fic, yeah, is derivative, but there's a lot of difference between reading *Hamlet* as a text or watching Ethan Hawke play Hamlet or watching Kenneth Branagh play Hamlet or watching, I imagine, Sarah Bernhardt play Hamlet. ... These are all very different characters, but they're all the same character. They're all delivering the same lines, more or less ... but there are different parts of this story being told in different ways. Stage plays, I think are probably the best illustration of this as an analogy. (jinjurly 2012)

jinjurly points to a vast difference in perceptions of iteration and variation in theater culture—where repertoire is the dominant logic—versus print culture—where archive is the dominant logic. In stage performance, variation and "versioning" are the norm, whereas print culture treats text as fixed and inviolable. I think that fan fiction, and especially podfic, uncovers the fact that print is not as fixed as is conventionally thought: even print texts are made meaningful by being received by readers and "performed" in their imaginations. It is because the "voices" of characters or narrators in transformational works—literally voices reading aloud, in the case of podfic—do not match the voices in the minds of the source text authors (in the case of podfic, the "source author" is a fan author) or source text fans that sparks their immediate, gut-level rejection of those transformations. But the culture of fan fiction and fan works, including audiofic, calls for a widespread acceptance that each reader's, each cultural receiver's, body is different, and so cultural works are brought to life differently by and in each body. This is true even in the case of fan fiction based on audiovisual media—that is, even when it seems that every fan has in mind the same composed bodies (what characters sound and look like, as performed by particular actors), there is still some difference in how each fan author, and fan reader, animates these bodies mentally. And once a reader/viewer/listener takes possession of a composed body through the act of media consumption, she will operate, script, and direct that body as she chooses. No source author or fan author can control or prevent this maneuver, this "invasion" (as Le Guin says) or appropriation of composed bodies by audiences, for it is a fundamental operation of cultural dissemination and reception.

Fan Casting

The importance of performers' bodies to fan authors and readers is made even more evident by "fan casting," which is a convention used by some fan authors of designating a popular actor as the "portrayer" of an original character (OC) included in a fanfic story (Fanlore, "Fan casting"). An author might indicate that an OC is "played by" a movie star, or that she had that star "in mind" when writing the OC. The author, knowing that fan readers will already have "in mind" the actors who portray the main characters in the source text when they read the fanfic, wish to provide as clear an image of the new, unfamiliar OC, and so she places the body and voice of a familiar performer on the same virtual stage as the other already-known bodies and voices. The primary characters who appear in fics have already been "cast" by the television series or the films in which they initially appear, so some fan authors feel compelled to "cast" any OCs they include, to ensure that all of the bodies playing out the fan-authored scenario in X-reality space are equally vivid for the reader. Since images of famous actors proliferate in the mainstream press and media, depicting them in a wide variety of poses and costumes (for example, actors may be photographed for a fashion magazine layout wearing sumptuous Victorian English period dress or futuristic sci-fi garb), fans can select the photos of an actor from the wider media archive in which the actor most looks like the fan author's OC (for example, if the fan author has written a story that takes place in Victorian England or in a twenty-fifth-century space station), and create photosets or montages of the actor "playing" their original character.

Recently, fans have also taken to recasting, especially through "raceswapping," "racebending," or "genderbending," familiar characters as well as original characters. For instance, one fan created a photoset from images and GIFs of African-British actor Idris Elba and African-American actress Kerry Washington playing various roles throughout their careers, images in which both performers look glamorous and dangerous, interspersed with images of the DC comic book and movie characters Batman and Catwoman (figure 6a.1). The caption of the photoset reads, "Idris Elba as Bruce Wayne/ Batman and Kerry Washington as Selina Kyle/Catwoman." Batman has never been portrayed by a black man on film or television, but the Elba–Washington fan work makes the case, with just a handful of images, that the fictional billionaire-vigilante could easily be played by Elba, whose confidence, sophistication, and widely respected acting talent would enable him to excel in the role. Moreover, Catwoman has been portrayed twice by black actresses (Eartha Kitt in 1967–68 on the *Batman* television series, and Halle Berry in the 2004 feature film *Catwoman*), so the notion of a black Batman is a logical extension of the precedent of Catwoman's being sometimes depicted as African American (indeed, some of the Catwoman images in the photoset are of Halle Berry in costume). Fan casting raceswaps such as this are fan fictions that do not need to provide much, if any, story or dialogue to fan readers, because the insertion of black faces, voices, and bodies into roles that are usually portrayed by white actors *is* the fanfic. Fans who have seen stories and scenes featuring Batman and Catwoman play out in films and television series, and who also are familiar with Elba and Washington's acting styles, can easily envision the performers enacting the famous DC-universe characters—except that Hollywood has never allowed Batman to be portrayed by, and as, a black man. What if Hollywood were willing to give audiences films in which black actors can play lead characters as heroic and as villainous, as romantic and strong and sexual, as complex and as important, as Batman and Catwoman are in Tim Burton's and Christopher Nolan's Batman films? The Elba–Washington photoset, and other fan raceswapping and genderbending castings, conjure up a fictional media industry for the fan reader, one that is entirely different than the media industry that audiences are currently "stuck with," one that is more attuned to the possibilities of foregrounding minority, female, and queer actors and characters. What makes possible the fan reader's understanding of this type of fan fiction is the operation, common to all transformative fan works, of appropriating embodied performances as the bases of composed bodies that can exist, and be deployed according to the fan author's directions, in virtual space.

Figure 6a.1
Fan casting raceswap: African-British actor Idris Elba and African-American actress Kerry Washington "cast" as Batman and Catwoman.

Performances without Moving Pictures

What about fan fiction that is based not on audiovisual recordings of live bodies but on other formats of source materials? Is fan fiction still a body medium when it is based on still recordings (photographs) of live bodies; hand-drawn or digitally rendered bodies such as one finds in graphic novels, comic books, manga, cartoons, animated films and videos, anime, and video games; bodies composed in text, such as one finds in novels and non-fiction books; bodies represented through musical performance and popular song recordings; and bodies that are not humans or humanoid robots, but are things/objects/animals (this type of fanfic is called "anthropomorphic fic")? I would say that fan fiction stories based on non-film/video/TV sources are still stories about bodies. I agree with Kurt Lancaster (2001) that when we see a person sitting in a chair reading a book, we are watching that person produce theater in his or her mind, for the solitary reader mentally animates the beings who initially exist only as words on the book's pages; the reader "sees" and "hears" the beings "come to life" in the spaces of his or her imagination. The fan author succeeds with her readers when she can write characteristics that all fans of a source text will quickly recognize as proper to the characters in that source text; in other words, as long as fan readers sense a close relation between the characters that they "know" and the fan author's version of those characters, they will be able to "see" and "hear" the fan author's enactments, using those appropriated bodies, "come to life" in the space, the X-reality, of their imaginations. They will be able to witness the performances that the fan author stages in the global theater.

One might also say that, when fans take on the task of transforming a source text that has never been visualized, it is the "voice" of the source author that the fan author attempts to replicate, rather than any physicality of the characters. For example, fan author via_ostiense (2012) states in her oral history interview, "When I write, or when I used to write in *Harry Potter* [fandom], I didn't have any trouble with it at all. But when I think about trying to write, I don't know, for Lymond, say [Francis Crawford of Lymond is the hero of Dorothy Dunnett's six *Lymond Chronicles* novels, published between 1961 and 1975, about sixteenth-century European and Mediterranean politics], it's much harder, just because the quality of Dorothy Dunnett's prose is excellent, and—and her writing has such a distinct feel, that it would—I have a really hard time with the idea of writing something not in her voice, but at the same time her voice is so damn hard to emulate. So I end up not writing it for anything at all" (via_ostiense 2012). via_ostiense here distinguishes between source authors whose literary voices are easy to replicate (J. K. Rowling) and those whose voices are difficult to replicate (Dorothy Dunnett).

The implication is that when via_ostiense *can* emulate a source text author's voice, she can write fanfic about the source text, and when she cannot emulate that voice, she cannot write fic about the source text, no matter how much she may wish to. I think that this need to emulate voice stems from the fan author wishing to evoke a resemblance for the fan reader: if fan readers do not recognize the characters or voices that the fan author writes as having any similarity to the characters or voices that they "know" from the source material, then the performance constituted by the fan work fails. Or rather, it never transpires; the stage of the fan reader's imagination remains empty of bodies and voices.

7 Archontic Production: Free Culture and Free Software as Versioning

New Media and the Archival Turn

So far, I have been discussing digital cultural memory as it is manifested in the building and maintenance of Internet archives. But digital cultural memory is composed of two threads, woven around one another like the double helix of biopolymer strands in a DNA molecule. One thread consists of actual archives, such as those I described in earlier sections. The other thread consists of conceptual archives. But what do I mean by "actual" and "conceptual" archives?

By "actual" archives, I mean archives as built repositories. By "conceptual" archives, I mean archives as thought constructs. Michel Foucault made this distinction in his 1969 book *Archaeology of Knowledge* (published in English in 1972), but it achieved widespread visibility in humanities and social science research beginning in the 1980s with what anthropologist Ann Stoler named the "archival turn": "a rethinking of the materiality and imaginary of collections and what kinds of truth-claims lie in documentation" (Stoler 2002, 94). The archival turn marked a moment when "archive" changed definition, when the term began to "represent neither a material site nor a set of documents," but served "as a strong metaphor for any corpus of selective forgettings and collections—and as importantly, for the seductions and longing that such quests, accumulations and passions for the primary, originary and untouched entail" (94). This "metaphoric move" (94, n. 29)—the transition of the referent of "archive" from material substrate to the register of abstraction and symbol—facilitated groundbreaking work such as Allan Sekula's "The Body and the Archive" (1986) and Mary Ann Doane's "The Instant and the Archive" (2002). Sekula's article examines the role that photography played in identifying, and making visible, class differences in the nineteenth century, helping to establish "a generalized, inclusive *archive*, a *shadow archive* that encompasses an entire social terrain while positioning individuals within that terrain" (10). Doane's essay argues that "What film archives, ... is first and foremost, a 'lost' experience of time as presence, time as immersion" (221–222), a loss keenly felt by those subjected to the nineteenth- and early twentieth-century industrialization of time, "[time's] rationalization and abstraction, its externalization and reification in the form of pocket watches, standardized schedules, the organization of the work day" through which "time becomes other, alienated" (221). Sekula's and Doane's influential pieces stand as only two examples of how scholars have rendered the archive figurative rather than physical. Kate Eichhorn (2008, 8, n. 2) summarizes the archival turn as "the archive's repositioning as a subject of investigation rather than [as a] mere site where research takes place."

So, before the archival turn—that is, before Eichhorn, Stoler, Doane, Sekula, and Foucault's *Archaeology*—what was the archive? One could say that it was a place of the dead, the still, the frozen. Foucault (1986), in his essay "Of Other Spaces" based on a 1967 lecture, argues that the archive, museum, and library resemble the cemetery. He states that the "idea of accumulating everything, of establishing a sort of general archive" that arises in the nineteenth century in the West, with the advent of modernity, reveals a "will to enclose in place all times, all epochs, all forms, all tastes...outside of time and inaccessible to its ravages" (Foucault 1986, 26). In "Archive Fever," Jacques Derrida (1995) gives the origin of "archive" as "the Greek *arkheion*: initially a house, a domicile, an address, the residence of the superior magistrates, the *archons*, those who commanded. ... It is at their home, in that *place* which is their house (private house, family house, or employee's house), that official documents are filed. The archons are first of all the documents' guardians. ... It is thus, in this *domiciliation*, in this house arrest, that archives take place" (9–10). From both Foucault and Derrida, we get a sense of the earliest meaning of archive as, first, a "material site" (in Stoler's phrasing), a physical place, and second, a site in which documents remain stationary, as if they are dead and mummified, "outside of time and inaccessible to its ravages." An archive is a "house" whose contents are under "arrest."

If that is what an archive was, what is an archive today, after the "archival turn"? As stated above, "archive" does not now *necessarily* refer to a material site; sometimes it is a metaphor. But, of course, some archives are still built repositories. Both of these categories—conceptual archives and actual archives—are being radically redefined by digital technologies. In this chapter, I will argue that new media have made possible archives that are designed to be fluid and constantly altered by crowdsourced updates.

We must conceive of information preservation sites very differently than the nineteenth century did, and regard them not as prisons for documents that optimize for stasis and timelessness, but as "dynarchives" (a term coined by Wolfgang Ernst) that invite interaction and remain (theoretically) forever in flux.

I will also argue that new media have facilitated the multiplication of what Eichhorn calls "archival genres," meaning types of cultural production that appropriate "images and texts culled from other sources." Eichhorn compares Internet blogs to Renaissance-era commonplace books; she argues that both the digital genre (blogs) and the much older handwritten genre (commonplace books) are "products of collecting and ordering" found content. Early modern readers copied "adages, sententia, and examples" and other "textual fragments ... from a myriad of sources" into their commonplace books, using the books "as memory aids and as rich storehouses of materials that might eventually be incorporated into composition[s] of one's own making" (Eichhorn 2008, 1). Similarly, states Eichhorn, most blogs consist of quotations of, and references to, media authored by others. Eichhorn argues that there is a "long, albeit largely neglected, history" of archival genres, a history that has spanned the centuries from the Renaissance to the dawn of the digital age and includes "everyday textual practices" such as scrapbooking, blogging, and social networking (3). I consider fan fiction, and all fan works, to be archival genres as Eichhorn defines them: texts composed of elements collected from other texts.

In a 2006 essay (Derecho 2006), I proposed "archontic literature" as a name for the body of derivative writing of which fan fiction is but one subset (this corpus also includes literary "classics" such as Jean Rhys's *Wide Sargasso Sea*, which retells the story of Charlotte Brönte's *Jane Eyre* from the point of view of the Caribbean-born "madwoman in the attic," and J. M. Coetzee's *Foe*, which narrates the tale of Daniel Defoe's *Robinson Crusoe* from a female castaway's perspective). I posited that archontic literature consists of fictional writings based on source texts, that is, texts that have been published; the writers of archontic literature are readers-turned-authors. Each source text is the foundation and core of an archive from which reader-authors make withdrawals (elements they wish to use) and into which they make deposits (their stories that incorporate those appropriated elements), thereby augmenting and enlarging the overarching archive.

However, digital derivations encompass much more than text-based stories, so I now think that *archontic production* is a more useful heading for the enormous, ever-growing category of appropriative writings, soundtracks, still and moving images, audiovisual works, games, and codes that constitutes a vast swath of digital culture today. My idea of archontic production includes Eichhorn's "archival genres" of blogs and commonplace books, which she defines as "plotless and meandering," "straddl[ing] autobiography and critical writing," and "accumulative" (2008, 7), and goes beyond them to also include transformative texts that are narrative driven, do not prominently foreground the reader-author's personality, and are not structured as compendia.

I argue that archontic production and rogue archives comprise the twin strands of digital cultural memory. Digital media accelerates archontic production, as it offers numerous affordances for remediation (Bolter and Grusin 2000), transmediation (Jenkins 2003, 2007b, 2011b), and remix (Lessig 2008)—that is, for the treatment of circulating texts *as archives*, "as rich storehouses of materials that might eventually be incorporated into composition[s] of one's own making" (Eichhorn 2008, 1). Digital media, as I have discussed, also contain multiple affordances for archive building, and many online archives—the majority of the rogue archives that I have described—are explicitly dedicated to the preservation of archontic production, the saving of the manifold variants that proliferate in the wake of the releases of source texts. Digital cultural memory therefore comprises both metaphorical and material archival activity.

The growth of digital cultural memory illustrates that the archival turn has reached far beyond the arenas of the heritage industry, the information sciences, and humanities research: new media culture writ large participates in, and elaborates on, the archival turn. But there are even greater ramifications of digital cultural memory's steady expansion. I will argue that the proliferation of actual archives of archontic production supports and strengthens a movement that legal scholar Lawrence Lessig calls *free culture*, which Lessig links to GNU Project founder Richard Stallman's free software movement. Free culture, like free software, is not a political movement per se, but it is a movement toward certain objectives and away from certain currently dominant structures. Free culture strives to legitimate and platform cultural production "from below," as Marxist historians would say. Free culture shunts aside print-era conceptions of copyright, authorship, textuality, and collective memory, and seeks to replace them with copyleft, a cultural commons that gives onto collaborative creativity, a widespread acknowledgment and acceptance of versioning (which resembles performance far more than writing), and rogue archives. Free culture wishes to usher in a new set of archons, whose subjectivity will dramatically diverge from that of print era's writers, readers, and archivists.

Archontic Production

Archontic production, as it pertains to reworkings of popular media, is the process by which audiences/receivers of mass-produced and mass-distributed cultural texts—the commodities sold by what Max Horkheimer and Theodor Adorno (2002) called the "culture industry"—seize hold of these commodities as a vast archive of usable resources, from which they select desirable parts as the raw material for their own revisions and variations.

Archontic production begins when the intended consumers of mass culture purposefully misperceive and reframe cultural commodities. Rather than regarding mass media texts as "end products" of the culture industry, which they are supposed to purchase and with which they are supposed to be satisfied, archontic producers treat mass media texts as starting points from which to launch their own narratives, images (still and moving), sounds, graphics, and/or animations—new, highly individualized texts that serve *their* ends and satisfy them far better than mass-produced culture ever can. The "they" in the previous sentence is the presumptive "audience," an undifferentiated body of paying customers, or rather, a body clumsily segmented, by the culture industry and its financers/advertisers, into brackets defined by age, ethnicity, nationality, location, and income level. Archontic producers are in fact *users* of culture rather than consumers, consisting of, and creating, individual and unique bodies.

Networked computing does not automatically work well as a memory machine in the sense of preserving everything that people do and share on the Internet—as I have argued, a great deal of human labor is required to make the Internet work like an archive—but it excels at facilitating a kind of culture making that is memory based. Networked computing allows for multiple transmediations and transformations of cultural texts, and the constant circulation, in online spaces, of those reworkings. Transmediations and transformations are, in part, rememberings of culture-that-came-before; they are premised on a large-scale understanding of both individual texts as archives and of culture-as-archive, with online sharings of such appropriations constituting augmentations of the cultural archive.

But then, does not the cultural archive become unwieldy in its gross enlargement by constant archontic production? In several places in their book *Audiences*, sociologists Nicholas Abercrombie and Brian Longhurst express some anxiety regarding the sheer quantity of audience-generated texts that now circulate on electronic media networks. They cite Barry Shank's theory of music "scenes" as a useful analogy for how the contemporary mediascape operates: Shank defines a "scene" as "an overproductive signifying community; that is, far more semiotic information is produced than can be rationally parsed" (1994, 22). Shank refers to scenes' "potentially dangerous overproduction and exchange of musicalized signs of identity and community" (1994, 122). In scenes, write Abercrombie and Longhurst (1998, 162), "conventional divisions between producers and consumers become blurred." And now, Abercrombie and Longhurst argue, everywhere is a "scene," that is, scenes are no longer limited to popular music cultures or to any specific medium's cultures. In every medium, and across media, audiences become fans become producers, and all participants become players and contributors. Thus, all media scenes are too prone to "potentially dangerous overproduction" to ever be "rationally parsed."

Abercrombie and Longhurst interestingly locate a solution to this problem of overproduction in a study of heritage institutions: Gaynor Bagnall's 1996 essay "Consuming the Past." Abercrombie and Longhurst cite Bagnall's notion that visitors to a museum or heritage institution first map the site physically, by "mov[ing] around the site in a very direct way" (Abercrombie and Longhurst 1998, 168) and then map the site emotionally, responding to different images and exhibits differently (Bagnall 1996, 236–239.). Abercrombie and Longhurst express a wish that future audience researchers will aim to elicit and study individuals' emotional maps of mediascapes in order to better understand "the relationships of different forms of media to the everyday life of participants" (170). The implication is that because "the mediascape to which [audiences] relate in [their] everyday life ... is increasingly complex and global" (170)—one reason for this is that audiences now create and circulate their own texts in addition to the texts made and distributed by "official" cultural producers—individuals *must* be creating emotional maps to help themselves navigate the vast quantity of media that they encounter. People have to make emotional maps of media in order to decide, of the overwhelming number of possible media performances presented to them, which ones they will consume and become involved with, which ones they will become fans of, which ones they will use as the bases of their own performances.

I find Abercrombie and Longhurst's turn to memory institutions to be provocative, because it allows me to understand the entire arena of media production and circulation, including literature, radio, cinema, comic books, television, recordings of live events, the Internet, art institutions and cultural memory institutions, plus audiences' responses and creations in all possible media—the Mediascape in the largest sense—as itself a giant memory institution, which fans must physically map (deciding which websites, TV programs, bands, and films to use and consume), and then

emotionally map (deciding which stories, shows, and songs they will affectively invest in and perhaps repeatedly consume). I like the strange image
of concentric rings of archives that this evokes: if all of media is already a
museum, then people make emotional maps of that museum in order to
decide what they are fans of and in order to gather with like-minded others
in organized fandoms; then fans within each fandom use their maps to create archives of the fan works that matter to them; and then users of those
fan archives must make emotional maps of what they find inside those
"museums," since fan repositories can also be overwhelmingly large (after
all, what Shank and Abercrombie and Longhurst are referring to when they
write about "overproduction" is the potentially limitless number of fan performances that can be produced within any given scene).

So, my concept of fan production as archontic production, combined
with Abercrombie and Longhurst's invocation of heritage institution mapping, opens up a perception of contemporary media use as a Russian doll set
of archiving-within-archiving-within-archiving. Individuals roam the enormous halls of the archive of media texts, they make selections and decide
which texts they will be fans of, they make another round of selections
when they decide what they will use as the sources for their own variants,
they build archives for those fan works, and they browse those archives of
fan works and make selections of those they like best. (Fans can then opt to
create new performances that archontically use other fans' performances,
such as remixes of remixes, which then augment actual archives of fan
works and virtual archives of source texts, and so on, and so on.)

Archontic production, then, reveals that digital popular culture is enacting its own archival turn, as audiences refuse the notion of "archive" as a
place where documents remain untouched and frozen, under "house arrest,"
and instead realize their power to seize upon all of culture, especially mass
media, *as* an archive, as an ever-expanding collection of archives that exist
for their use, that contain the raw matter for their generation of new narratives, new connections, new significations. Media audiences have begun
to perceive that they, themselves, are the archons, the ones who make the
laws that govern the textual archives they encounter, take possession of,
explore, and exploit. Audiences grasp the products of mass culture in their
hands, not to put them under arrest and keep them contained, static, and
still, but to subject the products to their manipulations. The law set forth
by the archon-authors who were previously known as "the audience," if it
were ever to be written down, would state that the archives of mass media
are open, capacious, permitting infinite withdrawals and welcoming of an
infinite array of additional entrants and entries; their potential for growth

is unbounded, they can hold and receive any contents that the archons see fit to deposit there. As many fans as there will *ever* be of Jane Austen's *Pride and Prejudice* ([1813] 2012), that is how large the *Pride and Prejudice* archive will become, for the archive will house all of those readers' interpretations and new versions, including all films and television miniseries and novels and Web series, all scholarly essays and commentaries, and all fan works as well.[1] The archive remains open to new entries, and each new entry changes the entirety of the archive.

In "Archive Fever," Derrida, as is his wont in most of his writings, reveals a definition of archives that appears to be the very opposite of the definition he initially gives. While he opens the essay with statements about archives as the sites of "house arrest," he eventually argues that a "new theory of the archive" is coming into being, one that marks it as "a movement of the promise of the future no less than of recording the past," and as the bearer of an "unknowable weight," that is, the weight of the unknowable future shape, size, and nature of the archive, which comprise the archive's "opening on the future," its "dependency with respect to what will come," and "all that ties knowledge and memory to the promise" (1995, 24). This archive that is never closed, but is always laden with promise, with the promise of what will come, and the promise of what it, the archive itself, will become each time new contents enter it through its opening, through its always-being-open: this is the archive that the new archons have discovered, and of which they make good use.

Free Culture

In the preface to his book *Free Culture*, legal scholar Lawrence Lessig (2004) writes, "The inspiration for the title and much of the argument of this book comes from the work of Richard Stallman and the Free Software Foundation. ... All of the theoretical insights I develop here are insights Stallman described decades ago. One could thus well argue that this work is 'merely' derivative" (xv). But of course, Lessig's goal in *Free Culture*, and in much of his subsequent writing (especially his book *Remix* [2008]), is to persuade his readers to begin perceiving derivative works as not "'merely' derivative" but as works that *develop a source*. In Lessig's, and Stallman's, view, derivations and iterations are not "mere" repetitions (rip-offs, knock-offs, copies, fakes) of original works by lesser authors; they are progressions, elaborations, and extensions, which are useful (if only to their makers), and are, therefore, necessary. Such developments of source material are not, in other words, redundant; they *must be done*, in order to fulfill the needs of the developers (and possibly additional users), and in order to fulfill the potentiality that would otherwise lie dormant, unused, in the source.

Both archontic production and rogue archives participate in and exemplify the free culture movement. What I call "the free culture movement" is not a highly visible, clearly organized series of direct actions, as were the civil rights movement or the women's rights movement of the twentieth century. Rather, it is a movement composed of everyday cultural practices, of minor and major appropriations and transmediations performed by individuals and collectives most of whom would not say, if questioned, that they were primarily or even slightly motivated by an ideological commitment to "free culture," but that they were simply doing what they wished to do with the new media tools, platforms, and networks available to them.

The free culture movement began taking shape in the 1990s, when new media became integral to the everyday life of millions of consumers, and when the culture industries began lobbying the US Congress and fighting numerous court battles to shore up the legal definition of US copyright, as a defense against digital technologies' affordances for copying, cutting-and-pasting, and remixing—in other words, as a defense against the threat that digital technologies pose to the culture industries' ability to own, control, and profit from the global flows of cultural content. Supporters of "free culture" believe that copyrights should not, by default, be extended indefinitely, without limit; that definitions of "fair use" must be expanded to include the types of transformation and sharing made possible by emerging technologies; and that cultural works must be allowed to enter the public domain so that audiences can transmute them without risk of committing a legal infringement. Free culture holds that culture should be free, as in freedom (not necessarily free, as in "free beer" [Lessig 2004, 106]). But to understand free culture, one must have at least a passing familiarity with free software.

The free software movement is a more cohesive and organized movement than the free culture movement. The free software movement has an identifiable founder, Richard Stallman, who writes and speaks on its behalf, it is guided by the nonprofit Free Software Foundation (FSF), and it counts legions of software engineers as its adherents. The FSF promotes four essential freedoms of computer users:

Freedom 0: The freedom to run a program as you wish.

Freedom 1: The freedom to study the source of the program and change it so that it does the work that you wish (i.e., the freedom to study and change the program's source code).

Freedom 2: The freedom to distribute exact copies to others.

Freedom 3: The freedom to distribute modified copies to others. (Stallman 2012; see also Weber 2009, 48)

The FSF has created many guidelines and apparatuses that explicitly invite users to practice these four freedoms, and that protect what users create when they practice them. For example, the FSF created the General Public License (GPL), which enforces a kind of legal right that Stallman calls "copyleft." "Copyleft uses copyright law, but flips it over to serve the opposite of its usual purpose: instead of a means of privatizing software, it becomes a means of keeping software free. ... For an effective copyleft, modified versions must also be free" (Stallman 2002, 22). What this means is that, according to political science scholar Steven Weber, "free software *and derivative works* from free software remain free. The central idea of the GPL is that it uses copyright law to extend the four freedoms by preventing any users from adding restrictions that could deny these rights to others" (Weber 2009, 48). So, if an individual (or a firm) releases software that she wants others to modify, but does not issue that software under the GPL, then another individual (or firm) can incorporate elements of that software into her own version, and release that modified version as proprietary software, disallowing any further modifications and reverting to the older "logic of keeping software source code secret" (Weber 2009, 48).

So, the FSF insists that the four freedoms be protected for all *future* users of all free software—that software must *remain* free, into perpetuity, rather than being transformed into copyrighted proprietary code. Again, free software code, whose programmers place it under copyleft rather than copyright, can be monetized and sold, but its source code can never be walled off from future users. "Copyleft says that anyone who redistributes the software, with or without changes, must pass along the freedom to further copy and change it. Copyleft guarantees that every user has freedom" (Free Software Foundation n.d.).

This may seem highly abstract to many who do not regularly write software or think about the writing of software, so an illustration of what free software produces may be useful here. Figures 7.1 and 7.2 show the history of the GNU/Linux operating system. The figures illustrate that GNU/Linux is a single operating system comprising numerous variants called "distributions" or "distros." (Many people call this set of variants "Linux distributions," but this is a misnomer. GNU is an operating system composed entirely of free software, whose development was initiated by Stallman and continued by the GNU Project, and Linux is an operating system initially developed by Linus Torvalds. What most people today call the "Linux system" is really the "GNU/Linux system," that is, "GNU with Linux added"

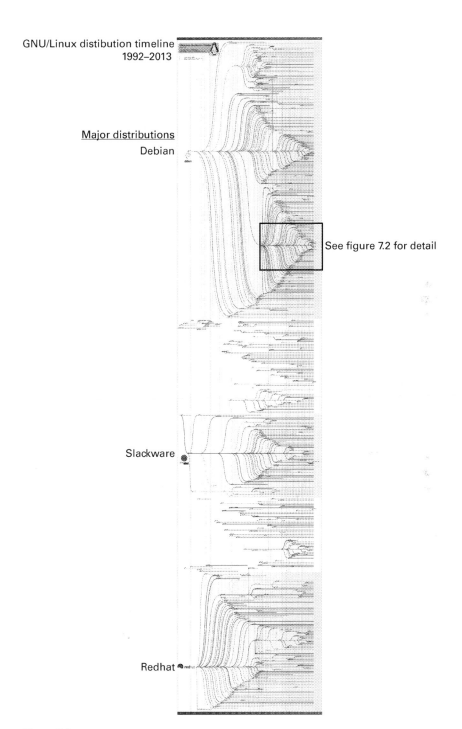

Figure 7.1
GNU/Linux Distribution Timeline, version 12.10, by A. Lundqvist and D. Rodic, October 29, 2012 (http://futurist.se/gldt/).

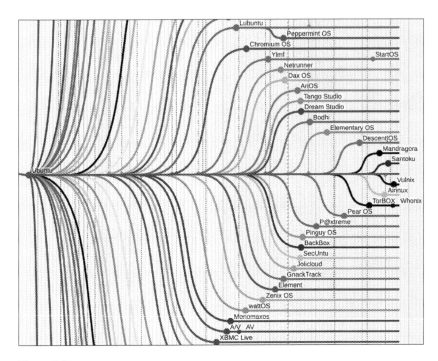

Figure 7.2
Detail of the top section of the GNU/Linux Distribution Timeline 12.10 (showing several forks of the Debian branch).

[Stallman 2012], or, the Linux kernel combined with many programs originally written by the GNU Project.) The first releases of GNU/Linux came out in the early 1990s, and since then, over six hundred distros have been released. Approximately half of these are being actively developed today, so there will undoubtedly be hundreds of additional GNU/Linux distros released in the next twenty years. Some of the distros were not well maintained, and so fell out of use, while other distros, such as Debian, proved so popular that they gave rise to multiple forks (and some of those descendent distros, such as Ubuntu from Debian, in turn earned followings that generated new forks). Not all GNU/Linux distributions are completely free (according to the FSF's definition), but many are.

The images that show the history of GNU/Linux distributions serve as useful visualizations of not only free software, but free culture. Think of the *Harry Potter* novels, authored by J. K. Rowling and appearing in print between 1997 and 2007, as composing the "kernel" of what we might call the "*Harry Potter* operating system." Now think of the culture industries and of ordinary individuals as "users" of the *Harry Potter* system, who, operating under the four freedoms (without necessarily understanding that they are doing so), decide to:

- run (that is, read, and comprehend) the (*Harry Potter*) program as they wish (Freedom 0);
- study the source of the program (the story and characters, as laid out in the books) and change it so that the program does the work that they wish, by adapting and transforming the books into films, video games, costumes, fan fiction, fan vids, and so on (Freedom 1);
- and distribute these modified copies to others, by writing essays about *Harry Potter* for school assignments or for academic journals, by dressing up as *Harry Potter* characters and attending fan conventions and posting selfies of their costume play ("cosplay") on Instagram, by making films based on Harry Potter and uploading them to YouTube, by posting fanfic stories to fic communities and archives, etc. (Freedom 3).

In this schema, *every variant* of Harry Potter, whether "official" (authorized and/or created by Rowling or Warner Bros., which purchased the media rights to Rowling's novels) or "unofficial" (created by readers-fans), whether high budget or low budget, whether consumed by millions or by only a handful of people, is a unique release, a unique distribution, of the *Harry Potter* system.

Some distros of *Harry Potter* have attracted more users, and generated more variants, than others: the films, for example, generated many fan works based more on their depictions of the *Harry Potter* stories than on the novels (just as some GNU/Linux distros, such as Debian, have generated many more new distros than others). But each distro belongs to, and expands, the system. While neither Rowling nor Warner Bros. assigned a Creative Commons license or any other license that adheres to the principles of copyleft, readers and fans still exercise their freedoms in relation to how they use the system kernel. My view is that the four freedoms are not only accessible and utile when certain legal designations are in place; the four freedoms are *innate* to media reception, consumption, and use, and legal designations, such as the GPL license or Creative Commons licenses, simply try to align with, formalize, and provide legal cover for, the freedoms that media users exercise with or without legal permissions (I discuss this idea at greater length in break 7).

Figures 7.1 and 7.2 show archontic production in operation. Archontic production is a crowdsourced multiplication of the contents of an archive. Archontic production does not treat the objects within an archive as discrete

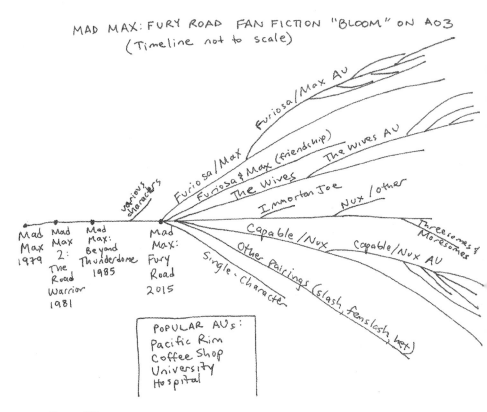

Figure 7.3
Hand-drawn visualization of fan fiction production based on the film *Mad Max: Fury Road* on Archive of Our Own, June 18, 2015.

and separate from one another. Rather, for the archontic producers, all of the stories that stem from a published storyworld are linked, branching off one another, just as all of the variants of the GNU/Linux operating system are linked. The GNU/Linux operating system constitutes a single metaphorical archive (or meta-archive) containing many variants, just as the *Harry Potter* metaphorical archive (meta-archive) contains millions of variants.

Figure 7.3 is my crude attempt to draw the archontic production within a specific fandom, the *Mad Max* fandom. Fan fiction stories branch out from source media texts in a way that is similar to GNU/Linux distros' forking from earlier versions of the operating system; I call this type of visualization "the bloom from the kernel" (which plays on the concept and phrasing of the "Linux kernel"). In figure 7.3, the "kernel" is the *Mad Max* universe, created by George Miller, consisting of four motion pictures (to date). I am depicting only the "bloom" of *Mad Max* fan fiction stories published and stored on the Archive of Our Own (AO3), and since AO3 had not yet launched when the first three *Mad Max* films were released, my bloom represents, for the most part, only the types of fanfic generated in response to *Mad Max: Fury Road* (*MMFR*), the fourth film, which premiered on May 14, 2015. A handful of fan stories, about various characters from the first three films, appeared on the archive prior to *MMFR*'s opening, but as soon as the fourth film appeared in cinemas, fans began to produce fic in much greater volume.

In the bloom generated by fans building on the *MMFR*, I have drawn a fork for each of the most popular fanfic genres in the fandom ("popular" meaning the most numerous: fans wrote more of these types of stories than any others). Each "genre" of *MMFR* fanfic is organized around specific characters, and usually also around those characters' relationship to one another. My bloom thus consists of forks for Furiosa/Max (the characters played by Charlize Theron and Tom Hardy) as a romantic pairing; Capable/Nux (the characters played by Riley Keough and Nicholas Hoult) as a romantic pairing; Furiosa and Max as a nonromantic pairing (these stories focus on the friendship or camaraderie between the two characters); the group of characters called the Wives (played by Keough, Rosie Huntington-Whiteley, Zoë Kravitz, Abbey Lee, and Courtney Eaton), whom Furiosa and Max rescue in the film; Immortan Joe (played by Hugh Keays-Byrne), the movie's primary villain; Nux paired with other characters; other boyslash pairings (e.g., Max/Nux), other femslash pairings (e.g., Furiosa/Capable), and other heterosexual (e.g., Furiosa and another male character) pairings; "Threesomes and Moresomes" (e.g., Furiosa/Nux/Max or Immortan Joe/ The Wives); and single-character (stories that only delve into the thoughts and experiences of one character, e.g., Furiosa).

The largest *MMFR* genres—Furiosa/Max, Capable/Nux, and the Wives— now have forks for "AU," or Alternate Universe, versions of those characters and pairings. I have indicated, at the bottom of the graphic, some of the most popular AU settings in the *MMFR* fandom: *Pacific Rim* (the 2013 Guillermo del Toro film in which pairs of characters who are "drift-compatible," i.e., whose minds can "meld" at a deep level, can pilot giant machines in combat against *kaiju*, which are giant dinosaur-like monsters—in most *MMFR*/*Pacific Rim* crossover AU stories, Furiosa and Max discover they are drift-compatible and become copilots); Coffee Shop (in which several of the characters work at a contemporary coffee shop, and get to know the other characters when they patronize the shop); University (in which the characters meet on a college campus); and Hospital (in which one or more of the characters works at a hospital, and meet the other characters when they need treatment). I have attempted to indicate the relative popularity of fic genres by the lengths of their forks, so the longer the fork, the more stories have been written in that genre, but this drawing is not data driven. The kernel—the horizontal line representing the official *Mad Max* franchise, whose official "author" is auteurist director George Miller—continues on, as Miller is about to launch several *Mad Max* comics and will possibly, depending on *MMFR's* box office receipts, make more *Mad Max* feature films.

Intertextuality and Feedback in Free Software and Free Culture

Both free software and free culture archives open onto the future, as Derrida would say. The branching structure of the GNU/Linux makes perceptible the conceptual archive that is opened by every new source text, and how that archive expands: through the activity of its users, who contribute modifications and variants. Christopher Kelty (2008) writes that Linux "privileges openness to new directions, at every level. ... It privileges the right to fork the software into new and different kinds of systems. ... It should be remembered that Linux is by no means an attempt to create something radically new; it is a rewrite of a Unix operating system, as [Linus] Torvalds points out, but one that through adaptation can end up becoming something new" (Kelty 2008, 222). Both free software and free culture value forking, rewriting, and adapting over "creat[ing] something radically new"—but both recognize that there can be originality, novelty, and innovation in derivation, modification, and modulation.

Literary scholars could argue that free software and free culture, both formations of the digital era, have not founded any new thinking but are only adapting ideas already developed by print-era theorists of intertextuality. In his 1967 essay "The Death of the Author," Roland Barthes argues,

We know now that a text is not a line of words releasing a single "theological" meaning (the "message" of the Author-God) but a multi-dimensional space in which a variety of writings, none of them original, blend and clash. The text is a tissue of quotations drawn from the innumerable centres of culture. ... In the multiplicity of writing, everything is to be *disentangled*, nothing *deciphered*; the structure can be followed, "run" (like the thread of a stocking) at every point and at every level, but there is nothing beneath: the space of writing is to be ranged over, not pierced. ... In precisely this way literature, ... by refusing to assign a "secret," an ultimate meaning, to the text, ... liberates what may be called an anti-theological activity, an activity that is truly revolutionary since to refuse to fix meaning is, in the end, to refuse God. (Barthes [1967] 1977, 146–147)

Barthes's poststructuralist idea that all language references all other language, that there is no originality in literary writing except in the recombination of known words, phrases, scenarios, and tropes, leads him to tear down the idea of an "Author-God," whose conscious intention or unconscious genius "fixes" the meaning of a text with finality. If the meaning of a text cannot be finally decided, then a text is simply a "space of writing to be ranged over," a space whose internal structure is borrowed from all preceding works of culture, and can be followed, can be traced like a run in a stocking. Anyone who has worn stockings knows that no "run" is final: any and every rip in a stocking's fabric is likely to extend and expand; runs beget runs. The multidimensional space brought into being by a text contains multiplicities, and gives on to further multiplicities. Barthes's metaphor of the stocking run evokes, in our digital period, software "runs," so we might say that, as a piece of software can be run on multiple machines, so a piece of culture (a text) can be run on multiple readers, and those readers can, in turn, run with the text they receive (or rather, run with the text *as they perceive it*) in any direction they choose. We might figure their run-ons as forkings or branchings-out from the text, and envision the multidimensional space of Barthes's text as tree-like in shape, similar to the above visualizations of GNU/Linux.

Rather than viewing transformative works as "'merely' derivative," or as repetitions, copies, rip-offs, knock-offs, or imitations, the free software/free culture framework allows us to see transformative works as development projects, as elaborations, extensions, modifications, and refinements of a source. We can think of GNU/Linux distros as fan productions. We can think of *Harry Potter* fan productions as distros. We can think of software engineers as "fanficcing" the GNU/Linux operating system kernel. We can think of fans as "engineering" new distributions of narrative/storyworld system kernels. We can conceive of the culture industries' mass media productions as releases of system kernels, on top of which fans/users constantly build new distributions.

A major difference between GNU/Linux software development and media fans' modes of cultural production is that GNU/Linux often seeks to stabilize code through incorporating variants. Free software does not wish for infinite forks, for, as Kelty writes, forking "implies dilution and confusion—competing versions of the same thing and potentially unmanageable incompatibilities" (2008, 233). Free software developers practice a range of methods to achieve some degree of reconciliation and standardization, that is, to decide what features and "mutations" (Kelty 2008, 156) will be included in official releases. If fans consider their source texts to be mass media titles, and their own works to be forkings of the commodities sold to them by the culture industries, they never expect their variations to be incorporated into later versions of the mass media texts. When a new season of a serial television program debuts, or when a film franchise such as *Star Trek* or *Star Wars* is relaunched or "rebooted" by Hollywood studios that own their copyrights, fans do not anticipate that they will be regarded as contributors to the development of these story worlds, and do not expect that a vote will be taken among all the users of these worlds as to which fan versions should be woven into the new canonical "releases." Fans do not require or desire their innovations or features to be incorporated into the source, and they do not view themselves as developers contributing to the improvement of the source.

However, GNU/Linux software development and fan production proceed similarly in some respects. Fans can be said to "improve" a source text for themselves and their fellow fans: fan productions come into being because users of these source materials deem them insufficient and inadequate, and/or in need of augmentation or elaboration. Fans also improve one another's work, through processes such as "beta-ing" (a beta reader reviews and edits a fan's work before the work is publicly posted; media fandom appropriated the term "beta" from the arena of software design [see also chapter 6, n. 4]). Fans occasionally incorporate one another's changes into their productions, resulting in the formation of what is called "fanon," or fan canon, which is a set of features of the larger story world, the meta-archive, that become constant in a great deal of fan production even though they never appear in the canonical, or source, texts. Fans' responses and opinions sometimes inform official makers' decisions, in the manner of a feedback loop. But this feedback is not collected or channeled formally, according to published procedures, as happens in free software development communities. Thus, remix collectives and free software communities do not mirror one another precisely, but share a family resemblance. Both groups define themselves by a strong commitment to what E. Gabriella Coleman (2012) calls "productive freedom" (3), which, she states, encompasses makers' rights to "autonomously improve on their peers' work, refine their technical [or creative] skills, and extend craftlike engineering [or cultural] traditions" (Coleman 2012, 3).

Archontic Production and New Media Literacies

Stallman (2012) states that none of the four freedoms of free software are compulsory. "You don't *have* to do any of these. You could run the program as you *don't* wish if you're a masochist. You don't have to distribute copies, and you don't have to distribute modified versions, you can run it privately." I view the four freedoms of free software as directly applicable to free culture, including their noncompulsory status. The existence and growth of free culture does not mandate that every cultural consumer must transform each work that they encounter and post all of their remixes online; even those who self-identify as fans do not generate modifications for all of the media they view, hear, read, or play, and some fans who do produce transformative works rarely or never share them with others. Like free software, free culture does not insist that every person who has access to the Internet become a fully and constantly participating member in the multidirectional flows of media content, but it seeks to defend the ability of *any* individual to contribute to those flows through archontic production, whenever and however they wish.

At the same time, a growing number of scholars in education studies and other fields are defining archontic production as a critical component of "new media literacies." Lessig quotes Elizabeth Daley of USC's Institute for Multimedia Literacy and the School of Cinematic Arts and Stephanie Barish, CEO of IndieCade, who have experimented with teaching new media literacies in inner-city Los Angeles high schools, on the importance of teaching children the skills to not only comprehend media, but to make media. Daley states, "From my perspective, probably the most important digital divide is not access to a box. It's the ability to be empowered with the language that the box works in. Otherwise only a very few people can write with this language, and all the rest of us are reduced to being read-only" (quoted in Lessig 2004, 37). The opposite of "read-only" is "read-write." As Lessig explains in his book *Remix*, in a read-only (RO) culture, the dominant mode of media consumption is to simply read (or listen to, or view, etc.) works as they are produced and packaged by their makers, but in a read-write (RW) culture, "reading ... is not enough." Lessig writes, in a read-write paradigm, "Ordinary citizens ... add to the culture they read by creating and re-creating the culture around them" (Lessig 2008, 28).[2] Lessig cites John Seely Brown, formerly chief scientist of Xerox Corporation, as another proponent of read-write culture, though Brown is more concerned with how young people learn engineering skills than with how they learn cultural production skills. Brown describes free and open-source software as a "completely new kind of learning platform." Brown endorses tinkering as an excellent learning methodology, and states that free and open source software encourages children to practice this methodology: "You are tinkering with other people's stuff. The more you tinker the more you improve" (quoted in Lessig 2004, 46).

In a paper for the John D. and Catherine T. MacArthur Foundation on digital media and learning, Henry Jenkins and his coauthors endorse an approach to education in which students use new media to learn how to engage in "participatory culture," which I read as overlapping with Lessig's "free culture." Participatory culture, write Jenkins et al., encourages "expressions" that include "digital sampling, skinning and modding, fan videomaking, fan fiction writing, zines, mash-ups," and teaches skills such as "appropriation—the ability to meaningfully sample and remix media content" (Jenkins et al. 2009, 3–4). Thinking critically about information and information networks; knowing how to acquire, interpret, and make media texts in multiple genres; understanding how to parse data and distinguish between sources; learning to quote from media texts, to gather evidence and form arguments from their contents for persuasion, critique, and entertainment; developing techniques for participation in small and large communities, in both real-world and online collaborations: these are only some of the learning objectives of an educational program focused on imparting "new media literacies," according to Jenkins et al. (2009, 28–104). In a similar vein as Lessig, Jenkins et al. claim that acquiring literacy in a digital age "involves the ability to both read and write across all available modes of expression" (48). Building on these perspectives, education scholars Rebecca W. Black and Angela Thomas argue that fan fiction is a genre of writing through which young people develop core literacy skills.[3] This body of work on new media literacies discusses read-write culture/participatory culture/free culture as key methods and desirable outcomes for contemporary education.

Archontic production, a practice in which media consumers treat existing media texts as archives, withdrawing elements they find interesting or appealing, tinkering with them, varying them, and incorporating them into original creations, thus stands at the heart of a recent reconceptualization of literacy. Therefore, while it will never be compulsory for individuals to make use of the freedoms of either free software or free culture, a major project of educators is to ensure that future generations at least know *how* to both "read" and "write" both code and culture.

Archontic Production and Minoritarian Cultures

Education theorists argue that archontic production is a critical component of the training of future generations, but this type of making has a
long history, particularly in minoritarian communities. Metaphorical uses
of "archive" and related terms to describe culture—especially "dominant"
culture in its many forms, often meaning Western "high" culture or, alter-
natively, "mass" culture—as well as references to acts of cultural plundering, extraction, withdrawal and deposit such as those I have described in
this chapter, can be found in many important texts of postcolonial studies,
critical race theory, and feminist theory. Below are a few key examples.

In "Of Mimicry and Man," Homi Bhabha (1984) writes of the colonial
subject's mimicry of the white colonizer as a "double articulation." The
colonized's performance of the colonizer, which is "*almost the same, but not
quite*" (126) (which, later in the essay, Bhabha rewrites, archontically, as
"*Almost the same but not white*" [130]) both "'appropriates' the [colonizing]
Other" and simultaneously stands as "the sign of the inappropriate," thus
"pos[ing] an immanent threat to both 'normalized' knowledges and disci-
plinary power" (126). The mimicking not quite/not white subject looks on
"the *founding objects* of the Western world" as "the erratic, eccentric, accidental *objets trouvés* [found objects] of the colonial discourse. ... It is then
that the body and the book [of the colonizer] lose their representational
authority" (132). Bhabha here presents the bodies and books of the imperial West as objects forming an archive waiting to be found by the colonized subject, readymade(s) in the Dadaist sense (*objets trouvés* is a Dadaist
phrase) available for "inappropriate" appropriations and deformations. As
an example of colonized subjects' proclivity for mimicry that destabilizes
colonial power, Bhabha quotes a piece of writing from a European missionary living and working in Bengal in 1817. The missionary writes that
the locals are quite happy to receive the Bibles he hands out, so that they
can use them as "waste paper" (133): a fanficcing of the Christian West's
holy book as trash, a conversion of the printed texts of the sacred archive
into disposables.

Nestor Canclini, in *Hybrid Cultures*, employs archival language to characterize local Latin American responses to the ascendance of tourism, met-
ropolitan cultures, and global economic and communication flows: "One
seeks to reconvert a *heritage or resource* ... in order to reintegrate it to new
conditions of production and distribution," Canclini writes, "not only in
the arts but in everyday life and in technological development" (Canclini
1995, xxvii, emphasis added). So techniques and possessions from the

past—those inherited as "heritage" or "resource"—become the source material for "reconversions," transformations, and updates, when, for instance, artisans "connect their traditional craftwork with modern uses in order to interest urban buyers" or when "indigenous movements ... renovate their demands in transnational politics or in an ecological discourse and learn to communicate these demands via radio, television, and the Internet" (xxvii). Drawing on another memory framework, Canclini states that there are "diverse ways in which the members of each group"—ethnic groups, national groups, and class groups—"appropriate the heterogeneous *repertoire* of goods and messages available in the transnational circuits" (xxviii; emphasis added). A link between Canclini's theory of hybridity and my idea of archontic production is suggested by Canclini's characterizations of culture as heritage, as a repository of resources, and as an inherited repertoire—that is, as a past rich with knowledges, skills, objects, and ways of doing, each of which can potentially be extracted and manipulated into something that will be valued in the postmodern, globalized, mediatized present.

Henry Louis Gates Jr. (1988) writes of "the black English vernacular tradition" as "the *repository* that contains the language that is the source—and the reflection—of black difference" (xxiii; emphasis added), and Houston Baker Jr. (1991) calls rap "the 'in effect' *archive* where postmodernism has been *dopely* sampled" (208; first emphasis added). Gates frames black English vernacular as a repository from which black authors extract valuable elements with which they can transform and rewrite "the canonical texts of the Western tradition" (1988, xxii). Gates writes, "Texts have a curious habit of generating other texts that resemble themselves. ... Black literature shares much with, far more than it differs from, the Western textual tradition. ... But black formal repetition always repeats with a difference, a black difference that manifests itself in specific language use" (xxii–xxiii). In this analysis, both the white Western literary tradition and the black English vernacular tradition are "repositories"—what Gates deems a "two-toned heritage" (xxiii)—from which black writers make withdrawals, and then enrich with their own creations, their repetitions-with-a-difference, which are the works of black American literature.

Baker pulls off a clever inversion with his reference to rap as "the 'in effect' archive where postmodernism has been *dopely* sampled." Rap routinely makes use of sampled music, that is, musical tracks constructed from excerpts of already recorded music, and so rap producers could be thought of as making liberal use of the existing archive of recorded sound. But Baker frames the makers of rap differently: as themselves the creators of an archive, the archive of rap, which Baker states is "now classical black sound," the source from which newer genres, such as "house" and "rap reggae," will "spin off" (Baker 1991, 208), but which will always acknowledge rap as the origin. However, in this framing, Baker does not efface rap's own origins in appropriation; he acknowledges that the archive of rap contains samples of preexisting material, but *what* rap has "dopely" sampled, Baker declares, is postmodernism itself, the entire artistic and cultural movement of unconstrained raids of past culture that is, writes Frederic Jameson, "stored up in the imaginary museum of a now global culture" (1984, 65). Against the stereotype of rap producers as "thieves" who sample without paying copyright holders, Baker characterizes rap producers as cultural sophisticates who take from the global postmodern movement what they wish, and practice postmodern stylistic flourishes to construct an archive of a new "classical" black music, an archive that will be highly generative, an open space rather than a closed room.

We also find an appearance of the archival motif in Gayatri Spivak's powerful interpretation of Jean Rhys's *Wide Sargasso Sea*: Spivak (1985) suggests that Charlotte Brontë's masterpiece *Jane Eyre* "can be read as the orchestration and staging of the self-immolation of Bertha Mason as 'good wife'" (259), and states that her reading of *Jane Eyre* derives from "a modest and inexpert 'reading' of '*archives*'" (emphasis added), by which she means "the archives of imperialist governance" (259). In other words, Spivak argues that we cannot understand the full meaning of Bertha Mason's actions "if we remain insufficiently knowledgeable about the history of the legal manipulation of widow-sacrifice in the entitlement of the British government in India" (Spivak 1985, 259). Spivak reads Bertha as archontically conceived, born of Brontë's engagement with "the archives of imperialist governance" (however unconsciously this archival research may have been done). But I would also position *Jane Eyre* as itself part of the imperialist archive, or as an instantiation of *an* imperialist (metaphorical) archive, from which Rhys, who was born and raised in the West Indies, felt compelled to extract the character of Bertha, so that she could transform and redeem the story of the West Indian "madwoman," locked for years in the attic by her English gentleman husband (under "house arrest," like the contents of a nineteenth century archive).

Thus, in minoritarian critics' explorations of appropriative writing, we find numerous invocations and allusions to archives as sources/source code whose contents are available to be reworked, revised, elaborated, extended, and expanded upon. Hence, my term "archontic production" does not name any altogether new, or specifically digital, ways of making culture, and does not attempt to theorize what has never been theorized before, but serves only as an overarching term for appropriative creativity, which has often been described through metaphorical references to archives, repositories, heritage, repertoires, and other forms of memory preservation and retrieval.

Political Potentialities

Archontic production definitely does not always serve the interests of minority discourses. It does not always take the form of counterhegemonic narratives. Education and gender studies theorists Peter McLaren and Rhonda Hammer underscore that media images are often manipulated in order to reinforce neocolonial capitalist power structures and racist/sexist/ classist/jingoistic stereotypes. They write: "Of serious concern in our own work is how electronic prophets ... have been able to turn wimp presidents into wrathful avengers and an often frustrated and self-hating citizenry into phallomilitary warrior citizens who are conditioned to redirect a media-instilled hatred of 'Sad'am' and various dark-skinned others against a familiar enemy within its own ranks: the poor, the homeless, people of color, those who comprise the detritus of capitalism and white man's democracy, those who are already oppressed by race, gender, caste, and circumstance" (McLaren and Hammer 1996, 109). In these examples, the US president, no matter who he is, is "fanficced" as a powerful warrior-leader, worthy of his constituents' devotion; Saddam Hussein is "fanficced" as a mass of abject and/or nonwhite Americans, deserving only of loathing and scorn. Even though McLaren and Hammer are here commenting on the power of right-wing media to edit news footage in ways that reinforce specific ideological messages, the authors acknowledge that it is not only broadcasting corporations who can treat recorded images as the source materials for freshly spun narratives.

In response to the power of both mass media and individual media makers to archontically produce reactionary, prejudiced, discriminatory, and imperialist media texts using the vast archive of recorded culture made electronically available, McLaren and Hammer desire an educational landscape that would teach all citizens to become aware of how archontic production operates, and how they personally can engage in it. Like other media literacy advocates, McLaren and Hammer call for the education of a populace that would be well versed in the use of media-as-archive, from which a potentially infinite number of divergent narratives can be constructed, so that individuals and communities, especially those occupying minority positions vis-à-vis existing hegemonies, can generate their own archontic "counternarratives." Citing Paul Willis's *Common Culture* (1990), McLaren and Hammer (1996) argue that "high culture or official culture has lost its dominance" (109), and that "the main seeds of cultural development are to be found in the commercial provision of cultural commodities" (110). Widespread media literacy, of which "reading" and "writing" archontically is a core component, would ensure that the power of archontic production is not concentrated in the hands of a select few—the professionals of the cultural industries—but is wielded by many, as what Willis terms "everyday symbolic work" (Willis 1990, 136) and what McLaren and Hammer (1996, 110) name "creative symbolic work within informal culture," which "offers important possibilities for 'oppositional, independent or alternative sym-bolizations of the self.'"

Willis, like the postcolonial, African-American, and feminist theorists cited above, frames culture as an archive to be mined when he states, "Where everyday symbolic work differs from what is normally thought of as 'education' is that it 'culturally produces'—from its own chosen cul-tural resources. Psychologically, at least, the informal symbolic workers of common cultures feel they really 'own' and can therefore manipulate their resources as materials and tools—unlike the books at school which are 'owned' by the teachers" (Willis 1990, 136). Media literacy then, involves a perspective on culture, all of culture, as a shared set of "resources" that each user *feels* she or he owns (whether they own copyright over specific cultural products or not), and therefore, feels entitled to "manipulate ... as materials and tools." Media literacy is less interested in legal definitions of intellectual property than with a perception, attitude, and belief system that should—even must—be encouraged among media audiences, which is: that every consumer is a potential *user* of media; that users can seize upon all of media and culture *as* an archive and plunder its elements as the bases for their own productions; and that when users circulate their archontic productions, either to their own communities (minority groups, fandoms, subcultures, activist organizations) or to a wider public, they exercise their power to make statements and stories that have meaning for them—personally, politically, or both—out of the images, texts, personas, data, and narratives that saturate their lives via global media. Advocates for media literacy wish for the "empire to write back," as Salman Rushdie (1982) put it. In coining this phrase, Rushdie was writing of the subjects of formal European and American imperial projects, but if we consider that the culture industries aim to colonize and occupy the minds and hearts of consumers, then it is audiences who are the subjects, who are the "empire"

conquered and won by global media, and who must individually and collectively assert their rights and abilities to govern and determine their own
emotional, psychological, and intellectual lives. This self-governance and
self-determination often takes the form of a negotiation with mass media
rather than an absolute resistance to it; it is a reduction of mass media to
base matter from which local meanings can be constructed, rather than a
rejection of all the riches that media has to offer.

Archontic production is not, therefore, necessarily or essentially minoritarian, but potentialities for democratizing, polyvocal, hybridizing, multi-
perspectival cultural production inhere in it. These political potentialities
have been fruitfully developed by scores of postcolonial, ethnic minority,
and women authors, who (as the theorists quoted above note) often are
culturally colonized by dominant power structures at the level of the very
languages they speak, the ideas they think, and the beliefs they hold, and
must therefore attempt to decolonize themselves and their communities by
launching new ways of speaking, thinking, and believing from *within* the
dominant discourse, by atomizing, mutating, and recombining that discourse into expressions of marginalized realities and fantasies.

Consumer Memory versus User Memory

Archontic production's most salient promise is the promise of transforming
mass media "markets" into media's masters—turning the targets of global
media flows into the containers and directors of those flows: archivists of
the mass of media texts, and liberal users and elaborators of those archives.

In *Acting Out* (2009; published in French in 2003), philosopher Bernard
Stiegler expresses similar concerns to those articulated by Max Horkheimer
and Theodor Adorno in their 1944 book *Dialectic of Enlightenment*, framing his anxiety about mass media not as a suspicion that they equal "mass
deception" but that they exercise control over human memory. For Stiegler,
human memory consists of three forms of retention: primary retention,
which belongs "to the present of perception," that is, listening to a melody
and remembering each note as it passes, so that one can link the stream
of notes together and make sense of the tune; secondary retention, which
Stiegler calls "the *past* of my consciousness," by which one remembers the
melody heard the day before and is able to "hear [it] again *in imagination*
by the play of memory"; and tertiary retention, "a prosthesis of exterior-
ized memory" (54), which can produce "the identical repetition of the
same temporal object" and exists in the forms of recording technologies
such as "phonograms, ... films, and radio and television broadcasts" (54).

Stiegler argues that tertiary retentions, "or "tertiarized temporal objects,"
"are materialized time, which overdetermines the relations between primary and secondary retentions in general, *thus*, in a sense, permitting their
control" (Stiegler [2003] 2009, 54; emphases in original). In other words,
Stiegler claims that by watching the same broadcasts (tertiary retentions) *en
masse*, at the same time of day every day (he gives the example of watching
the evening news), our primary and secondary retentions are becoming
more synchronized: "[Media audiences] end up being so well synchronized
that they have lost their *diachrony*, that is, their singularity, which is to say
their liberty, which always means their liberty *to think*" (55; emphases in
original).

Setting aside the fact that time-shifting has become a routine part of
television consumption for millions of people, and so television broadcasts
do not automatically require, or induce, precise synchronization among
viewers, I find it interesting that Stiegler identifies collective and individual
(he would say, *individuated*) memory as the battleground for determining
whether, and to what extent, mass media control audiences. I do not think
it is out of the question that people lose their "diachrony," "singularity,"
"liberty," or "liberty to think" by having their memory functions more or
less determined by the media they consume. But the person who surrenders
his or her memory function to mass media is a person whom I would characterize as a media illiterate.

My theory of archontic production is that a person literate in the contemporary cultural forms of her day, a person who can adequately "read"
the media formats that she regularly encounters, comprehends how these
forms work as tertiary memory, but does not let that imposed memory
wholly define, restrict, or limit her own primary and secondary memory
systems. Rather, a person with high media literacy treats tertiary memory
products as potentially useful and interesting wellsprings from which to
make new primary and secondary retentions—what I call archontic productions—which can be highly individual (experienced privately, as when
one has a personal interpretation of a cultural work, remembering specific
details about it both as one first encounters the work and then later, when
one recalls the work and perhaps imagines more detailed interpretations
or variations of the work), or can be collective and shared, as when one
"releases" one's interpretations or versions of a cultural work to a community of fellow developers/rememberers/memory workers. Media literacy
can be a kind of memory work in which tertiary memory is not the termi-
nus of cultural experience, but the beginning of a series of experiences—a
kind of memory work that spins out chains of unique and singular primary

and secondary retentions of ever-new derivations and transformations of an initial viewing or listening.

Thus, I locate archontic production's political stakes first of all in the question of whether the individuals who make up media markets can make themselves into media users, by learning and practicing the skills of media literacy, which are the skills of "reading" and then "writing" media. Members of marginalized groups may have maximal incentives to learn how to speak, write, and create from within hegemonic discourses, as appropriating the languages, literatures, and media of the groups who oppress them can be a first step in communicating their radical differences from those groups (Bertha Mason is Charlotte Brontë's "madwoman in the attic," but she is Jean Rhys's troubled West Indian heroine, seduced and then trapped by English colonial patriarchy). But archontic production's basic promise is that of striking the category of "media consumer" and replacing it with "media user": the archontic producer does not allow her consciousness, her singularity, her liberty to think, her memories, to be colonized or controlled by media, but engages with the media as a generative source for her own memory-based creativity. Write McLaren and Hammer, citing Willis (1990): "Human beings must not be regarded merely as human capital or labor power, but as 'creative *citizens*, full of their own sensuous symbolic capacities and activities and taking a hand in the construction of their own identities.' The pursuit of emancipation and equality, therefore, requires more than being made equal as workers. It calls for all to be fully developed as *cultural producers*" (McLaren and Hammer 1996, 110). Archontic production thus is not only political when it serves as a tool with which subordinate peoples critique or subvert dominant discourses. Insofar as the vast majority of people are potentially subjected to mass media, and are therefore perpetually in danger of becoming a subjected mass—what Martin Heidegger (2008) calls the *they* ("*das Man*")[4]—I see archontic production's primary political value as serving to constantly facilitate and affirm cultural expressions of what Stiegler calls "the *I*" or "an ensemble of *I*s in the interior of a *we*" ([2003] 2009, 80). Either the culture industries make of us a "they," or "I"/"we" use cultural commodities for our own ends.

Repertoire in Archontic Production

Although I have referred to the GNU/Linux software development as a model for understanding what I mean by archontic production, a much older model comes up again and again in the writings of cultural theorists to describe creative appropriation: performance.

In *The Uses of Literacy* (1957), Richard Hoggart, who would go on to found the Centre for Contemporary Cultural Studies at the University of Birmingham in 1964, defends the working-class culture that he grew up with in the 1930s. Hoggart argues that working-class people do not care much about mass marketed music recordings, "no matter how much Tin Pan Alley plugs them" (1957, 117), and become attached to popular songs only when they can "take them over": "'After the Ball is Over' is a melodramatic song; it is not even a people's song as the ballads were, but a commercial song taken over by the people; but they have taken it on their own terms, and so it is not for them as poor a thing as it might have been" (119). In their landmark writings on fandom and remix published decades later, Henry Jenkins and Lawrence Lessig both refer to nineteenth-century folk performance as a precedent for digital appropriation, Lessig discussing the preponderance of amateur reperformances of popular songs and ditties in the late 1800s and early 1900s (Lessig 2008, 23–28), and Jenkins pointing to the multitude of combinations of "folk traditions taken from various indigenous and immigrant populations" serving as the basis of US popular culture during that same period (Jenkins 2006, 135). Using a language of plunder that accords well with my concept of archontic production, Jenkins writes that in the United States in the second half of the 1800s, "there was no pure boundary between the emergent commercial culture and the residual folk culture: the commercial culture raided folk culture and folk culture raided commercial culture" (135).

Similarly, performance figures largely in Bhabha's concept of mimicry (which is, first and foremost, a *physical* act: Bhabha writes, for example, of "the white presence and its black semblance" [1984, 129] when discussing the uneasy coexistence of European colonizers and colonized Africans or Indians); in Gates's (1988) idea of the "black vernacular tradition"—a spoken tradition, a verbal tradition—as a repository whose contents suffuse black literature; and in Baker's "'in effect' archive" of rap music, whose success is judged more by the responses of live audiences than by record sales: "Technology can create a rap disc, but only the voice dancing to wheels of steel and producing a hip hopping, responsive audience gives testimony to a full-filled *break*. You ain't busted a move, in other words, until the audience lets you know you're in the groove" (Baker 1991, 202).

One of the clearest articulations of appropriation *as* performance can be found in Dick Hebdige's 1987 book on Caribbean popular music, *Cut 'n' Mix*. In the book's opening pages, Hebdige foregrounds the concept of "versioning," which he borrows from Jamaican reggae: "One of the most important words in reggae is 'version.' Sometimes a reggae record is released and literally hundreds of different versions of the same rhythm or melody will follow in its wake. Every time a version is released, the original tune will be slightly modified. ... 'Versioning' is at the heart not only of reggae but of *all* Afro-American and Caribbean musics" (Hebdige 1987, xiii). Hebdige goes on to argue that versioning is central not just to all black music but to all popular music (he cites Albert Goodman's description of young Elvis Presley as a "marvelous mimic," whose "art lay not in an act of substantive creation but in a recasting of one traditional style in terms of another" [xiv]), and not just to all music but to all creativity and scholarship:

Just as Elvis *used* the voices and the vocal styles of the other singers, so I have borrowed Albert Goldman's voice and style to say something about "versioning." That's what a quotation in a book or on a record is. It's an invocation of someone else's voice to help you say what you want to say. ... And every time the other voice is borrowed in this way, it is turned away slightly from what it was the original author or singer or musician thought they were saying, singing, playing. ... That's the beauty of quotation. The original version takes on a new life and a new meaning in a fresh context. Just like a rhythm or a melody which is brought in from another source in a record or in the live performance of a piece of music. They're just different *kinds* of quotation. And that's the beauty, too, of versioning. It's a democratic principle because it implies that no one has the final say. Everybody has a chance to make a contribution. And no one's version is treated as Holy Writ. (xv)[5]

Fan fiction has also been theorized in terms of performance. Francesca Coppa (2006b) argues that fan fiction offering new versions of familiar characters is akin to theater companies constantly reimagining and staging new productions of plays. "An endless number of Shakespearean productions supplement the texts, adding meanings that Shakespeare never intended and making them meaningful to twenty-first century audiences. There's no reason not to see this as a perfectly valid artistic activity," writes Coppa. Fan fiction revisions and extensions of media texts are "inevitable," states Coppa, "and they aren't any more redundant than multiple productions of *Hamlet*" (Coppa 2006b, 238). Thus, Coppa calls fandom "community theatre in a mass media world" (242).

Versioning is a key term in software development, and it is a key term in performance. Since performance has been integral to human culture far longer than computer programming has, and because all humans perform versions of the cultural works they consume (if only in their imaginations, when they recall and ponder works of art or media they have seen, or when they are alone and sing popular songs to themselves, or when they talk about their interpretations of books or television shows to their friends), the metaphor of performance, and actual genres of performance, provide useful reference points for writers who wish to explain media literacy, that is, the ability of media audiences to collectively create a plethora of variants of any given source. The fact that the language and concept of performance is so often invoked by cultural theorists to describe practices of transformation and remix permits an unusual perspective on free software development, bringing into focus a kinship between GNU/Linux programmers and folk, reggae, and rap artists, and drawing coding and community theater into relation. Jeremy Rifkin links performance to archontic production, versioning, and transformative reuse when he writes about what he calls "the new 'protean' generation": "Theirs is a world that is more theatrical than ideological and oriented more to a play ethos, than to a work ethos" (Rifkin 2001, 12).

So, my theory of archontic production turns out to be equally concerned with repertoires—cultural memory transmitted through performance—as with archives and archiving. In earlier sections, I argued that the structure of digital archives privileges repertoire, as every digital archive does not remain stable on its own, but depends on archivists constantly repeating certain routines of archive maintenance over time. The contents of digital archives often consist of versions and variations of source texts: archivists at Project Gutenberg and Open Library create digital versions of printed books; archivists at the Internet Archive create digital versions of film, video, and sound recordings; archivists at the AO3 store numerous elaborations on media sources; archivists at ibiblio preserve GNU/Linux developers' releases of their extensions of the Linux kernel. To say that these digital transmediations and appropriations are forms of "archontic production" references the memory mode of archive—the treatment of bodies of preexisting texts as archives from which any user can withdraw the raw materials for new projects—*and* the memory mode of repertoire—the process by which humans receive cultural matter *in their bodies* and, by using their bodies as playback machines, perform works that they record (via primary retention) in their own ways, making up their own imaginative transformations of the works (via process of secondary retention).

Humans are the models for all recording and playback devices, for storage and replay are faculties innate to the human body and psyche. Film and media historian Jane Gaines, writing on the development of intellectual property law around sound recording, argues that the "inevitability" of popular music's "use and re-use, imitation, and re-creation" is "prefigured by the body's own sound collection and reproduction apparatus, the prototype for the mechanical and electronic record/store/playback functions: listening, remembering, speaking, or singing" (Gaines 1991,

128–129). In "The Storyteller," Walter Benjamin shares a similar observation about the human listener as a memory-and-reproduction device: "It has seldom been realized that the listener's naïve relationship to the storyteller is controlled by his interest in retaining what he is told. The cardinal point for the unaffected listener is to assure himself of the possibility of reproducing the story. Memory is the epic faculty *par excellence*" (Benjamin [1936] 1968, 97).

Benjamin is not employing "epic" as an adjective here, as we would in contemporary vernacular speech, but as a noun. It is through memory that an epic story is disseminated, through the bodies of storytellers who reperform what they have heard and stored; it is through this combination of memory and reperformance that the epic is preserved. "The greater ... the story's claim to a place in the memory of the listener, the more completely it is integrated into his own experience, the greater will be his inclination to repeat it to someone else someday, sooner or later" (91), states Benjamin, describing the epic listener-turned-storyteller but also offering a strikingly accurate definition of the media fan. For what is a fan, but a listener, an audience member, who pays deep attention to a story, who awards it a place in her memory, who integrates it into her own experience, and then feels inclined to repeat it to someone else, someday, in her own fashion?

Benjamin and Gaines, like Hoggart, Lessig, Jenkins, Bhabha, Baker, Hebdige, and Coppa, recognize that the human receiver does not "purely" reproduce what she or he takes in, but delivers a new rendering of the recorded work. These theorists present creative appropriation as an act of memory that gives onto an act of versioning, which, in their shared view, is a performative act, an act best understood through references and comparisons to performance styles, such as singing and playing music, retelling a story, imitating another through gesture and voice, speaking in a vernacular, sampling and rapping on a record but then playing that record for a crowd. To engage in archontic production means to seize on a cultural work as an archive rich with usable resources, and it also means to put that work, or its elements, into one's personal repertoire. One dives into the archive of a work and expands that archive through versioning it, as a reggae singer versions, as a rapper or sampling artist versions, as a postcolonial subject versions, as Rhys versioned Brontë, as free software programmers version GNU/Linux. Versioning is what happens when you have something in your repertoire, and you play it, your way.

The Bloom from the Kernel, or The Dynarchive

Benjamin writes of an story from ancient Egypt that was told one way by Herodotus, and another way by Montaigne centuries later. Benjamin states, "it [the story] resembles the seeds of grain which have lain for centuries in the chambers of the pyramids shut up air-tight and have retained their germinative power to this day" (Benjamin [1936] 1968, 90). Benjamin mourns the passing of this style of storytelling; he regrets, to an extent, the rise of the novel and the short story, genres that circulate in the format of the single book that purports to stand alone and apart from other stories. The seemingly self-enclosed text "has removed itself from oral tradition and no longer permits that slow piling one on top of the other of thin, transparent layers which constitutes the most appropriate picture of the way in which the perfect narrative is revealed through the layers of a variety of retellings" (93).

The "picture" with which Benjamin presents us here—a layering of a variety of retellings of the same story, a cumulative, accretive progression that Benjamin claims does not obscure the "original" story, but instead reveals the perfect narrative, as if the perfection of the narrative is proven by its generative, "germinative" power—closely maps onto the image of the GNU/Linux Distribution timeline in figure 7.1, and onto my clumsy visualization of *Mad Max* fan fiction production in figure 7.3. Both figures illustrate branches stemming sideways from a single source; they are what Manuel Lima (2014) calls "horizontal trees." As I mentioned above, I call these types of diagrams, and the many-authored multiplications they represent, "the bloom from the kernel." Henry Jenkins, Sam Ford, and Joshua Green (2013) would say they show the "spread" of digital phenomena. Ernst (2013) would call these images of "the dynarchive."

If print culture suppressed Benjamin's picture of the "slow piling one on top of the other of thin, transparent layers" of narrative by installing the singular published book as the sole, complete bearer of a story, then digital culture lifts the ban on the "oral tradition" and assists a massive resurrection of its techniques: the piling, the layering, the retellings, all of which serve to reveal the robust life force of the seed, the kernel, the source, from which so many versions can germinate, sprout, bloom. Digital technologies do not only help users *metaphorically* use media as archives, they also enable users to actually archive their archontic productions. Many digital archives, if mapped, would be shown to follow a bloom-from-the-kernel pattern. Many digital archives, certainly all of the rogue archives in which I am interested, are committed to archiving versions. And again, we are forced to rethink how archive relates to repertoire, for what the bloom-from-the-kernel illustrates is the archiving of repertoire. Digital archives store, preserve, and keep accessible, the unfolding of whole repertoires over time; they are invested in saving each release, each new distribution. If only every performance of a play, no matter how good or bad, no matter how small or large, no matter the size of its audience, could be archived—this is the logic of digital archives.

Noah Wardrip-Fruin summarizes Ted Nelson's and others' "dream of hypermedia" and the dream of digital archiving to which it gave rise. The dream, which I also cited in chapter 1, is:

That in a not-so-distant future, we read and write (view and draw, hear and compose) most everything from and to a world-spanning computer network. That everyone have the ability to produce their own documents, and connect them with any other public documents. That the author may constantly create new versions of her or his own document, and individuals may create their own versions of any public document and that public connections made between one version of one document and another version of another will usually automatically place themselves in all the extant versions. That historical backtrack and degradation-proof storage allows us to visit any version, any moment in the network's history. To have the ultimate archive, and yet have each element of the archive constantly in process. Dynamism without loss. Impermanence enfolded within permanence. (Wardrip-Fruin 2000)

Ernst describes the dream of digital archiving thus: "The object-oriented archive … takes shape cumulatively, entailing a shift from read-only paradigms to a generative, participative form of archival reading. Source-oriented stock and classical file-oriented archive practices yield to the use-oriented ('to be completed') 'dynarchive'" (Ernst 2013, 81–82).

The hypothetical digital archive described by Wardrip-Fruin and Ernst is full of user contributions. The dynarchive constantly transforms and grows as it attracts and locks down new releases, and keeps a record of the links between entries, hosting entire families of entries and not just "final" versions (if there are such things). This dream of "impermanence enfolded within permanence," of repertoires stored within archives, has been realized to the extent that there exist archives and archivists whose mission it is to preserve the blooms that emit from kernels. Although there is no "dynamism without loss," and we must have serious questions and doubts regarding the "permanence" of any digital archive, the present moment is one in which archontic production takes place on a vast scale, and not all of it is lost.

Break 7   Licensing and Licentiousness

E. Gabriella Coleman writes that free software hackers have defended their right to exercise "productive freedom" in large part by constructing certain "legal devices" (2012, 3), that is, licenses. Licenses play a large part in the free software and free culture movements, which arose in opposition to far-reaching legal moves made by large copyright-holding organizations, beginning with the Copyright Act of 1976. Christopher Kelty states that this Copyright Act was "largely organized around new technologies like photocopier machines, home audiotaping, and the new videocassette recorders" (2008, 202). Over the next two decades, the new media developed into a robust infrastructure for a digital culture marked by, as Coleman writes, "information access, open content, and collaboration" (83), which rendered "major corporate copyright owners ... aghast at the promiscuous file sharing enabled by a broadband connection, a home desktop computer, and peer-to-peer systems" (Coleman 2012, 84). The copyright industries lobbied extensively for the US Congress to radically expand the reach of copyright law, and their efforts resulted in the passing of the Copyright Term Extension Act (CTEA) and Digital Millennium Copyright Act (DMCA) in 1998, which put severe restrictions on digital activities such as software hacking and cultural remixing, and sharply contracted the public domain. The free software and free culture communities responded by creating their own legal mechanisms, intended to protect reusers from being labeled "rogues, thieves, and pirates," in Kavita Philip's (2005) phrasing.

These legal mechanisms were new licenses, including the GNU General Public License (GPL), the GNU Free Documentation License, Creative Commons licenses, and the Open Content License, which digital content creators—what Philip calls "technological authors" in "amateur, educational, and entrepreneurial contexts" (2005, 203)—can employ to protect themselves and future reusers from prosecution for copyright infringement. Kelty argues that these licenses offer hackers and remixers "a back-door approach" to the CTEA and DMCA: "if the [new copyright] laws could not be changed, then people should be given the tools they needed to work around those laws" (2008, 260).

Licensing does not carry the same import in media fan communities that it does in free software communities and in many groups that explicitly operate in accord with Creative Commons principles. This is not to say that fans are unaware of, or unconcerned with, legal threats. Fans, like all categories of remixers, have received legal threats in the form of cease-and-desist letters (three people interviewed by my research team said they have dealt with legal notices claiming that fan fiction is a form of copyright infringement), and the Organization of Transformative Works (OTW) has a Legal Advocacy division designed to "be proactive in protecting and defending fanworks from commercial exploitation and legal challenge," which has (among other legal actions) successfully petitioned the US Copyright Office to approve exemptions to the DMCA that allow fans to legally make noncommercial, transformative videos. However, licensing does not take center stage in fans' debates and discussions around legal defense, probably because fans perceive themselves to always and only occupy the position of content users, and only content creators may append licenses such as the GPL or Creative Commons licenses to their productions.

Another way to interpret the situation of fans vis-à-vis licensing is that fans simply act "as if" official content creators license fans to make derivative works. In other words, fans have always behaved as though they already possess licenses to transform copyrighted texts for noncommercial uses. They have never waited for copyright holders to modify their legal rights through Creative Commons licenses. Fans have operated under a shared assumption that, so long as they do not sell their fannish productions for profit, they are not infringing on copyright—which amounts to an assumption that the culture industries' distribute their products under a Creative Commons Attribution-NonCommercial 4.0 International License, even though Hollywood studios and major publishing houses and record labels and game companies will likely never make use of this license. Fans do not think much about licensing, in other words, because they *take license* with copyrighted works, rather than founding new forms of legal protection.

That licensing is so foregrounded by free software and by some free culture communities, but does not carry the same significance in media fandom, illustrates that what Kelty calls "norms" of use precede legal devices such as licenses. Kelty writes, "For Creative Commons, norms are a prelegal and pretechnical substrate upon which the licenses they create operate. Norms *must* exist for the strategy employed in the licenses to make sense"

(2008, 293). Because licenses do not bring norms into being, but only serve to codify norms that are already in play, media fans could establish their norms of noncommercial, transformative uses of copyrighted works wholly apart from the licensing innovations of Stallman and Creative Commons.

Fans' tradition of behaving as if they are licensed to produce archontic works—their taking license with copyrighted media—marks them as rogues, according to Derrida's definition. As I discussed in the introduction, Jacques Derrida (2005) associates roguishness with democracy, and traces a convergence between the democrat's liberty and the *roué's* license. Derrida writes, "We must never forget that [Plato's] portrait of the democrat associates freedom or liberty (*eleutheria*) with license (*exousia*), which is also whim, free will, freedom of choice, leisure to follow one's desires, ease, facility, the faculty or power to do as one pleases" (2005, 22). Because "freedom is essentially the faculty or power to do as one pleases, to decide, to choose" (22), a question emerges about how a democracy can hope to service all the free people who make up its constituency. But the taking of liberties, the taking-license, the insistence on freedom that characterizes the rogue also, to some extent, enables the rogue's ability to thrive in democracy, for, states Derrida, "democracy contains all the different kinds of constitutions, of regimes or states. If one wants to found a state, all one has to do is go to a democracy to pick out the paradigm of one's choice. As in a market, there is no shortage of *paradeigmata*" (2005, 26). Democracy is not one kind of configuration or association or "constitution," it is a framework that offers the choice of many types of organization. Thus different segments of US society try to bring about different legal systems within that democracy, trying to "pick out" the legal paradigm that best suits their needs: the culture industries strive for heavy copyright protection; the free software movement and Creative Commons attempt to "defend the electronic commons against corporate privatization" by writing new licenses (Philip 2005, 207); and fans aim at a third paradigm, one in which they "do as they please" without seeking advance permission.

This is an important way in which free software and fandom do not coincide: fandom is more licentious than the license-based activity of free software development. Fans are even more likely than free software hackers to show a "subversive disrespect for principles, norms, and good manners, for the rules and laws that govern the circle of decent, self-respecting people, of respectable, right-thinking society" (Derrida 2005, 20)—to be "promiscuous" (Coleman 2012, 84) in the connections they make between media texts and digital networks, to hook up random elements of mass culture with their own imaginations and with unknown Internet users, to share liberally and connect somewhat indiscriminately—to be "rogues, thieves, and pirates" (Philip 2005). Rather than "distinguishing illegal sharing from good, creative sharing," seeking to make itself safe by distancing itself from piracy or other copyright-defiant practices as the Creative Commons and other licensing bodies do (Philip 2005, 207), media fandom on the whole does not dwell on the need to create new legal devices for its own protection (a specific body of fan volunteers within the OTW does pay a great deal of attention to legal matters and legal questions regarding fan production, and they do so precisely because so much of fandom does not think overmuch on these matters). Most fans, acting within the norms formed over time by their communities, simply act on their "whim, free will, freedom of choice, leisure to follow one's desires."

Kelty writes that conflicts between disciplines that have differing views of reuse and transformation

can be governed either by the legal specification of rights contained in … licenses … or by the customary means of collaboration enabled, perhaps enhanced, by software tools. The former is the domain of the state, the legal profession, and a moral and technical order that, for lack of a better word, might be called modernity. The latter, however, is the domain of the cultural, the informal, the practical, the interpersonal; it is the domain of ethics (prior to its modernization, perhaps) and of *tradition*. (2008, 291)

Fandom operates in the latter realm, adhering to its tradition, its ethic, its informal and practical history of licentiousness.

The roguish behavior that fans exhibit with regards to copyright; their unrestrained fooling around with culture; their assertion of what Derrida calls "the 'I can' … 'it is possible for me' … 'I am free to' … 'I can decide'" (2005, 23) with respect to products that are marketed to them as *fixed* and *final*; their seizure of commodity culture as a kind of inheritance, which prompts and fuels their leisure and pleasure; their treatment of mass media as a legacy that is not willed to them by its owners, but of which they nevertheless feel entitled to take possession, like presumptuous bastards; their enthusiastic generation of "bastard" derivatives of officially issued, legally owned texts; their positioning themselves as the heirs and successors to the paid professionals of the culture industries despite their lack of legal claim; their frequently performing, in the femaleness and queerness of their productions (their frequent and explicit focus on affect, romance, and sex, often exceeding the boundaries of narrative normativity *and* heteronormativity), what Derrida calls the "sexual connotations" of roguishness, the "playful and the lustful, the shameless, lewd, and dissolute, the licentious and libertine" aspects that always inhere in the idea of the rogue (2005, 22); their enthusiastically turning away from the neoliberal requirement of nonstop work in order to embrace "worklessness, the interruption of labor," which Derrida points out is the "original meaning of *debauchery*" (20), even as they work, *hard*, at growing and sustaining their derided tradition (the activities of the rogue look like nothing more than frivolous pastimes from the outside, but the rogue knows how much effort is required to be so much at ease): all of these licentious attitudes and acts of fandom make Internet fan communities and archives not utopic but heterotopic, not nonplaces but (in Michel Foucault's [1986] wording) "other spaces," whose alternate cultural logics and practices may ally with license-based movements such as free software and the Creative Commons, but which always exist before, and to a great extent apart from, matters of law.

If, as Derrida argues, the idea of democracy is inherently multiple, in that many democracies are possible ("democracy contains all the different kinds of constitutions, of regimes or states" [2005, 26]), then fan archives and communities call for a different notion of democracy than either copyright owners or copyleft activists. The democracy desired by fan sites would be one that would tolerate, or even invite, what Lawrence Liang (2005), citing the Raqs Media Collective, calls "seepage," that is, the transmutation of what appears to be a stable, long-standing structure—such as a structure of law (for instance, copyright) or a structure of culture (for instance, the state-founded archive)—initiated by elements that penetrate them unexpectedly, "that ooze through the pores of the outer surfaces into available pores within the structure, and result in a weakening of the structure itself …—and this produces an anxiety about the strength and durability of the structure" (Liang 2005, 14). For Raqs and Liang, digital networks are rife with seepage, as these networks facilitate, for "most people," a "lived experience of day-to-day negotiations with power that renders vacuous any neat binary of legal/illegal" (Liang 2005, 15), negotiations that take the shape of "citizens creating their own avenues of participation in the multiple worlds of media, modernity and globalization [which] demands that we ask fundamentally different questions of the relationship between law, legality, property (tangible and intangible) and that which we call the public domain" (Liang 2005, 16).

Fan archives, and all rogue archives, take many licenses with received culture, and archivists, archive users, and archive contributors perceive their licentiousness to be proper to the affordances of networks, the exigencies of Internet communication, and the social and cultural needs of humans. They have not sought out permission, nor have they felt much need to write new licenses for themselves (though again, they may work in sympathy and allegiance with those who do). Rather, they have assumed "the license to play with various possibilities," as Derrida (2005) puts it, which "presupposes … a freedom of play, an opening of indetermination and indecidability *in the very concept of democracy*, in the interpretation of the democratic" (25). Derrida finds this notion of democracy as a concept in play in Plato's *Republic*, in which Plato compares democracy to a "multi- and brightly colored garment," as it contains so much diversity ("all sorts of people, a greater variety than anywhere else" [Derrida 2005, 26]), an image which calls up "a 'milieu' of sexual difference where roués and voyous roam about" and which also evokes the "curiosity of women and children," who love "multicolored beauty," like "the fanning [*la roue*] of a peacock" (Derrida 2005, 26). Derrida states that Plato's noting of the interest of women and children in the "multicolored" weave of democracy is "politically signifi- cant," for in this metaphor Plato weaves into his definition of democracy those whom some other forms of government disenfranchise, foreground- ing democracy's potential for "freedom and multicoloredness" but also acknowledging that, if democracy truly is characterized by such diversity, then it must itself be open to transformation, and have "a changing, vari- able, whimsical character, complicated, sometimes obscure, ambiguous" (Derrida 2005, 26).

Let us remember that a great many of the people who take license with copyrighted cultural products are women and children. As media fans, women and children and queer-identifying people and people of color and people in the Global South and others who have not always been guaran- teed enfranchisement, politically or culturally, feel drawn to take liberties, to see what they can do with what they are given. Reading their actions through Derrida, we might say that their attraction to realizing the poten- tial for multicoloredness and variability in common cultural texts is linked to a "curiosity" about the potential woven into the very concept of democ- racy for changeability, transformability, recombination.

Rogues of digital culture do not "resist" culture or law. They seep into, disfigure, overtake, and reform (in "whimsical," "sometimes ambiguous" ways) structures of culture and of law. They do not anticipate how they might someday fit into "our neat categories of the liberal public sphere" (Liang 2005, 16); that is, they do not hope to see their works incorporated into official texts, they do not wait for authorization of their modes of practice by official laws, and they do not desire their archives to merge into official archives. Instead, they take liberties with the very concept of democracy, and take steps toward a "democracy to come" (Derrida 2005,

25), which would be a system that recognizes and sustains the "freedom of play," "indetermination," "indecidability," "diversity," "multicoloredness," "intrinsic plasticity," and "the curiosity of women and children" (Derrida 2005, 25–26), that stand at the core of the idea of democracy. A democracy aligned with digital culture, in other words, will remember its roots (in Plato, as read by Derrida), and will honor the memory play—the mutability of *objets trouvés* and the preservations of those mutations—beloved by its rogue constituents.

Conclusion   Fan Data: A Digital Humanities Approach to Internet Archives

Visualizing Vastness

This concluding chapter seeks to answer a question that readers of this book may have been asking from the very first pages: How big are "rogue" digital archives?

Here I will present data visualizations that illustrate the size and scale of Internet fan fiction archives, which make up a major sphere of activity within the larger trend of amateur digital archiving. I will present original quantitative research that establishes the volume and rate of fan fiction production that transpired on several key fan fiction archives over time. For all the archives that we analyzed, my research team counted the number of stories, and some archives allowed us to discern other metrics as well (such as the number of authors, hits [reads], and reviews).

To "count" all online rogue (amateur/hacker/fan/pirate/volunteer) archives would be impossible: I could never discover, let alone quantitatively analyze, every single amateur/fan/hacker/pirate/volunteer archive that exists on the Internet. Even to count all fan works archives is not an achievable goal: there are more fandoms than anyone can practically name, and more genres of fan production (commentaries, stories, art, and edited "vids" are only some of the most prominent ones; what about fanmixes and GIF sets, wallpapers and icons, in-character Twitter feeds and recorded reen-actments of entire films?), posted on more sites, than I will ever even know about. Even an attempt to count all fan fiction archives would be futile, as fan writers store their works in an incredibly diverse range of repositories, including private, password-protected or "friends-locked" blogs and torrent trackers. Therefore, I set out to count just a handful of fan fiction archives, selecting some of the largest, best-known, and most important archives according to volume (it was easy to tell at the outset which archives con-tained the most content) and according to reputation (as derived from our oral history interviews with fifty fans, many of whom named these archives as central to their fannish experiences).

What I want this conclusion to communicate above all is the quantitative significance of the world of Internet fan fiction. The size of fan fiction archives hints at the vastness of the universe of amateur archives, of which fan fiction archives make up but one subcategory. When we consider the largeness of these archives, we must also speculate about the enormous number of labor-hours that self-appointed archivists have dedicated to constructing and operating these sites. Even automated archives (i.e., archives that enable users to upload their own content, without intervention from an archivist) require a great deal of back-end maintenance and user support. I have made the case for greater recognition of the invisible work of rogue archivists; hopefully, that work will come into clearer focus for the reader via the data visualizations included below.

The Dream of Measuring Fandom

It has long been a dream of media studies scholars to quantify fan activity. John Fiske, whose groundbreaking publications on "active audiences" in the 1980s and the first half of the 1990s laid the foundation for the rise of fan studies in the 1990s and 2000s, "struggled across his writings to find some evidence which might convince his critics that popular struggles over meaning were widespread and impactful," according to Henry Jenkins (2011c, xxix), who studied under Fiske at the University of Wisconsin-Madison. In *Understanding Popular Culture*, Fiske ([1989] 2011) expresses dismay that "the products of this tactical consumption"—such as fan appropriations—"are difficult to study—they have no place, only the space of their moments of being, they are scattered, dispersed through our televised, urbanized, bureaucratized experience" (35; also cited in Jenkins 2011c, xxix). Because fan cultures were "operating in the shadows of mass culture" in the 1980s, Jenkins states, it was easy for Fiske's detractors to "dismiss such textual poachers as figments of our [fan scholars'] overactive imaginations" (Jenkins 2011c, xxix–xxx).

But wholesale dismissals of fan studies are less likely today, Jenkins writes, as "you can find fans all out in full force on the web. The Internet has made visible the invisible work of media audiences and the rise of social networking sites has also helped us to map the ways that such expression is collective rather than purely personal" (2011c, xxx). And now that we can see fan productions online—now that they are archived in digital cultural memory institutions made and maintained by fans—we can finally count them. In counting the numbers of participants and productions that make up online fan archives, I hope to deliver evidence that audience appropriations of mass cultural texts are "widespread and impactful," and "collective rather than purely personal"—to show, in other words, that audiences of mass media are not merely "cultural dopes," as Stuart Hall (1998) would say, but often engage in their own meaning-making practices and use commercial media as the bases for their own creative productions.

The Fan Data Project

With generous grants from the Hellman Fellows Fund, UC Berkeley's Committee on Research, and URAP (Undergraduate Research Apprentice Program), I developed and managed a project called "Fan Data." Our mission was to develop "data scrapers," or customize scrapers that had been developed for other purposes, that would allow us to count the numbers of stories and, in some cases, authors and reviews, of a variety of fan fiction archives. Data scrapers are computer programs that can analyze online information sets (such as databases) and extract and summarize key data about those information sets, such as how many users generated how many posts on a given day or in a given month. Scrapers can perform these "counting" tasks far more quickly and accurately than a person, or a team of people, can, given the vastness of the information sets that one finds on the Internet. (For example, a group of people would take days to count all of the posts made to a popular social media hashtag over the course of one month, but a data scraper could perform the task in hours.) Data scrapers are a type of tool that digital humanities scholars can use to accurately assess the numerical dimensions of the online communities that they wish to study, in terms of the population of those sites' participants and the volume of content they circulate in their shared space.

Fan Data launched in summer 2012 and concluded in summer 2014. The Fan Data team members in addition to myself, in alphabetical order, were (all are at UC Berkeley unless otherwise noted): Lisa Cronin, Anthropology major; Vera Cuntz-Leng, a visiting postdoctoral student who received her PhD in film studies from the Department of Media Studies, Eberhard Karls University of Tübingen in Germany; Professor Laurent El Ghaoui, electrical engineering and computer science (EECS); Andrew Godbehere, PhD candidate in EECS; Andrea Horbinski, PhD candidate in history; Zhiling Huang, double major in applied mathematics and EECS; Adam Hutz, PhD candidate in rhetoric; Renée Pastel, PhD candidate in film and media; Vu Pham, PhD candidate in EECS; and Kelsey Wong, double major in English and molecular cell biology. Crucial contributions were made by Molly Aplet, and also by Christof Leng at the International Computer Science Institute (ICSI), Berkeley. Undergraduates who contributed to the project as data collectors were Sean Huynh, Harry Heng, and Amelia Olson.

In my discussion of fan archives, I will first lay out two sets of case studies. The first set of archives I will examine pertain to one of the most prominent and productive online fandoms of the 1990s, the fandom centering on the sci-fi television series *The X-Files* (broadcast 1993–2002). The second set of archives I will analyze is one of fan fiction based on the *Harry Potter* novels by J. K. Rowling (published 1997–2007) and films (released 2001–2011). The *Harry Potter* fandom was one of the definitive Internet fandoms of the first decade of the 2000s. I am treating *The X-Files* and *Harry Potter* as representative fandoms of their respective decades, the 1990s and 2000s, and am choosing to delve deeply into these two sets of fan fiction archives, rather than attempting to mention all of the fandoms that have produced fan fiction in various archives over the last twenty years, which, as I have stated, would be impossible.

After examining *The X-Files* and *Harry Potter* fan data in detail, I will present the data extracted from the two major multifandom fan fiction archives operating today: Fanfiction.net (also called FF.net, founded in 1998), which is the largest archive, and the Archive of Our Own (also called AO3, opened to the public in 2009), which is the fastest-growing archive. Analyses of production and reception on these two massive archives will hopefully give the reader an idea of the scale of fan fiction as a contemporary cultural phenomenon.

The X-Files: ATXC and Gossamer

The first scraper built by Fan Data consisted of a two-step process, led by Horbinski. Horbinski managed a group of undergraduate students who culled HTML pages from fan sites, and then Horbinski asked Aplet to write a Python script that would extract the metadata from the HTML pages and generate an Excel file containing this metadata. Within Excel, Horbinski then produced graphs from the metadata. While the Horbinski team analyzed a number of fan sites, here I will include only one of their visualizations, which shows the number of posts made over time to ATXC (alt.x-files. tv.creative), the most popular Usenet newsgroup dedicated to fan fiction based on *The X-Files*. ATXC opened in 1994 and was highly active through the mid-2000s. In 2001, Google Groups acquired Deja News, which had been archiving Usenet newsgroups since 1995. The first Fan Data scraper

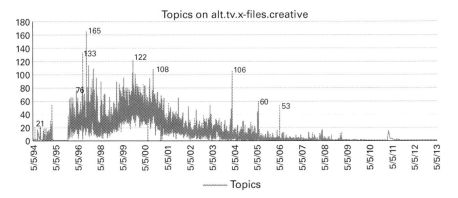

Figure 8.1
ATXC (alt.tv.x-files.creative, Usenet newsgroup for fan fiction based on *The X-Files*):
Posts (topics) per day, 1994–2013.

thus scraped ATXC as it was archived in Google Groups in May 2013, which
was fortunate timing, as in June 2013, a new version of Google Groups
was released that made it very difficult, if not impossible, to access all
but the most recent posts to ATXC. Since we were interested in the period
of ATXC's history with the highest frequency of postings, only the data
from 1994 through 2005 interested us. The Horbinski team was able to
access that data before the Google Groups redesign, and it is visualized in
figure 8.1.

The graph in figure 8.1 shows the number of posts made daily to the
ATXC newsgroup from May 1994 (the date of the earliest posts archived
on Google Groups) through May 2013 (the time of our scrape). Although
not all of the posts (labeled "Topics" in the graph itself) were fan fiction
stories, we can assume that many of them were either fan fiction stories
or comments and reviews pertaining to *X-Files* fan fiction in general, or to
individual stories. An additional bit of "noise" in the numbers represented
in the graph is that long fics were customarily divided into several parts, so
that multiple posts sometimes represent one story. Also, one can see that
in the importation of Usenet newsgroups into Google Groups, some posts
were lost; for example, a significant chunk of posts from 1995 to 1996 is
missing (where the daily post count drops to zero for an extended period).

Missing data aside, we can observe that from ATXC's launch in 1994 to
early 1997, the number of daily posts to the newsgroup increased steadily.
An early peak in the number of daily posts, reached in the fall of 1994,
was 21; in May of 1995, a new peak of 54 was achieved, and in fall 1996,

that was topped with a daily post count of 76. Then, sometime in the late fall/early winter of 1996, the daily post count increased by 75 percent, to 133. The highest number of daily posts on ATXC, 165, was achieved in the first few months of 1997. However, the daily post count still occasionally climbed above 100 from 1997 through late 2003. If we look at the numerical range that contains the bulk of the postings (the parts of the graph that are thickest)—the moving average of posts per day—we can see that the moving average climbed from about 30 in early 1996 to about 50 in spring 1997, not at the same time that the highest peak of 165 was reached but just after it, then fell to approximately 20 in late summer or early fall 1997, and then climbed steadily again until it reached approximately 50 in May 1999. From May 1999 onward, both the peaks and moving averages of daily posts fell off, with a short and sharp spike of the peak back up to above 100 (106) in late 2003.

We could propose a number of hypotheses to explain these numbers. For example, the peak in early 1997 was likely tied to the fact that *The X-Files* was then in the middle of its fourth season, which was one of its most critically acclaimed (lead actress Gillian Anderson won an Emmy, and the show won the Golden Globe for Best Drama, for that season), and was also the season when the series jumped from 55th to 11th place in the Nielsen ratings (Entertainment Weekly 1998). We might also hypothesize that many of the peaks in daily posts correlated with ratings sweeps months (November, February, and May), when television programs usually air their most exciting episodes.

However, my primary interest in sharing these numbers with readers is to offer some idea of the amount of activity that transpired on a highly popular online fan fiction community in the 1990s. The '90s were the first decade that fan fiction circulated online, and ATXC was among the first online communities founded for the distribution of fic in a fandom that did not previously have print-based mechanisms for publishing fic (in other words, while there were Usenet groups for fanfic pertaining to 1960s-era sci-fi television series such as *Star Trek* and *Doctor Who*, and some of these Usenet fic groups opened earlier than ATXC, *Star Trek* and *Doctor Who* fic both had significant zine traditions that preceded Internet fic publishing, whereas fanfic for *The X-Files* fic was "born digital," and thus ATXC was one of the earliest Internet fan fiction communities that was not a translation of, or "next step" for, an offline print-based fic community). Thus, I consider ATXC to be an exemplary 1990s Internet fanfic group. ATXC was built to be a discussion group, and as such, it was not quite an archive (stories posted on ATXC were more securely archived on other sites, the largest of which I will discuss below), and it was certainly not the only site that distributed *X-Files* fic, but I think most *X-Files* fans would acknowledge that ATXC was a major site of fic distribution and discussion in the fandom, and most media fans who were active in the 1990s would acknowledge that *The X-Files* was one of the largest fandoms online in that decade.

Therefore, from figure 8.1, we can understand the amount of activity that was typical for a thriving online fan community in the 1990s: between 30 and 50 daily posts on average, with the newsgroup collectively producing over 100 posts on its liveliest days. When one considers that the average number of (non-spam) business emails received per day per person in 2011 was 58 (Radicati 2011, 3), and that many people feel overwhelmed by the "information overload" conveyed by this number of messages (Bilton 2012), it is interesting that from 1998 through 2000, readers of ATXC had nearly this many *X-Files*-related posts per day to read on an average day, and sometimes had twice or even three times this number to get through. Of course, fandom-related postings are typically more pleasurable, and therefore easier, to consume than work-related emails. But if 58 business emails per day per person constitutes a glut of information in the early 2010s, then 30 to 50 *X-Files* fan posts per day on ATXC in the late 1990s surely constituted a tidal wave of online entertainment.

The ATXC daily post figures offer us some insight into what the everyday experience of participating in *The X-Files* online fandom might have been like. Let us now look at the cumulative story output of this fandom over time.

In the summer of 2013, Professor El Ghaoui and his doctoral student Godbehere joined the Fan Data project. Godbehere had earlier developed a tool for the purpose of extracting data from various social media sites, and at my behest, he refined his scraper so that it could extract data from online fan fiction database archives. Figure 8.2 is Godbehere's visualization of his "master scrape" of the largest *X-Files* fan fiction archive, called the Gossamer Project, which is widely known among fans simply as "Gossamer."

Most of the fan fiction posted to ATXC was archived in Gossamer, and Gossamer also archived stories posted to other *X-Files* electronic mailing lists and online communities. Gossamer is an opt-in archive (authors must give Gossamer explicit permission for every story they write to be added to the archive), so not every author who posted stories online allowed their stories to be saved in Gossamer; also, since 2007, 878 stories have been removed by author request.[1] Therefore, Gossamer cannot be said to contain every fan fiction story ever written for *The X-Files* narrative universe. But the fans that we interviewed who were active on Usenet and other

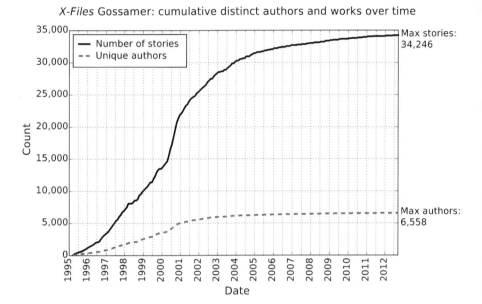

Figure 8.2

Gossamer: Cumulative *X-Files* fan fiction stories and authors, 1995–2013.

online spaces in the 1990s shared the opinion that Gossamer is as complete a single-fandom archive as was ever built. To my knowledge, Gossamer is the most comprehensive database archive built for fanfic based on one source text.

Figure 8.2 shows that between 1995 (Gossamer's opening) and 2013, 34,246 fan stories were archived, written by 6,558 unique authors, for an average production rate of 5.2 stories per author. This means that if an *X-Files* fan found the Gossamer archive today and set out to read one fan fiction on Gossamer every day, he or she would require about 94 years to work through the entire archive.

At the same time, 6,558 fan authors seems minuscule in comparison to the number of people who watched *The X-Files*: at its peak, during its fourth and fifth seasons (1996–97 and 1997–98, respectively), the show averaged over 19 million viewers per episode (Kavka n.d.). This means that only approximately 0.03 percent of the show's maximum number of viewers made the transition from audience to author. This can perhaps be taken as an indication of the effort that fiction writing requires—not everyone who watches or likes a source text will take the trouble to write stories about it. Also, the small number of fan authors relative to the number of viewers may underscore the "boutique" nature of fan fiction as a genre of writing and as a mode of entertainment—most people who enjoy consuming mass media do not want to write fanfic about that media, or perhaps do not know what fanfic is and for this reason, do not opt to participate in fic writing communities and archives. One question I will raise as we explore data from later time periods is whether we can detect a change in the overall awareness of fan fiction as a phenomenon over time, as measured by the number of people contributing stories to fic archives or the number of people using fic archives.

At the same time, based on the stories-per-author number of 5.2, it seems there is a "stickiness" to the practice of fan fiction writing: once a fan begins to write fiction, she keeps on doing it. So, while many fans never undertake the writing of fan fiction, or at least, never share their stories online, fans who do engage in this form of production appear to enjoy it enough that many or most of them produce multiple works. Few fans, we can surmise, write and post fan fiction only once. Learning to write and post fan fiction, then, might be regarded as a kind of skill acquisition—the acquisition of "media literacies," as I discussed in chapter 7—that media audiences learn: once they know how to create and share stories online in response to a media text they consume, they continue to respond to the text in this way. They turn definitively from consumers-only (who might limit their creative transformations of source texts to their private imaginations) into consumer-producers (who exteriorize these transformations in the form of fan fiction).

As for the number of stories produced by *X-Files* fans and stored in the Gossamer archive, however, we must acknowledge that fan authors have greatly augmented the total story universe, or what I call the meta-archive, of *The X-Files*.

Figure 8.3 is an infographic designed by Hutz based on Godbehere's master scrape of Gossamer. Between 1993 and 2008, 204 official installments of *X-Files* narrative were produced and distributed: 202 television episodes and two films (I am not including the three official *X-Files* video games in this count, nor ancillary material such as home media bonus features/extras). As stated earlier, between 1995 and 2013, 34,256 *X-Files* fan stories were archived in Gossamer. While 204 installments is not an insignificant number—at nine full seasons and two feature films, *The X-Files* is one of the most robust television-based media franchises ever made—this figure is dwarfed by the number of fan fiction stories written for the franchise.

What figure 8.3 illustrates is that, in the age of Internet fandom, when fan fiction is counted as part of an individual storyverse or meta-archive

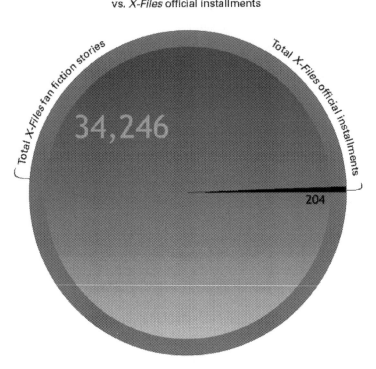

Figure 8.3
X-Files fan fiction stories (total stories on Gossamer), 1995–2013, versus official
X-Files installments (total TV episodes + films), 1993–2008.

(the total archive of narratives told about a given a source text), the quantity of fan-authored stories will constitute most of the meta-archive, just in
terms of the sheer number of stories told. Because there are far more fans
than official producers telling and distributing stories at lower costs, the
sum total of fan-made narratives will always swamp the sum total of official narratives in any given meta-archive. While the official installments
heavily influence the fan-authored stories, as they comprise the "canon"
of a meta-archive, an individual fan fiction reader interested in the *X-Files*
meta-archive can read up to 168 fan stories for every official *X-Files* episode
or film she views. Even if a fan reader discounts most of those stories as
not suited to her personal tastes, or poorly written according to her subjective standards, it is readily conceivable that, of the total time that an
individual fan spends consuming narratives within a given meta-archive
such as *The X-Files*, she spends a greater percentage of that time reading fan

texts rather than viewing official texts. In other words, fan stories can easily dominate the experiences that fan readers have of a meta-archive in terms of time spent on media consumption and quantity of media consumed, even though the canonical source texts may be often (though not always) more heavily "weighted" by the fan in terms of importance.

I have suggested that we can think of each source text as an archive that expands each time a reader/viewer/listener/player of the source text elaborates on the source, revises it, interprets it, or adapts it; this is my theory of archontic production. Each new version of the source is added to this conceptual meta-archive, enlarging it. Every meta-archive is infinitely expandable, as all new readers/viewers/listeners/players of a source text can add their own reworkings, retellings, and extensions to the archive, even if their archontic productions take place only in their imaginations. I also suggested that Internet fan fiction archives are the nearest we can come to concrete, perceptible instantiations of these meta-archives. Gossamer, as the most comprehensive database of *X-Files* fan fiction in existence, containing most of the written fanfic produced for this source text from 1995 to the present, is an excellent example of an online fic archive serving as a concretization of the conceptual meta-archive that grows and grows each time an audience member engages with the source text imaginatively.

Of course, Gossamer cannot archive all of the *X-Files* stories that have ever been dreamed up by *X-Files* fans; it houses only the stories that have been written out as fictional narratives and posted online. But figure 8.3 helps us to visualize that *every* meta-archive contains *mostly* nonofficial narratives. The vast majority of the stories told about a given source text are not told by the source text's authors/makers, but by its receivers/users. This is true whether or not a source text has a large online fic archive that can be examined, but visualizing the data of a central online fic archive such as Gossamer allows us to clearly see that every meta-archive contains a much greater number of "reader response" versions than official/source productions.

Harry Potter: LiveJournal and Fanfiction.net

If *The X-Files* fan community was a representative Internet fandom of the 1990s—meaning, a fandom that is often associated with the '90s because it began in that decade, was heavily populated, and was highly visible to online fans (whether or not they were "in" the fandom) at that time—then the most representative Internet fandom of the 2000s is surely the *Harry Potter* fan community. Just as *The X-Files* series was one of the highest-rated and most critically acclaimed sci-fi media texts of the 1990s, the *Harry Potter* novels and films were phenomenally popular fantasy texts of the 2000s (although the first three novels appeared in print in the 1990s, the online fandom around *Harry Potter* grew substantially with the premiere of the first film in 2001, and continued to swell throughout the 2000s). Both *The X-Files* and *Harry Potter* fandoms have generated copious amounts of fan fiction, particularly in their respective decades.

In the summer of 2013, Cuntz-Leng joined the Fan Data team and spearheaded the development of another Fan Data tool, one specifically designed to scrape LiveJournal (LJ). *Harry Potter* fan fiction was not concentrated in one specific single-fandom database archive, as *X-Files* fan fiction was in Gossamer. At the moment that *Harry Potter* fan fiction began to appear online in significant quantities, much of it was posted to the blogging platform LiveJournal, in communities or "comms" that were dedicated to specific *Harry Potter* fan fiction pairings. Thus, Cuntz-Leng selected the five *Harry Potter* LiveJournal fanfic comms that contained the greatest number of posts and extracted data from each of them. Here is Cuntz-Leng's description of the scrape:

> The data collection of five popular *Harry Potter* fan fiction communities on LiveJournal was done using a Bash shell script that counts the number of postings in each community in a given timeframe. It uses the LiveJournal web interface to enumerate all entries and produces a comma-separated text file with the number of posts for each day. The post-processing, including monthly aggregation, was performed with Microsoft Excel.
>
> The script counts all postings without distinguishing between actual fan fiction postings and other messages, e.g., of organizational nature. As the LiveJournal users can alter the post dates, the data collection only captures the shown dates, which may or may not be the actual posting dates. Outliers that have obviously been set to a date before the creation of the community have been removed in the post-processing step.
>
> The script only captures public postings. Postings that are only available for members of the probed communities are not included. This may bias the chronological distribution in special cases where the community changed the privacy settings over time. The data was collected on October 14 and October 15, 2013 and captures all postings till September 30, 2013. Future collection of the same time frame may yield different results, because postings can be added at an arbitrary date, be deleted, or moved to a different date. (personal communication with the author)

The five LJ communities that, as of mid-October 2013 (when Cuntz-Leng conducted the scrape), had the greatest number of public postings were (from greatest number of posts to least): harrydraco (dedicated to stories

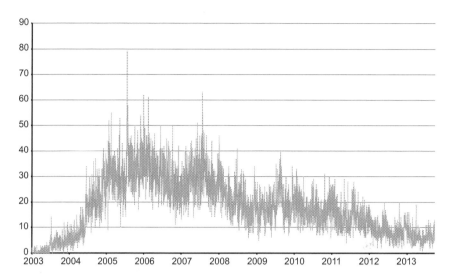

Figure 8.4
Five *Harry Potter* fan fiction communities on LiveJournal: Posts per day, 2003–2013.

about the characters Harry Potter and Draco Malfoy), remusxsirius (Remus Lupin/Sirius Black stories), harry-draco (another comm for Harry/Draco stories), hp_fanfiction (a general comm for *Harry Potter* fics), and snape_potter (Professor Severus Snape/Harry Potter stories).

Figure 8.4 shows the aggregate number of posts made daily to the five LJ comms between 2003 and 2013. It is an analogue to figure 8.1, which showed the number of posts made daily to the major *X-Files* community, ATXC. Like ATXC, the posts on the LJ comms are not exclusively fan fiction stories; members of LJ fan fiction communities often post links to interviews with members of casts and production staffs, icons and wallpapers, reviews and commentary, and other types of material related to the fandom (these materials often serve to inspire or inform the comm members' fan fiction production). However, fan fiction is a primary focus of these five LJ comms, as it was on ATXC.

It is striking that ATXC achieved higher peak numbers of daily postings in the 1990s than did the combination of five of the most productive *Harry Potter* LJs in the 2000s. Before seeing the data, I hypothesized that the most heavily trafficked *Harry Potter* LJ comms would beat ATXC for peak daily activity. Internet fandom was very new in the 1990s, when ATXC was most active, and I thought that fans in the 2000s would simply be more accustomed to participating in online comms and would therefore post more content than 1990s online fans. However, the five LJ comms we analyzed had peaks in aggregated daily post numbers ranging from the mid-teens to the mid-40s during their most active years (2005 to 2008), not greater than ATXC's 30 to 50 average daily posts in that community's years of peak participation. The LJs did see higher post numbers on some days, reaching the mid-50s or low-60s, but ATXC's highest-post days saw more than 100 messages circulated. On the *Harry Potter* LJ comms, the highest number of total daily posts reached was 79 in late summer or early fall of 2005 (perhaps driven by the publication of the sixth novel, *Harry Potter and the Half-Blood Prince*, and anticipation surrounding the premiere of the fourth film, *Harry Potter and the Goblet of Fire*, in November 2005). The moving average (the thickest part of the daily activity graph) was between 25 and 35 posts per day from 2005 through 2008, at which point it began to drop to around 20, then below, though the moving average spiked to around 30 in 2009, perhaps coinciding with the release of the film version of *Harry Potter and the Half-Blood Prince* that July.

That the daily average of the five combined *Harry Potter* LJs in the 2000s does not match the daily average of postings to ATXC in the 1990s is likely attributable to the shift from centralization to diffusion that took place in online fandom around the turn of the twenty-first century. In the 1990s, the first full decade of Internet fandom, Usenet newsgroups (such as ATXC), mailing lists, and custom-built database archives like Gossamer were sites for posting fan fiction for all characters and pairings in a fandom (so, Gossamer archives stories written about the show's main characters, Mulder and Scully, but it also archives every other pairing that *X-Files* fan authors wrote about). At the start of the 2000s, as social media platforms multiplied, offering fans without deep technical skills the tools to launch their own fan websites and communities, online fandom splintered. Many fan fiction communities organized around specific pairings; sites where all of the fan fiction written for a given source text could be found became rare. Thus, when I look at the combination of the daily posts on the five *Harry Potter* LJ comms in figure 8.4, I think that we would have had to combine the daily posts from many more than five LJs—perhaps as many as the top 70 *Harry Potter* LJ fanfic comms—to get a true sense of the daily activity of what we might call the "*Harry Potter* fan fiction community on LJ" in the largest sense.

However, when Cuntz-Leng and I examined the total numbers of posts for the top 70 *Harry Potter* LJ comms, there was a significant drop-off between the fifth and sixth most voluminous comms (a difference of over 2,600 total postings), and we decided to limit the scrape to the top five

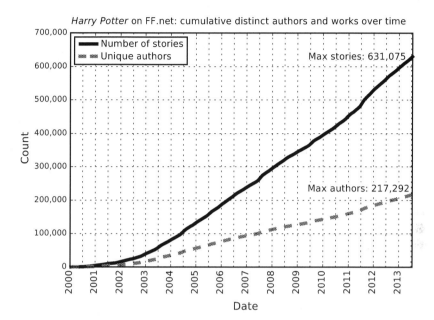

Figure 8.5

Fanfiction.net: Cumulative *Harry Potter* fan fiction stories and authors, 2001–2013.

comms. Perhaps we will execute a more comprehensive scrape at a later date. In any case, the fact that the five most active public *Harry Potter* LJs could not match the activity of ATXC is itself interesting, in that it shows that no single *Harry Potter* LJ could even come close to the single most popular fan fiction site for *The X-Files*—such was the difference between centralized and comprehensive fan fiction sites of the 1990s and diffuse, pairing-specific fan fiction sites of the 2000s.

However, when we examine the total number of *Harry Potter* stories stored in the largest multifandom database archive, Fanfiction.net (FF.net), we see a significant difference between this number and the number of total *X-Files* fan fiction stories archived in Gossamer.

Figure 8.5 is a visualization of the data extracted from the *Harry Potter* category of FF.net. The extraction was performed with Godbehere's scraper, and the visualization was rendered by Godbehere and Pham. In figure 8.5, we see that the total number of *Harry Potter* stories housed in the FF.net archive (631,075) is approximately 18 times the total number of *X-Files* stories housed in the Gossamer archive. Also, the number of unique authors who posted *Harry Potter* stories to FF.net (217,292) is 33 times the number of unique authors found on Gossamer. This shows that, while the top five *Harry Potter* LiveJournal communities show less daily activity than the *X-Files* ATXC community, the overall fiction production of the *Harry Potter* fandom was much greater than that of the *X-Files* fandom. Above, I attributed the lower levels of daily activity on the *Harry Potter* LJ comms to the fact that *Harry Potter* fan fiction activity was spread out over many individual fic comms, most of which were devoted to particular pairings. But figure 8.5 shows that when the fic production of *Harry Potter* fans is aggregated, inclusive of all characters and pairings, that the preeminent fandom of the 2000s generated more fan fiction than one of the preeminent fandoms of the 1990s. This is borne out by the fact that the four next most productive fandoms on FF.net after *Harry Potter* each show more stories than the 34K stories housed in Gossamer: *Twilight* (214K), *Lord of the Rings* (50.1K), *Percy Jackson and the Olympians* (46.1K), and *Hunger Games* (34.8K) are all media franchises that, like *Harry Potter*, comprise novels and big-budget Hollywood film series, and also like *Harry Potter*, all of the film versions were released in the 2000s and 2010s.

Internet fan fiction production increased substantially from the 1990s to the 2000s. This is perhaps the result of the media industries getting increasingly savvy about building successful multi-installment film franchises out of bestselling novels, but it may also be the result of the fact that online fandom has simply become a more popular pastime overall, as the Internet has attracted more users and become a more common site of entertainment and recreation. The number of US households with Internet access increased from 18 percent in 1997 (the first year that the Census Bureau asked about Internet use, and the year when ATXC daily activity reached its highest peak) to 50.4 percent in 2001 (when the first *Harry Potter* film opened) to 74.8 percent in 2012 (Census Bureau 2014). As Internet use has grown, so have Internet fan fiction archives; fandom is obviously a compelling activity, and fan fiction writing an engaging form of digital participation and production, for network users.

I stated that it would take an *X-Files* fan 94 years to read all of the stories in the Gossamer archive, if she read one story per day. In comparison, it would take a *Harry Potter* fan 1,729 years to get through all of the *Harry Potter* stories on FF.net at a rate of one story per day. However, there is one metric in which the 1990s *X-Files* fan fiction authors top the 2000s *Harry Potter* fan fiction authors: the number of stories per author (5.2 stories/author on Gossamer versus 2.9 stories/author in the *Harry Potter* section of FF.net). I am uncertain about what might have caused this gap in productivity,[2] but one possible explanation is that the *X-Files* in the 1990s may have been a more "cult" fandom than *Harry Potter* in the 2000s, if we define "cult" by some subjective notion of commitment or dedication—"cult" fans being more "hard-core," more deeply involved in their fan communities, than "casual" fans. It may be that fan fiction was, at the start of online fandom, an activity that only hard-core fans engaged in, but that as the 2000s progressed, fanfic writing became a form of online participation and, as I argued earlier, a type of media literacy that grew common enough among Internet users that casual fans practiced it alongside very dedicated cult fans.

However, with the average stories-per-author in the *Harry Potter* FF.net archive being close to three, fan fiction writing appears only slightly less the domain of "hard-core" fans in the 2000s than in the 1990s. Most fans who wrote and posted *Harry Potter* revisions and extensions did so more than once. Thus, "casual" may be the wrong descriptor for *Harry Potter* fan fiction writers—their repeated acts of fiction production show that these fans were quite immersed in their fandom, just perhaps not to the degree that *X-Files* fan fiction authors were committed to theirs. This hypothesis suggests that there is a spectrum of fan engagement, with not too great a distance separating *Harry Potter* fan fiction writers from *X-Files* fan fiction writers.

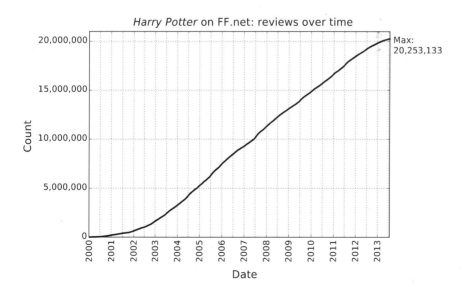

Figure 8.6
Fanfiction.net: Cumulative *Harry Potter* fan fiction reviews, 2001–2013.

Like figure 8.5, figure 8.6 was rendered by Godbehere and Pham based on a scrape of FF.net's *Harry Potter* subarchive. Figure 8.6 shows that, between 2000 and 2013, over 20.2 million reviews were posted in response to *Harry Potter* fan fiction stories on FF.net. On average, there are 32 reviews per *Harry Potter* story, and 93 reviews per unique author, on the archive. (Gossamer does not have a feedback or review feature, so we could not determine how many reviews were done per story on that archive.) While we cannot tell how many unique users the number of reviews represents (and since many *Harry Potter* stories on FF.net consist of multiple chapters, it is likely that the same readers left multiple reviews—one per chapter—on many stories). Nevertheless, I think it is fair to assume that many more people have read and reviewed *Harry Potter* fics than have written *Harry Potter* fics on FF.net. On the spectrum of fan engagement that I just proposed, we might think of reading fics as a practice located at the lower end of the spectrum, and writing fics being located at the higher end of the spectrum. As there are evidently far more readers/reviewers than writers, we might presume that writing fics takes more effort than reading and reviewing them. "Lurkers," or readers of fanfic who do *not* post reviews for what they read, would then be lower on the engagement spectrum than reviewers.

However, I also think that the terms I have been using to differentiate between kinds of fans—lurkers, reviewers, "casual" fan authors who write 2.9 stories each on average, and "cult" fan authors who write 5.2 stories on average—do not necessarily correspond to fans' levels of commitment or dedication to their fandoms. After all, we can easily imagine a lurker *feeling* as passionately about a fandom as a very prolific fan writer. The difference, then, is likely not the degree to which a fan feels immersed in her or his fandom, but the degree to which a fan feels comfortable exteriorizing—making public—her or his interior acts of archontic production. I thus revise my earlier proposal of a spectrum of fan engagement and now suggest that there is a spectrum of fan performativity. Some fans feel uncomfortable "performing" online in the "global theater" sense that I discussed in Break 0; by performing online, I mean any type of online communication, ranging from leaving a review on a fan fiction story to writing and posting a fan fiction story, or multiple stories, to running a fan fiction archive. Using this rubric, we might say that more people are willing to perform online by reviewing a fic than by writing a fic. This would explain the great discrepancy between the number of reviews and the number of stories/authors on the FF.net *Harry Potter* subarchive as well as a notion that fan engagement differs between reviewers and writers.

One final note about figure 8.6: 20.2 million reviews represents a significant amount of attention being paid to *Harry Potter* fan fiction. If 20.2 million viewers tuned in to a television show, that show would place second in the primetime broadcast ratings, coming in just after Sunday Night Football and ahead of all fiction and nonfiction television series, according to the most recent weekly Nielsen ratings available to me at the time of this writing (Bibel 2013). Of course, Sunday Night Football draws more than 20 million viewers on a single night, and the 20.2 million reviews on the FF.net *Harry Potter* subarchive accumulated over more than ten years. Nevertheless, figures 8.5 and 8.6 illustrates that fan fiction is not as "niche" or "boutique" a form of cultural production as it was in the 1990s. Fan fiction is rapidly approaching a size—in volume of stories and in quantity of users—that one might say is worthy of the title "mass," as in, "a genre of mass media production." This raises the question of what exactly constitutes "mass media" in terms of user-generated online content. How many stories, and how many readers/reviewers, would make fan fiction a form of crowdsourced, bottom-up, largely unmanaged, mass media?

Figure 8.7 is an infographic designed by Hutz based on Godbehere's scrape of the *Harry Potter* subarchives on Fanfiction.net and Archive of Our Own. Figure 8.7 offers another measure of the world of *Harry Potter* fan fiction: a comparison of the number of words contained in all of the *Harry Potter* fan stories on both archives to the number of words contained in all of Rowling's *Harry Potter* novels. Many fans of the *Harry Potter* books would say that they are among the longest books they have read, but as figure 8.7 illustrates, the total of all of the novels' words is minuscule compared to the total of words authored by fans based on those books and their film adaptations. Just as we saw in the case of *The X-Files* in figure 8.3, the meta-archive of *Harry Potter* is absolutely dominated by fan texts, not by the source texts, even when the source texts are voluminous in their own right.

Fanfiction.net and Archive of Our Own: Master Scrapes

I will now turn from examining fan fiction production and reception within individual fandoms to examining the entirety of two multifandom database archives FF.net and AO3. FF.net and AO3 are currently the most significant fanfic archives in operation, as FF.net is the largest and AO3 is the fastest-growing. Following are the results of the "master scrapes" of both FF.net and AO3, executed by Godbehere. Here are Godbehere's descriptions of his data collection processes (although in the following sections,

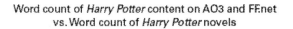

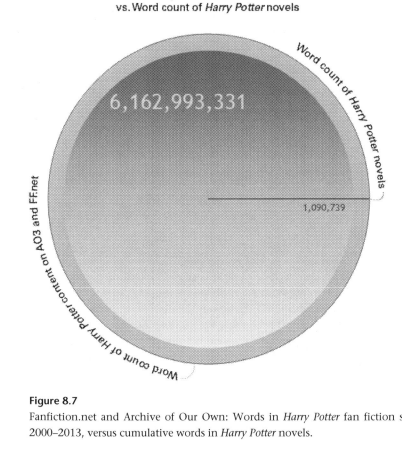

Word count of *Harry Potter* content on AO3 and FF.net
vs. Word count of *Harry Potter* novels

6,162,993,331

1,090,739

Figure 8.7

Fanfiction.net and Archive of Our Own: Words in *Harry Potter* fan fiction stories,
2000–2013, versus cumulative words in *Harry Potter* novels.

I discuss FF.net, the older archive, before AO3, Godbehere scraped AO3
before FF.net, and so AO3 precedes FF.net in his descriptions):

Archive of Our Own "Master Scrape":

Data collection began on July 29, 2013 and ended on August 2, 2013. The archive is
constructed hierarchically, listing fandom types (such as Anime & Manga, Movies,
TV Shows) at the highest level. In each fandom type, there is a list of fandoms (Harry
Potter, Marvel, etc.). These two categories serve as tags for works. Within each fandom, there is a list of works on which our data collection software iterated. (Note—
Works may appear in multiple fandoms. This led to over-counting. Currently trying
to resolve these duplicate entries in database for the correct counts. This error only
applies to the master count, not the individual fandom counts.)

Technical—Data collection (or "scraping") was performed with Python 2.7. The library urllib2 was used to load individual web pages and gather the page html:

html = urllib2.urlopen(url).read()

Data is stored in an SQLite database. A table in the database saves the following information on each work:

- title
- author (user name)
- fandom type
- fandom
- date (Date when published)
- summary (user-provided summary of the content)

Dates are represented as Unix timestamps, which count the number of seconds since the Epoch (Jan 01 1970 00:00 UTC). As of this writing, the Unix time is approximately 1377969792, indicating that nearly 1.4 billion seconds have elapsed since the epoch. Times before Jan 01 1970 are represented as negative numbers.

FanFiction.net "Master Scrape":

Data collection began on August 14, 2013 and ended on August 22, 2013. Technical—Fanfiction.net uses javascript to dynamically generate its web pages. This means that urllib2 is unable to correctly grab the HTML representation of the page. A more sophisticated means of data collection was required, with our Python 2.7 script needing to simulate a complete web browser. To this end, we used QtWebKit from PyQt4. (personal communication with the author)

Figure 8.8 is a visualization by Godbehere of the data he extracted from FF.net. In this graph, we can see that the rate of production of fan fiction has increased steadily from FF.net's opening in 1998 to the present. As active as *Harry Potter* fan authors were throughout the 2000s, through the release of the final film (*Harry Potter and the Deathly Hallows, Part 2*) in 2011, *Harry Potter* has obviously not been the only driver of fan fiction writing on FF.net; while there have been periodic dips, monthly production has grown overall. As of this scrape, which was done in the late summer of 2013, fan authors are now contributing over 80,000 new stories every month to the FF.net archive. The climbing rate of monthly production of fan authors indicates that fan fiction production did not cease or slow with the end of the *Harry Potter* franchise; as large a role as those books and movies played in fan fiction output throughout the 2000s, fan fiction has continued to thrive as a "media industry" after *Harry Potter*.

Let us recall that, on ATXC in the late 1990s, the high moving average was 50 daily posts, and the peak daily post count sometimes reached over 100; on the top five most active *Harry Potter* LJs in the 2000s, the high moving average was 35 daily posts, and the peak daily post count sometimes

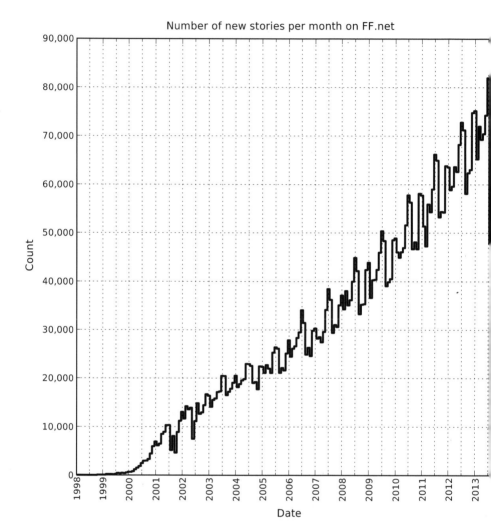

Figure 8.8

Fanfiction.net: Stories posted per month (8,101 fandoms), 1999–2013.

reached over 60. This means that, within a single fandom, in a thirty-day month of average-to-high production, a fan reader might have encountered between 1,050 and 3,000 new posts per month in the 1990s and 2000s. But combining all of the fandoms on FF.net, we get a much different sense of the rate of fan fiction production over the past fifteen years: figure 8.8 shows us that by 2010, fan authors were posting approximately 50,000 new stories per month, and that only three years later, fan authors were posting 60 percent more new stories per month than the 2010 figures. (Let us also keep in mind that not all of the posts on ATXC and the *Harry Potter* LJs contained fan fiction stories, as I explained above; however, all of the posts to FF.net are fan fiction stories.) Eighty thousand new narratives per month is an incredible rate of content generation. By contrast, at the time of this writing, only 251 new episodes of scripted television (inclusive of reality and fiction shows on broadcast, basic cable, and premium cable networks) air every week, meaning that 1,004 new episodes air in a month (Locate TV 2013). On FF.net, fan authors are currently publishing nearly 80 times that quantity of fresh content monthly.

Max Horkheimer and Theodor Adorno proposed in their 1944 essay "The Culture Industry" that the technologies of cinema and radio exemplified "the rationality of domination" (2002, 95), exposing all audience members "in authoritarian fashion to the same programs put out by different stations" (95–96), and thereby subjecting them to a set of unified ideologies, ideologies informed by and serving corporate interests. What if Horkheimer and Adorno could see that media audience members in the 2010s are not meekly consuming the narrow range of programming offered up by broadcast and cable TV, but are generating their own responses to, and revisions of, mass media content, in quantities that dwarf the number of cultural productions issued by media corporations? As I mentioned above, it would be an easy matter for an individual in the United States today to consume far more fan fiction stories, or fan productions/remixes in general, than episodes of television in any given week. Horkheimer and Adorno would likely say that it is difficult to ascertain whether a person who watches and reads more fan-made than corporate-made content subscribes to a different set of ideologies than one who consumes only what is put out by "the culture industry"—they might be quite skeptical that media fans can escape the "domination" of the industry's logics and beliefs (though I have argued in the chapters of this book that many fans produce counterhegemonic narratives and discourses). But Horkheimer and Adorno argued that many-to-many technologies (Poster 2012), such as the telephone, facilitate a very different type of use, and giving rise to a different type of user, than one-way technologies, such as film and broadcast radio—they write that the telephone "liberally permitted the participant to play the role of subject" while broadcast radio "makes everyone equally into listeners" (95)—and they might acknowledge that the Internet, as a many-to-many technology, enables participants to be "subjects"/makers of media and not merely "listeners"/receivers of media.

Might we one day be able to quantitatively measure something like "degrees of absorption" and "time spent on consumption" between different official and user-generated content types? Any such measure would be confused by the increasing amount of time people spend simultaneously engaging with multiple media platforms, for example, participating in a social media site while watching television or home media. One might also have to differentiate between long-form user-generated genres, such as novel-length fan fiction stories, and short-form user-made texts, such as 140-character tweets and six-second Vines.

A quantitative comparison of fan fiction production to television or film production may be an unfair one, as the barriers to entry and the costs of production are far higher in media production than in fan fiction writing. Let us then turn to book publishing, which is perhaps a more comparable media industry to fan fiction: according to the most recent data available from Bowker, the number of fiction books published (by US publishers) in 2011 was 43,016 (Bowker, "New Books Titles and Editions, 2002–2012"), and the number of total books (in every genre) self-published by authors, in either print or ebook format, in 2012 in the United States was 391,768 (Bowker 2013). If the number of stories published monthly on FF.net were to stay steady at 80,000 for a twelve-month period, FF.net would see a rate of publication of 960,000 fiction stories per year, which would be more than 22 times the number of fiction books issued by US publishers in 2011, and 2.4 times the number of books in *all* genres and formats self-published in the United States in 2012. But the rate of story production remaining steady of FF.net seems extremely unlikely, as this rate has, for the most part, only risen since the archive's founding.

Figures 8.9 and 8.10 were rendered by Godbehere and Huang based on Godbehere's data collection. Figure 8.9 shows that, as of the summer 2013 scrape, approximately 5.4 million stories in 8,101 fandoms, by 1.2 million authors, have been archived in FF.net, for an average of 4.5 stories per author (closer to the 5.2 stories/author we saw in *The X-Files* fandom on Gossamer than to the 2.9 stories/author we saw in the *Harry Potter* fandom on FF.net). Figure 8.10 shows that 139.5 million reviews have been left, an average of 25.6 reviews per story and 115.4 reviews per unique author.

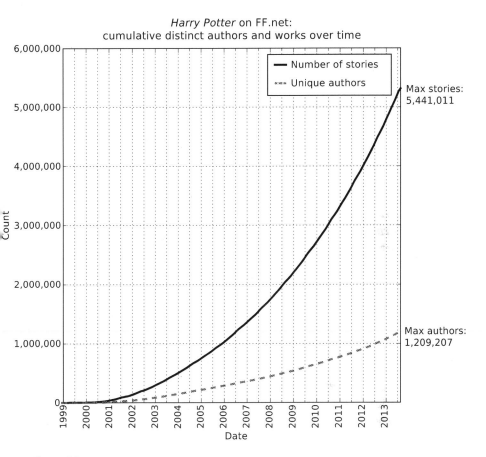

Figure 8.9
Fanfiction.net: Cumulative stories and authors (8,101 fandoms), 1999–2013.

At 5.4 million, FF.net's number of stories dwarfs Netflix's library of 60,000 television episodes and movies available for streaming (Levy 2013) and Project Gutenberg's 100,000 free ebooks (including the Project's affiliates and partners) (https://www.gutenberg.org/). It is slightly larger than the number of texts (5 million) available for download from the Internet Archive's Digital Books Collection (https://archive.org/details/texts),[3] and slightly smaller than the number of torrents (5.75 million) currently housed on the Pirate Bay (http://thepiratebay.se/). It falls far short of print-media and tangible-object collections such as the Smithsonian's repository of 137 million artifacts (Smithsonian, "Smithsonian Collections"), and the Library of Congress' total of over 158 million items (Library of Congress,

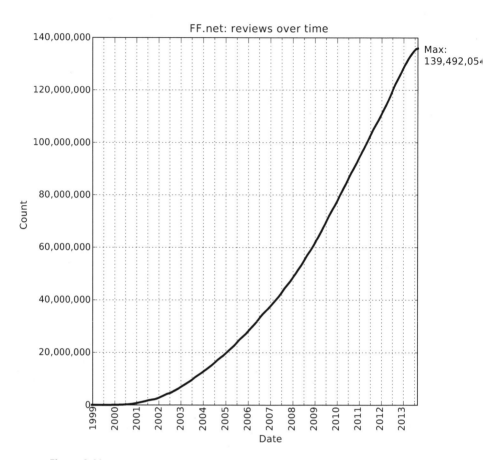

Figure 8.10

Fanfiction.net: Number of reviews (8,101 fandoms), 1999–2013.

"General Information: Year 2013 at a Glance"). So, when we compare the FF.net "library" to the largest print and artifact libraries in the United States, FF.net seems small, but when we compare FF.net to digital libraries and collections, it seems equivalent in volume to some of the larger repositories.

I am opting to compare FF.net to Netflix's streaming library, Project Gutenberg, the Internet Archive's Digital Books Collection, and the Pirate Bay because these are all digital archives from which a user can access complete content files—an entire fan fiction story, an entire book, or an entire movie or television episode—rather than content listings or content "previews" (parts of a book or audiovisual text). Thus, while many larger digital archives permit users limited access to content, like Google Books, or access to content catalogs, like many online library catalogs, I think that only full-access digital archives, such as those just listed, are comparable to online fan fiction archives. It is interesting to note that, barring Netflix, the full-access digital archives have a distinctive relationship to copyright law in each instance: Project Gutenberg and the Internet Archive's Digital Books Collections offer unrestricted access to texts that are in the public domain; both the Pirate Bay and FF.net violate copyright as it has been historically understood, as the Pirate Bay facilitates the networked exchange of media files that are primarily digitizations ("rips" or "scans") of Blu-rays, DVDs, printed books, and other hard-copy media that are traditionally sold commercially; and FF.net's authors appropriate copyrighted materials (that is, materials found in copyrighted print and audiovisual texts) such as names of characters and settings, plots, some dialogue, and so on. Netflix offers access to copyrighted material under a paid subscription model that has, so far, been successful, but Netflix's model has not gone unchallenged by copyright holders (for example, numerous film studios and television networks have ended their content licensing deals with Netflix, either because they wished to launch rival subscription services [Scoblete 2013] or because they decided that Netflix was not paying a high enough price for the licenses [Emerson 2012]); Netflix has lost thousands of titles because of these conflicts.

So, one way we can view fan fiction archives, and in fact, all rogue archives, is as part of a specific breed of online distribution service—the full-access, unrestricted (or nearly so) digital archive—and to note that many of these full-access archives are viewed as potential threats or enemies by industries protected by nondigital copyright norms. Fan fiction authors and archives have been the targets of legal action over the course of fan fiction's history, but not nearly as much as the Pirate Bay and other file-sharing sites. The point I wish to make with regard to FF.net is that it is remarkable that this fan fiction archive has been allowed to grow to its present size. FF.net is neither a repository of public domain content nor of Creative Commons–licensed content, nor does it pay for licenses for the content its authors appropriate. In many respects, it is closer to the Pirate Bay than to any of the other full-access digital archives, because it makes free use (in every possible sense) of copyrighted media, but probably because fan fiction is a *transformative* use of copyrighted media rather than a strict replication of that media, FF.net has been allowed to operate (so far) relatively unhindered, while the Pirate Bay has been the defendant in a number of high-profile legal disputes. That the two sites are of similar size but have received very different treatment by the legal representatives of copyright holders in the US media industries shows that, to some extent, media copyright holders consider fan fiction production to be "fair use," while they consider media piracy to be illegal infringement. (The question of what percentage of fans are actually media pirates—that is, how many people participate in *both* transformative and replicative appropriations of copyrighted media—remains open.)

Fanfiction.net is by far the largest online fan fiction archive operating. At a rate of one story per day, it would take a fan 94 years to read all of the *X-Files* stories on Gossamer, 1,729 years to read all of the *Harry Potter* stories on FF.net, and 14,907 years to read all of the stories, in all 8,000+ fandoms, on FF.net. The number of unique authors who have contributed to FF.net (1.2 million) is 9.3 times the number of writers and authors who were employed in the United States in 2012 (129,100, according to the Bureau of Labor Statistics [2014]). The number of reviews posted to stories on FF.net (139.5 million) over the past fifteen years is greater than the number of people who bought tickets to sporting events in the United States and Canada, inclusive of all games played in the National Football League, National Basketball Association, Major League Baseball, and National Hockey League, in 2012 (131 million) (Motion Picture Association of America 2012, 10). In my view, there is no question that FF.net is on the path to becoming a major content distributor, attracting significant quantities of makers and audiences. The FF.net data show that fan fiction is not a trend of media production and consumption that is slowing or shrinking. In regard to figure 8.8, I stated that the past three years show a 60 percent growth in the rate of fan fiction production. This is a rate that no other traditional media industry or entertainment genre can match: the number of films released in 2012 was only 21.5 percent higher than the number of films released in 2009 (Motion Picture Association of America 2012, 20), and the number of fiction books published in 2011 was 19 percent lower than in 2008 (Bowker, "New Books Titles and Editions"). One new media industry, self-publishing in print and in ebook formats, is outpacing the increase in the rate of fan fiction production: 252 percent more texts were self-published in 2012 than in 2009 (Bowker 2013, 1). Fan fiction *is* a form of self-publishing, so perhaps one conclusion we can draw from these data is that self-publishing in all genres, including media fans' self-publishing their fiction works digitally, is an industry on the rise.

In any case, I argue that at 5.4 million archived works—90 times as many works as are housed in Netflix's streaming library—with 80,000 new works currently being added every month, FF.net can be considered a mass media

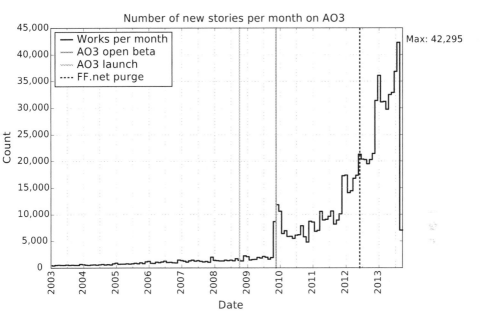

Figure 8.11
Archive of Our Own: Stories posted per month (12,023 fandoms), 2008–2013.

channel. The FF.net data show that fan fiction is a fast-growing type of media content production and distribution, and that it is attracting signifi- cant numbers of consumers. If one could invest in the "stock" of FF.net—if one could bet on whether the site will see continuing growth in its numbers of works, authors, and consumers—it would be a relatively safe investment.

However, while FF.net is unquestionably the largest fan fiction archive, it is not the only major archive, it is not the fastest-growing archive, and it is not a well-liked archive by many fans. An alternative archive, to which many fan authors and readers have flocked in recent years, is the Archive of Our Own, or AO3.

Figures 8.11 and 8.12 are visualizations by Godbehere based on his mas- ter scrape of AO3. AO3 was launched in closed beta on October 3, 2008 (during closed beta, only a limited number of people were allowed to create accounts and upload works), and then entered open beta on November 14, 2009, and is still in open beta today (newcomers may register for accounts on the archiveofourown.org website, and once they have accounts, they may upload works). AO3 allows users to assign any dates they wish to the works that they upload, hence some of the stories have dates that precede

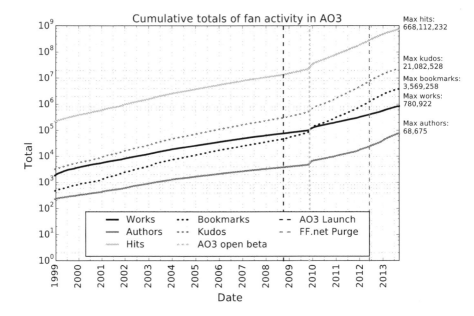

Figure 8.12

Archive of Our Own: Cumulative authors, stories, bookmarks, kudos, and hits (12,023 fandoms), 2008–2013.

the 2008 closed beta launch of the archive (and figures 8.11 and 8.12 show these predated stories—all numbers prior to the "AO3 Launch" marker in 2008—these are likely stories that fans *wrote* earlier than 2008, but posted to AO3 after the 2008 launch). But figures 8.11 and 8.12 clearly show that open beta was the archive's true launch. And, in figure 8.11, looking at the rate of new works added per month following the November 2009 open beta, we can see that there was a large uploading push as soon as users could get accounts, and then a decrease in the rate of uploading in early 2010, then an increase starting at the beginning of 2011, and then sharp climbs in the rate of uploading continuing to mid-2013, when the rate of new works added per month is 42,295.

We can also see that several surges in this rate took place after the FF.net "purge" of June 2012: on AO3, the rate of new works added went from 18,000 per month in spring 2012 to over 20,000 right after the purge, then rose above 30,000 at the end of 2012, spiked to about 35,000 right at the beginning of 2013, and, after a dip back down to 30,000 in spring 2013, has climbed steadily to its current peak of over 40,000. The FF.net purge consisted of FF.net choosing to remove approximately 62,000 stories from its site, without notifying authors before the removals, because those stories allegedly violated the site's content rating policies (FF.net removed stories that, in the moderators' opinions, deserved an "MA" rating—stories containing "detailed descriptions of physical interaction of sexual or violent nature" [Wikinews 2012]).

It is likely that FF.net's deletion of stories drove many fan fiction authors to seek out AO3 as a "safe harbor" for their fics. Although FF.net's 60 percent increase in productivity over the last three years seems remarkable, AO3's increase in productivity over the same period has been 323 percent. Granted, this is the growth over the entire period of time that AO3 has been in open beta, but even if we look only at the increase from the FF.net purge in June 2012 through summer 2013, that figure is 101 percent. Therefore, in part because of FF.net's imposition of what many fans call censorship of adult content, AO3 is a faster-growing archive than FF.net, and while it is not yet as large as FF.net in any category (works, authors, or reviews), it is well on its way to catching up with the much older archive.

As I noted in earlier chapters, AO3 is an archive for fan works (not only fan fiction stories, but fanvids, fan art, and other genres of transformative works, though the vast majority of works uploaded to date have been stories) that has, from its inception, been designed, maintained, and managed by fans. AO3 is run by a not-for-profit fan organization called the Organization for Transformative Works (OTW), its governing board members are voted in via online elections open to OTW members, and it is financially supported by donations from fans. The FF.net, in contrast, is a for-profit company whose governance is not transparent to the public, which generates revenue through advertising on the site. FF.net's owners and moderators can therefore implement content restriction policies and delete users' stories without advance warning or permission-seeking; the OTW and AO3 were specifically structured so that fans would have greater control over, and input into, their archives than FF.net and other archives have allowed.

Throughout AO3's initial planning, closed beta, and open beta phases, it has welcomed feedback and requests from fans as to its affordances. AO3's designers and users have had the benefit of years of prior experience with fan fiction archives (Usenet newsgroups, Gossamer, LiveJournal comms, and FF.net, among others); therefore, much collective intelligence about what fans desire and need from fan archives has explicitly informed the architecture of AO3. AO3 combines utilities offered by previous archives (Gossamer and FF.net's database format, FF.net's author-uploading, review, and bookmarking features) with new functions, such as the reader being able to hit a "Kudos" button for a fic without commenting on it, and authors being able to see how many "Hits," or views, one of their stories has received, apart from how many "Comments," or reviews, have been left for that particular story. We were able to scrape all of these categories for AO3, and thus the visualization of AO3's cumulative data is more detailed than our visualizations of any other archive.

In its five years of existence (four if we take the open beta entry date as the launch date), AO3 has accumulated 780,922 works, across 12,023 fandoms, by 68,675 authors. The average number of works per author is 11.4, higher by far than FF.net's 4.5 or Gossamer's 5.2 average works per author. Also, while AO3's average number of works per fandom (65) is far lower than FF.net's (672), it is noteworthy that AO3, a smaller and newer archive, has 48 percent more fandoms than FF.net (12,023 fandoms in AO3 versus 8,101 fandoms in FF.net). Thus, AO3's authors are far more productive than FF.net's, and AO3 is a much more diverse archive, in terms of the range of fandoms that it houses.

To my earlier proposition that a high productivity-per-author figure within a fandom suggests that that fandom's members have a high level of comfort with online performativity, let me add another proposal: perhaps AO3's mission as a fan-built and fan-run institution makes it a "safer space" for online performance—a safer *stage*, we might say—than FF.net, and thus AO3 is already seeing higher rates of productivity in its authors and greater diversity in its content. In other words, FF.net's content purge in 2012 could have signaled to fan authors that some of their content, and perhaps even entire fandoms, were not welcome on that archive, and thus fans migrated to AO3, where they felt free to contribute whatever content, in whatever fandoms, they wished.

An archive whose policies specifically do not place limits or constraints on fans' productions will be preferable, as a space/stage for fans' online performativity, to an archive that announces and enacts content restriction policies seemingly (to its users) at random. High output-per-author and diversity of fandoms may not be desirable to all fic archives—and FF.net may have had understandable reasons for initiating their purge, for example, in order to minimize risk of legal action on the part of media watchdog organizations that seek to shut down websites that expose minors to sexual content—but I think that most fans want authors to write a great deal, as much as they can and as much as they want to, in as many fandoms as they wish. AO3 is a "better" archive than FF.net by the metrics of author productivity and fandom diversity.

There are other interesting lessons from AO3's data: the number of bookmarks in AO3, accumulated from its 2008 launch through summer 2013, is 3,569,258 (4.6 bookmarks per work on average); the cumulative number of kudos left on works is 21,082,528 (27 kudos per work on average); and the cumulative number of hits is 668,112,232 (855.5 hits per work on average). The fact that there are more kudos than bookmarks left per work is especially interesting given that AO3 offered the bookmark function from its 2008 launch, but only introduced the kudos function on December 15, 2010 (Archive of Our Own 2010), so fan readers were not even able to leave kudos for works they appreciated for the first two years of AO3's existence; the data show a clear overwhelming preference for kudos over bookmarks, but knowing that kudos were not even an option until two years into AO3's history makes the preference for kudos even more emphatic. While there are many more kudos than bookmarks left on works on AO3 as feedback for authors, most readers choose not to leave any formal feedback for authors: the number of hits far exceeds the numbers of kudos or bookmarks.

AO3 is the first fan archive that tracks the number of hits (not reviews, bookmarks, or kudos) left on works. Thus, this is the first indication we have of how large the readership of fan fiction may be, apart from any purposeful traces that readers leave of their attention. In other words, AO3 is the first archive that allows us to grasp the actual dimensions of fanfic's readership, inclusive of "lurkers." The figure that we discover—855.5 average hits per work—leads me to wonder: What if 855.5 views per fan fiction work is typical? What if this were the average hits per story on FF.net? Then we would postulate that the 5.4 million total stories archived on FF.net have attracted a total readership of 4,654,784,910. We have no way of knowing how many people have read stories on FF.net, but if our guess, based on the AO3 ratio of readers to stories, of more than 4.6 billion hits on the largest fan fiction archive over the past fifteen years is even in the ballpark of accuracy, that would be an extraordinary figure. That number is more than the number of movie tickets sold in the United States and Canada between 2009 and 2012 (3.98 billion tickets [Motion Picture Association of America 2012]). If each hit represented one user reading one story on FF.net over the past decade and a half, the size of this readership would be the equivalent of 65 percent of the world's population (7.1 billion). Again, this is just a thought exercise, since it is well known that fans do not read just one fan story each; each fan consumes multiple fanfics over a lifetime. But it is yet another prompt for readers to consider the world of fan fiction to be more than a niche subculture.

Appendix: Oral History Project, Demographics, and Ethical Considerations

Fan Fiction and Internet Memory

Much of the primary qualitative data used in this book was collected through an oral history project called "Fan Fiction and Internet Memory" (FFIM), directed by the author. The FFIM project took place from June 16, 2012 through March 2, 2013, with the approval of the University of California, Berkeley's Committee for the Protection of Human Subjects (CPHS). The CPHS Protocol Number for the project was 2012-01-3948. The project was funded by several grants from the UC Berkeley Committee on Research and the Doreen B. Townsend Center for the Humanities' Geballe Research Opportunities for Undergraduates Program (GROUP). The author and two UC Berkeley students, Andrea Horbinski and Lisa Cronin, conducted fifty-six interviews with fifty individuals who have participated in Internet fan fiction archives as founders, archivists, moderators, contributors, and/or users. Interviewers followed CPHS guidelines and requirements, and the Principles and Best Practices for Oral History established by the Oral History Association (2009): all participants gave "informed consent" to being interviewed after reviewing written materials stating the goals and terms of the interviews and a list of possible interview questions, and all were given the choice to be interviewed anonymously, pseudonymously, or using their actual names. Participants received gift cards to online retailers following their interviews.

Demographics

All FFIM participants were given the option to answer demographic questions to any degree of specificity and in any words they chose, or to not answer the questions if they chose.

Name	Age	Ethnicity	Gender	Sexual Orientation	Nationality	Location
Adruinna	47	White	Female	Heterosexual	USA	Boston
Aethel	31	White	Cis female	Heterosexual	USA	Maryland
Aja	32	White	Female/blank	Queer	USA	New York City
Alexia	32	White	Female	Bisexual	USA	Colorado
Alexis Lothian	30	White	Feminine, Cis female, femme	Queer	UK (Scotland)	Pittsburgh
Anonymous I	37	Jewish	Female	N/A	USA	Northeast
Anonymous II	40+	White	Female	Heterosexual	USA	Blue state
Azurelunatic	32	Caucasian	Genderqueer	Sapiosexual	USA (Alaska)	Pacifica
Caffeine Junkie	30	White	Female	Heterosexual	USA	France
Chael	35+	White	Male	Heterosexual	USA	Chicago
Cofax	47	White	Female	Heterosexual	USA	SF Bay Area
Constable Katie	55	Caucasian, Multiethnic	Female	Heterosexual	USA	Philadelphia
Cynthia Jenkins	55	White	Female	Hetero/Queer	USA	Los Angeles
Deirdre	34	White	Female	Heterosexual	USA	Chicago
elfwreck	42	White	Female	Bisexual	USA	SF Bay Area
Ellen Fremedon	36	White	Female	Heterosexual	USA	DC area
Eruthros	31	White	Female	Queer	USA	New York state
Francesca Coppa	42	White, Italian American	Female	Heterosexual	USA	New York City
Henry Jenkins	54	White	Male	Bisexual	USA	Los Angeles
HL	26	White	I don't know	Bisexual	Argentina	Buenos Aires
Inkstone	33	Asian	Female	Heterosexual	USA	DC area
Jacqueline	56	Russian, Jewish	Female	Queer	USA	New York City
jinjurly	42	White	Cis female	Hetero/Queer	USA	Midwest
Julia Price	23	White	Cis female	Queer	USA	San Francisco, CA
Julie Levin Russo	34	White	Female	Queer	USA	Massachusetts
Karan Hellekson	45	White	Female	Heterosexual	USA	Jay Maine
Kate (Megami Tenchi)	28	European	Female	Heterosexual	USA	Ohio
Kristina Busse	44	White	Female	Heterosexual	Germany	Alabama
litotease	56	White	Female	Ambiguous	USA	SF Bay Area
Liviapenn	32	White	Female	Heterosexual	USA	Portland, OR
Meri Oddities	52	Jewish	Female	Heterosexual	USA	Maryland
Morgan Dawn	56	Greek, German, English	Female	Heterosexual	USA	SF Bay Area
Nele Noppe	29	White	Female	Bisexual	Belgium	Kyoto, Japan
Nightflier	39	Asian-American	Female	Heterosexual	USA	SF Bay Area
Olivia Breckenridge	27	White, Jewish	Female	Queer	USA	New York City
Oxoniensis (Signe)	37	White, British	Female	Heterosexual	UK	Southeast England
Rachel Sabotini/Wickedwords	50	White	Female	Bisexual	USA	Pacific Northwest
Rebecca Tushnet	39	White	Female	Heterosexual	USA	Virginia
Robin	36	White	Female	Heterosexual	USA	Minnesota
Sam Starbuck	32	White	Female	Bisexual	USA	Chicago
starlady	27	White	Female	Asexual	USA	SF Bay Area
Tari Gwaemir	27	Korean-American	Female	Heterosexual	USA	SF Bay Area
Te	36	Black	Female	Queer	USA	New York City
Therienne	42	White	Female	Heterosexual	USA	New England
Thingswithwings	30	White	Cis female	Queer	Canada	New York state
Vera Heinau	53	White	Female	Heterosexual	German	Berlin
Via_ostiense	27	Korean-American	Female	Queer	USA	SF Bay Area
Vicki Tubridy	31	White	Female	Heterosexual	Ireland	Limerick City, Ireland
Victoria P	42	White	Female	Heterosexual	USA	New York City
Vincent Juodvalkis	42	White	Male	Heterosexual	USA	Columbus, OH

Figure A.1
Demographic information of FFIM oral history project participants.

Figure A.1 provides the fifty FFIM participants' demographic information. The table was created by UC Berkeley doctoral student Adam Hutz, under the author's supervision.

Figures A.2 and A.3 provide visualizations of the demographic information of the FFIM oral history participants. The visualizations were designed by UC Berkeley doctoral students Andrew Godbehere, Andrea Horbinski, and Adam Hutz, and were generated by Godbehere, under the author's supervision.

In figures A.2 and A.3, the size of the circles is indicative of the number of FFIM participants who gave the same response to a specific question about demographics; for example, the more participants who responded "Female" to the question about their gender identification, the larger the circle containing the trait descriptor "Female." The thickness of the connecting "band" between the circles indicates the frequency with which two traits were given by the same participant; in other words, the more frequently "White" (as a racial/ethnic identification) and "Female" were given by the same participant as demographic traits, the thicker the band that connects those two traits in the visualization.

We opted not to merge any of the participants' answers. In figure 9.2, for example, while "White" appears as the most frequently stated racial/ethnic identification, some participants also gave answers such as "Jewish-American," "White British," "European," and so on, which might be construed as the equivalent of "White"; however, we chose to leave each participant's self-identifications exactly as he or she stated them. This resulted in a visualization that does not contain a circle for "Non-White," but instead shows circles for "Korean American," "Black," "Asian American," and so on. Similarly, we include circles for the gender identifications such as "Cis female" and "Female blank," rather than combining these with "Female."

Similarly, in figure 9.3, we created circles for every response that participants gave to a question about their sexual identification, so that in addition to a circle for the trait "Queer," there are also circles for "Bisexual," "Hetero Queer," "Asexual," "Ambiguous," as well as a blank circle representing the participants who opted not to answer this question.

Ethical Considerations

In accordance with the "Ethical Guidelines for Research Online" formulated by Amy Bruckman (2002), all websites cited in this book (except one, the website "Sly," discussed below) are officially, publicly archived, requiring no password for archive access and lacking any policy prohibiting

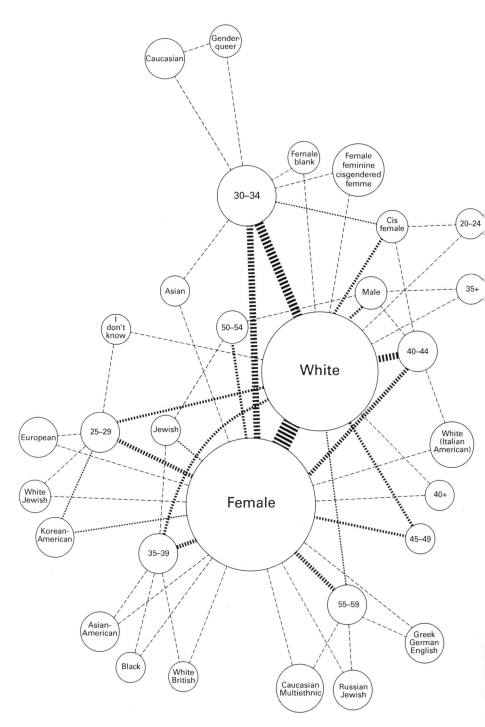

Figure A.2
Age, ethnicity, and gender of FFIM oral history project participants.

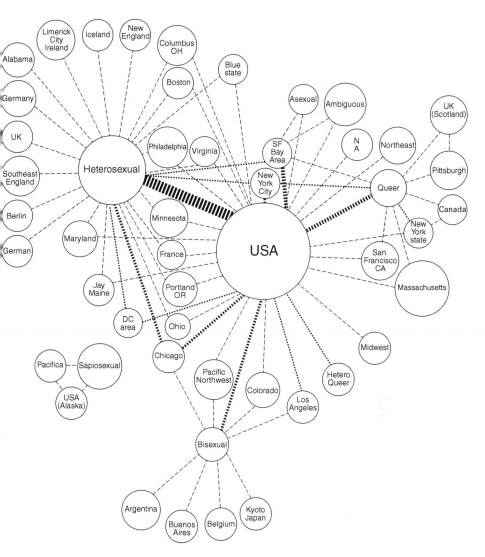

Figure A.3
Locale, nationality, and sexual orientation of FFIM oral history project participants.

citation. Given the preponderance of scholarly publications on the topic of fan fiction and fan cultures generally that have appeared since the early 1990s, I do not consider online fandom or fan fiction to be a "highly sensitive" topic. However, I acknowledge that many individuals may think of fandom and fan productivity as "private" (i.e., limited to consumption and interpretation by members) rather than "public." As a number of Internet researchers have noted,[1] scholars currently lack consensus as to what online sites and communities scholars should be considered private as opposed to public; Radhika Gajjala argues that "ideas of private/public, closed and open spaces are blurred and reconfigured" (2002, 182) in online research methodologies. The same uncertainty applies to quantitative, "Big Data" analyses, such as those that I present in the conclusion, and it may be the case in the future that fan archives ban data scraping or other third-party studies of their contents, to protect the privacy of their participants and the health of the communities that they serve. However, as of this writing in 2014, the websites that are explicitly quoted and the archives scraped have no stated restrictions on such studies, and I consider them to be public sites.

I have chosen to pseudonymize one website, the private torrent tracker (password-protected peer-to-peer media file-sharing site) that I discuss in several chapters, as "Sly." Although other scholarly publications have named this site in the past, I have found none that cite text from the site; since I quote text and data from the site, I have decided not to name it, to protect the site from any potential unwanted discovery.

Notes

Introduction

1. At the same time, Mbembe argues that a state often detests its archives, for archives record the state's past violence and crimes, and for this reason, states secretly "long to abolish the archive and anaesthetise the past" (Mbembe 2002, 23). Some states indeed have attempted to "silence" or "destroy" their archives—but more commonly, states "have sought to 'civilise' the ways in which the archive might be consumed," for example through instituting commemorations of past events, the ultimate objective of which is "less to [cause the people to] remember than to forget" (23–24).

2. See "History of the Internet" (Brady and Eikner 2011) and Brügger 2010, 2–3.

3. I first articulated this theory of appropriation as an archival operation in my 2006 essay, "Archontic Literature" (Derecho 2006). In *Technologies of History*, Steve Anderson makes a similar argument about the recent ascendance of a conception of "history" as available for constant access and reorganization, and for possible re-renderings as multiple diverse histories, owing largely to the rise of computing and the subsequent proliferation of databases of historical records (and database logics, as Manovich [2001] describes in *The Language of New Media*). Anderson defines "recombinant or 'database histories'" as "histories comprised of ... collections of infinitely retrievable fragments [that] offer users, whether they are artists, gamers, or geeks, both the materials and structures by which the past may be conceived as fundamentally mutable and reconfigurable ... offering us a relation to the past that is always already open to continual revision and reinterpretation" (Anderson 2011, 122).

4. "Digital divide" refers to the separation between people privileged by ethnicity (white), gender (male), class (middle and upper class), sexuality (heterosexual), and/ or nation and region (Global North), and people who do not enjoy these privileges, in terms of access to computer devices and networks. Paul DiMaggio and Eszter Hargittai advocate for a shift in terminology from "digital divide" to "digital inequality," as they call for more investigations of differences in skills, types of equipment,

and purposes for which technology is used—in other words, investigations into how diverse demographics interact with digital devices that expand beyond the question of access (DiMaggio and Hargittai 2001). See also: Hargittai 2002, 2003; Schradie 2013.

5. "Fuck Yeah" was a popular genre of individual blog names on the social media Tumblr from approximately 2009 to 2012 (see Know Your Meme 2012 for a data visualization of the number of Fuck Yeah blogs created daily from 2007 to 2012). For example: "Fuck Yeah Dykes" is the name of a Tumblr dedicated to lesbian culture, "Fuck Yeah Hermione Granger" is a Tumblr devoted to the Hermione Granger from the *Harry Potter* books and films, and "Fuck Yeah The Beatles" is a site for Beatles fandom.

6. See De Kosnik 2009, 2013a, 2013b.

7. hooks (1994, 76) also notes that many such "'safe' spaces" for women, in "the early years of [the] contemporary feminist movement," tended to be characterized by internal dispute and disagreement rather than harmony. Similarly, Internet fan fiction communities have never been free of conflict or "flame wars." The "safety" of offline and online women's spaces is experienced by many members as occasional and contingent. We might also conceive of open disagreement as integral to "safe" spaces, as most women would not associate being silenced with feelings of safety.

8. As bell hooks did with in-person women's groups, fans have criticized the notion that women's online fan communities are always "safe," or even that they should be. Katherine Larsen and Lynn Zubernis cite one fan, named kalichan, who posts, "We talk a lot about 'safe' spaces here in internet fandom. ... Safety is, perhaps, overrated. ... The world I want to live in is filled with both peril and enchantment. To discard one, is to discard the other." Larsen and Zubernis interpret kalichan's post as an argument "for the continued existence of open dialogue in fandom" (Zubernis and Larsen 2012, 142). For additional discussions of fandoms as "safe spaces," see M I C H I, "on fandom, bullying, and respectful spaces," and Fanlore, "Fandom as a Safe Space."

9. "TOS'ing" or "Terms of Service-ing" refers to the imposition of unwanted rules and regulations about what content may or may not appear on a website. If a corporation owns a site, it may determine the terms of service by which all users of the site must abide, and can therefore require users to take down, or can refuse, any types of content categorized as undesirable by its terms of service.

Break 0: A Glossary of Key Terms

1. See also Blouin and Rosenberg 2006; Boswell and Evans 1999.

2. See Keen 2007; Gorman 2003; Isaksen 2008.

3. See Terras 2010, 436–437; Finnegan 2005; Burke 2000.

4. The *Phaedrus* contains a famous exchange between two Egyptian gods, Theuth and Thamus. Theuth tells Thamus that he has invented writing in order to aid humans' memories. Thamus replies that writing will not improve humans' memories, but "will create forgetfulness in the learners' souls, because they will not use their memories; they will trust to the external written characters and not remember of themselves."

5. See Olick, Vinitzky-Seroussi, and Levy 2011; Winter 2001.

6. See Harth 2008; A. Assmann 1996; J. Assmann 2008.

7. See Meyers, Zandberg, and Neiger 2009; Van Dijck 2007; Kuhn and McAllister 2006; Morley and Robins 2002; Naficy 1993; Strong 2011.

8. I stress that new media *potentially* constitutes a "global theater," but this potential has not yet been fully actualized. As research on the "digital divide" shows (see introduction, note 4), great differences in people's access to, and education in, digital networked technologies persist, and many regions in the Global South do not have the capacity to participate in the "global theater" of the Internet. In addition, as Paul Dourish and Scott D. Mainwaring note, many attempts by Global North organizations to introduce new media to areas that lack them are highly problematic, as they replicate and reenact colonialist attitudes and fail to account for "polyvocality, diversity, and multiple perspectives" with regards to technology among local users (Dourish and Mainwaring 2012, 8). That said, the two largest archives that I will discuss in this book, Fanfiction.net and Archive of Our Own, accept stories in thirty languages and fifty-six languages, respectively, demonstrating that participatory digital culture does reach many regions in the world, and is not confined to the Global North.

9. See Chan 2000; Waskul 2005; boyd 2006b; boyd and Heer 2006; boyd and Ellison 2007; Pearson 2009; Aspling 2011; Markham 2013.

10. Several performance scholars have published excellent studies of how new media are utilized in live performance works (see Auslander 2008; Dixon 2007; Benayoun 2010; Jones 2006). While this is a very significant area of research, it is outside the purview of my investigation.

11. I am aware that the term "meta" refers to an entire genre of fan works; what fans call "meta" writings are what most people would call "commentaries" or "analyses" of source texts. However, by "meta-archive," I mean something like an overarching archive, not an archive of "meta" written by fans.

12. See Henry Jenkins's (2013) *Textual Poachers*, xxvii–xxviii and chap. 8: "'Strangers No More, We Sing': Filk Music, Folk Culture, and the Fan Community," 250–276, for a discussion of fan works in relation to folk culture.

13. In "A Brief History of Media Fandom," Francesca Coppa discusses earlier fanzines and Amateur Press Associations (APAs), dating to the 1930s and organized by

fans of science fiction literature (Coppa 2006a, 42–43), but in my view, most fan fiction communities operating today would acknowledge a direct debt, and trace their genealogy, to the 1960s *Star Trek* fandom and the zines that they produced, and would not recognize the same type of relation to the 1930s fandoms that organized around sci-fi literature. Coppa names both *The Man from U.N.C.L.E.* and *Star Trek* fandoms of the 1960s as the direct predecessors of contemporary media fandom, and credits the *Trek* fandom with going beyond "the critical discussion typical of science fiction fandom" to produce "creative responses to their favorite show," in the form of fan art and fanfic (43–45).

14. See Katz and Lazarsfeld (1955) 2009; Lowery and DeFleur 1995; Berger 2012.

15. See Fiske 1987.

16. See Fiske 1987; Lewis 1991; Hall 1998; Hebdige 1988; McRobbie 2000.

1   Memory Machine Myth: The Memex, Media Archaeology, and Repertoires of Archiving

1. See Engelbart 1962, "Augmenting Human Intellect: A Conceptual Framework"; Nelson (1972) 1991, "As We Will Think."

2. Bush may in fact have been *the* father of the bomb, or at least the instrumental decision maker with regard to the question of whether or not to build the bomb. In a 1992 article, Stanley Goldberg presents persuasive evidence that Vannevar Bush was the driving force behind the United States' development of atomic weapons. Goldberg writes that, in "the absence of a strong consensus" among American scientists who were evaluating the prospect of fission bombs, it was Bush who "engineered the decision that the U.S. government would undertake an all-out, emergency effort to develop weapons using nuclear fission" (Goldberg 1992, 450).

3. A description of the mission of the US Task Force on Archiving of Digital Information, and a link to its Final Report and Recommendations, called "Preserving Digital Information," released in 1996, can be found at "Digital Information Preservation— The Landmark Study," http://oclc.org/research/activities/digpresstudy.html.

4. Today, the "IWM" is simply called "Wayback Machine," and is a resource available on the Internet Archive's website.

5. The gerund form, "infrastructuring," was coined by Helena Karasti and Anna-Liisa Syrjänen (2004).

Break 1: Canon and Repertoire

1. See, e.g., Sontag (1964) 2001; Huyssen 1984; Jameson 1984.

2. For traditionalists, see, e.g., E. D. Hirsch, *Cultural Literacy* (1988); for reformists, see, e.g., Ronald A. T. Judy, *(Dis)Forming the American Canon* (1993).

3. The person who initiated the use of hashtags on Twitter was Chris Messina (Edwards 2013).

2 Archival Styles: Universal, Community, and Alternative Digital Preservation Projects

1. "Sly" is a pseudonym torrent tracker (a password-protected site on which peer-to-peer file-sharing of copyrighted material takes place). Owing to ethical considerations, I am not naming the site or providing a citation for the text or data that I quote from it (see the appendix for more details).

2. See Electronic Frontier Foundation, "A Guide to YouTube Removals."

3. See Phelan 1993.

4. The Internet Archive's grants and donations, from sources including Alexa Internet (a for-profit Internet analytics company founded by Kahle), a number of high-profile foundations such as the William and Flora Hewlett Foundation, and ordinary users, support the Archive's $10 million annual budget (Internet Archive, "Frequently Asked Questions").

5. The Rosetta Project is also inscribed on a four-inch nickel sphere that is designed to protect its contents for thousands of years.

6. "Bandom" usually refers to fandom centering on the rock bands My Chemical Romance, Fall Out Boy, and Panic! at the Disco.

7. Some scholars and critics might say that fans immerse themselves in fic archives because they are "addicted" to the consumption of media texts, and because they have little control over themselves when it comes to their recreational uses of media machines, such as televisions and digital devices. Lynn Spigel (2001) efficiently summarizes this line of discourse as "master-slave fantasies" (86–87), in which humans are, inappropriately, slaves to their consumer technologies, and must strive to assert dominance over their entertainment and leisure apparatuses.

8. See, e.g., Murray 1997; Stone 1991; Rheingold 1993.

9. Here, I am paraphrasing and transforming Deleuze and Guattari's (1986) statement, "A minor literature doesn't come from a minor language; it is rather that which a minority constructs within a major language" (16).

3 Queer and Feminist Archival Cultures: The Politics of Preserving Fan Works

1. See Fanlore, "Strikethrough and Boldthrough" for a detailed recounting of Strikethrough and another journal-deletion wave that soon followed, called Boldthrough.

For descriptions and analyses of FanFiction.net's purges, see Wikinews 2012; Ellison 2012; AllianceCommand 2012; Fletcher 2012.

2. See De Kosnik 2009, Cupitt 2008, Jenkins 2007a, and Fanlore, "FanLib" for discussions of FanLib and fans' extreme disapproval of the company's attitude toward fan productions.

3. Full disclosure: I am a member of the editorial board of the academic journal *Transformative Works and Cultures*, which is an OTW project.

4. While AO3's achievements in recruiting women coders warrant celebration, it must be noted (as I described in break 2) that great demands have been made on AO3's technical volunteers, and a number of them have suffered burnout as a result. Techno-volunteerism almost always helps a worker increase their skills, but its emotional payoffs are less predictable. The experience of volunteering over a long period of time may produce very positive or very negative emotions, or a confusing mixture of these, or a frustrating alternation between the two poles. See Coleman 2012, 11, for a description of how "adept craftspeople, such as hackers," can be prone to burnout. A comparison can also be made between techno-volunteers' burnout and activist burnout, as described in Activist Trauma Support, "Sustainable Activism"; Rettig 2006; Hoffman 2014.

5. "Mary Sue" stories are fan fiction stories in which the author inserts an original character (the "Mary Sue"), who might be construed as the fan author's idealized version of herself, who becomes the center of the narrative universe that the fan author appropriates. For example, a Mary Sue character in a *Star Trek* fic will likely be described as so attractive and compelling that one or several of the main *Trek* characters fall in love with her right away. "Mary Sue" is generally used as a term of derision in fandom, and the category of Mary Sue stories is widely despised, as the authors of Mary Sues are thought to be immature and unskilled as writers. The Fanlore entry for "Mary Sue" (Fanlore, "Mary Sue") thoroughly explores the origins and debates over Mary Sue stories.

Break 3: Fan Time versus Media Time

1. See Rubin 1970; Rothenberg 1981; Schechner 2003; Friedman 1998.

4   Repertoire Fills the Archive: Race, Sexuality, and Social Justice in Fandom

1. Because this site is private (access is limited to registered members), I am using a pseudonym ("Sly") and will not give citation information for the text and data I quote from the site (see the appendix for more details).

2. There are also popular variants of Big Bang challenges: for example, in Reverse Bangs, the creation of fan artworks precedes (and inspires) the writing of long fan

fiction stories, and the 2008 Bandom Big Bang matched fan authors with fans who created soundtracks, rather than artwork, to complement their stories.

3. Only stories from Yuletide 2009 onward can be found on the AO3, as Yuletide previously took place on LiveJournal. The Yuletide moderators intend to import stories from earlier Yuletides to the AO3 at some point in the future in order to make the complete Yuletide collection available at one archive (Archive of Our Own, "Yuletide").

4. Since the number of fandoms is greater than the number of works, there must have been a number of "crossover" stories—stories that merge multiple source text universes, for example bringing together characters from *Star Wars* and *Star Trek*.

5. The Nickelodeon animated series *Avatar: The Last Airbender* featured lead characters who "were clearly Inuit and Asian," according to NPR's Alicia Montgomery (2010), but in the 2010 live-action film adaptation, *The Last Airbender*, directed by M. Night Shyamalan, "most of the top roles in the film cast went to white actors." This "whitewashing" of the source material was met with outrage by fans and cultural critics, and sparked calls for a boycott of the film (see Martin et al. 2010).

6. Each square on a kink_bingo card contains the name of a kink—a turn-on, an activator of libidinal excitement—and to make "bingo," players must incorporate all of the kinks in a horizontal, vertical, or diagonal line on their card.

7. For a detailed summary of the events constituting RaceFail '09, see Fanlore, "RaceFail '09." For fan scholars' analysis of RaceFail and its fallout, see Sarah N. Gatson and Robin Anne Reid's (2011) "Race and Ethnicity in Fandom."

8. See Rachael's (2011) "How to Be a Fan of Problematic Things."

9. See *Transformative Works and Cultures'* Symposium, "Pattern Recognition: A Dialogue on Racism in Fan Communities" (TWC Editor 2009).

Break 4: "Works" or "Performances"?

1. "Picspams" are online posts that contain series of photographs of particular actors or characters (or character pairings). "Icons" are small digital images (for example, the maximum file size specified by LiveJournal is 40 KB)—usually GIFs, PNGs, or JPGs—that are typically uploaded by participants to their social media sites to represent their accounts, as their "userpics." Most fans will select an icon of a favorite character or actor as their userpic.

2. The definition of "meta" is contested among fans; some fans consider "meta" posts to be posts about fandom itself, such as whether a certain trope that recurs in fan fiction is sexist or misogynist, while other fans consider "meta" posts to be any posts that are not "fan works," such as essays about the prominent themes within a source text.

3. Fanmixes resemble mixtapes; a fanmix is a list of songs that a fan feels are especially relevant to a source text or a favorite character or pairing at a given time. When a fan posts a fanmix to a fan community, the list is usually accompanied by a work of fan art whose emotional tone echoes and reinforces the overarching tone of the songs included in the fanmix.

5 Print Fans versus Net Fans: Women's Cultural Memory at the Threshold of New Media

1. "APA" stands for "Amateur Press Association." According to the Fanlore entry on "APA," an APA "is a kind of fan publication in which all the materials, generally letters, would be sent to a central person, who would simply copy the entire packet in the cheapest possible way (e.g. mimeograph, spirit duplicating, xerography, offset printing; APAs far predate the photocopy machine)" (Fanlore, "APA"). See also Francesca Coppa's (2006a) "A Brief History of Media Fandom."

2. The *Professionals* Circuit, or Pros Circuit, was a practice engaged in by fans of the UK television program *The Professionals*: fan fiction writers would circulate their typewritten stories via mail. According to the online Circuit Archive (which contains digital versions of many of the original typewritten stories, as well as more recently authored fanfics): "Originally, fans wrote stories for each other and put them 'on the circuit'; i.e., they circulated paper copies by snail mail. Eventually, some particularly industrious fans gathered these circuit stories together and established 'circuit libraries.' Fans who joined a library would receive stories in the mail, which they could read and/or copy and then return for more stories" (The Circuit Archive, "About the Archive").

3. The first *Star Trek* text that contains this "full" version of the Borg's assimilation speech is *Star Trek: First Contact* (1996).

4. Steven Levy, author of *Hackers: Heroes of the Computer Revolution* (1984), helped Brand coordinate a 1984 Whole Earth conference attended by legendary engineers such as Apple cofounder Steve Wozniak, hypertext innovator Ted Nelson, and free software pioneer Richard Stallman, and a transcript of the "Future of the Hacker Ethic" forum that Levy moderated was printed in the *Review* (Turner 2006, 138).

5. See also historian Londa Schiebinger's *Nature's Body* (1993) for an extensive discussion of how "natural" gender differences were formulated during the seventeenth and eighteenth centuries. Schiebinger argues that Enlightenment philosophers' deep interest in "natural" rights extended to an interest in defining "natural" differences, and that classificatory science—which yielded natural history and anthropological taxonomies that stood for centuries—established women and nonwhite people as essentially inferior to white men, closer to animals (because of their innate instincts for nurturing) than to rational thinkers.

6. While the class-based digital divide was, and remains, very real, I agree with oral history participant Jacqueline's statements (quoted above) that print-based fandom was not necessarily free of cost, and that the large-scale transition of print fans to the Internet in the late 1990s indicates that print fans' strenuous objections to Net fandom in the early 1990s was not primarily about the cost of computing.

7. *B7 Complex* was a popular *Blakes 7* zine published from 1981 to 1988 (see Fanlore, "B7 complex"). *Blakes 7* was a UK television show that aired on BBC1 from 1978 to 1981.

Break 5: A Femslash Parable of the Print-to-Digital Transition

1. See Fanlore, "Just Between series," for a description of the "Just Between" fan fiction stories, including several fan readers' reviews of it.

6   The Default Body and the Composed Body: Performance through New Media

1. In the series, the "X-Files" is the name of the FBI department dedicated to investigating paranormal, extraterrestrial, and otherwise inexplicable events, staffed by only two agents: Dana Scully and Fox Mulder. Over the course of the series, Mulder and Scully uncover evidence of a vast conspiracy, helmed by a small band of US and international government insiders, to facilitate the Earth's invasion and colonization by a confederacy of highly intelligent and technologically superior alien species, the "police" arm of which is a species of shape shifters.

2. A disclaimer is a statement by which a fan authors declares that they do not own the copyright to the source text. Although such a statement, usually condensed to "Not mine" or "Don't own anything," is *pro forma*, many fan writers think that including disclaimers in their story headers means that they cannot be accused of copyright infringement by the copyright holders of the source material.

3. Of The Compass, the first improvisational theater in the United States (founded in Chicago in 1955), Janet Coleman writes that "with no set script and no fixed lines," the Compass Players "improvised much of their stage material by playing off the shouted concerns of their audience," and that the company's popularization of improvisation "change[d] the course of comedy" in the nation, for example by launching the careers of Mike Nichols, Elaine May, and numerous other comedians, writers, and directors, and spawning the legendary improv troupe, the Second City (Coleman 1990, xi).

4. "Beta reading," "betaing," or "beta-ing" means editing or proofreading a fan fiction story. Fan authors frequently seek out "betas" to read and edit their works before they publish them. Fanlore's entry on "Beta" states that "The word 'beta' comes from the world of software design, in which an unfinished version of the

software (the beta version) is released to a limited audience outside of the programming team. The metaphor was applied to fanfiction, fanart, and vids; a story, piece of art or vid is tested by outsiders to see if it's working" (Fanlore, "Beta").

5. In "Save As," Taylor (2010) argues, "We have always lived in a 'mixed reality,'" referring to actions such as "losing oneself in a literary work of fiction, or getting caught up in the as if-ness of a performance, or entering a trance state in Candomblé," which "have long preceded the experience of living an alternate reality provided by the virtual realm online" (3). I agree with Taylor that people grew accustomed to "mixed realities" long before digital computing and networking, and would only add that the new media have given rise to the development of many different kinds of realities.

6. The televised event that Fiske describes was the low-speed chase of O. J. Simpson by police cars and helicopters on June 17, 1994, four days after Simpson's ex-wife, Nicole Brown Simpson, and her acquaintance, Ronald Goldman, were killed; Simpson was the prime suspect in the murders.

7. "Rickrolling" is a bait-and-switch practice that rose to popularity on YouTube in 2007. To be "rickrolled" means to begin watching a video because it appears to have interesting content, and then to be surprised when, part way through the viewing, the video switches to the 1987 video of R&B artist Rick Astley's hit single "Never Gonna Give You Up." (See D'Orazio 2014.)

8. However, Hellekson states that the "gifts" fans make and give to one another can be of any genre or medium: "They may be artworks, as in vids, ... podcasts, fan fiction, or manipulated images. But they may also be narrative analysis, known as *meta*, of the primary source or of a fan artwork. They may be fan fiction archives, bulletin board forums, screen capture galleries, fandom-specific wikis, or other aggregates of information" (Hellekson 2009, 114–115).

7 Archontic Production: Free Culture and Free Software as Versioning

1. For example, what I would call the *Pride and Prejudice* archive includes the 1995 BBC television miniseries *Pride and Prejudice*; the film *Bridget Jones's Diary* (2001) and its sequels; the 2005 film adaptation for which Keira Knightley received an Academy Award nomination; the novels *Fitzwilliam Darcy, Gentleman* by Pamela Aidan (2003), *Austenland* by Shannon Hale (2007), *Pride and Prejudice and Zombies* by Seth Grahame-Smith (2009), and *Death Comes to Pemberley* (2011); *The Lizzie Bennett Diaries*, a Web series that premiered in April 2012 and concluded in March 2013; over 3,300 stories on FanFiction.net, the largest fan fiction archive, at the time of this writing (June 2014) (Fanfiction.net, "Books: Pride and Prejudice"); and all of the lectures on the novel delivered by the late literary scholar Ian Watt at Stanford University, where I took Watt's (1990) course on Jane Austen.

2. Lessig explains in *Remix* that read-only and read-write are terms borrowed from computing culture: "If the user has 'RW' permissions, then he is allowed to both read the file and make changes to it. If he has 'Read/Only' permissions, he is allowed only to read the file" (Lessig 2008, 28).

3. See Black 2007 and Thomas 2007.

4. See also Van Camp 2012 and Carman 2008.

5. There is an interesting coincidence between Hebdige's statement that "no one's version is treated as Holy Writ" and Bhabha's (1984) example of the European missionary handing out free Bibles in Bengal in 1817 and then watching those Bibles being put to use by local recipients as "waste paper." In some cases, archontic producers do not even treat the Holy Writ as Holy Writ.

Conclusion: Fan Data: A Digital Humanities Approach to Internet Archives

1. Noted in private communication from Chael to De Kosnik, dated November 3, 2013.

2. It is also possible that what I am calling a "productivity gap" between *X-Files* fan authors and *Harry Potter* fan authors, based on the difference between the average number of stories per author, is illusory. What if, for example, the average number of *words* produced per author is equivalent between the two fandoms? Here we run into the limitations of data scrapers: Gossamer does not include word count in the metadata of their story listings, so we were unable to compare the number of words produced by *X-Files* authors and compare it to the number of words produced by *Harry Potter* FF.net authors.

3. Between the time that I initially wrote this chapter in 2014 and the time when I reviewed it in copyedits in 2015, the "Digital Books Collection" on the Internet Archive was renamed "ebooks and Texts." That section of the Internet Archive now includes other archives discussed in this book—Project Gutenberg and Open Library—and makes nearly 8.7 million texts publicly accessible. Because I have left the data for all fan archives and other archives, such as the Pirate Bay, the same as in my original draft, I have also left the data for the Internet Archive's "Digital Books Collection" unchanged.

Appendix: Oral History Project, Demographics, and Ethical Considerations

1. See, e.g., Milner 2011 and Gajjala 2002.

References

Abbate, Janet. 2012. *Recoding Gender: Women's Changing Participation in Computing.* Cambridge, MA: MIT Press.

Abercrombie, Nicholas, and Brian Longhurst. 1998. *Audiences: A Sociological Theory of Performance and Imagination.* Thousand Oaks, CA: Sage.

Activist Trauma Support. Sustainable activism and avoiding burnout. *Activist Trauma Support.* https://www.activist-trauma.net/assets/files/burnout_flyer_rightway.pdf.

Aeschylus. 1984. *The Ortesia.* Ed. W. B. Stanford. Trans. Robert Fagles. New York: Penguin Books.

Aidan, Pamela. 2003. *Fitzwilliam Darcy, Gentleman.* Coeur d'Alene, ID: Wytherngate Press.

Allen, Robert C., ed. 1995. *To Be Continued …: Soap Operas around the World.* New York: Routledge.

AllianceCommand. 2012. The purge, or "Why I left FanFiction.net." *DeviantArt.* June 7. http://alliancecommand.deviantart.com/journal/The-Purge-or-quot-Why-I-left-FanFiction-net-quot-306989587.

Anderson, Steve F. 2011. *Technologies of History: Visual Media and the Eccentricity of the Past.* Lebanon, NH: Dartmouth College Press.

anythingbutgrey. 2011. At the close: A Harry Potter wars comment ficathon. *Anything But Grey.* LiveJournal. July 16. http://anythingbutgrey.livejournal.com/797887.html.

Archive of Our Own. 2009. The yuletide FAQ. December 17. http://archiveofourown.org/collections/yuletide/profile#faq.

Archive of Our Own. 2010. Release notes for Release 0.8.3. December 15. http://archiveofourown.org/admin_posts/100.

Archive of Our Own. About the OTW. http://archiveofourown.org/about.

Archive of Our Own. Big Bang challenge. http://archiveofourown.org/tags/Big %20Bang%20Challenge/works.

Archive of Our Own. Chromatic remix redux. http://archiveofourown.org/ collections/chromatic_remix_redux.

Archive of Our Own. Chromatic yuletide. http://archiveofourown.org/collections/ chromatic_yuletide_2009.

Archive of Our Own. Chromatic yuletide. http://archiveofourown.org/collections/ chromatic_yuletide_2010.

Archive of Our Own. Trope bingo. http://archiveofourown.org/collections/ tropebingo.

Archive of Our Own. We invented the remix ... redux. http://archiveofourown.org/ collections/Remix.

Archive of Our Own. Yuletide. http://archiveofourown.org/collections/yuletide.

Archive Team. About. Internet Archive. https://archive.org/details/archiveteam &tab=about.

Arditi, Benjamín. 2007. *Politics on the Edge of Liberalism: Difference, Populism, Revolution, Agitation.* Edinburgh: Edinburgh University Press.

Arduinna [pseud.]. 2012. Interview by Lisa Cronin. Audio recording. August 4 and September 8. Transcript available at University of Iowa Libraries.

Arnold, Matthew. (1961) 2009. *Culture and Anarchy.* Ed. Jane Garnett. New York: Oxford University Press.

Aspling, Frederik. 2011. The private and the public in online presentations of the self: A critical development of Goffman's dramaturgical perspective. Thesis, Stockholm University. http://www.diva-portal.org/smash/get/diva2:431462/FULLTEXT01 .pdf.

Assmann, Aleida. 1996. Texts, traces, trash: The changing media of cultural memory. *Representations* 56 (autumn): 123–134.

Assmann, Aleida. 2008. Canon and archive. In *Cultural Memory Studies: An International and Interdisciplinary Handbook*, ed. Astrid Erll, Ansgar Nünning and Sara B. Young, 97–108. New York: Walter de Gruyter.

Assmann, Jan. 1995. Collective memory and cultural identity. Trans. John Czaplicka. *New German Critique* 65:125–133.

Assmann, Jan. 2008. Communicative and cultural memory. In *Cultural Memory Studies: An International and Interdisciplinary Handbook*, ed. Astrid Erll, Ansgar Nünning and Sara B. Young, 109–118. New York: Walter de Gruyter.

Audiofic. About this site. http://www.audiofic.jinjurly.com/.

Auslander, Philip. 2008. *Liveness: Performance in a Mediatized Culture*. New York: Routledge.

Austen, Jane. 2012. *Pride and Prejudice*. Champaign, IL: Project Gutenberg.

Azure Lunatic [pseud.]. 2012. Interview by Lisa Cronin. Audio recording. July 3. Transcript available at University of Iowa Libraries.

Bagnall, Gaynor. 1996. Consuming the past. *Sociological Review* 44 (S1): 227–247.

Baker, Houston A., Jr. 1991. Hybridity, the rap race, and pedagogy for the 1990s. In *Technoculture*, ed. Constance Penley and Andrew Ross, 197–210. Minneapolis: University of Minnesota Press.

Bakhtin, Mikhail. (1963) 1993. *Problems of Dostoevsky's Poetics*. Ed. and trans. C. Emerson. Minneapolis: University of Minnesota Press.

Bakhtin, Mikhail. (1965) 1984. *Rabelais and His World*. Trans. H. Iswolsky. Bloomington: University of Indiana Press.

Balsamo, Anne. 1987. Un-wrapping the postmodern: A feminist glance. *Journal of Communication Inquiry* 2 (1): 64–72.

Barthes, Roland. (1967) 1977. *Image Music Text*. Trans. S. Heath. London: Fontana Press.

Bastian, Jeannette A. 2003. *Owning Memory: How A Caribbean Community Lost Its Archives and Found Its History*. Westport, CT: Libraries Unlimited.

Bayley, Alex Skud. 2009. Standing out in the crowd: My OSCON keynote. Keynote address at the Open Source Convention. San Jose, California. July 20–24. *Infotropism*. http://infotrope.net/2009/07/25/standing-out-in-the-crowd-my-oscon-keynote/.

Bear, Elizabeth. 2009. Whatever you're doing, you're probably wrong. *Throw Another Bear in the Canoe* LiveJournal. January 12. http://matociquala.livejournal.com/1544111.html.

Benayoun, Maurice. 2010. The nervous breakdown of the global body: An organic model of the connected world.Maurice Benayoun's art installations virtual reality and interactive art works. http://www.benayoun.com/projetwords.php?id=158.

Benjamin, Walter. (1936) 1968. The storyteller: Reflections on the work of Nikolai Leskov. In *Illuminations*, ed. Hannah Arendt, trans. Zohn, 69–82. New York: Harcourt, Brace & World.

Benkler, Yochai. 2006. *The Wealth of Networks: How Social Production Transforms Markets and Freedom*. New Haven, CT: Yale University Press.

Bennett, Tony. 1995. *The Birth of the Museum: History, Theory, Politics*. New York: Routledge.

Berger, Arthur Asa. 2012. *Media and Society: A Critical Perspective*. Lanham, MD: Rowman & Littlefield.

Berlant, Lauren. 1997. *The Queen of America Goes to Washington*. Durham, NC: Duke University Press.

Berlant, Lauren. 2008. *The Female Complaint: The Unfinished Business of Sentimentality in American Culture*. Durham, NC: Duke University Press.

Bhabha, Homi. 1984. Of mimicry and man: The ambivalence of colonial discourse. *October* 28 (spring): 125–133.

Bibel, Sara. 2013. TV Ratings Broadcast Top 25: "Sunday Night Football" tops week 9 with adults 18–49 and with total viewers. *TV by the Numbers*. November 26. http://tvbythenumbers.zap2it.com/2013/11/26/tv-ratings-broadcast-top-25-sunday-night-football-tops-week-9-with-adults-18-49-with-total-viewers/218076/.

Bilton, Nick. 2012. Disruptions: Life's too short for so much e-mail. July 8. http://bits.blogs.nytimes.com/2012/07/08/life%E2%80%99s-too-short-for-so-much-e-mail/.

Björgvinsson, Erling, Pelle Ehn, and Per-Anders Hillgren. 2012. Agonistic participatory design: Working with marginalised social movements. *CoDesign: International Journal of CoCreation in Design and the Arts* 8 (2–3): 127–144.

Black, Rebecca W. 2007. Digital design: English language learners and reader reviews in online fiction. In *A New Literacies Sampler*, ed. Michele Knobel and Colin Lankshear, 115–136. New York: Peter Lang.

Blouin, Jr., Francis X., and William G. Rosenberg. 2006. *Archives, Documentation and Institutions of Social Memory: Essays from the Sawyer Seminar*. Ann Arbor: University of Michigan Press.

Bolter, Jay David, and Richard Grusin. 2000. *Remediation: Understanding New Media*. Cambridge, MA: MIT Press.

Boswell, David, and Jessica Evans, eds. 1999. *Representing the Nation: A Reader: Histories, Heritage, and Museums*. New York: Routledge.

Bowker. 2013. Self-publishing in the United States, 2007–2012. October 9. http://media.bowker.com/documents/selfpublishingpubcounts_2007_2012.pdf.

Bowker. New books titles and editions, 2002–2012. http://media.bowker.com/documents/isbn_output_2002_2012.pdf.

boyd, danah. 2006a. Discrimination in gaming: World of Warcraft bans queer community. *Apophenia*. January 30. http://www.zephoria.org/thoughts/archives/2006/01/30/discrimination.html.

boyd, danah. 2006b. Friends, friendsters, and top 8: Writing community into being on social network sites. *First Monday* 11 (12): 4. http://journals.uic.edu/ojs/index .php/fm/article/view/1418/1336.

boyd, danah, and Nicole Ellison. 2007. Social network sites: Definition, history, and scholarship. *Journal of Computer-Mediated Communication* 13 (1): 210–230.

boyd, danah, and Jeffrey Heer. 2006. Profiles as conversation: Networked identity performance on Friendster. In *Proceedings of the Hawai'i International Conference on System Sciences (HICSS-39)*. Kauai, HI: IEEE Computer Society. January 4–7. http:// www.danah.org/papers/HICSS2006.pdf.

Brady, Will, and Jeffrey Eikner. 2011. History of the Internet. In *Introduction to Information and Communication Technology*. http://openbookproject.net/courses/ intro2ict/internet/history.html.

Brand, Stewart. 1999. Escaping the digital dark age. *Library Journal* 124 (2): 46–49.

Brontë, Charlotte. 2010. *Jane Eyre*. London: William Collins.

Brough, Melissa M., and Sangita Shresthova. 2012. Fandom meets activism: Rethinking civic and political participation. *Transformative Works and Cultures* 10: n.p. http://journal.transformativeworks.org/index.php/twc/article/view/303/265.

Bruckman, Amy. 2002. Ethical guidelines for research online. College of Computing, Georgia Institute of Technology. April 4. http://www.cc.gatech.edu/~asb/ ethics/.

Brügger, Niels, ed. 2010. *Web History*. New York: Peter Lang.

brynnmck. 2005. Brightly shone the moon. *My Addictions Have Failed to Fail Me* LiveJournal. December 5. http://brynnmck.livejournal.com/36945.html.

Burdick, Anne, Johanna Drucker, Peter Lunenfeld, Todd Presner, and Jeffrey Schnapp. 2013. *Digital Humanities*. Cambridge, MA: MIT Press.

Bureau of Labor Statistics. 2014. Writers and authors. *Occupational Outlook Handbook, 2012–13 Edition*. January 8. http://www.bls.gov/ooh/media-and -communication/writers-and-authors.htm.

Burke, P. 2000. *A Social History of Knowledge: From Gutenberg to Diderot*. Cambridge: Polity Press.

Burrows, Peter, and Les Morgan. 2010. *The Language of Learning by Design: An Elaborated Glossary*. https://teacherrefresher.wikispaces.com/file/view/Elaborated+Glossar y+LbyD+amended+July+2010.doc.

Bush, Vannevar. 1945. As we may think. *Atlantic*, July 1. http://www.theatlantic .com/magazine/archive/1945/07/as-we-may-think/303881/.

Busse, Kristina. 2009. The organization for transformative works: I want us to own the goddamned servers. *Writercon.* August. http://www.kristinabusse.com/cv/research/writercon09otw.html.

Busse, Kristina. 2012. Interview by Abigail De Kosnik. Audio recording. July 30. Transcript available at University of Iowa Libraries.

Caldwell, John Thornton. 2008. *Production Culture: Industrial Reflexivity and Critical Practice in Film and Television.* Durham, NC: Duke University Press.

Canclini, Néstor García. 1995. *Hybrid Cultures: Strategies for Entering and Leaving Modernity.* Minneapolis: University of Minnesota Press.

Carman, Taylor. 2008. *Foreword to Being and Time, by Martin Heidegger.* New York: Harper & Row.

Carstensen, Jeanne, and Richard Kadrey, eds. 1989. Is the body obsolete? A forum. *Whole Earth Review* 63 (summer): 37–41.

Castells, Manuel. 2012. *Networks of Outrage and Hope: Social Movements in the Internet Age.* London: Polity Press.

Chael [pseud.]. 2012. Interview by Abigail De Kosnik. Audio recording. July 20. Transcript available at University of Iowa Libraries.

Chan, S. Y. 2000. Wired selves: From artifact to performance. *Cyberpsychology and Behavior* 3 (2): 271–285.

Chun, Wendy. 2008. The enduring ephemeral, or The future is a memory. *Critical Inquiry* 35 (autumn): 148–171.

Clark, Jessica, Nick Couldry, Abigail De Kosnik, Tarleton Gillespie, Henry Jenkins, Christopher Kelty, Zizi Papacharissi, Alison Powell, and José van Dijck. 2014. Participations: Dialogues on the participatory promise of contemporary culture and politics, part 5: Platforms. *International Journal of Communication* 8:1446–1473.

Coetzee, J. M. 1988. *Foe.* New York: Penguin Books.

cofax7 [pseud.]. Interview by Andrea Horbinski. Audio recording. July 17. Transcript available at University of Iowa Libraries.

Coleman, Beth. 2011. *Hello Avatar: Rise of the Networked Generation.* Cambridge, MA: MIT Press.

Coleman, E. Gabriella. 2012. *Coding Freedom: The Ethics and Aesthetics of Hacking.* Princeton: Princeton University Press.

Coleman, Janet. 1990. *The Compass: The Improvisational Theatre That Revolutionized American Comedy.* Chicago: University of Chicago Press.

Collins, Suzanne. 2014. *The Hunger Games Trilogy.* New York: Scholastic Press.

Conrad, Jessica. 2014. Brewster Kahle. *On the Commons*. January 27. http://onthecommons.org/magazine/brewster-kahle.

Constable Katie [pseud.]. 2012. Interview by Abigail De Kosnik. Audio recording. November 1. Transcript available at University of Iowa Libraries.

Conway, Paul. 1996. Preservation in the digital world. Report for the Council on Library and Information Resources. March. http://www.clir.org/pubs/reports/reports/conway2/index.html.

Cooper, Joel. 2006. The digital divide: The special case of gender. *Journal of Computer Assisted Learning* 22:320–334.

Coppa, Francesca. 2006a. A brief history of media fandom. In *Fan Fiction and Fan Communities in the Age of the Internet*, ed. Karen Hellekson and Kristina Busse, 41–60. Jefferson, NC: McFarland.

Coppa, Francesca. 2006b. Writing bodies in space: Media fanfiction as theatrical performance. In *Fan Fiction and Fan Communities in the Age of the Internet*, ed. Karen Hellekson and Kristina Busse, 225–244. Jefferson, NC: McFarland.

Coppa, Francesca. 2012. Interview by Abigail De Kosnik. Audio recording. July 19 and July 24. Transcript available at University of Iowa Libraries.

Correa, Teresa. 2010. The participation divide among "online experts": Experience, skills, and psychological factors as predictors of college students' Web content creation. *Journal of Computer-Mediated Communication* 16 (1): 71–92.

Cossman, Brenda. 2013. Censor, resist, repeat: A history of censorship of gay and lesbian sexual representation in Canada. *Duke Journal of Gender Law and Policy* 21 (45): 45–66. http://scholarship.law.duke.edu/cgi/viewcontent.cgi?article=1246&context=djglp.

Craig, Edward Gordon. (1907) 2002. The actor and the über-marionette. In *The Twentieth-Century Performance Reader*, 2nd ed., ed. Michael Huxley and Noel Witts, 159–166. New York: Routledge.

Craig, Hannah. 2014. Safe spaces and the Internet nerd. *Dorkadia*. July 7. http://www.dorkadia.com/2014/07/07/internet-safe-spaces/.

Creative Commons. About. http://creativecommons.org/about (last accessed October 15, 2015).

Cupitt, Cathy. 2008. Nothing but Net: When cultures collide. *Transformative Works and Cultures* 1. http://journal.transformativeworks.org/index.php/twc/article/view/55/57.

Cvetkovich, Ann. 2003. *An Archive of Feelings: Trauma, Sexuality, and Lesbian Public Cultures*. Durham, NC: Duke University Press.

dark_administrator. 2011a. Kaleidoscope fanwork exchange FAQ. June 26. http://archiveofourown.org/collections/kaleidoscope/profile#faq.

dark_administrator. 2011b. Racebending revenge challenge fanworks and resources. Dreamwidth. June 1. http://dark-agenda.dreamwidth.org/21052.html.

Darnton, Robert. 2008. The library in the new age. *New York Review of Books*, June 12. http://www.nybooks.com/articles/archives/2008/jun/12/the-library-in-the-new-age/.

Dartt, G. L. Just between us. http://users.eastlink.ca/~ginadartt/JBSeries/Season1/jb01us.htm.

Dawn, Morgan [pseud]. 2012. Interview by Lisa Cronin. Audio recording. July 21. Transcript available at University of Iowa Libraries.

Defoe, Daniel. 2013. *Robinson Crusoe*. London: Penguin Classics.

Deirdre [pseud.]. 2012. Interview by Abigail De Kosnik. Audio recording. July 27. Transcript available at University of Iowa Libraries.

De Kosnik, Abigail. 2009. Should fan fiction be free? *Cinema Journal* 48 (4): 118–124.

De Kosnik, Abigail. 2013a. Fandom as free labor. In *Digital Labor: The Internet as Playground and Factory*, ed. Trebor Scholz, 98–111. New York: Routledge.

De Kosnik, Abigail. 2013b. Interrogating "free" fan labor. *Spreadable Media*. http://spreadablemedia.org/essays/kosnik/.

Deleuze, Gilles, and Félix Guattari. 1986. *Kafka: Toward a Minor Literature*. Trans. D. Polan. Minneapolis: University of Minnesota Press.

Derecho, Abigail. 2006. Archontic literature: A definition, a history, and several theories of fan fiction. In *Fan Fiction and Fan Communities in the Age of the Internet: New Essays*, ed. Karen Hellekson and Kristina Busse, 61–78. Jefferson, NC: McFarland.

Derrida, Jacques. 1995. Archive fever: A Freudian impression. Trans. Eric Prenowitz. *Diacritics* 25 (2): 9–63.

Derrida, Jacques. 2005. *Rogues: Two Essays on Reason*. Trans. P.-A. Brault and M. Naas. Stanford, CA: Stanford University Press.

DiMaggio, Paul, and Eszter Hargittai. 2001. From the "digital divide" to "digital inequality": Studying Internet use as penetration increases. Working Paper Series, 15. Center for Arts and Cultural Policy Studies. https://www.princeton.edu/~artspol/workpap/WP15%20-%20DiMaggio%2BHargittai.pdf.

Dixon, Laura J., Teresa Correa, Joseph Straubhaar, Laura Covarrubias, Dean Graber, Jeremiah Spence, and Viviana Rojas. 2014. Gendered space: The digital divide between male and female users in Internet public access sites. *Journal of*

Computer-Mediated Communication 19:991–1009. http://onlinelibrary.wiley.com/doi/10.1111/jcc4.12088/epdf.

Dixon, Steve. 2007. *Digital Performance: A History of New Media in Theater, Dance, Performance Art, and Installation*. Cambridge, MA: MIT Press.

Doane, Mary Ann. 2002. The instant and the archive. In *The Emergence of Cinematic Time: Modernity, Contingency, the Archive*, 206–234. Cambridge, MA: Harvard University Press.

Dockterman, Eliana. 2014. What is #gamergate and why are women being threatened about video games? *Time*, October 16. http://time.com/3510381/gamergate-faq/.

D'Orazio, Dante. 2014. The "original" Rickroll video has disappeared from YouTube. *The Verge*. July 19. http://www.theverge.com/2014/7/19/5918645/the-original-rickroll-video-has-disappeared-from-youtube.

Doty, Alexander. 1993. *Making Things Perfectly Queer: Interpreting Mass Culture*. Minneapolis: University of Minnesota Press.

Dourish, Paul, and Scott D. Mainwaring. 2012. Ubicomp's colonial impulse. In *UbiComp '12 Proceedings of the 2012 ACM Conference on Ubiquitous Computing*, 133–142. New York: ACM Press.

Dreamwidth. 2013. List of Racebending Revenge Challenge fanworks and resources. Last updated May 19, 2013. http://dark-agenda.dreamwidth.org/21052.html#cutid1.

Dreamwidth. 2014. Community profile: Dark Agenda. Last modified April 25, 2015. http://dark-agenda.dreamwidth.org/profile.

Dreamwidth. Trope bingo. http://trope-bingo.dreamwidth.org/.

Duggan, Maeve. 2013. It's a woman's (social media) world. *Pew Research Center*. September 12. http://www.pewresearch.org/fact-tank/2013/09/12/its-a-womans-social-media-world/.

Duggan, Maeve, and Joanna Brenner. 2013. The demographics of social media users—2012. *Pew Research Center*. February 14. http://www.pewinternet.org/2013/02/14/the-demographics-of-social-media-users-2012/.

Duncombe, Stephen. 2003. "I'm a Loser Baby": Zines and the creation of underground identity. In *Hop on Pop: The Politics and Pleasures of Popular Culture*, ed. Henry Jenkins, et al., 227–250. Durham, NC: Duke University Press.

Duncombe, Stephen. 2012. Imagining no-place. *Transformative Works and Cultures* 10: n.p. http://journal.transformativeworks.org/index.php/twc/article/view/350/266.

Dunnett, Dorothy. 1997. *The Lymond Chronicles, 1961–1975*. New York: Vintage Books.

Dzodan, Flavia. 2011. Come one, come all! Feminist and social justice blogging as performance and bloodshed. *Tiger Beatdown.* October 17. http://tigerbeatdown. com/2011/10/17/come-one-come-all-bloggers-bear-it-all-out-feminist-and -social-justice-blogging-as-performance-and-bloodshed/.

Edensor, Tim, Deborah Leslie, Steve Millington, and Norma M. Rantisi, eds. 2010. *Spaces of Vernacular Creativity: Rethinking the Cultural Economy.* New York: Routledge.

Edney, Matthew H. 1999. Reconsidering enlightenment geography and map making: Reconnaissance, mapping, archive. In *Geography and Enlightenment,* ed. David N. Livingstone and Charles W. Withers, 165–198. Chicago: University of Chicago Press.

Edwards, Jim. 2013. The inventor of the Twitter hashtag explains why he didn't patent it. *Business Insider.* November 21. http://www.businessinsider.com/chris -messina-talks-about-inventing-the-hashtag-on-twitter-2013-11.

Edwards, Paul N. 1996. *The Closed World: Computers and the Politics of Discourse in Cold War America.* Cambridge, MA: MIT Press.

Eichhorn, Kate. 2008. Archival genres: Gathering texts and reading spaces. *Invisible Culture: An Electronic Journal for Visual Culture* 12 (May): n.p. http://www.rochester .edu/in_visible_culture/Issue_12/eichhorn/eichhorn.pdf.

Electronic Frontier Foundation. A guide to YouTube removals. https://www.eff.org/ issues/intellectual-property/guide-to-youtube-removals.

Electronic Frontier Foundation. About EFF. https://www.eff.org/about (last accessed October 15, 2015).

Elliot, Shanti. 1999. Carnival and dialogue in Bakhtin's poetics of folklore. *Folklore Forum* 30 (1–2): 129–139.

Ellison, Hannah. 2012. The book burning that wasn't: Thousands of works of fiction destroyed and no one pays attention. *HuffPost Culture United Kingdom.* June 13. http://www.huffingtonpost.co.uk/hannah-ellison/fanfiction-the-book-burning- that-was_b_1592689.html.

embolalia. 2014. The way it should be. Archive of Our Own. February 15. http:// archiveofourown.org/works/1186762.

Emerson, Ramona. 2012. Netflix losing Starz Play: Over 1,000 Starz movies, TV shows to be cut. *Huffington Post.* February 28. http://www.huffingtonpost. com/2012/02/27/netflix-starz-play_n_1304611.html.

Engelbart, Douglas. 1962. Augmenting human intellect: A conceptual framework. Report for Director of Information Sciences, Air Force Office of Scientific Research. October. http://web.stanford.edu/dept/SUL/library/extra4/ sloan/mousesite/EngelbartPapers/B5_F18_ConceptFrameworkInd.html.

Entertainment Weekly. 1998. The final countdown. May 29. http://www.ew.com/ew/article/0,283382,00.html.

Ernst, Wolfgang. 2005. Let there be irony: Cultural history and media archaeology. *Art History* 28 (5): 582–603.

Ernst, Wolfgang. 2013. *Digital Memory and the Archive.* Minneapolis: University of Minnesota Press.

eruthros [pseud.] and thingswithwings [pseud.]. 2012. Interview by Andrea Horbinski. Audio recording. July 16. Transcript available at University of Iowa Libraries.

FAMA Collection: Siege of Sarajevo 92–96. http://www.famacollection.org/eng/.

Famous Monsters of Filmland. 1958–1983. New York: Warren.

FanFiction.net. Books: Pride and Prejudice. https://www.fanfiction.net/book/Pride-and-Prejudice/ (last accessed December 13, 2015).

Fanlore. APA. Last modified April 27, 2015. http://fanlore.org/wiki/APA.

Fanlore. B7 complex. Last modified November 10, 2015. http://fanlore.org/wiki/B7_Complex.

Fanlore. Beta. Last modified August 28, 2015. http://fanlore.org/wiki/Beta.

Fanlore. Fan casting. Last modified February 10, 2015. http://fanlore.org/wiki/Fan_Casting.

Fanlore. Fandom and the Internet. Last modified November 8, 2015. http://fanlore.org/wiki/Fandom_and_the_Internet.

Fanlore. Fandom as a Safe Space. Last modified April 17, 2015. http://fanlore.org/wiki/Fandom_as_a_Safe_Space.

Fanlore. FanLib. Last modified October 20, 2015. http://fanlore.org/wiki/FanLib.

Fanlore. Just Between series. Last modified August 22, 2015. http://fanlore.org/wiki/Just_Between_Series.

Fanlore. Leave a light on for me. Last modified November 19, 2012. http://fanlore.org/wiki/Leave_a_Light_On_for_Me.

Fanlore. Mary Sue. Last modified November 18, 2015. http://fanlore.org/wiki/Mary_Sue.

Fanlore. RaceFail '09. Last modified November 30, 2015. http://fanlore.org/wiki/RaceFail.

Fanlore. Scullyfic. Last modified August 17, 2015. http://fanlore.org/wiki/Scullyfic.

Fanlore. Spockanalia. Last modified June 12, 2015. http://fanlore.org/wiki/Spockanalia.

Fanlore. Strikethrough and Boldthrough. Last modified November 10, 2015. http://fanlore.org/wiki/Strikethrough_and_Boldthrough.

Fanlore. Zines and the Internet. Last modified on September 8, 2015. http://fanlore.org/wiki/Zines_and_the_Internet.

Ferguson, Sian. 2014. 6 reasons why we need safe spaces. *Everyday Feminism.* August 5. http://everydayfeminism.com/2014/08/we-need-safe-spaces/.

Finnegan, Ruth. 2005. Introduction: Looking beyond the walls. In *Participating in the Knowledge Society: Researchers Beyond the University Walls*, ed. Ruth Finnegan, 1–19. Basingstoke, UK: Palgrave-MacMillan.

Fiske, John. 1987. *Television Culture.* New York: Methuen.

Fiske, John, ed. (1989) 2011. *The John Fiske Collection: Understanding Popular Culture.* Boston: Unwin Hyman; New York: Routledge.

Fiske, John. 1992. The cultural economy of fandom. In *Adoring Audience: Fan Culture and Popular Media*, ed. Lisa A. Lewis, 30–49. New York: Routledge.

Fiske, John. 1996. *Media Matters: Everyday Culture and Political Change.* Minneapolis: University of Minnesota Press.

Fleischman, Glenn. 2014. Internet permanence: Down the memory hole. *Economist.* January 15. http://www.economist.com/blogs/babbage/2014/01/internet-permanence.

Fletcher, Challa. 2012. The purge. *You Write What?!* July. http://bloggingfanfiction.blogspot.com/2012/07/the-purge.html.

Fletcher, Dan. 2009. Internet atrocity! Geocities' demise erases Web history. *Time,* November 9. http://content.time.com/time/business/article/0,8599,1936645,00.html.

Flinn, Andrew. 2007. Community histories, community archives: Some opportunities and challenges. *Journal of the Society of Archivists* 28 (2): 151–176.

Flinn, Andrew, and Mary Stevens. 2009. "It is noh mistri, wi mekin histri." Telling our own story: Independent and community archives in the UK, challenging and subverting the mainstream. In *Community Archives: The Shaping of Memory*, ed. Jeannette Bastian and Benjamin F. Alexander, 3–27. London: Facet Publishing.

Florini, Sarah. 2014. Tweets, tweeps, and signifyin': Communication and cultural performance on "Black Twitter." *Television and New Media* 15 (3): 223-237.

Fluck, Winfried. 1997. *Das kulturelle Imaginäre: Eine Funktionsgeschichte des amerikanischen Romans, 1790–1900.* Frankfurt: Suhrkamp.

Forrest, Conner. 2014. Diversity stats: 10 tech companies that have come clean. *TechRepublic.* August 28. http://www.techrepublic.com/article/diversity-stats-10-tech-companies-that-have-come-clean/.

Foucault, Michel. 1972. *The Archaeology of Knowledge*. Trans. A. Sheridan. New York: Pantheon Books.

Foucault, Michel. 1986. Of other spaces. Trans. Jay Miskowiec. *Diacritics* 16 (1): 22–27.

Free Biflows. About. http://freebitflows.t0.or.at/f/about/introduction (last accessed October 15, 2015).

Freeman, Elizabeth. 2010. *Time Binds: Queer Temporalities, Queer Histories*. Durham, NC: Duke University Press.

Free Software Foundation. What is copyleft? https://www.gnu.org/copyleft/ (last accessed October 13, 2015).

Friedman, Ken, ed. 1998. *The Fluxus Reader*. New York: Academy Editions.

Fuchs, Christian. 2012a. Dallas Smythe today—the audience commodity, the digital labour debate, Marxist political economy and critical theory. Prolegomena to a digital labour theory of value. *Triple C: Communication, Capitalism, and Critique: Journal for a Global Sustainable Information Society* 10 (2): 692–740.

Fuchs, Christian. 2012b. Some reflections on Manuel Castells' book *Networks of Outrage and Hope: Social Movements in the Internet Age*. *tripleC* 10 (2): 775–797.

Gaines, Jane M. 1991. *Contested Culture: The Image, the Voice, and the Law*. Chapel Hill: University of North Carolina Press.

Gajjala, Radhika. 2002. An interrupted postcolonial/feminist cyberethnography: Complicity and resistance in the "cyberfield." *Feminist Media Studies* 2 (2): 177–193.

Ganeshananthan, V. V. 2011. Digital diaspora: The South Asian American digital archive. *Sepia Mutiny*. August 1. http://sepiamutiny.com/blog/2011/08/01/digital_diaspor/.

Garrels, Machtelt. 2004. Inside TLDP. *The Linux Documentation Project*. March. http://www.tldp.org/history.html.

Gates, Henry Louis, Jr. 1988. *The Signifying Monkey: A Theory of Afro-American Literary Criticism*. New York: Oxford University Press.

Gatson, Sarah N., and Robin Anne Reid. 2011. Race and ethnicity in fandom. *Transformative Works and Cultures* 8: n.p. http://journal.transformativeworks.org/index.php/twc/article/view/392/252.

Genette, Gérard. 1997. *Paratexts: Thresholds of Interpretation*. New York: Cambridge University Press.

Gibson, William. 1984. *Neuromancer*. New York: Ace Books.

Gleick, James. (1998) 2002. The digital attic: Are we now amnesiacs? Or packrats? In *What Just Happened: A Chronicle from the Information Frontier*, 196–201. New York: Pantheon Books.

GLSEN (Gay, Lesbian & Straight Education Network). 2013. *Out Online: The Experiences of LGBT Youth on the Internet.* July 10. http://www.glsen.org/press/study -finds-lgbt-youth-face-greater-harassment-online.

Goffman, Erving. (1956) 1959. *The Presentation of Self in Everyday Life.* Edinburgh: University of Edinburgh, Social Science Research Centre. New York: Anchor Books.

Goggin, Gerard. 2006. *Cell Phone Culture: Mobile Technology in Everyday Life.* New York: Routledge.

Goldberg, Stanley. 1992. *Inventing a Climate of Opinion: Vannevar Bush and the Decision to Build the Bomb.* Philadelphia: History of Science Society.

Goofusgallant. 2012. Book post: How authors feel about fan-fiction. *Oh No They Didn't!* LiveJournal. April 19. http://ohnotheydidnt.livejournal.com/68332629.html.

Gorman, Michael. 2003. Cataloguing in an electronic age. *Cataloging and Classification Quarterly* 36 (3–4): 5–17.

Grahame-Smith, Seth. 2009. *Pride and Prejudice and Zombies: The Classic Regency Romance—Now with Ultraviolent Zombie Mayhem.* San Francisco, CA: Chronicle Books.

Gray, Jonathan. 2010. *Show Sold Separately: Promos, Spoilers, and Other Media Paratexts.* New York: New York University Press.

Gray, Jonathan. 2012. Of snowspeeders and imperial walkers: Fannish play at the Wisconsin protests. *Transformative Works and Cultures* 10: n.p. http://journal .transformativeworks.org/index.php/twc/article/view/353/296.

Halberstam, Jack. 1992. Queer creatures. *On Our Backs* 9 (November/December): 10–11, 44.

Halberstam, Jack. 2005. *In a Queer Time and Place: Transgender Bodies, Subcultural Lives.* New York: New York University Press.

Halbwachs, Maurice. 1992. *On Collective Memory.* Ed. and trans. L. A. Caser. Chicago: University of Chicago Press.

Hale, Shannon. 2007. *Austenland: A Novel.* New York: Bloomsbury.

Hall, Stuart. 1998. Notes on deconstructing "the popular." In *Cultural Theory and Popular Culture: A Reader,* ed. John Story, 442–453. Toronto: Pearson Educational.

Hallam, Elizabeth, and Tim Ingold. 2007. Creativity and cultural improvisation: An introduction. In *Creativity and Cultural Improvisation,* ed. Elizabeth Hallam and Tim Ingold, 1–24. New York: Berg.

Hamscha, Susanne. 2013. *The Fiction of America: Performance and the Cultural Imaginary in Literature and Film*. Frankfurt: Campus.

Hansberry, Lorraine. 1994. *A Raisin in the Sun*. New York: Vintage Books.

Haraway, Donna. (1985) 2000. The cyborg manifesto. In *The Cyberculture Reader*, ed. David Bell and Barbara M. Kennedy, 291–324. New York: Routledge. Citations refer to Routledge edition.

Hardt, Michael, and Antonio Negri. 2000. *Empire*. Cambridge, MA: Harvard University Press.

Hargittai, Eszter. 2002. Second-level digital divide: Differences in people's online skills. *First Monday* 7 (4) (April 1). http://firstmonday.org/article/view/942/864.

Hargittai, Eszter. 2003. *The Digital Divide and What to Do about It*. Pre-Print Version. New Economy Handbook. San Diego, CA: Academic Press.

Hart, Michael. 1992. Gutenberg: The history and philosophy of Project Gutenberg. *Project Gutenberg*. August. http://www.gutenberg.org/wiki/Gutenberg:The_History_and_Philosophy_of_Project_Gutenberg_by_Michael_Hart.

Harth, Dietrich. 2008. The invention of cultural memory. In *Cultural Memory Studies: An International and Interdisciplinary Handbook*, ed. Astrid Erll, Ansgar Nünning and Sara B. Young, 85–96. New York: Walter de Gruyter.

Harvey, David. 1989. *The Condition of Postmodernity: An Enquiry into the Origins of Cultural Change*. Cambridge, MA: Blackwell.

Hayles, N. Katherine. 1996. How cyberspace signifies. In *Immortal Engines: Life Extension and Immortality in Science Fiction and Fantasy*, ed. George Edgar Slusser, Gary Westfahl and Eric S. Rabkin, 111–121. Athens: University of Georgia Press.

Hayles, N. Katherine. 2007. Hyper and deep attention: The generational divide in cognitive modes. *Profession*: 187–199.

Hebdige, Dick. 1983. *Subculture: The Meaning of Style*. London: Methuen.

Hebdige, Dick. 1987. *Cut 'n' Mix: Culture, Identity, and Caribbean Music*. New York: Methuen.

Hebdige, Dick. 1988. *Hiding in the Light: On Images and Things*. New York: Routledge.

Heidegger, Martin. (1962) 2008. *Being and Time*. Trans. J. MacQuarrie and E. Robinson. New York: Harper & Row.

Heinau, Vera. 2012. Interview by Abigail De Kosnik. Email. August 12. Transcript available at University of Iowa Libraries.

Hellekson, Karen. 2009. A fannish field of value: Online fan gift culture. *Cinema Journal* 48 (4): 113–118.

Hellekson, Karen. 2012. Interview by Abigail De Kosnik. Audio recording. July 27. Transcript available at University of Iowa Libraries.

Hess, Amanda. 2014. Why women aren't welcome on the Internet. *Pacific Standard*. January 6. http://www.psmag.com/health-and-behavior/women-arent-welcome-internet-72170.

Hill, Matt. 2002. *Fan Cultures*. New York: Routledge.

Hirsch, E. D. 1988. *Cultural Literacy: What Every American Needs to Know*. New York: Vintage.

Hoffman, Piper. 2014. How an activist headed toward burnout can change course: Four ways to cope with compassion fatigue. *Our Hen House*. October 9. http://www.ourhenhouse.org/2014/10/how-an-activist-headed-toward-burnout-can-change-course-four-ways-to-cope-with-compassion-fatigue-2/.

Hoffmann, E. T. A. 1979. The sand-man. In *The Best Tales of Hoffmann*, 183–214. New York: Dover.

Hoggart, Richard. 1957. *The Uses of Literacy: Aspects of Working-Class Life with Special References to Publications and Entertainments*. London: Chatto & Windus.

Holcomb, Julie. 2000. Preserving digital archives, preserving cultural memory. *Journal for the Association of History and Computing* 3 (3) (November): n.p. http://quod.lib.umich.edu/j/jahc/3310410.0003.320/--preserving-digital-archives-preserving-cultural-memory?rgn=main;view=fulltext.

hooks, bell. 1994. *Outlaw Culture*. New York: Routledge.

Horkheimer, Max, and Theodor W. Adorno. 2002. The culture industry: Enlightenment as mass deception. In *Dialectic of Enlightenment: Philosophical Fragments*. Ed. Gunzelin Schmid Noerr. Trans. Edmund Jephcott. Stanford: Stanford University Press.

Huffington Post. 2012. Rafael Morelos, gay Washington teen, commits suicide after reportedly enduring anti-gay bullying, cyberbullying. *HuffPost Gay Voices*. February 6. http://www.huffingtonpost.com/2012/02/06/rafael-morelos-gay-washington-suicide_n_1258471.html.

Huyssen, Andreas. 1984. Mapping the postmodern. *New German Critique* 33 (autumn): 5–52.

Hwang, David Henry. 1993. *M. Butterfly*. New York: Plume.

Ibsen, Henrik. 2013. *Heda Gabbler*. Trans. William Archer and Edmund Gosse. Project Gutenberg. May 1. http://www.gutenberg.org/ebooks/4093?msg=welcome _stranger.

Intel Corporation. 2012. Women and the Web: Bridging the Internet gap and creating new global opportunities in low and middle-income countries. http://www .intel.com/content/dam/www/public/us/en/documents/pdf/women-and-the-web .pdf.

Internet Archive. 2010. 1968 Demo—FJCC Conference Reel #1 (December 10, 1968). Last accessed December 13, 2015. https://archive.org/details/XD300-23_68Highlight sAResearchCntAugHumanIntellect.

Internet Archive. Frequently asked questions. https://archive.org/about/faqs.php (last accessed October 15, 2015).

Isaksen, Leif. 2008. Pandora's box: The future of cultural heritage on the World Wide Web. Presentation at the Cultural Heritage Imaging Conference on Digital Heritage in the New Knowledge Environment: Shared Spaces and Open Paths to Cultural Content, Athens, Greece, August 10–11, 2008. Hellenic Ministry of Culture.

Ito, Mizuko. 2006. Japanese media mixes amateur cultural exchange. In *Digital Generations: Children, Young People, and New Media*, ed. David Buckingham and Rebekah Willett, 49–66. Mahwah, NJ: Erlbaum.

Jackson, Shannon. 2004. *Professing Performance: Theatre in the Academy from Philology to Performativity*. New York: Cambridge University Press.

Jackson, Shannon. 2011. *Social Works: Performing Art, Supporting Publics*. New York: Routledge.

Jacqueline [pseud.]. 2012. Interview by Lisa Cronin. Audio recording. July 6. Transcript available at University of Iowa Libraries.

James, E. L. 2012. *Fifty Shades of Grey*. New York: Random House.

James, P. D. 2011. *Death Comes to Pemberley*. New York: Knopf.

Jameson, Frederic. 1984. Postmodernism, or The cultural logic of late capitalism. *New Left Review*, no. 146 (July/August): 53–92.

Jardin, Xeni. 2007. LiveJournal/6A re: mass strikethrough—"we screwed up." *Boing Boing*. May 31. http://boingboing.net/2007/05/31/livejournal6a-re-mas.html.

Jedi Buttercup. 2013. Not one to settle. Archive of Our Own. June 1. http:// archiveofourown.org/works/34105.

Jenkins, Henry. 1992. *Textual Poachers: Television Fans and Participatory Culture*. New York: Routledge.

Jenkins, Henry. 2003. Transmedia storytelling. *MIT Technology Review*. January 15. http://www.technologyreview.com/news/401760/transmedia-storytelling/.

Jenkins, Henry. 2006. *Convergence Culture: Where Old and New Media Collide*. New York: New York University Press.

Jenkins, Henry. 2007a. Transforming fan culture into user-generated content: The case of Fanlib. *Confessions of an Aca-Fan*. May 22. http://henryjenkins.org/2007/05/ transforming_fan_culture_into.html.

Jenkins, Henry. 2007b. Transmedia storytelling 101. *Confessions of an Aca-Fan: The Official Weblog of Henry Jenkins*. March 22. http://henryjenkins.org/2007/03/ transmedia_storytelling_101.html.

Jenkins, Henry. 2011a. Aca-fandom and beyond: John Edward Campbell, Lee Harrington, and Catherine Tossenberger (part two). *Confessions of an Aca-Fan: The Official Weblog of Henry Jenkins*. July 29. http://henryjenkins.org/2011/07/aca -fandom_and_beyond_harringt_1.html.

Jenkins, Henry. 2011b. Transmedia 202: Further reflections. *Confessions of an Aca-Fan: The Official Weblog of Henry Jenkins*. August 1. http://henryjenkins.org/2011/08/ defining_transmedia_further_re.html.

Jenkins, Henry. 2011c. Why Fiske still matters. In *The John Fiske Collection: Understanding Popular Culture*, ed. John Fiske, xii–xxxviii. New York: Routledge. First published 1989 by Unwin Hyman.

Jenkins, Henry. 2012. "Cultural acupuncture": Fan activism and the Harry Potter Alliance. *Transformative Works and Cultures* 10: n.p. http://journal .transformativeworks.org/index.php/twc/article/view/305/259.

Jenkins, Henry. 2013. *Textual Poachers: Television Fans and Participatory Culture*. New York: Routledge.

Jenkins, Henry, Sam Ford, and Joshua Green. 2013. *Spreadable Media: Creating Value and Meaning in a Networked Culture*. New York: New York University Press.

Jenkins, Henry, and Cynthia Jenkins. 2012. Interview by Abigail De Kosnik. Audio recording. August 14. Transcript available at University of Iowa Libraries.

Jenkins, Henry, with Ravi Purushotma, Margaret Weigel, Katie Clinton, and Alice J. Robison. 2009. *Confronting the Challenges of Participatory Culture: Media Education in the 21st Century*. Cambridge, MA: MIT Press.

Jesemie's Evil Twin. 2000. Night giving off flames. The Gossamer Project. June 6. http://fluky.gossamer.org/display.php?NightGivingOffFlames.Twin.

jinjurly [pseud.]. 2012. Interview by Andrea Horbinski. Audio recording. July 7 and July 19. Transcript available at University of Iowa Libraries.

Jones, Caroline A. 2006. *Sensorium: Embodied Experience, Technology, and Contemporary Art.* Cambridge, MA: MIT Press.

Judy, Ronald A. T. 1993. *(Dis)Forming the American Canon.* Minneapolis: University of Minnesota Press.

Juodvalkis, Vincent. 2012. Interview by Abigail De Kosnik. Audio recording. July 23. Transcript available at University of Iowa Libraries.

Kahle, Brewster. 1997. Archiving the Internet. *Scientific American.* March. http://www.uibk.ac.at/voeb/texte/kahle.html.

Kahle, Brewster. 2013. Aaron Schwartz, hero of the open world, dies. Internet Archive Blogs. January 12. http://blog.archive.org/2013/01/12/aaron-swartz-hero-of-the-open-world-rip/.

Karasti, Helena, and Anna-Liisa Syrjänen. 2004. Artful infrastructuring in two cases of community PD. Paper presented at the Eighth Conference on Participatory Design: Artful Integration: Interweaving Media, Materials and Practices, Toronto, Canada, July 27–31.

Katz, Elihu, and Paul F. Lazarsfeld. (1955) 2009. *Personal Influence: The Part Played by People in the Flow of Mass Communications.* Glencoe, IL: Free Press; New Brunswick, NJ: Transaction Publishers.

Kavka, Ondrej. Nielsen ratings. *The X-Files Compilation.* URL no longer accessible.

Keen, Andrew. 2007. *The Cult of the Amateur: How Today's Internet is Killing our Culture.* New York: Doubleday/Currency.

Kelly, Kevin. 2006. Scan this book! *New York Times.* May 14. http://www.nytimes.com/2006/05/14/magazine/14publishing.html?pagewanted=print&_r=2&.

Kelly, Kevin. 2008. Very long-term backup. Kevin Kelly's Lifestream. August 20. http://kk.org/kk/2008/08/very-longterm-backup.php.

Kelty, Christopher M. 2008. *Two Bits: The Cultural Significance of Free Archives.* Durham, NC: Duke University Press.

Ketelaar, Eric. 2001. Tacit narratives: The meanings of archives. *Archival Science* 1:131–141.

Kirschenbaum, Matthew G. 2012. *Mechanisms: New Media and the Forensic Imagination.* Cambridge, MA: MIT Press.

Kirschenbaum, Matthew G., et al. 2009. *Approaches to Managing and Collecting Born-Digital Literary Materials for Scholarly Use.* Washington, DC: National Endowment for the Humanities Office of Digital Humanities. http://mith.umd.edu/wp-content/uploads/whitepaper_HD-50346.Kirschenbaum.WP.pdf.PDF.

Klein, Hugh, and Kenneth S. Shiffman. 2009. Underrepresentation and symbolic annihilation of socially disenfranchised groups ("out groups") in animated cartoons. *Howard Journal of Communications* 20:55–72.

Knott, Judson, and Paul Jones. 1996. SunSITE: Serving your needs since 1992. *D-Lib Magazine.* February. http://www.dlib.org/dlib/february96/02knott.html.

Know Your Meme. 2008a. LOLcats. Last modified 2014. http://knowyourmeme .com/memes/lolcats.

Know Your Meme. 2008b. Rickroll. Last modified September 2015. http:// knowyourmeme.com/memes/rickroll.

Know Your Meme. 2011. Ryan Gosling "Hey Girl." Last modified August 2015. http://knowyourmeme.com/memes/people/ryan-gosling.

Know Your Meme. 2012. Tumblr—Fuck Yeah Fuck Yeah blogs. Last modified 2012. http://knowyourmeme.com/photos/302572-tumblr.

Kuhn, Annette, and Kirsten Emiko McAllister, eds. 2006. *Locating Memory: Photographic Acts.* New York: Berghahn Books.

Kuny, Terry. 1997. A digital dark ages? Challenges in the preservation of electronic information. Paper presented at the 63rd IFLA Council and General Conference, Copenhagen, Denmark. August 31–September 5. http://archive.ifla.org/IV/ifla63/63kuny1.pdf.

Lancaster, Kurt. 2001. *Interacting with Babylon 5: Fan Performance in a Media Universe.* Austin: University of Texas Press.

Latour, Bruno. 1994. On technical mediation. *Common Knowledge* 3 (2): 29–64.

Latour, Bruno. 2005. *Reassembling the Social: An Introduction to Actor-Network-Theory.* New York: Oxford University Press.

Laurel, Brenda. 1991. *Computers as Theatre.* Reading, MA: Addison-Wesley.

Lauzen, Martha M. 2013. Boxed in: Employment of behind-the-scenes and on-screen women in 2012–13 prime-time television. Center for the Study of Women in Television & Film, San Diego State University. http://womenintvfilm.sdsu.edu/files/2012-13_Boxed_In_Report.pdf.

Lazzarato, Mauricio. 1996. Immaterial labor. In *Radical Thought in Italy: A Potential Politics,* ed. Paolo Virno and Michael Hardt, 133–147. Minneapolis: University of Minnesota Press.

Leadbeater, Charles, and Paul Miller. 2004. *The Pro-Am Revolution: How Enthusiasts are Changing our Society and Economy.* London: Demos.

Lebert, Marie. 2008. Project Gutenberg (1971–2008). *Project Gutenberg.* October. http://www.gutenberg.org/cache/epub/27045/pg27045.html.

Lee, Aileen. 2011. Why women rule the Internet. *TechCrunch*. March 20. http://techcrunch.com/2011/03/20/why-women-rule-the-internet/.

Lesk, Michael. 1995. Preserving digital objects: Recurrent needs and challenges. http://www.lesk.com/mlesk/auspres/aus.html.

Lesk, Michael. 1996. Preserving digital objects: Recurrent needs and challenges. In *Multimedia Preservation: Capturing the Rainbow. Proceedings of the Second National Conference of the National Preservation Office*, ed. Hilary Berthon and Ronda Jamieson, 106–125. Canberra: National Library of Australia.

Lessig, Lawrence. 2004. *Free Culture: How Big Media Uses Technology and the Law to Lock Down Culture and Control Creativity*. New York: Penguin Press.

Lessig, Lawrence. 2008. *Remix: Making Art and Commerce Thrive in the Hybrid Economy*. New York: Penguin Press.

Levy, Adam. 2013. Comcast's VOD library may rival Netflix. The Motley Fool: To Educate, Amuse & Enrich. October 22. http://www.fool.com/investing/general/2013/10/22/comcasts-vod-library-may-rival-netflix.aspx.

Levy, Steven. 1984. *Hackers: Heroes of the Computer Revolution*. Garden City, NY: Anchor Press/Doubleday.

Lewis, Justin. 1991. *The Ideological Octopus: An Exploration of Television and Its Audience*. New York: Routledge.

Lewis, Lisa A., ed. 1992. *Adoring Audience: Fan Culture and Popular Media*. New York: Routledge.

Liang, Lawrence. 2005. Porous legalities and avenues of participation. *Sarai Reader 05: Bare* Acts: 6–17.

Library of Congress. General information: Year 2013 at a glance. http://www.loc.gov/about/general-information/#year-at-a-glance.

Licklider, J. C. R., et al. 1965. *Libraries of the Future*. Cambridge, MA: MIT Press.

Lima, Manuel. 2014. *The Book of Trees: Visualizing Branches of Knowledge*. New York: Princeton Architectural Press.

Linshi, Jack. 2015. 6 charts showing tech's gender gap is more complicated than you think. *Time*, March 26. http://time.com/3758017/ellen-pao-gender-diversity-tech-valley/.

Litotease [pseud.]. 2012. Interview by Abigail De Kosnik. Audio recording. June 12. Transcript available at University of Iowa Libraries.

Liviapenn [pseud.]. 2012. Interview by Lisa Cronin. Audio recording. August 16. Transcript available at University of Iowa Libraries.

Livingstone, Sonia, and Ellen Helsper. 2007. Gradations in digital inclusion: Children, young people, and the digital divide. *New Media and Society* 9 (4): 671–696.

Locate TV. 2013. New TV episodes this week. December. http://www.locatetv.com/new-tv-episodes.

Lothian, Alexis. 2012a. Archival anarchies: Online fandom, subcultural conservation, and the transformative work of digital ephemera. *International Journal of Cultural Studies* 11 (September). http://queergeektheory.org/docs/LothianArchivalAnarchiesIJoCS.pdf.PDF.

Lothian, Alexis. 2012b. Interview by Abigail De Kosnik. Audio recording. July 20. Transcript available at University of Iowa Libraries.

Lothian, Alexis, Kristina Busse, and Robin Anne Reid. 2007. "Yearning void and infinite potential": Online slash fandom as queer female space. *English Language Notes* 45 (2): 103–111.

Lovink, Geert. 2011. *My First Recession: Critical Internet Culture in Transition.* Amsterdam: Institute of Network Cultures.

Lowery, Shearon, and Melvin DeFleur. 1995. *Milestones in Mass Communication Research: Media Effects.* White Plains, NY: Longman Publishers.

Löwgren, Jonas, and Bo Reimer. 2013. *Collaborative Media: Production, Consumption, and Design Interventions.* Cambridge, MA: MIT Press.

Löwgren, Jonas, and Eric Stolterman. 1998. Developing IT design ability through repertoires and contextual product semantics. *Digital Creativity* 9 (4): 223–237.

Lukács, György. (1923) 1971. *History and Class Consciousness: Studies in Marxist Dialectics.* Cambridge, MA: MIT Press.

Lulu. 2013. Heterosexual female slash fans. The Slow Dance of the Infinite Stars Tumblr. October 4. http://centrumlumina.tumblr.com/post/63112902720/heterosexual-female-slash-fans.

MacKenzie, Donald, and Judy Wajcman. (1985) 1999. *The Social Shaping of Technology,* 2nd ed. Milton Keynes, UK: Open University Press; Philadelphia: Open University Press.

Malone, Paul. 2000. Cyber-Kleist. In *Mediated Drama, Dramatized Media: Papers Given on Occasion of the 8th Annual Conference of the German Society for Contemporary Theatre and Drama in English,* ed. Eckart Voigts-Virchow, 57–66. Trier, Germany: Wissenschaftlicher Verlag, Trier.

Manovich, Lev. 2001. *The Language of New Media.* Cambridge, MA: MIT Press.

Maraffi, Christopher. 2011. Roots of a performatology: From uber-marionette to performative embodied agents. http://users.soe.ucsc.edu/~topherm/Maraffi_Poster _DH2011_ACM.pdf.

Markham, Annette. 2013. The dramaturgy of digital experience. In *The Drama of Social Life: A Dramaturgical Handbook*, ed. Charles Edgley, 279–294. Burlington, VT: Ashgate.

Martin, Michel, et al. 2010. Summer movies, in white and white? *NPR*. June 30. http://www.npr.org/templates/story/story.php?storyId=128215446.

Martín-Barbero, Jesús. 1995. Memory and form in the Latin American soap opera. In *To Be Continued ... Soap Operas from Around the World*, ed. Robert C. Allen, 276–284. New York: Routledge.

Marx, Karl. (1867) 2011. *Capital*, vol. 1: *A Critique of Political Economy*. Ed. Friedrich Engels. New York: Dover.

Mbembe, Achille. 2002. The power of the archive and its limits. In *Refiguring the Archive*, ed. Carolyn Hamilton, 19–26. Cape Town: Clyson Printers.

McLaren, Peter, and Rhonda Hammer. 1996. Media knowledges, warrior citizenry, and postmodern literacies. In *Counternarratives: Cultural Studies and Critical Pedagogies in Postmodern Spaces*, ed. Henry A. Giroux, 81–116. New York: Routledge.

McLuhan, Marshall. 1970. *From Cliché to Archetype*. New York: Viking Press.

McLuhan, Marshall, and Barrinton Nevitt. 1972. *Take Today: The Executive as Dropout*. New York: Harcourt Bruce Jovanovich.

McRobbie, Angela. 2000. *Feminism and Youth Culture*, 2nd ed. New York: Routledge.

melannen. 2010. Science, y'all. Dreamwidth. January 16. http://melannen .dreamwidth.org/77558.html.

Mellor, Hugh D. 1980. On things and causes in spacetime. *British Journal for the Philosophy of Science* 31 (3): 282–288.

Merskin, Debra. 1998. Sending up signals: A survey of Native American media use and representation in the mass media. *Howard Journal of Communications* 9:333–345.

Meyer, Stephanie. 2009. *The Twilight Saga Collection*. New York: Little, Brown and Co.

Meyers, Oren, Eyal Zandberg, and Motti Neiger. 2009. Prime time communication: An analysis of television broadcasts on Israel's memorial day for the Holocaust and heroism. *Journal of Communication* 59 (3): 456–480.

Meyrowitz, Joshua. 1985. *No Sense of Place: The Impact of Electronic Media on Social Behavior*. New York: Oxford University Press.

M I C H I. on fandom, bullying, and respectful spaces. *M I C H I Tumblr*. http://traumachu.tumblr.com/post/116469030779/on-fandom-bullying-and-respectful-spaces (last accessed October 15, 2015).

Michigan/Trans Controversy Archive. http://eminism.org/michigan/.

Milner, R. M. 2011. The study of cultures online: Some methodological and ethical tensions. *Graduate Journal of Social Science* 8 (3): 14–35.

Modine, Austin. 2009. Web 0.2 archivists save Geocities from deletion: Preserving history one hideous webpage at a time. *Register*. April 28. http://www.theregister.co.uk/Print/2009/04/28/geocities_preservation/.

Modleski, Tania. 2007. The search for tomorrow in today's soap operas. In *Loving with a Vengeance: Mass-produced Fantasies for Women*, 77–102. New York: Routledge.

Montgomery, Alicia. 2010. The white washing of "The Last Airbender." *NPR*. June 29. http://www.npr.org/blogs/tellmemore/2010/06/29/128196842/the-white-washing-of-a-nickelodeon-hit.

Morley, David, and Kevin Robins. 2002. *Spaces of Identity: Global Media, Electronic Landscapes, and Cultural Boundaries*. New York: Routledge.

Morrison, Toni. 1992. *Playing in the Dark: Whiteness and the Literary Imagination*. Cambridge, MA: Harvard University Press.

Morrissey, Charles T. 2007. Oral history interviews: From inception to closure. In *History of Oral History: Foundations and Methodology*, ed. Thomas L. Charlton, Lois E. Myers and Rebecca Sharpless, 160–196. Lanham, MD: Rowman & Littlefield.

Motion Picture Association of America. 2012. Theatrical market statistics 2012. http://www.mpaa.org/wp-content/uploads/2014/03/2012-Theatrical-Market-Statistics-Report.pdf.

Mouffe, Chantal. 2000. *The Democratic Paradox*. London: Verso.

Murray, Janet Horowitz. 1997. *Hamlet on Holodeck: The Future of Narrative in Cyberspace*. New York: Free Press.

Naficy, Hamid. 1993. *The Making of Exile Cultures: Iranian Television in Los Angeles*. Minneapolis: University of Minnesota Press.

Nakamura, Lisa. 2008. *Digitizing Race: Visual Cultures of the Internet*. Minneapolis: University of Minnesota Press.

Nelson, Robin. 2012. Interview by Abigail De Kosnik. Audio recording. July 23. Transcript available at University of Iowa Libraries.

Nelson, Theodore H. (1972) 1991. As we will think. In *From Memex to Hypertext: Vannevar Bush and the Mind's Machine*, ed. James M. Nyce and Paul Kahn, 245–260. Boston: Academic Press.

Nelson, Theodore H. 1993. *Literary Machines: The Report on, and of, Project Xandu Concerning Word Processing, Electronic Publishing, Hypertext, Thinkertoys, Tomorrow's Intellectual Revolution, and Certain Other Topics Including Knowledge, Education and Freedom.* Sausalito, CA: Mindful Press.

Nestle, Joan. 1990. The will to remember: The Lesbian Herstory Archives of New York. *Feminist Review* 34 (spring): 86–94.

Newsom, Jennifer Siebel, and Martha M. Lauzen. 2013. Hollywood pipeline: Still a pipe dream for women? *The Blog, Huffington Post.* February 22. http://www .huffingtonpost.com/jennifer-siebel-newsom/hollywood-pipeline-still-_b_2743371 .html.

New Tactics. 2013. Creating safe spaces: Tactics for communities at risk. *New Tactics in Human Rights.* https://www.newtactics.org/conversation/creating-safe-spaces -tactics-communities-risk.

New York Times. 2012. Tyler Clementi. *New York Times,* March 16. http://topics .nytimes.com/top/reference/timestopics/people/c/tyler_clementi/index.html.

Nigam, Hemanshu. 2012. The Internet remembers and so we must. *Huffington Post.* December 13. http://www.huffingtonpost.com/hemanshu-nigam/the-internet-remembers-an_b_2294619.html.

nightflier [pseud.]. 2012. Interview by Lisa Cronin. Audio recording. June 13. Transcript available at University of Iowa Libraries.

Nora, Pierre. 1984. *Les lieux de mémoire,* vol. 1: *La République.* Paris: Gallimard.

Novak, Marcos. 1992. Liquid architectures in cyberspace. In *Cyberspace: First Steps,* ed. Michael L. Benedikt. Cambridge, MA: MIT Press.

OCLC Research. Digital information preservation—the landmark study. http://oclc .org/research/activities/digpresstudy.html (last accessed October 15, 2015).

Ohye, Bonnie Y., and Jessica Henderson Daniels. 1999. The "other" adolescent girls: Who are they? In *Beyond Appearance: A New Look at Adolescent Girls,* ed. Norine Johnson, Michael Roberts and Judith Worell, 115–130. Washington, DC: American Psychological Association.

Olick, Jeffrey, Vered Vinitzky-Seroussi, and Daniel Levy, eds. 2011. *The Collective Memory Reader.* New York: Oxford University Press.

Oral History Association. 2009. Principles and best practices. Last accessed December 13, 2015. http://www.oralhistory.org/about/principles-and-practices/.

O'Reilly, Tim. 2005. What is Web 2.0: Design patterns and business models for the next generation software. *O'Reilly.com.* September 30. http://oreilly.com/pub/a/ web2/archive/what-is-web-20.html?page=1.

Organization for Transformative Works. Legal advocacy. *Organization for Transformative Works*. http://transformativeworks.org/projects/legal (last accessed October 15, 2015).

Organization for Transformative Works. Our projects. *Organization for Transformative Works*. http://transformativeworks.org/our-projects (last accessed October 15, 2015).

Organization for Transformative Works. What we believe. *Organization for Transformative Works*. http://transformativeworks.org/about/believe (last accessed October 15, 2015).

O'Riordan, Kate, and David J. Phillips. 2007. Introduction. In *Queer Online: Media Technology and Sexuality*, ed. Kate O'Riordan and David J. Phillips, 1–9. New York: Peter Lang.

oxoniensis [psued.]. 2012. Interview by Abigail De Kosnik. Email. August 5–26. Transcript available at University of Iowa Libraries.

Parikka, Jussi. 2013. Archival media theory: An introduction to Wolfgang Ernst's media archaeology. In *Digital Memory and the Archive*, by Wolfgang Ernst, 1–22. Minneapolis: University of Minnesota Press.

Parks, Lisa. 2004. Flexible microcasting: Gender, generation, and television-Internet convergence. In *Television after TV: Essays on a Medium in Transition*, ed. Lynn Spigel and Jan Olsson, 133–156. Durham, NC: Duke University Press.

Paschalidis, Gregory. 2008. Towards cultural hypermnesia: Cultural memory in the age of digital heritage. In *Digital Heritage in the New Knowledge Environment: Shared Spaces and Open Paths to Cultural Content*, ed. Metaxia Tsipopoulous, 179–181. Athens: Hellenic Ministry of Culture.

Pearson, Erika. 2009. All the World Wide Web's a stage: The performance of identity in online social networks. *First Monday* 14 (3). http://firstmonday.org/ojs/index.php/fm/article/view/2162/2127#author.

Pessach, Guy. 2008. [Networked] memory institutions: Social remembering, privatization, and its discontent. *Social Science Research Network*: n.p. http://papers.ssrn.com/sol3/papers.cfm?abstract_id=1085267.

Pettitt, Tom. 2007. Before the Gutenberg parenthesis: Elizabethan-American compatibilities. Paper presented at Media in Transition 5: Creativity, Ownership and Collaboration in the Digital Age, Cambridge, Massachusetts, April 27–29.

Phelan, Peggy. 1993. *Unmarked: The Politics of Performance*. New York: Routledge.

Philip, Kavita. 2005. What is a technological author? The pirate function and intellectual property. *Postcolonial Studies* 8 (2): 199–218.

Pitts, Byron. 2010. Gay student's death highlights troubling trend. *CBSNews.com*. September 30. http://www.cbsnews.com/news/gay-students-death-highlights-troubling-trend/.

Plato. 2005. *Phaedrus*. Trans. C. Rowe. New York: Penguin Classics.

Plato. *Cratylus*. Trans. Benjamin Jowett. The Internet Classics Archive. http://classics .mit.edu/Plato/cratylus.html.

Pockets: Just Another WordPress.com Weblog. Sven Konig. http://pocketsfull .wordpress.com/sven-konig/ (last accessed October 15, 2015).

Poster, Mark. 2012. Postmodern virtualities. In *Media and Cultural Studies: Keyworks*, 2nd ed., ed. Meenakshi Gigi Durham and Douglas M. Kellner, 442–451. Malden, MA: Wiley-Blackwell.

purple_cube. 2013. Identity. Archive of Our Own. April 25. http://archiveofourown .org/works/774032?view_adult=true.

Rachael. 2011. How to be a fan of problematic things. *Social Justice League*. September 18. http://www.socialjusticeleague.net/2011/09/how-to-be-a-fan-of-problematic -things/.

Radical Content Collective. 2011. RadFem Archives. Last accessed December 13, 2015. http://www.radicalcontent.org/radfem-archives/.

Radicati, Sara, ed. 2011. *Email Statistics Report, 2011–2015*. Palo Alto: Radicati Group.

Radway, Janice. 1991. *Reading the Romance: Women, Patriarchy, and Popular Literature*. Chapel Hill: University of North Carolina Press.

Raley, Rita. 2009. *Tactical Media*. Minneapolis: University of Minnesota Press.

Ralph J. Bunche Center for African American Studies at UCLA. 2014. 2014 Hollywood Diversity Report. February. http://www.bunchecenter.ucla.edu/wp-content/ uploads/2014/02/2014-Hollywood-Diversity-Report-2-12-14.pdf.PDF.

Raqs Media Collective. Seepage. *Issuu*. http://issuu.com/raqsmediacollective/docs/ seepage/89 (last accessed October 15, 2015).

Rayner, Alice. 2006. *Ghosts: Death's Double and the Phenomena of Theatre*. Minneapolis: University of Minnesota Press.

Repertoire of Practice. *The Language of Learning by Design: An Elaborated Glossary. New Learning: Transformational Designs for Pedagogy and Assessment*. http://newlearningonline .com/learning-by-design/glossary/repertoire-of-practice (last accessed October 15, 2015).

Rettig, Hillary. 2006. Honesty vs. burnout. *The Lifelong Activist*. http://www .lifelongactivist.com/part-i-managing-your-mission/honesty-vs-burnout/.

Rheingold, Howard. 1993. *The Virtual Community: Homesteading on the Electronic Frontier*. Reading, MA: Addison-Wesley.

Rhizome.org. 1996. HILUS Vienna send sad news. Last accessed December 13, 2015. http://rhizome.org/discuss/view/29298/.

Rhizome.org. About the Rhizome ArtBase. http://rhizome.org/artbase/about/ (last accessed October 15, 2015).

Rhizome.org, and Rhizome Commissions. http://rhizome.org/commissions/ (last accessed October 15, 2015).

Rhys, Jean. 1992. *Wide Sargasso Sea: A Novel*. New York: W. W. Norton.

Rice, Anne. 2011. *The Vampire Chronicles Collection*. New York: Random House.

Rich, Adrienne. 1986. Compulsory heterosexuality and lesbian existence. In *Blood, Bread, and Poetry: Selected Prose, 1979–1985*, 23–75. New York: W. W. Norton.

Rifkin, Jeremy. 2001. *The Age of Access: The New Culture of Hypercapitalism, Where All of Life is a Paid-for Experience*. New York: Jeremy P. Tarcher/Putnam.

Riordan, Rick. 2005–2007. *Percy Jackson and the Olympians*. New York: Hyperion Paperbacks for Children.

Roach, Joseph R. 1996. *Cities of the Dead: Circum-Atlantic Performance*. New York: Columbia University Press.

Ross, Andrew. 2009. *Nice Work if You Can Get It: Life and Labor in Precarious Times*. New York: New York University Press.

Rothenberg, Jerome. 1981. New models, new visions: Some notes toward a poetics of performance. In *Pre-Faces and Other Writings*, 165–174. New York: New Directions.

Rowling, J. K. 2005. *Harry Potter Collection*. New York: Arthur A. Levine Books, Scholastic Press.

Rubin, Gayle. 1984. Thinking sex: Notes for a radical theory of the politics of sexuality. In *Pleasure and Danger: Exploring Female Sexuality*, ed. Carole S. Vance, 267–319. Boston: Routledge & Kegan Paul.

Rubin, Jerry. 1970. *DO IT! Scenarios of the Revolution*. New York: Simon & Schuster.

Rushdie, Salman. 1982. The Empire writes back with a vengeance. *London Times*, July 3.

rushlight75. 2003. Slash survey results. *Rushlight's Musings* LiveJournal. October 14. http://rushlight75.livejournal.com/2003/10/14/.

Russ, Joanna. 1985. Pornography by women, for women, with love. In *Magic Mommas, Trembling Sisters, Puritans, and Perverts: Feminists Essays*, 79–99. Trumansburg, NY: Crossing Press.

Russo, Julie Levin. 2012. Interview by Abigail De Kosnik. Audio recording. July 24 and August 1. Transcript available at University of Iowa Libraries.

Sabotini, Rachael [psued.]. 2012. Interview by Lisa Cronin. Audio recording. August 20. Transcript available at University of Iowa Libraries.

Saliou, Philippe, and Vincent Ribaud. 2004. Bootstrapping and empty repertoire of experience: The design case. Workshop on Human Aspects of Software Engineering, 24th ACM SIGPLAN Conference, Orlando Florida, Octrober 25–29.

Samuels, Julie, and Corynne McSherry. 2012. Thank you, Internet! And the fight continues. *Electronic Frontier Foundation*, January 18. https://www.eff.org/deeplinks/2012/01/thank-you-internet-and-fight-continues.

Sassen, Saskia. 1991. *The Global City: New York, London, Tokyo*. Princeton, NJ: Princeton University Press.

Sauerberg, Lars Ole. 2009. The encyclopedia and the Gutenberg Parenthesis. Paper presented at Media in Transition 6: Stone and Papyrus, Storage and Transmission, Cambridge, Massachusetts, April 24–26.

Schechner, Richard. 1985. *Between Theater and Anthropology*. Philadelphia: University of Pennsylvania Press.

Schechner, Richard. 2003. *The Future of Ritual: Writings on Culture and Performance*. New York: Routledge.

Schechner, Richard. 2013. *Performance Studies: An Introduction*, 3rd ed. New York: Routledge.

Schiebinger, Londa L. 1993. *Nature's Body: Gender in the Making of Modern Science*. Boston, MA: Beacon Press.

Schneider, Rebecca. 2012. It seems as if … I am dead. *Drama Review* 56 (4): 150–162.

Scholz, Trebor. 2013. *Digital Labor: The Internet as Playground and Factory*. New York: Routledge.

Schradie, Jen. 2013. 7 myths of the digital divide. *The Society Pages*, April 26. http://thesocietypages.org/cyborgology/2013/04/26/7-myths-of-the-digital-divide/.

Scoblete, Greg. 2013. Netflix cutting almost 2,000 movies, is a bigger content bleed coming? Real Clear Technology. May 1. http://www.realcleartechnology.com/articles/2013/05/01/netflix_cutting_almost_2000_movies_399.html.

Scott, Jason. 2013. Still life, with emulator: The JSMESS FAQ. Internet Archive Blogs. December 31. http://blog.archive.org/2013/12/31/still-life-with-emulator-the-jsmess-faq/.

Sekula, Allan. 1986. The body and the archive. *October* 39 (winter): 3–64.

Seiter, Ellen. 1999. *Television and New Media Audiences*. Oxford: Oxford University Press.

Shakespeare, William. 1997. *The Tragedy of Macbeth*. Project Gutenberg. December. http://www.gutenberg.org/cache/epub/1129/pg1129.html.

Shakespeare, William. 2006. *Hamlet*. London: Bloomsbury Arden Shakespeare.

Shank, Barry. 1994. *Dissonant Identities: The Rock 'n' Roll Scene in Austin, Texas*. Hanover, NH: University Press of New England.

Shaviro, Steven. 2011. What is the post-cinematic? *The Pinocchio Theory*. http://www.shaviro.com/Blog/?p=992.

Shirky, Clay. 2008. *Here Comes Everybody: The Power of Organizing without Organizations*. New York: Penguin Press.

Sholette, Gregory. 2011. *Dark Matter: Art and Politics in the Age of Enterprise Culture*. New York: Palgrave Macmillan.

Sierra, Kathy. 2014. Why the trolls will always win. *Wired*, October 8. http://www.wired.com/2014/10/trolls-will-always-win/.

Skylar. 2007. FANFIC: Incense and peppermints. *Kamikaze Waffle* LiveJournal, September 24. http://kamikazewaffle.livejournal.com/12136.html.

Smith, Hazel, and Roger Dean. 1997. *Improvisation, Hypermedia, and the Arts Since 1945*. Amsterdam: Harwood Academic Publishers.

Smithsonian. Smithsonian Collections. http://www.si.edu/Collections (last accessed October 15, 2015).

Sontag, Susan. (1964) 2001. Notes on "camp." In *Against Interpretation and Other Essays*, 275–292. New York: Picador.

South Asian American Digital Archive. First Days Project. http://www.saadigitalarchive.org/firstdays (last accessed October 15, 2015).

Spigel, Lynn. 2001. *Welcome to the Dreamhouse: Popular Media and Postwar Suburbs*. Durham, NC: Duke University Press.

Spivak, Gayatri Chakravorty. 1985. Three women's texts and a critique of imperialism. *Critical Inquiry* 12 (1): 243–261.

Springer, Claudia. 1996. *Electronic Eros: Bodies and Desire in the Postindustrial Age*. Austin: University of Texas Press.

Stallman, Richard. 2002. *Free Software, Free Society: Selected Essays of Richard M. Stallman*. Ed. Joshua Gay. Boston: Free Software Foundation.

Stallman, Richard. 2012. Free software, GNU and GCC. Keynote presentation at the Annual GNU Tools Cauldron, Prague, Czech Republic, July 9–11.

Stallman, Richard. Linux and the GNU System. Free Software Foundation. https://www.gnu.org/gnu/linux-and-gnu.html (last accessed October 15, 2015).

Starlady [pseud.]. 2012. Interview by Abigail De Kosnik. Audio recording. June 18. Transcript available at University of Iowa Libraries.

Stebbins, Robert. 1992. *Amateurs, Professionals, and Serious Leisure.* Montreal: McGill-Queen's University Press.

Stebbins, Robert. 2001. *New Directions in the Theory and Research of Serious Leisure.* Lewiston, NY: Edwin Mellen Press.

Stein, Louisa. 2002. Subject: "Off topic: Oh my God: US terrorism!" Roswell fans respond to 11 September. *European Journal of Cultural Studies* 5 (4): 471–491.

Stein, Louisa. 2012. Interview by Abigail De Kosnik. Audio recording/email/chat. August 16. Transcript available at University of Iowa Libraries.

Stevens, Mary, Andrew Flinn, and Elizabeth Shepherd. 2010. New frameworks for community engagement in the archive sector: From handing over to handing on. *International Journal of Heritage Studies* 16 (1–2): 59–76.

Stiegler, Bernard. 1998. The fault of Epimetheus. In *Technics and Time*, vol. 1. Stanford, CA: Stanford University Press.

Stiegler, Bernard. (2003) 2009. *Acting Out*. Trans. David Barison, Daniel Ross, and Patrick Crogan. Stanford, CA: Stanford University Press.

Stoler, Ann Laura. 2002. Colonial archives and the arts of governance. *Archival Science* 2: 87–109.

Stone, Allucquère Rosanne. 1991. Will the real body please stand up? In *Cyberspace: First Steps*, ed. Michael Benedikt, 81–118. Cambridge, MA: MIT Press.

Stone, Allucquère Rosanne. 1996. *The War of Desire and Technology at the Close of the Mechanical Age*. Cambridge, MA: MIT Press.

Storey, John, ed. 2009. *Cultural Theory and Popular Culture: A Reader*, 4th ed. Essex: Pearson Education.

Strong, Catherine. 2011. *Grunge: Music and Memory*. Burlington, VT: Ashgate.

sublimeglass. 2013. On slash fandom, queerness, and a queer predominant space. Sublimeglass Tumblr. October 15. http://sublimeglass.tumblr.com/post/64443103638/on-slash-fandom-queerness-and-a-queer-predominant.

Supernatural Wiki. 2011. LJ Strikethrough 2007. Last modified May 30, 2011. http://www.supernaturalwiki.com/index.php?title=LJ_Strikethrough_2007.

Taormino, Tristan, Constance Penley, Celine Parrenas Shimizu, and Mireille Miller-Young, eds. 2013. *The Feminist Porn Book: The Politics of Producing Pleasure*. New York: Feminist Press at the City University of New York.

Tari [pseud.]. 2012. Interview by Andrea Horbinski. Audio recording. July 5. Transcript available at University of Iowa Libraries.

Taylor, Diana. 2003. *The Archive and the Repertoire: Performing Cultural Memory in the Americas*. Durham, NC: Duke University Press.

Taylor, Diana. 2010. Save as …: Knowledge and transmission in the age of digital technologies. *Imagining America*. Paper 7. http://surface.syr.edu/ia/7.

Te [psued.]. 2012. Interview by Lisa Cronin. Audio recording. August 3. Transcript available at University of Iowa Libraries.

Terranova, Tiziana. 2004. *Network Culture: Politics for the Information Age*. Ann Arbor, MI: Pluto Press.

Terras, Melissa. 2010. Digital curiosities: Resource creation via amateur digitization. *Literary and Linguistic Computing* 25 (4): 425–438.

Theall, Donald F. 1999. The carnivalesque, the Internet, and control of content: Satirizing knowledge, power, and control. *Continuum* 13 (2): 153–164.

The Circuit Archive. About the archive. http://www.thecircuitarchive.com/tca/about_the_archive.php (last accessed October 15, 2015).

the-other-sandy. 2007. No more zines? :-(. *Dr. Terror's House of Pancakes* LiveJournal, August 15. http://the-other-sandy.livejournal.com/25076.html.

The Porn Battle. Chromatic entries. Porn Battle XI—Eleven Days of Porn. http://battle.oxoniensis.org/battle11chromatic.html (last accessed October 15, 2015).

The Porn Battle. Chromatic prompts. Porn Battle XI—Eleven Days of Porn. http://battle.oxoniensis.org/battle11chromaticprompts.html (last accessed October 15, 2015).

The Rosetta Project. The Rosetta Project—Texts. https://archive.org/details/rosettaproject (last accessed October 15, 2015).

Thomas, Angela. 2007. Blurring and breaking through the boundaries of narrative, literacy, and identity in adolescent fan fiction. In *A New Literacies Sampler*, ed. Michele Knobel and Colin Lankshear, 137–166. New York: Peter Lang.

Tinnell, John. 2011. All the world's a link: The global theater of mobile world browsers. *Enculturation: A Journal of Rhetoric, Writing, and Culture* (December): n.p. http://www.enculturation.net/all-the-worlds-a-link.

Tolkien, J. R. R. 1954–1956. *The Lord of the Rings*. London: Allen & Unwin.

trope_bingo. 2013. Trope list for rounds two & three. Dreamwidth. June 13. http://trope-bingo.dreamwidth.org/47961.html.

Tuchman, Gaye. 1978. Introduction: The symbolic annihilation of women by the mass media. In *Hearth and Home: Images of Women in the Mass Media*, ed. Gaye Tuchman, Arlene Kaplan Daniels, and James Benét, 3–38. New York: Oxford University Press.

Turkle, Sherry. 1995. *Life on the Screen: Identity in the Age of the Internet*. New York: Simon & Schuster.

Turner, Fred. 2006. *From Counterculture to Cyberculture: Steward Brand, the Whole Network, and the Rise of Digital Utopianism*. Chicago: University of Chicago Press.

Tushnet, Rebecca. 2012. Interview by Abigail De Kosnik. Audio recording. August 22. Transcript available at University of Iowa Libraries.

Tushnet, Rebecca. 2013. Performance anxiety: Copyright embodied and disembodied. Georgetown Law Library. http://scholarship.law.georgetown.edu/cgi/viewcontent.cgi?article=2225&context=facpub.

TWC Editor. 2009. Pattern recognition: A dialogue on racism in fan communities. *Transformative Works and Cultures* 3: n.p. http://journal.transformativeworks.org/index.php/twc/article/view/172/119.

Ulmer, Gregory L. 2005. *Electronic Monuments*. Minneapolis: University of Minnesota Press.

United States Census Bureau. 2014. Computer and Internet access in the United States: 2012—table 4. Last modified January 31. http://www.census.gov/hhes/computer/publications/2012.html.

Uprichard, Lucy. 2013. In defence of call-out culture. *The Blog, Huffington Post*, December 27. http://www.huffingtonpost.co.uk/lucy-uprichard/call-out-culture_b_4507889.html.

Van Camp, Nathan. 2012. From biopower to psychopower: Bernard Stiegler's pharmacology of mnemotechnologies. *Ctheory.net*, May 9. http://www.ctheory.net/articles.aspx?id=706#_edn16.

Van Dijck, José. 2007. *Mediated Memories: Personal Cultural Memory in the Digital Age*. Stanford, CA: Stanford University Press.

via_ostiense [psued.]. 2012. Interview by Andrea Horbinski. Audio recording. August 8. Transcript available at University of Iowa Libraries.

Victoria P. [pseud.]. 2012. Interview by Andrea Horbinski. Chat. August 7. Transcript available at University of Iowa Libraries.

Vint, Sherryl. 2007. *Bodies of Tomorrow: Technology: Subjectivity, Science Fiction*. Toronto, Ca: University of Toronto Press.

Walsh, Deb. 2010. Presentation and purpose. My Life in Fandom: Fanzines, Fiction and Friends through the Years. October 1. http://debwalsh.com/mylifeinfandom/?p=332.

Wardip-Fruin, Noah. 2000. Hypermedia, eternal live, and the impermanence agent. *TechnoOasis*. ACM Siggraph Online. http://www.siggraph.org/artdesign/gallery/S99/big/techoasis/index.html.

Wardip-Fruin, Noah, and Nick Montfort. 2003. *The New Media Reader*. Cambridge, MA: MIT Press.

Waskul, Dennis. 2005. Ekstasis and the Internet: Liminality and computer-mediated communication. *New Media and Society* 7 (1): 47–63.

Watkins, S. Craig. 2005. *Hip Hop Matters: Politics, Pop Culture, and the Struggle for the Soul of a Movement*. Boston: Beacon Press.

Weber, Steven. 2009. *The Success of the Open Source*. Cambridge, MA: Harvard University Press.

Wikinews. 2012. FanFiction.Net adult content purge felt across fandom two weeks on. June 16. http://en.wikinews.org/wiki/FanFiction.Net_adult_content_purge_felt_across_fandom_two_weeks_on.

Wikipedia. 2014. Wikipedia: WikiProject open barn raising 2014. Last modified August 17, 2015. http://en.wikipedia.org/wiki/Wikipedia:WikiProject_Open_Barn_Raising_2014.

Williams, Joan C. 2014. Hacking tech's diversity problem. *Harvard Business Review*, October. https://hbr.org/2014/10/hacking-techs-diversity-problem.

Williams, Raymond. (1958) 2002. Culture is ordinary. In *The Everyday Life Reader*, ed. Ben Highmore, 91–100. New York: Routledge.

Williams, Raymond. (1961) 2001. *The Long Revolution*. Westport, CT: Greenwood Press.

Williams, Raymond. 1963. *Culture and Society, 1780–1950*. Harmondsworth: Penguin Books.

Williams, Raymond. 2009. The analysis of culture. In *Cultural Theory and Popular Culture: A Reader*, 4th ed., ed. John Storey, 32–40. Essex: Pearson Education.

Willis, Paul. 1990. *Common Culture: Symbolic Work at Play in Everyday Cultures of the Young*. Boulder, CO: Westview Press.

Willis, Paul. 1997. Symbolic creativity. In *Studying Culture: An Introductory Reader*, ed. Ann Gray and Jim McGuigan, 206–216. London: Arnold.

Winter, Jay. 2001. The memory boom in contemporary historical studies. *Raritan* 21 (1): 52–66.

Wojnarowicz, David. 1991. *Close to the Knives: A Memoir of Disintegration*. New York: Vintage Books.

Zubernis, Lynn, and Katherine Larsen. 2012. *Fandom at the Crossroads: Celebration, Shame and Fan/Producer Relationships*. Newcastle upon Tyne: Cambridge Scholars Publishing.

Media Texts

Angel. 2010. Directed by James A. Contner, Joss Whedon, et al. Broadcast 1999–2004. Beverly Hills, CA: 20th Century Fox Home Entertainment. DVD.

Avatar: The Last Airbender. 2008. Created by Michael Dante DiMartino and Bryan Konietzko. Broadcast 2005–2008. Hollywood, CA: Paramount Pictures. DVD.

Babylon 5. 2004. Created by J. Michael Stracynski. Broadcast 1994–1998. Burbank, CA: Warner Home Video. DVD.

Batman. 2014. Directed by Oscar Rudolph, James B. Clark, et al. Broadcast 1966–1968. Burbank, CA: Warner Home Video. DVD.

Battlestar Galatica. 2010. Directed by Michael Rymer, Michael Nankin, et al. Broadcast 2004–2009. Universal City, CA: Universal Studios Home Entertainment. DVD.

Beauty and the Beast. (1991) 2002. Directed by Gary Trousdale and Kirk Wise. Burbank, CA: Walt Disney Studios Home Entertainment. DVD.

Beauty and the Beast. 2008. Created by Ron Koslow. Broadcast 1987–1990. Hollywood, CA: Paramount Pictures. DVD.

Beyond the Valley of the Dolls. (1970) 2006. Directed by Russ Meyer. Beverly Hills, CA: 20th Century Fox Home Entertainment. DVD.

The Bionic Woman. 2011. Created by Kenneth Johnson. Broadcast 1976–1978. Universal City, CA: Universal Studios Home Entertainment. DVD.

Blakes 7. 2004. Created by Terry Nation. Broadcast 1978–1981. London: BBC. DVD.

Bridget Jones's Diary. (2001) 2005. Directed by Sharon Maguire. Universal City, CA: Universal Studios Home Entertainment. DVD.

Catwoman. (2004) 2005. Directed by Pitof. Burbank, CA: Warner Home Video. DVD.

Cinderella. (1950) 2005. Directed by Clyde Geronimi, Wilfred Jackson, and Hamilton Luske. Burbank, CA: Walt Disney Studios Home Entertainment. DVD.

The Dark Knight Rises. 2012. Directed by Christopher Nolan. Burbank, CA: Warner Home Video. DVD.

Doctor Who. 2009–2012. Createdy by Sydney Newman. Broadcast 1963–1989. Burbank, CA: Warner Home Video. DVD.

Doctor Who. 2013. Directed by Graeme Harper, Euros Lyn, et al. Broadcast 2005–ongoing. Burbank, CA: Warner Home Video. Seasons 1–7. DVD.

Due South. 2014. Directed by Paul Haggis. Broadcast 1994–1999. LaCrosse, WI: Echo Bridge Home Entertainment. DVD.

Firefly. 2003. Directed by Joss Whedon, Vern Gillum, et al. Broadcast 2002–2003. Beverly Hills, CA: 20th Century Fox Home Entertainment. DVD.

Forever Knight. 2003. Created by Barney Cohen and James D. Parriott. Broadcast 1992–1996. Culver City, CA: Tristar Home Entertainment.

The Good Wife. 2014. Created by Michelle King and Robert King. Broadcast 2009–2016. Seasons 1–5. Hollywood, CA: Paramount Pictures. DVD.

Gossip Girl. 2013. Created by Stephanie Savage and Josh Schwartz. Broadcast 2007–2012. Burbank, CA: Warner Home Video. DVD.

Harry Potter: The Complete 8-Film Collection. 2011. Directed by Chris Columbus, Alfonso Cuarón, Mike Newell, and David Yates. Broadcast 2001–2011. Burbank, CA: Warner Home Video. DVD.

Her. 2013. Directed by Spike Jonze. Burbank, CA: Warner Home Video. DVD.

Highlander: The Complete Series (Seasons 1–6). 2005. Created by Davis-Panzer Productions. Broadcast 1992–1998. Beverly Hills, CA: Anchor Bay Entertainment. DVD.

Homicide: Life on the Street. 2009. Directed by Kenneth Fink, Alan Taylor, et al. Broadcast 1993–1999. New York: A&E Home Video. DVD.

House M.D. 2012. Created by David Shore. Broadcast 2004–2012. Universal City, CA: Universal Studios Home Entertainment. DVD.

The Hunger Games. 2012. Directed by Gary Ross. Santa Monica, CA: Lionsgate. DVD.

The Hunger Games: Catching Fire. (2013) 2014. Directed by Francis Lawrence. Santa Monica, CA: Lionsgate. DVD.

Inception. 2010. Directed by Christopher Nolan. Burbank, CA: Warner Home Video. DVD.

La Jetée. (1962) 2007. Directed by Chris Marker. Irvington, NY: Criterion Collection. DVD.

The Last Airbender. 2010. Directed by M. Night Shyamalan. Hollywood, CA: Paramount Pictures. DVD.

The Little Mermaid. (1989) 2013. Directed by Ron Clements and John Musker. Burbank, CA: Walt Disney Studios Home Entertainment. DVD.

The Lizzie Bennet Diaries: An Online Modernized Adaptation of Jane Austen's Pride and Prejudice. Broadcast 2012–2013. Created by Hank Green and Bernie Su. http://www.lizziebennet.com/.

The Lord of the Rings Trilogy. 2004. Directed by Peter Jackson. Broadcast 2001–2003. Los Angeles, CA: New Line Home Entertainment.

Mad Max: Fury Road. 2015. Directed by George Miller. Hollywood, CA: Warner Bros. Pictures.

The Man from U.N.C.L.E: The Complete Series. 2008. Created by Sam Rolfe. Broadcast 1964–1968. Burbank, CA: Warner Home Video. DVD.

The Matrix Trilogy. 2008. Directed by The Wachowski Brothers. Broadcast 1999–2003. Burbank, CA: Distributed by Warner Home Video. DVD.

Metropolis. (1927) 2004. Directed by Fritz Lang. Hollywood, CA: Paramount Pictures. DVD.

Percy Jackson and the Olympians: Sea of Monsters. 2013. Directed by Thor Freudenthal. Beverly Hills, CA: 20th Century Fox Home Entertainment. DVD.

Percy Jackson and the Olympians: The Lightning Thief. 2010. Directed by Chris Columbus. Century City, CA: Fox Searchlight. DVD.

Pride and Prejudice. (1995) 2010. Directed by Simon Langton. New York: A&E Home Video. DVD.

Pride and Prejudice. (2005) 2006. Directed by Joe Wright. Universal City, CA: Universal Studios Home Entertainment. DVD.

The Princess and the Frog. (2009) 2010. Directed by Ron Clements and John Musker. Burbank, CA: Walt Disney Studios Home Entertainment. DVD.

The Professionals. 2002. Created by Brian Clemens. Broadcast 1977–1983. London: Contender Films. DVD.

Roswell. 2008. Directed by Patrick R. Norris, Paul Shapiro, et al. Broadcast 1999–2002. Beverly Hills, CA: 20th Century Fox Home Entertainment. DVD.

The Sentinel. 2006. Created by Danny Bilson and Paul De Meo. Broadcast 1996–1999. Hollywood, CA: Paramount Pictures. DVD.

Sleeping Beauty. (1959) 2008. Directed by Clyde Geronimi. Burbank, CA: Walt Disney Studios Home Entertainment. DVD.

Smallville. 2011. Created by Alfred Gough and Miles Millar. Broadcast 2001–2011. Burbank, CA: Warner Home Video DVD.

Stargate. (2003) 1994. Directed by Roland Emmerich. Santa Monica, CA: Lionsgate. DVD.

Stargate: Atlantis. Created by Robert C. Cooper and Brad Wright. Broadcast 2004–2009. Century City, CA: MGM Home Entertainment, 2009. DVD.

Stargate SG-1. 2007. Directed by Peter DeLuise, Martin Wood, et al. Broadcast 1997–2007. Century City, CA: MGM Home Entertainment. DVD.

Star Trek. 2008. Directed by Marc Daniels, Joseph Pevney, et al. Broadcast 1966–1969. Hollywood, CA: Paramount Pictures. DVD.

Star Trek: Deep Space Nine. 2004. Created by Rick Berman and Michael Piller. Broadcast 1993–1999. Hollywood, CA: Paramount Pictures. DVD.

Star Trek: Enterprise. 2005.Created by Rick Berman and Brannon Braga. Broadcast 2001–2005. Hollywood, CA: Paramount Pictures,. DVD.

Star Trek: First Contact. 1996. Directed by Jonathan Frakes. Hollywood, CA: Paramount Pictures. VHS tape.

Star Trek: The Next Generation. 2007. Directed by Cliff Bole, Les Landau, et al. Broadcast 1987–1994. Hollywood, CA: Paramount Pictures. DVD.

Star Trek: Voyager. 2004. Created by Rick Berman, Michael Piller, and Jeri Taylor. Broadcast 1995–2001. Hollywood, CA: Paramount Pictures. DVD.

Star Wars: The Complete Saga. 2011. Directed by George Lucas. Beverly Hills, CA: 20th Century Fox Home Entertainment. DVD.

The Terminator. (1984) 2004. Directed by James Cameron. Beverly Hills, CA: 20th Century Fox Home Entertainment. DVD.

The Terminator 2: Judgment Day. (1991) 2003. Directed by James Cameron. Santa Monica, CA: Artisan Home Entertainment. DVD.

Twilight. (2008) 2009. Directed by Catherine Hardwicke. Universal City, CA: Summit Entertainment. DVD.

Twilight Forever: The Complete Box. 2013. Directed by Catherine Hardwicke, Chris Weitz, David Slade, and Bill Condon. Broadcast 2008–2012. Universal City, CA: Summit Entertainment. DVD.

The Twilight Saga: New Moon. 2009. Directed by Chris Weitz. Los Angeles, CA: Summit Entertainment.

The X-Files. 2013. Directed by Kim Manners, Rob Bowman, et al. Broadcast 1993–2002. Beverly Hills, CA: 20th Century Fox Home Entertainment. DVD.

The X-Files: Fight the Future. (1998) 2008. Directed by Rob Bowman. Beverly Hills, CA: 20th Century Fox Home Entertainment. DVD.

The X-Files: I Want to Believe. 2008. Directed by Chris Carter. Beverly Hills, CA: 20th Century Fox Home Entertainment. DVD.

X-Men: First Class. 2011. Directed by Matthew Vaughn. Beverly Hills, CA: 20th Century Fox Home Entertainment. DVD.

FanFic Sites, LiveJournals, Websites, and WebBlogs

Archive of Our Own. https://archiveofourown.org/.

Archive Team. http://archiveteam.org/index.php?title=Main_Page.

Artstor. http://www.artstor.org/index.shtml.

Archive, Audiofic. http://www.audiofic.jinjurly.com/.

BitTorrent. http://www.bittorrent.com/.

B. S. G. Femslash Archive. https://delicious.com/bsg_femslash/.

Cornell University's Rose Goldsen Archive of New Media Art. http://goldsen.library
.cornell.edu/.

Creative Commons. http://creativecommons.org/.

Download Finished. http://download-finished.com/.

Dreamwidth. http://www.dreamwidth.org/.

Due South Fiction Archive. 2005. Last modified January 9. https://www.squidge.org/
dsa/.

EEBO. Early English Books Online. http://eebo.chadwyck.com/home.

Eldritch Press. http://eldritchpress.org/.

Europeana: Think Culture. http://www.europeana.eu/.

F.A.M.A. Collection. http://famacollection.org/eng/.

FanFiction: Unleash Your Imagination. https://www.fanfiction.net/.

Fan Fiction and Internet Memory. An Oral History Project. http://fanficmemory
.wordpress.com/.

Femslash Fiction. http://www.ralst.com/Femslash.html.

Fuck Yeah. The Beatles. http://fuckyeahthebeatles.tumblr.com/.

Fuck Yeah Dykes. http://fuckyeahdykes.tumblr.com/.

Fuck Yeah Hermione Granger. http://fuckyeahhermionegranger.tumblr.com/.

Getty Images. http://www.gettyimages.com/.

The Gossamer Project. The X-Files Fan Fiction Archive. http://fluky.gossamer.org/.

Gossip-Fic.net. http://gossip-fic.net/.

harry-draco LiveJournal. http://harrydraco.livejournal.com/.

Harry Potter Fan Fiction. The Story Continues ... http://www.harrypotterfanfiction
.com/.

Hemispheric Institute's Digital Video Library. http://hemisphericinstitute.org/hemi/
en/hidvl/.

hp_fanfiction LiveJournal. http://hp-fanfiction.livejournal.com/.

ibiblio. http://ibiblio.org/.

Internet Archive. https://archive.org/.

Jstor. http://www.jstor.org/.

LiveJournal. http://www.livejournal.com/.

Michigan/Trans Controversy Archive. http://eminism.org/michigan.

Museum of Online Museums. http://www.coudal.com/moom/.

Nanowrimo. http://nanowrimo.org/.

Netbase. http://netbase.org/t0.

Open Library. https://openlibrary.org/.

Organization for Transformative Works. http://transformativeworks.org/.

The Pirate Bay. http://thepiratebay.se/.

The Porn Battle. http://battle.oxoniensis.org/.

Project Gutenberg. http://www.gutenberg.org/.

snape_potter LiveJournal. http://snape-potter.livejournal.com/.

South Asian American Digital Archive. http://www.saadigitalarchive.org/.

RadFem Archive. http://radfem.org/.

remusxsirius LiveJournal. http://remusxsirius.livejournal.com/.

Rhizome ArtBase. http://rhizome.org/artbase/.

Rosetta Project. http://rosettaproject.org/.

Smallville Slash Archive. http://smallville.slashdom.net/.

Trekiverse. http://www.trekiverse.org/.

Tumblr. https://www.tumblr.com/.

Twitter. https://twitter.com/.

Warp 5 Complex: Star Trek Enterprise Fan Fiction Archive. http://fiction
.entstcommunity.org/.

Wayback Machine on Internet Archive. http://archive.org/web/web.php.

Wikileaks. https://wikileaks.org/.

Wikipedia. http://www.wikipedia.org/.

World of Warcraft. http://us.battle.net/wow/en/.

YouTube. http://www.youtube.com/.

Index

Page numbers in italics indicate figures.

Printed in the United States
by Baker & Taylor Publisher Services